The Secrets of Wildflowers

The Secrets of Wildflowers

A Delightful Feast of Little-Known Facts, Folklore, and History

JACK SANDERS

with photographs by the author

Guilford, Connecticut
An Imprint of The Globe Pequot Press

The Lyons Press is an imprint of The Globe Pequot Press

10 9 8 7 6 5 4 3 2

Text design by Casey Shain

Spot images: www.clipart.com

Printed in the United States of America

Library of Congress Cataloging-in-Publication Data
Sanders, Jack, 1944-
    The secrets of wildflowers / by Jack Sanders.
        p. cm.
    ISBN 1-58574-668-1 (hc : alk. paper)
      1. Wild flowers—North America. I. Title.
    QK110.S26 2003
    582.13'097—dc21
                                        2002154440

AUTHOR'S WARNING:

While this book contains many descriptions of herbal uses of plants, the author does not endorse
any of these plants as medicines. Except for spreading jewelweed on his poison ivy rashes, he does
not practice herbal medicine and does not recommend herbal treatments to others unless a licensed
medical doctor prescribes them. Some widely used herbs are, in fact, dangerous. By using them, you
could wind up among the dearly departed. Descriptions of medicinal uses are included in the book
to tell the history of the plants and their relationship with people, to note species that are under
study as possible medicines (and there are many of those), and to explain the origins of some often
obscure folk names.

To my wife, Sally, who helped me with this project in countless ways over many years; to Betty Grace Nash, who encouraged me to keep at it; to Jim Hodgins, who published many of my essays in the pages of *Wildflower* magazine; and to Tom McCarthy, the editor who believed in the book, *The Secrets of Wildflowers* is dedicated.

CONTENTS

Acknowledgments   XI

Introduction   XIII

(Arranged approximately by blooming seasons)

Skunk Cabbage: First Flower of Winter   3
Hepatica: Gem of the Woods   7
Spring-Beauty: A Pink Potato   11
Anemones: Flowers of the Wind   14
Coltsfoot: Roadside Cough Medicine   18
Bloodroot: A Bloody Early Bloomer   22
Dandelion: Our Tulip in the Grass   25
American Columbine: An Elfin Beauty   31
Dutchman's Breeches: Rude Little Trousers   34
Garlic Mustard: A Tasty Foe   37
Trout Lily: A Lily by Any Other Name   40
Ginsengs: The Man-Plants   44
Violets: Love in the Springtime   48
Trilliums: Dead Meat   55
Speedwells: Diamonds in the Rough   58
Pussytoes: The Feet in the Lawn   62
Buttercups: Bitter Beauties   65
Celandine: A Golden Poppy   69
Marsh Marigold: Friend of the Farmer   72
Blue Flag: Born to the Purple   76
Solomon's Seals: The Several Seals of Solomon   80
Wild Ginger: An Overlooked Crank   83
Jack-in-the-Pulpit: The Silent Preacher   86
Saxifrages: Rock Crushers?   90
Lady's Slippers: The Secretive Slippers   92
May Apples: The Green Umbrellas   97
Daisy: A Flower Loved and Hated   101
Wild Geranium: The Catapulted Crawler   105
Baneberries: Two-Season Treats   107

CONTENTS

Summer

Goatsbeard: The Geodesic Clock 113
Bedstraws: Creepers for Runners 115
Cinquefoil: A Rose by Another Name 117
Forget-Me-Nots: Legendary Flowers 120
Chickweeds: For the Birds 124
Black-Eyed Susan: A Pretty Face 128
Bindweeds: The Pretty Stranglers 131
Deptford Pink: Tiny but Divine 135
Milkweed: A Sweet Grabber 137
Butterflyweed: A Neglected Beauty 142
Clovers: Ubiquitous and Useful 145
Jewelweed: Nature's Salve and Toy 150
Black Cohosh: Candles of the Fairies 154
Chicory: The Roadside Peasant 157
Bergamots: The Monster Mints 161
Nightshades: Beautiful, but Deadly? 164
Pokeweed: Bounty for Man and Bird 168
Sundews: The Carnivores 173
Purple Loosestrife: Summer's Deadly Glow 176
Yarrow: The First-Aid Kit 180
Queen Anne's Lace: The Royal Carrot 185
Dayflowers: An Embarrassing Memorial 188

CONTENTS

Late Summer & Fall

Knotweeds: Knots Underfoot 192

Indian Pipes: Ghosts of Summer's Woods 198

Mulleins: The Bearded Weeds 202

St. Johnsworts: Chasing the Blues with Yellows 207

Avens: Both Blessed and Cursed 211

Mints: Old and Lively Scents 213

Cardinal Flower: America's Favorite 217

Bouncing Bet: Soap with Bounce 221

Evening-Primrose: An Owl-Like Sweet 223

Toadflax: Old Toad Face 227

Goldenrods: The All-Americans 230

Ragweeds: The Season for Sneezin' 236

Joe-Pye Weed: A Noble Lummox 240

Boneset: A Bitter Tea for the Ailing 243

Sunflowers: Beauty and Bounty 246

Turtleheads: The Talking Heads 251

Vervain: A Favorite of Priests and Witches 254

Groundnut: Sweet from Tip to Toe 257

Ladies'-Tresses: Orchids of Autumn 261

Dogbane: A Fly's Worst Friend 264

Thistles: Watch Your Step! 267

Asters: The Stars of Autumn 271

Gentians: The Royal Family 276

Websites 281

A Brief Glossary 283

Bibliography 284

Index 294

Acknowledgments

In preparing this book, I received help from many people for which I am very thankful. Editors Tom McCarthy and Pamela Benner kept my prose on the straight and narrow. Barry Meyers-Rice, Ph.D., of the University of California at Davis provided expert assistance on carnivores. Dr. Bernd Blossey of Cornell University kept me up-to-date on purple loosestrife parasites. John C. Semple, Ph.D., of the University of Waterloo explained the intricacies involved in the renaming of the asters. Dr. A. Randall Olson, curator of the A. E. Roland Herbarium and head of the Department of Environmental Science at the Nova Scotia Agricultural College, advised me on Indian pipe, of which he's been a lifelong fan. Michael Lloyd Charters helped with some challenging plant names. Professor Peter Bernhardt of St. Louis University, an author of several important books on the plant world, assisted with the genus *Erythronium*. Naturalist and author Ed Kanze provided information, important photographs (sundew and dogbane), and a lot of encouragement.

Introduction

What's so interesting about wildflowers and why would you care to know any "secrets" they may have? Many people, after all, consider wildflowers little more than pests at odds with a putting-green lawn. The fact is, though, that few things in nature beautify the world more than wildflowers. Their countless colors and endless designs are found almost anywhere the sun strikes the earth—from fields to woods, deserts to ponds, and even in junkyards, dumps, and cracks in shopping-center parking lots. Without them, the world would be a pretty dull place.

More than just decorations, however, wildflowers are essential parts of our environment and even our lives. They feed insects, birds, animals, and even humans; they hold together and condition the soil; they are the "parents" of our garden flowers; and they provide many modern medicines or the inspirations for them. How they work and what they do is often overlooked, and how they have been used has largely been forgotten. *The Secrets of Wildflowers* will provide a thorough introduction to the natural and cultural history of more than 100 representative species of North American wildflowers.

What is a wildflower? Simply put, it is a blooming plant that can survive without the help of humans. More than 10,000 kinds exist in North America, many of them rare and limited in territory, hundreds of them abundant and widespread. They range from odd-looking orchids whose locations are whispered only among trusted friends, to "weeds" that pop up in lawn and garden and keep herbicide manufacturers in business. While many trees and shrubs could be considered "wild flowers," this book covers only herbs—plants whose aboveground parts die back in the winter or after their season of life.

The Secrets of Wildflowers is not a substitute for a good field guide, several of which are listed in the bibliography. Rather, it picks up where field guides leave off, describing what's interesting about the plants you've already identified, such as their natural history, folklore, habitats, horticulture, uses, origin of their names, and even their place in literature. I've tried to include many of the most widespread, interesting, and recognized species you are apt to find on a walk or in the backyard, and I've deliberately excluded plants that would be found only in restricted environments such as the seashore, desert, or high mountains.

NATIVES AND ALIENS

Many common wildflowers are natives that evolved long before humans set foot in North America. Many others were recently imported, deliberately or accidentally, from Europe, Africa, or Asia. *The Secrets of Wildflowers* covers natives and immigrants, friends or foes, because both kinds are here and both are interesting.

In the world of North American wildflowers, a lot has happened in the last 500 years. Many native plants are either more common or more rare today than they were when the Europeans arrived and began redesigning the surface of the continent. Anthropologists and historians are still trying to figure out just what North America looked like in 1491. For instance, while we once thought the East was covered with forest, indications are that the American Indian population was much larger than was long believed and that the natives had cleared much of the land for agriculture and kept it clear by regular, controlled burns. From the very earliest contacts with Europeans, however, the Indians picked up previously unknown diseases that killed a huge number of them, some historians now say. So many Indians died that most of the land they had kept open filled in with trees during the two centuries after their first contact with Europeans. These forests were eventually felled as the colonists increased in number and needed more land for farms.

This history presents the possibility of an unusual chain of events. Sun-loving native plants that thrived before the Europeans' arrival were pushed out by the post-1492 spread of the woodland, and when the colonists cleared those forests, species they accidentally or deliberately introduced from Europe spread across the reopened landscape. Some immigrant species overpowered the native plants because the newcomers lacked enemies. In their home territories, most were kept in check by insects and other predators, and by careful cultivation. Here, they lacked natural controls and had a vast land available to them. The alien species often made enemies with the very farmers who had carried them across the Atlantic and given them the sunlight they needed.

As fields turned to woods, and then the woods to fields, many native species died out or declined in number. As wetlands were drained or filled for fields, habitats of many native species were eliminated, and those plants were often made rare or rarer.

WEEDS OR WILDFLOWERS?

Someone once called a wildflower "a weed with a press agent." Our most common wildflowers are often called weeds, one definition of which is a plant growing where it's not wanted, usually profusely. Many imports—and some natives—are indeed pests and a few might be called villains—ragweeds, purple loosestrife, Japanese knotweed, and garlic mustard, chief among them. However, many weeds are also among the most successful wildflowers. Success is a trait that we usually admire in humans and beasts, and it's a quality that can be appreciated, if not enjoyed, in plants as well. Many weeds that are exceedingly common are simply those wildflowers that are best able to adapt and survive. Often, they are among the most highly evolved plants on the evolutionary scale.

In most cases, weeds also have humans to thank for their success. Some, like purple loosestrife and garlic mustard, were given a land without enemies. Others have had their native land "improved" —in the case of ragweed, for instance, by the increasing amounts of carbon dioxide in the atmosphere, caused by the burning of petrochemicals. Black-eyed Susan, once limited chiefly to the Midwest, is now found in almost every state and province because farmers opened the land to this plant and transported its seeds by rail and road to new territories.

Of course, we are also responsible for the scarcity or loss of many native plants, pushed out when we introduced alien invaders, when we drained swamps or bulldozed woods and fields. (The house, condominium, or apartment where you're reading this book stands on land that was once home to many kinds of plants—perhaps even a rare orchid.)

Some of our effects on plant life may be subtler. In my part of the Northeast, for example, restrictions on hunting and the destruction of natural enemies have contributed to an explosion in the white-tailed deer population. In its effort to find food, the burgeoning herd is turning to plants normally shunned. Lady's slipper orchids, jewelweed, and other natives are becoming harder and harder to find in my neighborhood because the hungry deer are decimating their numbers—a domino effect of human-induced changes in the environment.

ETHNOBOTANY

Those who came before us appreciated the wild plants, for both their decorative and practical uses—alleged or proven. Commonplace field or roadside flowers that few people today could name might well have been valued as medicines by your great-great-grandmother. American Indians, who seemed to find a use for almost anything that sprouted from the earth, may have cherished that weed in your lawn. In fact, some of our weediest wildflowers have been cultivated since ancient times as medicines, foods, flavorings, scents, dyes, and fibers.

Herbalists and naturopaths have written countless books on how to use plants to heal or to improve our health. Almost half of the medicines in use today employ substances first found in nature, so there's no doubt to the validity of using some plants to treat some ailments. However, I am not a herbalist, nor do I practice herbal medicine. This book merely points out uses to which plants have been put and does not recommend or endorse any plant as a treatment for any illness, except perhaps jewelweed as a poison ivy salve.

MUCH VARIETY

Wildflowers come in countless designs. The form, size, color, scent, positioning, and other characteristics of the blossoms all result from eons of evolution. Botanists have figured out the purpose of some of the often intricate floral patterns, usually aimed at luring or guiding insects. Other characteristics remain mysteries. Wherever possible, I have tried to point out the known or probable purposes of the intriguing designs.

Like birds and other creatures of nature, wildflowers have ranges. Most of the plants in this book range from at least the East Coast to the Rockies, and many are found coast to coast.

However, like other forms of life, many wildflowers are changing their ranges. Some are becoming more widespread, heading westward and occasionally eastward or northward. Conversely, for the sensitive, less adaptable species, ranges tend to grow smaller. Some plants have become so rare that about the only place you can see them is in special wildflower preserves, the zoos of the plant world.

Of course, uncommon plants should not be picked. Nor should they be dug for transplantation—unless they are in the path of a builder's bulldozer. Many plants are uncommon because they've been overpicked or overdug, or because they are sensitive to their surroundings, which are difficult to duplicate. If you want to try growing rare or fussy flowers, do it with stock from a reputable nursery or with a few seeds gathered from the wild ones you've found. Certainly, many flowers can be picked for bouquets or dug for transplanting without endangering the species' or colony's survival. Oddly enough, these flowers—such as many asters and goldenrods—are also the ones that usually look best as a decoration on a dining room table or growing in or near your backyard.

Whether you view them in your lawn, on a roadside, or way off in the woods, enjoy wildflowers for the marvelous creations they are. They have survived much longer than humans, despite our carelessness and callousness, and they bring color and beauty to a world that needs both.

The Secrets of Wildflowers includes an extensive, annotated bibliography; I hope it will help readers find more books on wildflowers. The Internet has exploded upon the world and with it the ability to quickly find used copies of almost any book ever published. Because of these innovations, the bibliography is especially useful as a guide to further reading.

The Internet's World Wide Web has also given the wildflower fan a tremendous database of information about plants—from photographs and range maps to the latest in botanical research. The appendices include select Websites to help the enthusiast learn more about wildflowers.

In the 25 or so years since I began writing about wildflowers, the scientific names of hundreds of well-known plants have changed. In many cases scientists have found that species were simply miscast and did not belong in the genus to which they had been assigned, sometimes centuries ago. In some cases, one species has been determined to be a subspecies of another, not a species of its own, and some subspecies have become their own species. In still other cases, scientists discovered earlier and more appropriate names for species. For the latest names, we have relied upon the U.S. Department of Agriculture's Plants Database.

Finally, the book's 74 chapters begin with the earliest flowering plants and end with the last to bloom. It just seems a more natural configuration than arranging them by taxonomic designations or alphabetically by names. In addition, because we all seem to be attuned to seasons, I have divided the chapters into three approximate seasons. The breaks are somewhat arbitrary—the blooming seasons of flowers, of course, cross our calendric definitions of seasons. What's more, times of blooming vary with region and climate. Most wild plants, however, seem to be generally known as spring, summer, or fall flowers, and so they are presented here by season.

Spring

Skunk Cabbage

FIRST FLOWER OF WINTER

Skunk cabbage is a hot plant with a loyal following.

In much of North America, the skunk cabbage has earned the popular reputation as the first flower of spring. It might be more accurate, however, to call it the first flower of winter. In fact, skunk cabbage appears so early that, reports naturalist John Burroughs, it "may be found with its round green spear-point an inch or two above the mould in December. It is ready to welcome and make the most of the first fitful March warmth."

Henry David Thoreau observed that almost as soon as the leaves wither and die in the fall, new buds begin pushing upward. In fact, he counseled those afflicted with the melancholy of late autumn to go to the swamps "and see the brave spears of skunk cabbage buds already advanced toward the new year."

Many people in the colder parts of eastern North America watch for skunk cabbage as an early sign of spring. The plant's spathe, or sheath, pushes through the still-frosty earth and stands tall when the first breaths of warmer air begin blowing. That can happen with a long January thaw, a "goosethaw," as some New Englanders call it, or it can occur as late as March.

Skunk cabbage's tiny flowers are located on a thick round spadix hidden within the large purple and green spathe. Insects, particularly bees and flies, flock to these small but early blossoms.

Fly Delight

While skunk cabbage frankly *stinks*, it is a fascinating plant in many ways, including its scent. Naturalist Neltje Blanchan described the smell as combining "a suspicion of skunk, putrid meat, and garlic." The scent is actually less like skunk than rotten meat or even dung. In fact, two of the scent-producing substances in skunk cabbage are skatole and cadaverine, the same chemicals found in a variety of decaying animal and vegetable matter. There are at least two uses for this smell. One is that it helps make the plant unappetizing to most grazing animals. But equally important is its ability to attract insects. Certain varieties of flies can detect the smell from long distances and find it delightful. They provide an important source of transportation for the flowers' golden pollen. Sometimes hundreds of flies can be seen swarming around skunk cabbages.

Part of the spathe of this skunk cabbage has been torn away to show the flower-bearing spadix inside.

Obligate

Topography and land investigators, conservationists, surveyors, and cartographers use skunk cabbage as a certain sign that the soil is wetland. The plant is considered "obligate"—that is, its probability of appearing in a wetland is 99 percent.

A Hideous Smoke

"I dryd & smoakt some on't but it stunk so wretchedly as to make me spew; but the Indians have a way of dressing it so as to make it less hideous."
—*Thomas More* (1725)
on smoking skunk cabbage leaves

Skunk cabbage's scent also attracts certain kinds of carrion beetles, whose usual meal is the thawing corpses of animals that died over the winter. They crawl about in the pollen that falls to the base of the clublike spadix inside the sheath and also wander about the flower-bearing spadix itself, no doubt looking for the source of that mouthwatering aroma. Thus tricked into thinking there's a dead body about, they pick up enough grains of pollen to fertilize the next skunk cabbage that similarly fools them. According to scientists, the smooth and slippery interior of the spathe keeps the beetles from wandering across parts of the plant on which they will find no pollen.

Not only scent but color figures into the skunk cabbage's techniques for drawing flies and beetles. The spathe is reddish purple, a shade that resembles meat—or carrion. Skunk cabbage shares this color with other carrion-imitating flowers of spring such as the red trillium and wild ginger.

I must admit that I was surprised when an internationally known beekeeper who lives in my neighborhood told me that skunk cabbage was a popular plant with his hives. One would think that bees would shun this plant, which lacks flashy flowers, sweet scent, or any nectar to speak of. However, the flowers do produce plenty of golden pollen, a food for bees. And despite the bad odor and hidden flowers, the skunk cabbage offers an ideal design for feeding bees in the cold of early spring. Through a process called thermogenesis, skunk cabbage can heat its spadix to around 70 degrees Fahrenheit. The air surrounding the spadix and enclosed by the spathe is thus kept much warmer than the outside air, even when the temperature is below freezing. This bit of Florida-like climate in the midst of the cold northern spring is ideal for insects, such as bees and flies.

Beekeepers call these plants "heat stops." My neighborhood beekeeper once described to me how his honeybees, which dislike temperatures under 65 degrees, deal with the cold of a spring day. Each hesitates at the mouth of the warm hive, as if screwing up the courage to go out into the cold air. It eventually takes off and makes a "beeline" for a nearby skunk cabbage and, crawling through an opening in the spathe, goes to the pollen—and warmth—inside. In a little while the bee reappears at the opening and again hesitates in the face of the cold. Finally, the bee departs to visit another flower or to return to the hive with its load of pollen.

Despite such designs aimed at attracting the "right" insects and protecting the pollen for them, skunk cabbages are apparently susceptible to pollen theft by slugs, which are attracted to the plant and which will also eat holes in the leaves. In addition, nearly a dozen kinds of spiders visit or live on skunk cabbage. Some weave webs across the spathe's entrance, snaring insects that would have pollinated the flowers. What's more, the spathe occasionally and unintentionally entraps larger bees, and the plant becomes their tomb.

After the flowers come the leaves, which by midsummer are usually huge—up to several feet across. Their large size captures as much food-producing sunlight as possible in shaded wetlands. The leaves also create shade, preventing competing plants from establishing themselves near the skunk cabbage's root system. These natural umbrellas also provide shelter for various creatures, including birds, frogs, and lizards. The yellowthroat, a variety of warbler, sometimes builds its nest in the hollow of the spathe, using the foul odor to mask its own scent and discourage investigation by four-footed predators.

Indian Medicine

This native-American plant has a long history of medicinal use among the Native Americans. The huge leaves were used in poultices, and Indians also dressed wounds with a powder obtained from the dried roots. Root hairs treated toothaches. Delawares made a tea for whooping cough from the root, and epileptics among them chewed the leaf to avoid seizures. Nanticokes used it in a cold medicine. Micmacs sniffed bundles of leaves to relieve headaches, though botanical explorer Peter Kalm found that the smell gave him a headache. Skunk cabbage has also been employed in treating asthma, rheumatism, hysteria, dropsy, and other maladies.

One of the more unusual medicinal uses for the plant was in tattooing, an art practiced on the ill by such tribes as the Menominees. Skunk cabbage powder was mixed with pigments and other ingredients, moistened, and then inserted into the skin with a sharp fish tooth. The resulting designs were not so much decorative as they were charms to prevent return of the diseases.

Some American Indians made flour from the dried roots; thorough drying in the sun removes the mouth-blistering calcium oxalate that the plant uses as a defense against grazing animals. Indians also ate the early spring leaves, which had to be first dried or repeatedly boiled to remove the calcium oxalate. In large enough doses, the skunk cabbage can cause nausea, vomiting, dizziness, and temporary blindness. Yet, though the plant is acrid and even toxic to humans, bears in the spring reportedly relish the raw roots, which they dig up to eat. However, as one author put it, bears emerging from hibernation will eat almost anything in sight.

Skunk cabbage can be found from Canada to the Carolinas and beyond the Mississippi. Among its many folk names are skunkweed, polecat weed, meadow cabbage, fetid hellebore, rockweed, swamp cabbage, Midas ears, parson in a pillory, clumpfoot cabbage, polkweed, and collard.

Scientists have disagreed over what to officially name the plant, with some authorities having called it *Spathyema foetida* and others *Ictodes foetidus* (with *ictodes* meaning "skunk oil"). However, today they've pretty much settled on *Symplocarpus foetidus*. *Symplocarpus* is from the Greek words for "connection" and "fruit," and is descriptive of the seeds. *Foetidus*, of course, refers to the fetid smell of the plant.

Dr. Harold Moldenke of the New York Botanical Garden wrote in 1949 that the skunk cabbage's nearest relatives are in distant Malaysia. This suggests that when the Northern Hemisphere was warmer, the ancestors of our skunk cabbage worked their way up the east coast of Asia, across to Alaska via the Aleutians, and headed south. Subsequent ice ages cut the plant's range and the long line between *Symplocarpus foetidus* and those East Asian ancestors was broken. A similar plant, *Lysichiton americanus* of the Pacific Coast states and British Columbia, may share those same ancestors. Called the yellow skunk cabbage, western skunk cabbage, or American skunk cabbage, the species is so handsome it has been imported to Europe as a garden plant and has escaped into the wild there.

Skunk cabbage is not likely to find its way into fancy seed catalogues, however. While the flower structure is unusual—and typical of the Arum family, one of the smallest and most

Oldest Wildflower?

Skunk cabbages may be our oldest wildflowers. If conditions are right and have remained stable, a skunk cabbage's roots may live more than 200 years.

Titan Arum

The largest flower in the world is the titan arum (*Amorphophallus titanum*), a native of Sumatra whose flowers are as big as 10 feet wide and can weigh 145 pounds. Like skunk cabbage, it gives off a foul odor aimed at attracting sweat bees, and earning it the name "corpse flower" among natives. The flower has a spathe and spadix design similar to that of skunk cabbage, but more like Jack-in-the-pulpit (see page 86), another arum.

primitive clans of flowering plants—they are not the symmetrical, fragrant beauties we usually associate with large wildflowers. Nonetheless, some people have noticed that the flower-bearing spadix, removed from the sheath, is not unattractive. In fact Nelson Coon, in *The Dictionary of Useful Plants*, calls them an example of "beauty within the beast" and says he often decorates his dining table with a bouquet of skunk cabbage flowers in the spring. For many years a doctor who lived in Connecticut grew skunk cabbages in pots to give to her friends each spring in celebration of the new season.

The showy clusters of leaves are also decorative additions to wet areas and, once established, the plants are long lasting. Though it is hard to imagine wetlands that lack skunk cabbage, if yours does and you'd like some, simply dig up a smaller-size plant in the spring or stick some of the late-summer seeds into the moist soil.

And if you're like Thoreau, you may find hope in their December buds.

Hepatica

GEM OF THE WOODS

The hepatica wraps itself in fur to bring its early blooms.

Early-spring flowers can be a double treat. They cheer the spirit with the first signs of the new season's life, and they can also provide fascinating examples of nature's survival techniques. The beautiful and seemingly delicate hepatica is just such a survivalist plant.

Some observers claim hepatica is the earliest flower of spring, excepting what one author describes as "the plebeian skunk cabbage that ought scarcely be reckoned among true flowers" (see page 3). Although I have seen hepaticas as early as mid-April in Connecticut, friends have spotted them in late March. John Burroughs said that some years he found the coltsfoot appearing first while in others, he found the hepatica first.

F. Schuyler Mathews participated in the debate, noting that some folks felt the trailing arbutus was the earliest flower in New England. "I have found the hepatica in some seasons earlier than the trailing arbutus, but this is a matter of personal experience," Mathews wrote. "William Hamilton Gibson asserts positively that the flower is really the first to appear, and I believe he is quite right. It is the easiest thing in the world to pass the hepatica without noticing it, so closely does it snuggle among the withered leaves; on this account, I am inclined to believe it comes and goes quite undiscovered, while the conspicuous arbutus never fails to attract attention."

When the buds push through the leaves, or even the snow, they bear many little hairs. "Someone has suggested that the fuzzy little buds look as though they were still wearing their furs as a protection against the wintry weather which so often stretches late into our spring," wrote Mrs. William Starr Dana.

Hairs also coat the stems and probably have two purposes: warmth and defense. They may help the plant retain heat during the cool spring days and cold nights. They may also dissuade ants from climbing to the flowers and stealing the nectar. Later, however, the plant makes use of the ants. Hepaticas are among the spring wildflowers that practice myrmecochory, encouraging ants to collect and bury their seeds by offering them tasty treats (see also the chapter on violets, page 48).

The hepatica leaves are also furry. Moreover, they are "evergreen," lasting a full year. After each spring's blooming, new leaves appear and the old ones take on a rusty, liver-like color as they die and dry up. Frederic William Stack, who was a Vassar botanist, suggested that the long-

Some consider the round-lobed hepatica the first flower of spring. The flowers seem too delicate for such a harsh season.

lived leaves are a survival technique. They are available for the entire growing season to manufacture plenty of food to store in the roots. This gives the hepatica the ability to produce a flower so early the next season.

What's more, the leaves provide protection. "The evergreen leaves offer shelter from the frosts and assist in accumulating a blanket of fallen leaves and similar litter, until they are covered by the snow and made triply snug and secure for the winter," Stack said. "Again in the spring these leaves are first to catch the warm rays of the sun, and the ground about them is first to become freed from the frost crystals and to arouse their roots to activity."

Name Game

Until recently scientists said we had two species of hepaticas, round-lobed (*Hepatica americana*) and sharp-lobed (*H. acutiloba*), so called because of the shapes of the leaves. A couple from Missouri made identification simpler for us, and now there's only one species, called hepatica (*Hepatica nobilis*), though the taxonomists admit there is a round-lobed subspecies (*H. nobilis obtuse*) and a sharp-lobed subspecies (*H. nobilis acuta*). The reclassification was the work of Julian and Cora Steyermark; Julian (1909–1988) has been called "the finest taxonomist in the world." The Steyermarks studied both hepatica varieties in a part of Lake County, Illinois, and found the round-lobed tended toward forested uplands with rich soil, and the sharp-lobed the bottomlands near streams, but that they shared territory in between and often intermingled and crossbred. They decided the two varieties were not different enough to warrant being separate species. Not all botanists agree and some still use the old names.

Hepatica is a flower of variety in more ways than this. The blossoms may appear in any of several colors, including white, pink, lavender, purple, and blue, each in a pastel shade that seems too delicate for the harsh weather of April. The flowers may bear from six to eight sepals that look like petals.

The blossoms may or may not be scented. Naturalist John Burroughs, who called hepatica "the gem of the woods," wondered about this oddity in several of his essays. "This flower is the earliest, as it is certainly one of the most beautiful, to be found in our woods, and occasionally it is fragrant," he wrote in *A Bunch of Herbs*. "Group after group may be inspected, ranging through all shades of purple and blue, with some perfectly white, and no odor to be detected, when presently you will happen upon a little brood of them that have a most delicate and delicious fragrance." Elsewhere he wrote that more often than not the scent will be found in the white flowers, but that one year after a particularly severe winter almost every blue hepatica he came upon was scented—another of the little unexplained peculiarities of wildflowers that make them so fascinating.

The hepatica flower, incidentally, does not require visiting insects for pollination and can fertilize itself. Considering the dearth of insects in the north in March or April, that's not surprising. However, some early flies, bees, and butterflies visit the flowers, including the small blue azure butterfly, among the first of its kind to emerge each year, whose color is not unlike the pastel blue found in many hepaticas.

Ozark Courtship

Julian and Cora Steyermark, the botanists from Missouri whose work reclassified the hepaticas, met over a wildflower. Cora had discovered an Ozark wake-robin; she told Julian about it, and he asked her to show it to him. They spent the rest of their lives together, researching and writing on botany.

Silent Token

All the woodland path is broken
By warm tints along the way,
And the low and sunny slope
Is alive with sudden hope,
When there comes the silent token
Of an April day,—
Blue hepatica.
—Dora Read Goodale
    (1866–1915)

The Liverwort

The dying leaves of the plant resemble a liver in color and shape, so it's not surprising that *Hepatica* comes from the Greek word for liver. Centuries ago people used the shape, color, or form of a plant as a sign of its value, a practice known as "the doctrine of signatures." Thus, herbs with leaves that were ribbed like a snake's flesh were often used to treat snakebites. As a result a European version of the hepatica was used long ago as a cure for liver ailments. "It is a singular good herb for all diseases of the liver, both to cool and cleanse it, and helps inflammations in any part, and the yellow jaundice," wrote Nicholas Culpeper, who also recommended it for the "bites of mad-dogs." Some herbals still list hepatica as a remedy for kidney, liver, and bladder ailments, and for certain gastric problems, but most modern herbalists don't recommend it for anything. Hepatica tea was long used to treat bronchitis and as a diuretic. (A once-popular laxative, called Sal Hepatica, or "liver salt," did not use the plant, just the name.) In the mid-1800s there was a popular patent medicine called Dr. Rogers' Liverwort and Tar, used for lung afflictions. By the 1880s, hepatica treatments were all the rage, so much so that in 1883 alone, more than 200 tons of hepatica leaves were imported from Europe to meet the needs of patent-medicine manufacturers.

Chippewas used hepatica as a treatment for convulsions, especially in children. They called the plant *gabisanikeag*, which means "it is silent," possibly a reference to its effect on convulsing people. Other natives used it to try to straighten out the cross-eyed. Perhaps Cherokees had the most peculiar use. They dreaded dreams about snakes and if they had one, they would drink a tea made of hepatica and walking fern to make them vomit, thereby banishing snake dreams. The fresh plant is said to be irritating to the skin, and large amounts taken internally can cause poisoning.

Other Names

The use and shape of the leaves and the appearance of the flower itself have led to a variety of folk names, including liverwort, liverleaf, heart-leaf liverwort, liver-moss, mouse-ears, spring beauty, crystalwort, golden trefoil, ivy flower, herb trinity, and squirrel cup.

Hepaticas are members of the crowfoot or buttercup family, and fewer than a half-dozen hepatica species are known in the world. Their next of kin is the anemone, which can often be found blooming at the same time in the same places. In fact, hepaticas were once classified under the genus *Anemone*, and over the years round-lobed hepatica has been known to scientists by at least four names: *Anemone hepatica, Hepatica hepatica, H. triloba,* and *H. americana.*

Hepaticas are found from the central states and provinces east to the Atlantic. They favor rich soils in woods that include maples, beeches, and oaks, but may sometimes be found in pastures. The plants grow to about six inches in height.

The temptation for woodland walkers to pick this flower is great because it is so colorful among the bleak, dead remnants of last season and so full of promise of the flowers to come. Yet picking is one reason we don't find it more widespread in our woods, and picking should be avoided. The hepaticas have survived because they are hearty and spread readily. Where left alone, they

Spring Race

"The well-developed flower beds of the Liverworts can hardly await the final thaw and the first warm rain to start them as pace-makers in Nature's annual spring race for first honors. They are probably the earliest of our spring flowers, earlier even than the Bloodroot, and if we except the cold, stiff and unattractive Skunk Cabbage, the beautiful Hepaticas invariably lead them all."
—*Frederic William Stack* (1913)

thrive. They can be successfully transplanted but should never be removed from the wild unless threatened with certain destruction.

Hepaticas are considered easy to grow from seeds, which appear a little later in the spring. Use a small bag to grab and handle the tiny seeds. Plant them immediately in appropriate soil. The seeds will germinate in the fall, and in the next season will send up only two little seed leaves during the summer. But they should produce attractive blossoms the next spring at just about the time you're anxious to see the first flowers of the season.

Spring-Beauty

A PINK POTATO

If you eat them, they won't come.

In much of North America, March and April bring out hordes of the winter-weary. They wander the woods in search of reassurance that the season of cold and snow is passing and life is returning to the dead, brown earth. These woodland quests draw them to flowers they might otherwise ignore in the more lush months ahead. For early spring is a season of small flowers. Many barely sneak through the carpet of last year's leaves, and often open only when the sun beckons. Yet, these dainty blossoms are designed to handle the harshness of frigid nights, fierce winds, and heavy rains that come with the changing seasons.

Spring-beauty is among the earliest of the forest flowers. Despite its vainglorious name, it is small, simple, and perhaps even bland compared to fancier, more colorful brethren of late spring and early summer. But its being among the first flowers of the season has earned it the affection of many a woodland trekker. One of its pleasing characteristics is its tendency to colonize and carpet large areas of woodland, making up for its small size with large numbers. These colonies can easily spread since the flowers produce pods that explode and fire seeds as far as two feet. In some places, as June Carver Roberts said in her book, *Born in the Spring*, spring-beauty "marches right into towns, scattering pink across lawns here and there."

How does such a small flower survive at a time of year when few insects are about to pollinate it and when temperatures may dip below freezing? The spring-beauty is a showman. Its white petals glisten in the sunlight, bearing many tiny reflective beacons to catch the eye of the earliest bees and flies. Once they move in, those eyes follow the several pink lines that radiate from the base of each of the five petals. These lines or "bee guides" direct the insect to the nectar at the bottom of the corolla cup at the center of the petals. Pink is especially attractive to bumblebees, but since relatively few of them are out so early in the season in much of the plant's range, spring-beauty also makes use of smaller bees and flies, attracted perhaps by the white. In my neighborhood, spring-beauty tends to be white with faint pink lines. In other areas, the lines are deeper, more visible; and in still other places, the entire petals are blushed pink. Could the coloration reflect the kinds of insects prevalent in each region? Do pinker blossoms occur where the climate is a bit warmer and more bumblebees are available as pollinators? Through eons of natural selec-

Spring-beauty's flowers come in light and dark shades of pink, but invariably have lines radiating from the center.

Legal Natives

Some nurseries selling spring-beauty offer plants dug from the wild, perhaps illegally. While growing spring-beauty from seed requires time and effort, reputable nurseries do so. For a list of places that carry nursery-grown native plants, visit the Virginia Native Plant Society's Website at www.vnps.org and look for its nurseries listing.

tion, with bees favoring the pink blossoms over the white, entire colonies of pink flowers could easily develop in warmer areas while in cooler areas, where flies and less fussy bees are more readily available, whiter flowers may have developed.

When I posed this idea to an electronic gathering place of people interested in botany, one correspondent reported a different possibility. "It is generally true that brighter colored flowers are found nearer the Equator," she said, noting that the "natural range of white Eastern dogwood reaches to central New York, but the pink ones are found only much farther south. One theory is that more light is required for plants to develop colored flowers."

Surviving the Elements but Not Humans

Spring-beauty has other techniques for survival. Scurrying about the forest floor early in the season, ants are only too happy to steal a sip of nectar when it's available. Spring-beauty has protected itself from most crawlers by evolving a very slender stem that most ants cannot negotiate to reach the blossom. These stems are also quite flexible, able to bend without breaking in the often harsh winds of March and early April.

To help deal with the cold, the spring-beauty closes its flower when the sun is low in the sky or when rain threatens. This helps conserve heat and also prevents rainwater from diluting the nectar and washing away the pollen.

Most spring flowers of the forest floor have broad leaves, the better to collect the sparse rays of the sun during the shady days of late spring and summer. Spring-beauty's leaves are different—slender and grasslike. Because it is one of the earliest bloomers, this leaf form suits the plant well. Easily positioned toward the sun, the blades can capture the sunlight coming in at the relatively low angle found in the early spring. (Slender leaves are more often found on plants that live in the full sun of the open fields. These summertime species can aim the tips of their long leaves right at the sun so its desiccating rays don't strike the leaves broadside.)

Though it's well able to deal with the cold, spring-beauty has been less able to deal with humans. Naturalist and wildflower gardener Frank C. Pellett wrote in the 1930s that "this is one of the plants which suffers greatly from the common practice of picking great bunches of flowers. Since there is but one stem, bearing both flowers and leaves, nothing is left to support the root and ripen the tuber for another year's growth." Often, the corm whose flower has been picked will die. Ironically, picking spring-beauty is useless from the start: they quickly wilt and are wasted.

North America is home to several species of spring-beauty. On the East Coast, Virginia spring-beauty or just plain spring-beauty (*Claytonia virginica*) and Carolina spring-beauty (*C. caroliniana*) both have about the same ranges—from southern Canada into the mountains of the southern states and out to the Mississippi River region. They differ chiefly in the width of their leaves and in their favored habitats. *C. virginica* likes moist woods and clearings, often near streams, while *C. caroliniana* is usually found in mountains.

On the West Coast, *C. lanceolata* is the chief representative of the genus. Like the eastern species, this is a white or pink flower, though there is a yellow version, *C. lanceolata* var. *flava*, which is rare enough to be on or considered for endangered species lists in the Pacific Northwest. The Rockies are home to several mountain-loving species. In a book on Utah wildflowers, Dixie Rose observed: "Blossoms of spring-beauty are like innocent little girls in pinstriped pinafores."

Indian or miners' lettuce, *C. perfoliata*, is found on the Pacific Coast to the Dakotas. The plant was so popular as a salad green and cooked vegetable that it was imported into Europe where it grows wild today. The English call it water weed because it prefers wet feet.

Claytonia, the generic name, recalls John Clayton, who came to Virginia as a child in 1705. Though he was an official of the Gloucester County government for a half century, Clayton's real interest was botany, and he spent much of his life collecting specimens. He sent them to a botanist named Johann Friedrich Gronovius who named and categorized them in *Flora Virginica*, published in 1739 and 1743. Clayton died in 1773.

Candy

Spring-beauties are members of the Portulaca, or Purslane, family, a relatively small group of about 20 genera and 600 species of herbs and shrubs found around the world, but mostly in western North and South America. The clan includes the namesake genus, *Portulaca*. These purslanes are generally weedy plants that have been used as foods and medicines for thousands of years.

Spring-beauties are not only edible, but considered delicious. The tasty part is the corm, small and nutlike, and while it takes time and effort to gather enough to make worthwhile servings, fans swear it's worth the trouble. American Indian children were especially fond of digging up this underground "candy." Spring-beauty tubers have been prepared mashed, fried, baked, boiled, or raw, and are, when cooked, invariably likened to potatoes or chestnuts, though some say they are sweeter and more flavorful. Raw, they are said to taste like radishes. They may be cooked with or without their potato-like skin or jacket. Both the taste and the skin have led to some of its folk names, including fairy-spuds and wild potatoes.

Of course, eating spring-beauty corms in quantity may threaten populations of a plant that's already in short supply in some parts of its range. I'd recommend enjoying the flowers and leaving the roots to return each year and re-create new editions. However, I wouldn't press that point with one of its biggest fans, the grizzly bear.

Green Gold

During the California gold rush, fresh vegetables and fruit were hard to find, and many miners contracted scurvy and other diseases caused by vitamin deficiencies. From the Spanish or maybe even the local American Indians, many miners learned of a nutritious and tasty plant that would keep them healthy and that grew profusely in the wet spring woods. The plant, *Claytonia perfoliata*, became known as miners' lettuce.

Anemones

FLOWERS OF THE WIND

Loved by poets and feared by peasants, anemones
are sure signs of spring.

Wood anemone uses the spring winds to pollinate its flowers.

Early spring is the windy season, when nature sweeps away the cold and snow, and awakens long-sleeping roots with gusts of warmer air. In my neighborhood, among the first plants to stir under these beckoning blasts is the appropriately named "windflower."

Also known as the wood anemone, this plant and its closely related cousin, the rue-anemone, seem too small and delicate to force their way through the recently thawed earth and survive this chilly season. Yet on inspection, the wood anemone is ideally designed to bear the brunt of the strongest spring winds.

"The practical scientist sees in the anemone, trembling and bending before the wind, a perfect adaptation to its environment," noted Neltje Blanchan, a naturalist at the turn of the 20th century. It is "anchored in the light soil by a horizontal rootstock (and is) furnished with a stem so slender and pliable no blast can break it."

Anemones not only are protected against the wind but also take advantage of it. When the weather is cloudy—and clouds often accompany the spring winds—the white flowers nod. The breezes jar loose pollen and carry it to nearby blossoms, thus fertilizing without the need for insects that are few in number so early in the season. The blossoms consequently have no nectar and little scent, devices used by other plants to attract pollinators.

Windy Ways

Anemone is based on the Greek word for "wind," whose root word means "breathes" or "lives," the same root from which words like *animated* and *animal* stem. Some authorities say the generic name means "wind" because the flower was believed to bloom when the wind blows. Another theory is more specific, maintaining *anemone* is a combination of *anemos*, meaning "wind," and *mone*, "habitat," suggesting that the plant lives in windy places. Others say the genus was named for Anemone, a nymph who was loved by Zephyr but who was transformed into a flower by the jealous Flora. Still others believe it comes from *Namaan,* a Semitic name for the god Adonis; one story had it that these flowers sprang from the drops of Adonis's blood after he was killed by a boar, and another says they grew from the tears of Aphrodite as she wept for Adonis, who was her lover. Take your pick.

Anemones are members of the Buttercup, or Crowfoot, family of about 1,100 species in 35 genera worldwide. The genus, *Anemone,* has some 85 species, about 25 of which are found in North America, mostly in colder climates.

Gay Circles

Wood anemone, *Anemone quinquefolia,* is usually found growing in woods, particularly around the roots of trees. Although the flower is solitary, plants usually cluster together, probably the better to effect pollination by wind. William Cullen Bryant observed:

> Within the woods,
> Whose young transparent leaves scarce cast
> A shade, gay circles of anemones
> Danced on their stalks.

Wood anemone, one of the most common anemones in the East, is found from Nova Scotia down to the Georgia highlands and westward to Minnesota. *Quinquefolia* describes the leaves that usually, but not always, come in sets of five; in many anemones, leaves are in threes. The plant's folk names include woodflower, mayflower, nimbleweed, and wild cucumber.

Rue-anemone is often confused with the wood anemone. Both have white, similarly shaped flowers, blooming at the same times and in the same places. However, wood anemone has clusters of three to five deeply cut leaves while rue-anemone has roundish leaves with three to five tips. In addition, wood anemone sends up single flowers while rue-anemone has clusters of several blossoms. Both can have between 5 and 10 petal-like sepals; neither has petals. Wood anemone usually bears 5 sepals and its cousin, usually 6. Bryant's "gay circles of anemones" may have been rue-anemone, often found growing near, even intermixed with, the wood anemone. Rue-anemone is found from Ontario as far south as Florida and as far west as Kansas.

For a long time, rue-anemone was considered a monotypic species called *Anemonella thalictroides*—literally, "little anemone thalictrum-like." *Thalictrum* is the generic name for the meadowrues, summer-blooming plants that have leaves very similar to rue-anemone's. (*Thalictrum* is a Greek word for a plant whose identity today is unknown.) Around 1990 rue-anemone was moved to the sizable *Thalictrum* genus, the name was changed to *Thalictrum thalictroides,* and the result is what sounds like botanical silliness. While the name has a certain rhythm, it means: "A rue anemone that's like a rue-anemone."

Rue, incidentally, has nothing to do with sorrow or regret, as in the English noun and verb, but is from the Latin, *ruta,* or the Greek, *rhute,* words that refer to the rue plant.

Anticipation

Beside a fading bank of snow
A lovely anemone blew,
Unfolding to the sun's bright glow
Its leaves of heaven's serenest hue.
'Tis spring, I cried; pale winter's fled;
The earliest wreath of flowers is
    blown;
The blossoms, withered long and
    dead,
Will soon proclaim their tyrant
    flown.
—James Gates Percival
    (1795–1856)

Thunderbolt

In Staffordshire, England, "the natives gave it the name of thunderbolt, and explained to me very carefully that I must on no account pluck it. If I did, it would certainly bring on a thunderstorm, and without a doubt, I would be struck."
—E. Deacon, (1930)

Elaiosomes

Anemones are among the many spring woodland plants that make use of ants to spread their seeds. The seed casings bear tasty tidbits called elaiosomes. The ants haul the seeds to their nests—as far as 75 yards or more—where they eat the elaiosomes, then discard the seeds in an unused tunnel where they can sprout in a protected environment (see page 49 in the chapter on violets).

For some anemones, such as European wood anemone, *Anemone nemorosa,* protection may be important. The embryo isn't developed when the seed leaves the plant but forms slowly during the fall and winter, and is ready by germination in the spring.

Among the many North American members of the genus are such eastern woodland species as the thimbleweeds, *A. virginiana* and *A. cylindrica,* named for their thimble-like seed clusters, and the Canada anemone, *A. canadensis.* All look like bleached buttercups, and were popular with North American Indian medicine men. More showy are the spectacular pasque flowers of the western prairies, so called because they bloom around Easter. *A. patens* is a handsome white flower, cuplike and much bigger than the eastern anemones. The western pasque flower, *A. occidentalis,* a mountain species of the far West, has large yellow flowers.

Life and Death

Anemones have a long history of folk recognition, for better or worse. The ancient Greeks believed that Anemos, the wind, used the flowers to herald the coming of spring. Romans carefully picked the first anemone of the year, with a prayer to protect them from fevers.

Crusaders are said to have returned from the Middle East with the beautiful poppy anemone (*A. coronaria*). The sudden appearance in Europe of this red-and-white flower sparked tales of its having sprung from the drops of Christ's blood, and it became a popular flower in the gardens of medieval monasteries. In fact, some believe that since this flower grew in great numbers in the somewhat bleak hills of its native Palestine, the poppy anemone was the flower Christ spoke of when he said: "Consider the lilies of the field . . . even Solomon in all his glory was not arrayed like one of these." This species, which has graced gardens for centuries, is the parent of many colorful cultivated anemones.

Oddly enough, however, many European peasants avoided some anemones as if they carried the plague. When they came upon a field of the flowers, they would hold their breath and run by, fearing they would fall ill if they inhaled the vapors of the blossoms. Egyptians considered the flowers a symbol of sickness, and in China they were planted on graves and called the flowers of death.

Nonetheless, old herbalists found the plant useful for headaches, gout, leprosy, eye inflammations, and ulcers. Typical of the buttercups, anemones are generally acrid plants, and many species are said to be somewhat poisonous. North American Indians of Quebec used an anemone tea for just about any ailment, while other native nations employed it in treating boils, lung congestion, and eye illnesses. Virgil J. Vogel, in *American Indian Medicine,* reported that

Meskwakis burned seeds to make a smoke that was supposed to revive unconscious persons. Some Ojibwas used the plant to soothe and prepare their throats for singing.

Modern authorities usually advise against such practices because the plant has some poisonous constituents. Carolus Linnaeus, the Swedish botanist who developed the modern system of classifying and naming plants and animals, reported that underfed cows died from eating *A. nemorosa*.

Culture

Though certainly not endangered, neither the wood anemone nor rue-anemone is particularly common, and neither should ever be picked, nor should transplanting be attempted unless it will save them from being destroyed. To try to establish them, use seeds collected in the spring or purchased from a wildflower seed house. Plant anemone seeds in the spring and rue-anemone in the fall. They favor slightly acid soils in situations similar to those found in open deciduous woods—not too dry and not too wet.

Whether you enjoy them in your wildflower garden or in the woods, native anemones (true and rue) remain among the sure signs that the hosts of spring wildflowers are on their way. I have seen anemones blooming as early as April 15, and as late as May 15. Only the skunk cabbage, coltsfoot, arbutus, certain violets, spring-beauties, and hepaticas (which are related) may appear earlier in my woods.

Perhaps we can be more happy about seeing them than was the winter-weary Nathaniel Hawthorne when he was writing his fiancée in the spring of 1841: "There has been but one flower found in this vicinity—and that was an anemone, a poor, pale, shivering little flower that had crept under a stone wall for shelter."

Prating Physicians

Nicholas Culpeper extolled the anemone's bitterness in urging that the plant be chewed to relieve headaches. "And when all is done," he wrote in the early 1600s, "let physicians prate what they please, all the pills in the dispensary purge not the head like to hot things held in the mouth."

Coltsfoot

ROADSIDE COUGH MEDICINE

Coltsfoot, a dandelion look-alike, is an excellent example of survival of the fittest.

Coltsfoot flowers are often confused with dandelions but have a center disc that dandelions lack.

The first beacons of spring rise from the ground at just about the equinox in my neighborhood, and among the showiest are the yellow and orange heads of the coltsfoot. Big, bright bunches of them assure us that the drabness of winter is ending, and that color is returning to the land.

Commonly seen along roadsides in northern states and southern provinces, the coltsfoot is a European import that has been marching from the Atlantic Coast westward for more than a century. It settles in some of our poorest soils; one sizable patch near my house thrives in a roadside shoulder composed chiefly of salty highway sand from years of winter storms. The plants' only demands seem to be open sunlight and moist ground.

At a distance the flower is often mistaken for the dandelion, to which it bears a strong resemblance. But viewed up close, the flowers are distinctly different. Coltsfoot has yellow rays surrounding an orangish disk in daisy-like fashion, while dandelions have mostly rays and no disk. Coltsfoot has a stout stem covered with hairy, scale-like projections while the dandelion has a smooth, slender stem. Also, coltsfoot blooms well before the leaves emerge while dandelions show flowers and leaves together.

One of a Kind

In fact, no flower is really like coltsfoot. *Tussilago farfara* is the only species within its genus, making it "monotypic." Its native territory is northern Europe, North Africa, and Asia. In North America, it has moved westward from the Atlantic states and provinces into Minnesota, Manitoba, and perhaps beyond, favoring cooler climates and blooming in March or, if the winter has been harsh or late, in early April.

Few people associate the roundish leaves, which appear later in the spring and last till fall, with the flowers that bloomed months earlier. The leaves are rather large and similar to the hoofprint of an unshod horse, earning the plant its common name. Coltsfoot has a bad reputation among farm-

ers in England, where the plant sometimes would infest fields. The wide leaves arose around the same time as the grain crop and could blanket large areas of the fields.

Coltsfoot, however, has largely been considered a friend of humans. In fact, in 1971, Czechoslovakia issued a commemorative postage stamp in its honor. Coltsfoot was so widely used as a medicine that, for many years, the hanging-sign symbol of apothecary shops in France was the shape of its leaf. A popular remedy for the cough, the plant contains much mucilage, which coats and soothes an irritated throat. The generic name is based on the Latin, *tussis*, and means "cough dispeller." Robitussin, the popular line of patent cough medicines, uses the same root word.

When youngsters in New England came down with a cough or cold in the 19th century, they were often given coltsfoot candies, made from an extract of the leaves and lots of sugar. Strange as it may seem, asthmatics used to smoke coltsfoot to gain relief. "The fume of the dried leaves taken through a funnell or tunnell, burned upon coles, effectually helpeth those that are troubled with the shortnesse of breath, and fetch their winde thicke and often," wrote John Gerard, the 16th-century herbalist. Gypsies smoked the dried leaves for pleasure. These leaves were an important ingredient in an English pipe mixture called British Herb Tobacco.

While Coltsfoot was employed mainly for respiratory problems, Nicholas Culpeper, another early herbalist, listed all sorts of unpleasant maladies it would handle, among them "St. Anthony's fire, and burnings, and (it) is singular good to take away wheals and small pushes that arise through heat, as also the burning heat of the piles or privy parts, cloths wet therein being thereunto applied." Coltsfoot was also used to treat diarrhea, insect bites, inflammations, leg ulcers, and phlebitis. Dried coltsfoot leaves were brewed as an aromatic tea, and the ashes obtained by burning the leaves were once used to season foods.

Modern research indicates, however, that the coltsfoot is a plant best used with care. Studies in Japan found that the flowers fed to rats caused liver tumors. Some authorities say that alkaloids in the flowers and leaves can cause liver damage, though a Swedish study concluded that simmering them for at least a half hour removed the alkaloids. Nonetheless, the plant is best used for nonmedicinal purposes. For instance, you could stuff mattresses with the seed hairs, as the Scottish Highlanders did, or soak the leaves in a saltpeter solution to produce a taper that burns as bright as a torch, as English peasants did.

Coltsfoot is an important bee plant, providing nectar early in the season when flowers are uncommon. Coltsfoot can self-pollinate so it does not depend entirely on bees to perform this service. Self-pollination occurs when the flowers close up, pressing male and female parts together.

A Study in Survival

Coltsfoot is a study in highly evolved survival techniques. The flowers flourish at a harsh time of the year when temperatures may vary dozens of degrees, often dipping below freezing. To retain heat and insulate against icy blasts, the stalk, or "scape," is covered with hairy scales. Some scientists think these scales are tinged red because red is supposed to better absorb the heat of the sun.

The Coltsfoot Gold

A thousand years will come and go,
And thousands more will rise,
My buried bones to dust will grow
And dust defile my eyes.
But when the lark sings o'er the world
And the swallow weaves her nest,
My soul will take the Coltsfoot gold
And blossom on my breast.
—Alfred Williams (1877–1930)

As the new stalk arises, the closed flower head is usually turned toward the ground to protect the plant against both cold and rain. When the plant blooms, the head straightens up and looks directly at the sun to absorb maximum radiation. However, the flower closes at night and stays closed on cloudy or cold days, conserving heat and displaying the blossom only when insects are least likely to appear.

The disk is composed of about 40 tightly packed florets, shaped like upside-down bells. These florets serve the male function of giving off pollen. The many ray florets around the outside of the disk possess female parts, and project pollen-catching stigmas. Thus, an insect drawn to the bright flower wanders around the disk, easily extracting nectar from the conveniently compact collection of florets and in the process picking up pollen. The insect takes off for another flower, lands on the rays (which act as landing strips), and brushes against the ray-flower stigmas, which rake off some pollen and are fertilized. This typical Composite-family design has thus used its colony of two different floret forms to efficiently attract, reward, and extract payment from the insect.

When sufficiently fertilized, the head folds up and again droops for protection. Any flower parts no longer of value, such as the disk florets, the rays, and the bracts that supported the flower, quickly wither, focusing the plant's strength on developing the seeds. A few days later the head stands up again and displays a dandelion-like "clock" of fuzz-topped seeds, all set for the spring breezes to catch and carry to distant fields. Coltsfoot seeds have been known to travel more than 8.6 miles (14 km).

While the seeds are important for creating new colonies, coltsfoot can also expand existing ones through underground runners. Even if broken off from the parent plant, these runners can establish new plants—a survival technique that makes it difficult to eradicate a colony simply by digging or plowing.

Though the task of the flower is now complete, the coltsfoot's work is hardly done. As the flowers die away, the leaves appear, growing only a few inches off the ground but up to 10 inches across. At first they wear a coating of "fur" on the top to protect them from the cold but shed it as the weather warms. (Cottony hair under the leaf, retained to keep moisture and dust away from the breathing pores, or "stomata," was once gathered by English villagers for tinder.)

The leaves manufacture food to store as starch in the roots, nourishment for the next year's flowers. However, those large leaves perform other functions. They shade the ground underneath, cutting off light to any other plants that might compete with the coltsfoot. The leaves' shade also helps prevent evaporation of the moist ground—the plant likes wet feet. Finally, the leaves collect rain and direct it down the stalk to the roots below.

Coltsfoot Candies

Coltsfoot candies, the cough drop of the 19th century, were made by boiling down a mixture of fresh leaves and water, removing the leaves, adding lots of sugar, boiling again till there's a thick syrup, and dropping spoonfuls of it into cold water.

Farmyard Names

Its medicinal properties have earned the plant its other common name, coughwort, but it has a whole farmyard full of folk names, including horsefoot, horsehoof, dovedock, sowfoot, colt-herb, hoofs, cleats, ass's-foot, bull's-foot, foalfoot, foalswort, ginger, clayweed (reflecting the habitat it likes), butter-bur, and dummy weed. One of its oldest names is *filius-ante-patrem*, Latin for "son before father," because the flowers show up before the leaves do. *Farfara*, incidentally, is an old word for the white poplar tree, whose leaves are similar to the coltsfoot's. (The name coltsfoot is sometimes applied to our marsh marigold, which is not related to true coltsfoot. There's also a clan of plants that is related and is called sweet coltsfoot, or petasites, usually found in more northern climates.)

A perennial, coltsfoot is easy to establish from seed, readily obtained from the freshly opened clocks and planted in wet, clayish soil. The plants will quickly spread, as witness the fact that 100 years ago coltsfoot was so uncommon that even North American wildflower experts had trouble figuring out what it was. Now it's widespread in the cooler East, and will probably work its way across the continent, and maybe into more southern states in the coming decades.

The arrival of another early flower, especially one that inhabits waste places, should please many who enjoy wildflowers, for spring flowers are often the most cherished, especially in regions where cold winters kill the plant life or force it into hibernation. Spring flowers bring color to eyes accustomed to the monotony of brown and white. And for splashes of lively color after the snows melt, coltsfoot can't be beat.

Coltsfoot Tea

Coltsfoot was a common treatment for coughs due to colds, bronchitis, and asthma. Here's how a decoction was typically made:

1 ounce coltsfoot leaves and/or flowers (collected in late spring)
1 quart water
Boil down to a pint. Add sugar, honey, or licorice to taste.
Served by the teacupful.
—*Maude Grieve*

Bloodroot

A BLOODY EARLY BLOOMER

Bloodroot's red juice may help keep teeth white.

Perhaps because we have been so long without flowers, the earliest seem to be among the most beautiful: exotic, orange red columbine; dainty, pastel hepatica; bright, golden coltsfoot; and ivory anemone. Among the largest-flowered of the early bloomers is the bloodroot. It is ironic that a plant named for so strong a color bears flower petals of such pure white, but the namesake "blood" is the plant's orange red juice, which can be seen in the reddish stem and on your fingers if you pick one.

Bloodroot rises from the cold earth as soon as it can. "It is singular how little warmth is necessary to encourage these . . . flowers to put forth," wrote naturalist John Burroughs in 1871. "It would seem as if some influence must come on in advance underground and get things ready, so that, when the outside temperature is propitious, they at once venture out. I have found the bloodroot when it was still freezing two or three nights a week . . ."

I've found bloodroot flowers as early as April 13 in Connecticut, but they are more common at the beginning of May. Flowering requires a lot of work for a plant, and work requires energy and food. Bloodroot and other March and April flowers can put on their floral shows so early because they have stored food over the previous season in their thick roots, corms, or bulbs. Most plants that flower in late spring, summer, or fall rely on food gathered in the current season.

The protective leaves of the bloodroot are still wrapped around the flower stalks of these just-opened blossoms.

Endearing Arrival

Bloodroot's arrival is almost endearing. Both the budded stalk and the plant's single leaf arise together, but in no ordinary fashion. The leaf is wrapped around the stem and bud, like a mother protecting its baby with a cloak. When the bud is ready to blossom, the stalk pushes the bud just a bit higher than the leaf so that when the petals open, they are still given a degree of protection by the enveloping leaf.

And well they should be protected. The petals, from 7 to 12 of them, are so delicate that the blossoms often last only a day or two before a strong wind or a heavy shower rips them away. Probably for this reason, wild bloodroot has never evolved into a particularly popular garden plant.

"This is the reason why some of our most beautiful wild flowers are not cultivated by florists," wrote naturalist F. Schuyler Mathews in 1901. "It does not pay to spend much time over such ephemeral lives."

A half century after Mathews wrote those words, one freak bloodroot plant, found in the midwestern United States, would produce a variety whose flowers are more durable. "Peony flowers," or double bloodroot (*Sanguinaria canadensis multiplex*, or *florepleno*), have all descended from that one plant.

A Poppy

As its shape suggests, *Sanguinaria canadensis* is a member of the Poppy family (Papaveraceae), a small group of some 115 species in 23 genera, found mostly in north temperate zones. Its generic name refers to the orange red, bloodlike color of the juice and to a portion of its range; it was probably first identified in Canada. The only member of its genus in the world, bloodroot is found wild from Nova Scotia to Florida and as far west as Manitoba and Nebraska. It has been imported to Europe, where it also does well.

Other names for the plant include coon root, snakebite (from its poisonous characteristic), sweet slumber (it was used to induce sleep), red root, corn root, turmeric, and tetterwort (a "tetter" is a skin disease).

The plant's juice is so abundant and such a potent dye that several wildflower manuals warn against picking the flowers because the fluid will stain anything it touches. The American Indians knew this, and used the juice mixed with animal fat to paint their faces (whence another name, "Indian paint"). Bloodroot juice would also dye baskets, decorate weapons and implements, and color clothing. Colonists were quick to catch on, and used the plant to dye cloth—particularly wool—a reddish orange, using alum as a "mordant," or stabilizing agent. Even the French once imported it as a dye.

Medicinal Uses

Medicine men in various tribes noticed that, when injured, the plant "bled" like a human, and they took this as a sign that bloodroot was good for treating ulcers, ringworm, and other skin afflictions. Learning this, a London physician of the mid-19th century concocted a treatment for skin cancers, consisting of bloodroot, zinc chloride, flour, and water. The treatment was extensively used at London's Middlesex Hospital and eventually fell out of use, but was resumed in the 1960s for minor cancers and polyps of the nose and ear. Authorities still debate its cancer-treating value.

The juice's color may have also led to its widespread use among the Algonquian nations as a blood purifier. Calling the plant puccoon or paucon, a name that refers to the red juice, some tribes used it to treat cramps, stop vomiting, induce abortions, and even repel insects. According to Gladys Tantaquidgeon, a Mohegan who wrote of the folk medicines of northeastern U.S. tribes, "For general debility, a pea-sized piece of root is taken every morning for 30 days."

Milky Way

What time the earliest ferns unfold
And meadow cowslips count their
    gold;
A countless multitude they stood,
A Milky Way within the wood.
White are my dreams, but whiter
    still,
The bloodroot on the lonely hill;
Lovely and pure my visions rise,
To fade before my yearning eyes;
But on that day I thought I trod
'Mid the embodied dreams of God.
Tho' frail those flowers, tho' brief
    their sway,
They sanctified one perfect day;
And tho' the summer may forget,
In my rapt soul they blossom yet.
—Danske Dandridge
    (1854–1919)

First Line

". . . Sanguinaria extract may significantly reduce concentrations of oral microorganisms for short periods of time and should be recommended for a first line of defense."
—*University of Colorado Health Services Center*

Puccoons

At least a half-dozen North American plants, besides bloodroot, bear the name puccoon or something similar. Though they may not be related to one another, they share the color red, be it in petals, leaves, or juice. *Puccoon* comes from the Virginia Algonquian word, *pak*, meaning "blood." *Pokan* meant anything used as a red dye, and thus we also have pokeweed, pocan-bush, and poke-root.

The plant contains protopine, also found in opium, and the tinctures and powder obtained from the rootstock have also been used by North Americans to treat a variety of ailments. *The Ladies' Indispensable Assistant* (1852) said bloodroot "is excellent in coughs and croup. It is an emetic, and narcotic; produces perspiration, and menstrual discharge; is good in influenza, hooping cough, and phthisic [lung disease]. It is good in bilious complaints, combined with black cherrytree bark, also in cases of scarlet fever and catarrh." Indians and colonists would put a few drops of the juice on a lump of maple sugar, which they'd suck to relieve coughs and sore throats. The sugar was necessary because the taste is so nauseating that it can cause "expectorant action."

Many modern herbalists warn that if the juice gets on the skin, it may cause an allergic reaction similar to that of poison ivy. Modern herbals describe its uses but often warn that the plant is so strong that it should never be ingested or used without medical supervision. An overdose can kill a person, though its taste is so awful it's hard to believe anyone could consume an overdose.

Medicine men and herbalists alike apparently overlooked bloodroot's chief modern use. In 1983 Vipont Pharmaceuticals—a company formed in the late 1960s by a rodeo cowboy from Colorado—began marketing Viadent toothpaste and mouth rinse, both containing an extract of bloodroot considered excellent for reducing the growth of plaque. The American Dental Association said the extract, called sanguinarine, was a promising plaque-fighter, and a former surgeon general of the Army Dental Corps was quoted as calling it "the best thing that's happened since fluoride. What fluoride has done in fighting tooth decay, this material will do in preventing gum disease." However, recent research has suggested that for sanguinarine to be effective, both the mouthwash and the toothpaste must be used.

Trickery

Bloodroot is a fine early-spring plant for rich woods or shady borders. Although it transplants readily in the spring, it is not overly common in many areas and should not be removed from natural habitats, unless the locality is in danger of destruction or has an overabundance of plants. It's better to obtain the seeds, which have a good germination rate, or to buy plants from a reputable nursery. Because they will self-sow, the plants can, in good situations, form large colonies. And if the weather's not too harsh, the blossoms can last for a week or more.

Bloodroot flowers manage pollination by trickery. The blossoms have no nectar, but their inviting petals and the bright yellow anthers (the part of the stamen that bears the pollen) attract insects, which transfer pollen picked up during their hopeless search for sweets. However, the visit isn't a total loss for bees and other insects that are pollen eaters.

An Ontario man told me the flowers bloom in his area long before any bees appear. His observations suggested the plants readily self-pollinate. "This is corroborated to some extent by examination: the stamens form a tight ring around the stigma and it is quite easy for the pollen, ejected from their sacs, to hit the stigma." No doubt, the colder the climate, the less likely this early bloomer is to be visited by bees. Like other flowers, especially in spring, they are apparently able to produce seed with or without insect help.

Dandelion

OUR TULIP IN THE GRASS

The dandelion could be our most valuable and useful "weed."

To many homeowners the dandelion is little more than a prolific, pesky weed. To others, however, this abundant yellow-flowering plant provides not only beauty but also food, drink, medicine, entertainment, and even inspiration for poetry.

Perhaps no one has praised the dandelion better than Wallace Nutting, the noted early-20th-century photographer and author. "The dandelion is the greatest natural agent of decoration in our part of America," he wrote in *Connecticut Beautiful* (1923). "In some fields it is so abundant that there is no more than enough grass visible to give it a setting . . . . It is so thoroughly at home that we feel it to be the most prominent and persistent native American, whatever its origin. Coming as it does in the early spring, it clothes an entire landscape with its gorgeous color, and rejoices the heart of man. . . . It is our tulip in the grass."

Among our thousands of species of wildflowers, the common dandelion may be the most common; probably its only close competitor is the common chickweed. Not only are its numbers great, but also its flowering season is one of the longest of any of our plants. Although they are most common in spring, I have seen them blooming in every month of the year in Connecticut, though finding one in January or February is rare.

Most authorities report that the common dandelion came here from Europe but originated in Asia Minor. It spread like wildfire across the continent, as it has across most of the civilized world. Even the most casual observer of flora knows why. The dandelion's highly efficient system of transmitting seeds makes use of the wind, which can carry its fuzz-topped fruits long distances.

While they are targets of lawn herbicides, dandelions have been much admired—and eaten—over the centuries.

Timeless Toys

Besides ensuring the species' survival, these seeds provide entertainment for millions of children. What youngster has never blown or waved the seed-laden stalks and watched with glee as the "fuzzies" floated off? Years ago, children used to "tell" the hour of the day by counting the number of times they had to blow before all of the seeds would separate from the head or by counting the number of seeds remaining after one good blow. That's why the fuzz-heads are often called clocks, and the plant is sometimes called blowball.

Maidens would blow at the ball, and the remaining seeds would foretell the number of children they'd have when they were grown and married. Instead of picking the petals of daisies, some youngsters would play "he loves me, he loves me not" (or the "she" version) by blowing the clocks down to the last seed.

In England, children well into the 20th century believed the flying seeds were fairies. If you caught one, you made a wish. But you had to let the fairy go on its way for the wish to be granted.

Another favorite pastime of children, particularly girls, was making chains, bracelets, and curls from the hollow flower stems, called "scapes." Here's how a scientist, Charles F. Millspaugh, used his technical training to describe in *American Medicinal Plants* a child's work on a dandelion: "The curls are formed as follows: a split is started in four directions at the smaller end of a scape, into which the tongue is deftly and gradually inserted, causing a slow separation into sections that curl backward, revolutely, being kept up to their form by the tongue, when the scape is curled to the end it is drawn several times through the operator's mouth and partially uncurled into graceful ringlets."

Much less technical is the poet. "My childhood's earliest thoughts are linked with thee," wrote James Russell Lowell in "To the Dandelion," in which he described the

> *Dear common flower, that grow'st beside the way,*
> *Fringing the dusty road with harmless gold*
> *First pledge of blithesome May,*
> *Which children pluck, and, full of pride uphold,*
> *High-hearted buccaneers, o'erjoyed that they*
> *An eldorado in the grass have found,*
> *Which not the rich earth's ample round*
> *May match in wealth, thou are more dear to me*
> *Than all the prouder summer-blooms may be.*

Little Flowers

Unless you inspect the dandelion closely, you may think the bloom is just a mass of yellow petals or "rays." Each of the 100 to 200 rays is actually a tiny tube-shaped flower. Long, straplike rays extend from part of the top, outside edge of those tubes. Thus, one flower is actually a "composite" of many little ones, which is why the dandelion is a member of the huge Composite family of plants. The Composites are considered the most advanced and successful family of flowers, and surely the dandelion is a leader of the clan.

Dandelions open in the morning and close in the evening. The flowers will also quickly close with the first few drops of rain, perhaps a remnant of the stage in its evolution when it needed to protect its nectar and pollen. However, closing the flower head also helps to preserve heat on cool, early-spring nights. Its shut-tight appearance has given the flower one of its less attractive folk names, swine's snout.

Golden Kisses

"You cannot forget it, if you would, those golden kisses all over the cheeks of the meadow, queerly called dandelions."
—*Henry Ward Beecher*
(1813–1887)

It is interesting to observe that the dandelion flowers are usually only a little higher off the ground than the surrounding vegetation. In a frequently cut lawn or on waste ground without much vegetation, they tend to stay low; in a field, their scapes will send them up 12 to 18 inches off the ground—whatever's needed to best catch those seed-dispersing breezes.

Apomixis

Unlike most Composites, the dandelion does not need its showy flower display to attract insects, though many insects do stop by for its nectar; a German scientist counted 93 species that visited the dandelion. The genus is "apomict"; that is, it produces seeds without pollination. Because such seeds are genetically identical to those of the parent plant, apomixis tends to make life tough for botanists because countless "microspecies" of the genus are created. Every time a significant mutation occurs and a plant successfully produces seeds that spread and germinate, technically a new "species" is born.

Thus, while most texts identify only a handful of dandelion species in a given area, expert botanists can find enough differences that are transmitted from parent to child to identify hundreds of microspecies. In England alone, more than 150 dandelions have been identified this way. Yet the United States Department of Agriculture (USDA) lists more than 50 names of dandelion species that are really other names for *Taraxacum officinale*.

You, too, can notice different types or subspecies of the common dandelion. For example, in dry open fields at higher elevations, dandelions tend to have small flowers; in waste places, such as along roadsides, they tend to be large and coarse; and in wetlands, they often develop red leaf-veins.

To the scientist, the common dandelion is known as *Taraxacum officinale*. It is one of about eight recognized *Taraxacum* species found in North America, and around 25 known in the world. Some of these are natives. The USDA plant database recognizes five native dandelions, including the northern dandelion (*T. phymatocarpum*) and the fleshy dandelion (*T. carneocoloratum*), both found only in Alaska; the California dandelion (*T. californicum*), found only in California; the wool-bearing dandelion (*T. eriophorum*), found in the upper Rockies; and the harp dandelion (*T. lyratum*) of the Rocky Mountain states. Several other introduced species are also found.

The generic name, *Taraxacum*, is from the Persian, meaning "bitter herb," referring to the flavor of the leaves. *Officinale* is a Latin word that means "a shop where things are sold," and is meant to suggest that this was a plant that a professional herbalist would keep among his wares. Botanists never seem satisfied with a name, though, and this plant has also been known off and on since 1753 as *Leontodon taraxacum*, with *Leontodon* meaning literally "lion's tooth."

When each dandelion's blooming period is completed, the flower head folds up for several days and then reopens with an array of "fuzzies" to catch the wind. When the seeds have blown away, a smooth, rounded, white button remains, the inspiration for such names as monk's head and priest's crown. These names refer to the medieval custom of tonsure, in which the top of a priest's or monk's head was shaven clean as a sign of his eschewing vanity and other worldly ways.

Children's Flower

Dear dandelion, you sunshiny thing,
How many toys for the young folks
    you bring;
Watchchains for Nanny, and trum-
    pets for Ned,
Funny green curls for the baby's bald
    head;
Next your white seeds fly, which
    way the winds blow,
Friend of the barefoot boy, gold of the
    poor,
You're a wee playhouse at every
    child's door.
—Author unknown

Dandelion Dinner

The town of Vineland, New Jersey, known as the Dandelion Capital of the World, has about a dozen farmers who grow hundreds of acres of dandelions for the salad market. Each April, the chamber of commerce sponsors the Dandelion Dinner Festival with a meal that includes dandelion salad, dandelion soup with dandelion sausage, dandelion chicken Alfredo, and dandelion ravioli, all served with dandelion wine.

The dandelion has also been called milk gowan by the English, reflecting the whitish juice that also made an impression on Chippewas, who called it by a name that meant "milk root." That "milk" is sticky and contains latex. The Russians have done considerable experimentation with hybrids of the Russian dandelion or chew-root (*T. kok-saghyz*), which may yield three or four times the latex that ordinary dandelions can. In the United States there have been experiments with getting rubber from our dandelions, but none has proved commercially feasible.

Dandelion is a corruption of the French, *dents de lion*, "tooth of the lion," a name that is applied to the plant in almost every European tongue. Experts disagree on the origin of the name. Most think it's related to the deeply toothed leaves that could be said to resemble lion's teeth. Some, however, maintain the name is connected with the flower's color, which is the same as the yellow used for heraldic lions.

Other names for the plant include doon-head, puffball, yellow gowan (gowan is an Old World daisy-like flower), Irish daisy, cankerwort, and lion's tooth.

Remedies

While our English word for the plant is from the French, the French have often called the plant *pissenlit*—politely translatable as "wetting the bed"—because of a belief among children of many European nations that eating or even picking the flowers would cause them to wet their beds at night. Perhaps it's one of the hazards of curl making. One wag has gone so far as to suggest that instead of a potherb, dandelion could be considered a "potty herb."

The bed-wetting belief may have been connected with the fact that since the Middle Ages, dandelion root was used as a diuretic in the treatment of liver and kidney disorders. One modern British herbalist maintains that the plant is far better as a diuretic than drugs chemically produced by pharmaceutical companies. According to Mr. Millspaugh, the dandelion "is one of those drugs, overrated, derogated, extirpated, and reinstated time and again by writers upon pharmacology."

Indeed, the plant's deep-growing root has had many uses besides sparking the ire of lawn-loving homeowners and helping keep herbicide manufacturers in business. The root has been an ingredient in many patent medicines for such problems as dyspepsia, constipation, gallstones, insomnia, dropsy, and jaundice. Nicholas Culpeper, the Elizabethan herbalist, even claimed "this herb helps one to see farther without a pair of spectacles."

The roasted and ground root has been used for dandelion coffee and, some feel, it improves the taste of real coffee when added to the ground beans. Euell Gibbons maintained that the roasted root produces the best-tasting coffee substitute found in the wild on the North American continent. Many people, especially French Canadians, Europeans, and immigrants to America, dig up the roots in spring, slicing them into salads or boiling them as one would a parsnip, to which they are alike in consistency but not in taste.

To the plant, the deep root is important in survival. It enables the dandelion to go far down in the earth for water and thus to withstand dry spells that would kill other plants or make them dormant. The deep root also makes it difficult for animals—including humans—to destroy the plant, by eating, by digging, or by pulling. In these respects and in the root's popularity for food and drink, the dandelion is much like its cousin, the chicory.

Good Eating

The young leaves have long been used in salads and are sold in many grocery stores. Many people boil the leaves and serve them like spinach. "Young dandelion leaves make delicious sandwiches, the tender leaves being laid between slices of bread and butter, sprinkled with salt," wrote Maude Grieve in *A Modern Herbal* (1931). "The addition of a little lemon juice and pepper varies the flavor. The leaves should always be torn to pieces, rather than cut, in order to keep the flavor."

A friend of mine boils the fresh spring leaves about six minutes until they are tender and then mixes them with some salt pork that's been rendered with a little garlic. "It's super," she says. Bradford Angier, who wrote *Feasting Free on Wild Edibles*, liked his leaves scrambled with eggs. Apaches were said to be so fond of dandelions that they'd search for days to find enough to satisfy themselves. The amount that would be consumed by one Apache was said to exceed belief.

It should be emphasized that only the young leaves are used; older, mature leaves are too bitter to eat unless they are boiled twice, changing the water after the first boiling. True dandelion-leaf aficionados, doing what the chicory and endive fans do to produce "witloof," keep roots in the cellar, forcing them in winter—even year-round—to obtain blanched, tasty leaves for salads. A hundred years ago, many seed catalogues carried dandelions, even "improved" hybrids.

Nutritious, Too

The dandelion is able to bloom so early in the season, often long before the last frost, because the flowers are formed at the top of the root and are protected by a couple of inches of soil. As soon as the weather turns nice for a bit, the buds—all ready to go—quickly shoot up and open. Picked before they spring from the ground, these buds can be boiled and served with butter and seasoning. Buds and blossoms may also be dipped in batter and fried as a fritter, although Gibbons insists that the developing buds dug from beneath the ground are always better tasting than the ones that have seen the light of day.

The blooming flowers are often used in the preparation of an excellent wine. I have never had the patience to make dandelion wine but have had several bottles of homemade stock over the years. It was a thick, rather sweet, and tasty beverage.

The consumption of sundry parts of the dandelion dates back to ancient times. Its popularity may be related not only to its flavor and availability but also to recognition of its food value. Ancient Egyptians were known to prescribe the plant for various ailments that were probably caused by dietary deficiencies. Today it is known that the plant is rich in vitamins and minerals, especially in vitamin A. In fact, 3.5 ounces of dandelion leaves have much more vitamin A than the equivalent

Propaganda?

Could it be that somewhere along the line, dandelion aficionados hired a propaganda expert to assure the plant's survival? The propagandist could have spread stories about bed-wetting to scare children into not picking the flower but could also have circulated tales about blowing on the seed head to tell time or forecast events—thus encouraging the kids to disperse the seeds.

amount of carrots, known as a source of vitamin A. Ounce for ounce, dandelion leaves have more potassium than bananas, a popular source of that mineral. The leaves are also rich in thiamine, riboflavin, and calcium.

Animals also find the dandelion a tasty treat. Birds, of course, eat the seeds, as do small animals, such as mice. Rabbits, pigs, and goats enjoy the entire plant. While cows usually shun the plant because of its rather bitter-tasting juice, it has been said that a cow's eating the plant will increase its yield of milk.

For bees and about 100 other kinds of insects, the dandelion is an important supply of food, not only because it produces nectar but because it produces it at a time of year when other flowers may not be abundant.

However, to poet Lowell, the dandelion was much more than food and medicine. He concluded his poem:

> How like a prodigal doth nature seem,
> When thou, for all thy gold, so common art!
> Thou teachest me to deem
> More sacredly of every human heart,
> Since each reflects in joy its scanty gleam
> Of heaven, and could some wondrous secret show,
> Did we but pay the love we owe,
> And with a child's undoubting wisdom look
> On all these living pages of God's book.

Without a doubt, the dandelion is no ordinary weed, if we only "with a child's undoubting wisdom look." Opus, Berke Breathed's famous comic strip character of the 1980s and '90s, had this wisdom. When life became too stressful, Opus could be seen seated among the flowers in a lawn, taking a "dandelion break." He was a penguin of good taste.

American Columbine

AN ELFIN BEAUTY

This columbine is an all-American plant,
right down to its name.

Few plants have generated as much admiration as the American columbine. "Our columbine is at all times and in all places one of the most exquisitely beautiful of flowers," wrote John Burroughs. In fact, in a 1940s survey of hundreds of North American naturalists, the American columbine ranked as the seventh most popular native wildflower. Indeed, Europeans long ago admired its beauty and started importing the American columbine to their gardens in the early 1600s after John Tradescant, a noted naturalist of his time, first collected it.

This perennial likes rocky cliffs or outcroppings and limy soils—it's not unusual to find a clump of columbine growing from what seems like a handful of soil in a pocket on a huge boulder. "The early wild flowers seem to have selected the Columbines for their reception committee, and to have stationed them along the rocky balconies of woodland ridges during their spring festival, to extend a hearty welcome to all strangers who happen to pass," wrote Frederic William Stack in *Wild Flowers Every Child Should Know*. Such stony surroundings emphasize the flowers' charm but unfortunately have also encouraged some people to "rescue" it for their own gardens. "It contrives to secure a foothold in the most precipitous and uncertain of nooks, its jewel-like flowers gleaming from their lofty perches with a graceful insouciance which awakens our sportsmanlike instincts and fires us with the ambition to equal it in daring and make its loveliness our own," wrote Mrs. William Starr Dana. "Perhaps it is as well if our greediness be foiled and we get a tumble for our pains, for no flower loses more with its surroundings than the columbine."

Some people try to "rescue" it, moving it from a barren, rocky home to a crowded garden, where it loses much of its natural attractiveness and proper habitat. Or, worse, others succumb to the temptation to pick it, often pulling up the shallow roots in the process.

Lest those who have never seen the American columbine (*Aquilegia canadensis*) confuse it with the garden varieties, there is no real comparison. "Although under cultivation the columbine nearly doubles its size," wrote Neltje Blanchan, "it never has the elfin charm in a conventional garden that it possesses wild in nature's."

The American columbine is designed to be pollinated by hummingbirds.

Nor do cultivated varieties, most of which descend from a European species, possess the color or elegant form of wild American columbine. No other wildflower east of the Rockies has the same scarlet color, brightened by a sort of translucence. The rich exterior is complemented by a bright, yellow interior and yellow around the mouth.

Clever Design

The color and unusual shape of the blossom are part of nature's clever design, long in evolution. Each flower consists of five extended tubes or spurs that hold the nectar deep inside and away from most thieving insects. These tubes are longer in the native wild species than in the European or cultivated varieties. The common European wild columbine is blue, a color that attracts bees, which can easily reach into the shorter tubes to extract the sweets.

American columbine is red, a color that most attracts the ruby-throated hummingbird. Not coincidentally, hummingbirds are the only creatures that can easily sip the nectar from the flowers and, in so doing, pollinate them. The yellow opening and interior are said to guide the bird into the flower. Ms. Blanchan went so far as to suggest in 1900 that probably to the hummingbird "and no longer to the outgrown bumblebee, has the flower adapted itself." Although some bees, wasps, and other insects cheat the system by nibbling through the nectar end of the spur, only the largest, strongest, and longest-tongued insects, such as bumblebees, can draw nectar from the tube.

Hummingbirds, incidentally, are not found in Europe, where the native columbine is designed for insect pollination. It is interesting to note, too, that many of the columbines of western North America are white, yellow, or blue—colors that don't attract the hummingbird. These varieties use insects for pollination and consequently many have evolved forms more convenient for bees and flies. While American columbine is tubular, many western columbines are more open, with a display of beckoning petals. In addition, the western flowers are positioned horizontally, convenient to insects, while the American columbine dangles flowers upside down, which is fine for hummingbirds.

Several insects rely on the green parts of the American columbine for food and shelter. The larvae of two species of columbine leafminers (*Phytomyza*) eat serpentine "trails" through the leaves—consuming the flesh of the leaf and leaving mostly veining behind. There is also a columbine aphid, a columbine borer, and a columbine skipper. The last, *Erynnis lucilius*, is a kind of moth whose larva eats holes in the leaves. When it's time to rest, the caterpillar rolls up a leaf like a sleeping bag and hides inside.

A Buttercup

Few people who find this oddly shaped flower would guess it is a member of the Buttercup family and that it is closely related to anemones (see page 14) and hepaticas (see page 7), which bloom a bit earlier in spring than the columbine.

Aquilegia is a small genus of 50 species worldwide, but limited to north temperate zones. While Easterners have only one native, *A. canadensis*, more than a dozen species live in the West,

particularly in the Rockies, where they find the kind of cold they seem to like. Colorado's state flower is the Rocky Mountain blue columbine, *A. caerulea*.

Aquilegia may come from the Latin for "eagle" because of a fancied resemblance of the flower's spurs to an eagle's talons. Or it may be a combination of *aqua*, "water," and *lego*, "to collect," a reference to the nectar-holding spurs. A bird of peace, not of war, figures into the common English name. Columbine is from the Latin, *columba*, meaning "dove." Some say the name stems from an imagined likeness of the flowers—probably of a European species—to a flight of doves. Others say the resemblance is to a circle of doves or pigeon heads, a design commonly painted on dishes and other circular objects long ago. Other folk names for the plant include culverwort (from the Saxon, *culfre*, meaning "pigeon," and *wyrt*, "plant"), rock bells, rock lily, bells, meeting houses, cluckies, and jack-in-trousers—a name that sounds rather risqué, and may well be.

Poisoning the Kids

Years ago New Englanders used to honor veterans, especially on Memorial or Decoration Day, by garnishing their graves with wild columbine and other flowers that would produce a red, white, and blue combination. Children, who used to call the flowers honeysuckle, would bite off the tips of the tubes for the sweets inside. At one time early in the 20th century, American columbine was touted as a candidate for the national flower. But there were less noble uses for the columbine. Giving a woman a bouquet of the flowers was a sign that her husband or lover was unfaithful.

The plant has some medicinal history, although few people today would think of ruining one to make a lotion for sore mouths or throats. "The seed taken in wine causeth a speedy delivery of women in childbirth," wrote the English herbalist Nicholas Culpeper. The common European or garden variety (*A. vulgaris*) was once fairly frequently used in Europe for this and other ailments—until physicians found that children were being poisoned by overdoses of it and that other herbs served their purposes better and more safely.

Young Meskwaki Indians mixed ripe seed capsules with smoking tobacco to improve its smell. They believed the seeds smoked or added to a potion yielded a "love perfume," handy when courting. Other Indians ate the roots and used the seeds in a tea for headaches and fever.

We might better use the seeds in establishing and spreading this uncommon perennial. Columbine favors dry rocky woods and outcroppings with a soil that has a pH of from 5 to 7.5 and that is not too rich. It spreads well from seeds, which can be gathered in July or purchased from wildflower nurseries, some of which also carry the plants. Columbine should never be transplanted from the wild unless threatened with certain destruction.

Remember to plant columbine in a situation similar to what it frequents naturally. "Nothing is daintier or more beautiful than the color effect of this graceful blossom among the gray rocks of a hillside pasture," said F. Schuyler Mathews. And once it is established, you, too, might be able to feel a little of the healing properties that Ralph Waldo Emerson once described: "A woodland walk, a quest for river-grapes, a mocking thrush, a wild rose or rock-living columbine, salve my worst wounds."

National Flower?

"I wonder where Uncle Sam could find a more beautiful or emblematic national flower than the columbine. Its range is general throughout the United States; the name of columbine as well as Columbia is derived from *colomba*—a dove, and is significant of our love for peace; its generic name—*Aquilegia*—is without doubt derived from the Latin, *aquila*, an eagle . . . the long spurs suggest horns of plenty while in another position they resemble a liberty cap; and if one takes into consideration the Rocky Mountain variety—*Aquilegia caerulea*—that appears in blue as well as white, we have the national colors—red, white, and blue."
—*Arthur Craig Quick* (1939)

Dutchman's Breeches

RUDE LITTLE TROUSERS

Dutchman's breeches sparked a Victorian controversy.

Some wildflower enthusiasts seem almost to swoon over Dutchman's breeches, an unusual species once subject of a fiery debate. John Burroughs counted it "among our prettiest spring flowers," though I prefer the description of the author who called it one of the daintiest.

What you call a flower can be a matter of controversy, especially if you lived in Victorian times. For it was then that one Dr. Abbott raged: "To think that such a plant should be called 'Dutchman's breeches'! If this abomination were dropped from *Gray's Manual*, perhaps in time a decent substitute would come in use." Dr. Abbott offered *Dicentra*, the generic name, as an alternative.

Although he admitted the name is "rather rude," F. Schuyler Mathews defended its use. Unlike *Dicentra*, a Latin word that would be "enigmatic or meaningless" to most Americans, "Dutchman's breeches means something, and it does not seem quite abominable if we look at it from the right point of view. I like the name because of its Knickerbocker flavor, and although it is suggestive of a bit of rude humor, it is not without a certain poetic significance," he wrote.

The flowers are, after all, peculiar things, much like the garden bleeding hearts to which they are closely related. However, they lack the color of the cultivated *Dicentra spectabilis* and bear flowers that are mostly white with a bit of yellow. And they are shaped like an old-fashioned pair of knickers.

But to most Victorians, talking about the clothing that covered *that* part of the body was not the stuff of garden club meetings, and even Mr. Mathews, perhaps knowing that the original meaning of *breech* is "buttocks" or "rump," agreed that "breeches . . . sounds a bit unrefined." However, if we were to use the more proper *pants*, we'd lose the flavor of the name, he said. Imagine Henry Hudson clothed in "Dutchman's pants," he said. "Presto! all the poetry attached to the romantic vigils in the Catskills is gone."

Dutchman's breeches are wild siblings of the garden bleeding heart.

Butterfly Banners

The unusual form of the flowers has generated a variety of imaginative folk names that demonstrate how one shape can conjure up different ideas: soldier's cap, white hearts, eardrops (they hang like earrings), monk's head, butterfly banners, flyflower, plus a variety of pants-oriented names such as kitten-, bachelor's-, leather-, and little boy's breeches. Another old-fashioned name is "boys and girls," which was often employed by children when the Dutchman's breeches were found with a similarly shaped but pinkish sibling, squirrel corn.

Scientists were not so imaginative. Squirrel corn's name is *Dicentra cucullaria*, which simply describes the plant as "two-spurred" and "hooded."

Dicentra is a small genus of only 16 species worldwide. Seven species are found in North America and the rest in Asia. Dutchman's breeches is the type species, the species theoretically most typical of the genus and the one from which the genus was named.

Dicentra in turn belongs to the small Fumitory family of only 18 genera and 450 species. Dutchman's breeches are widespread in the northern United States from the Atlantic to the Dakotas and Kansas, and out along the Columbia River in Washington, Idaho, and Oregon. Squirrel, or turkey, corn (*D. canadensis*), which has a pink "waistband" instead of a yellow one, has a similar range, though not as western. The plant is named for its yellowish kernel-like bulbs, perhaps a delicacy for squirrels and wild turkeys. The West Coast has several colorful species, including the bright pink Pacific bleeding heart (*D. formosa*).

Strange Form

Dutchman's breeches are actually four-petaled flowers. Two of the petals unite to form the two legs of the pantaloons while the two others are inside, but project like lips over the stamens. Why these flowers evolved so strange a form must be left to conjecture. The shape has its advantages. Each "upside-down" blossom is sealed from the effects of rain and wind on the pollen. It's also sealed from invasion by most crawling or small flying insects that might steal the nectar without carrying the pollen to the next flower. In fact, only the long, strong tongue of the female bumblebee is said to be able to reach from the flower's bottom opening up into each of the two long petal-spurs to lap up the sweets—in the process, picking up and depositing pollen. John Eastman, in *The Book of Forest and Thicket*, reports that a bumblebee's eight-millimeter-long tongue is just long enough to reach the nectar while the honeybee, at only six millimeters, can't quite make it and must be satisfied with feeding only on pollen. Both insects, however, wind up pollinating the plant.

Dutchman's breeches are not perfect vaults, however. Certain wasps, carpenter bees, and even bumblebees have learned to chew holes through the tips of the spurs to gain direct access to the nectar.

Big Britches

Why would Dutchmen wear such
  britches,
Bloated so their legs looked huge?
Was it so they'd not have itches—
From tight woolies, a refuge?
Or did they see the plant Dicentra
And decide its blooms looked swell,
And, with that fashion pattern, went
  ta
A tailor who'd cut the pants from
  hell.
—J. S.

Ample Pants

Dutchman's breeches—worn, not grown—could be sizable affairs, and F. Schuyler Mathews tells the story of a settler who induced some Indians to sell him for a pittance all the land that could be enclosed by a pair of these voluminous trousers. The Indians thought they had the best of the deal until the Dutchman sliced up his ample drawers into narrow strips, sewed them end to end, and made a ribbon that enclosed several acres!

Dutchman's breeches are early-spring arrivals. "As soon as bloodroot has begun to star the waste, stony places, and the first swallow has been heard in the sky, we are on the lookout for *Dicentra*," wrote Burroughs. I've seen the flowers in bloom in my part of western Connecticut as early as April 18 and as late as mid-May.

Elfin Trousers

The plants favor rocky hillsides of open woods, often forming sizable colonies. Mabel Osgood Wright once described "a bed among rocks of much-cleft silver-green foliage, set with flower-sprays of two-pointed white and yellow bloom that might be pairs of elfin trousers hung out to bleach." They like limestone regions but, paradoxically, their soil should be rich woodland humus, neutral to slightly acid.

Their bulbs transplant easily, but because the plants are uncommon—mostly because their favorite habitats have been developed or damaged by development-related erosion—they should be left alone unless threatened with certain destruction. You can gather seeds in late spring, but don't sow them until September.

Unlike many of the wildflowers described in this book, Dutchman's breeches have no notable history as a practical plant. The species has never been popular as a food or a medicine, although one of its old-time names—colicweed—suggests that it may have been used to treat that ailment. There is also record of its use for skin infections and as a tonic, a diuretic.

Perhaps the fact that it is somewhat toxic and narcotic has limited its use. The plant is unpopular with farmers whose grazing cattle could suffer convulsions, even death, from eating too much of the leaves. Ranchers called it staggerweed because of the effect it had on livestock.

The Fumitory family is very closely related to the Poppy family, and one of *Dicentra*'s constituents is a poppy-like hallucinogen, which may explain its unusual use by the Menominees of upper Michigan and Wisconsin. According to a 1923 paper by Huron H. Smith, Dutchman's breeches "is one of the most important love charms of the Menominees. The young swain tries to throw it at his intended and hit her with it. Another way is for him to chew the root, breathing out so that the scent will carry to her. He then circles around the girl, and when she catches the scent, she will follow him wherever he goes, even against her will." Do perfume manufacturers know about this?

While Dr. Abbott considered the name an abomination and Burroughs called it "absurd," it can also be annoying. When one writes about the plant, the mind asks whether to say: "The Dutchman's breeches is . . ." or "the Dutchman's breeches are . . ." If you come across only one, do you have a Dutchman's breech? Not, I suppose, unless you can wear a pair of pant.

Garlic Mustard

A TASTY FOE

Lacking any enemies, garlic mustard has become
one. Perhaps the answer is to eat it.

Like an alien army reeking of garlic, *Alliaria petiolata* has been marching
across North America, reshaping woodlands and wiping out native
wildlife. No less an authority than the U.S. National Park Service calls
garlic mustard "a severe threat to native plants and animals in forest com-
munities in much of the Eastern and Midwestern United States."

When I began studying the wildflowers in my region of
Connecticut around 1970, garlic mustard was an occasionally seen curiosity. Today, hordes inhabit many places where favorite May natives used to
bloom. Garlic mustard shares the same territory and season as bloodroot,
Dutchman's breeches, spring-beauty, wild ginger, hepaticas, toothworts,
trilliums, and others that suffer at its hands—or roots.

Species that depend on natives for food are also in danger. For
instance, the National Park Service reports that garlic mustard threatens
the West Virginia white butterfly (*Pieris virginiensis*). "Several species of
spring wildflowers known as 'toothworts' (*Dentaria*), also in the mustard
family, are the primary food source for the caterpillar stage of this butterfly," the Park Service said. "Invasions of garlic mustard are causing local
extirpations of the toothworts, and chemicals in garlic mustard appear to
be toxic to the eggs of the butterfly, as evidenced by their failure to hatch
when laid on garlic mustard plants."

*Garlic mustard, an invasive plant from
Europe, is driving out native species in its
march across North America.*

No Enemies

Because it is a vigorous biennial that relies on seeds to survive and spread, garlic mustard can
quickly take over a piece of land and push out the locals.

Seed power aside, the main reason for garlic mustard's success in North America is its
complete lack of natural enemies. Scientists at the Department of Natural Resources at Cornell
University report that in its native Europe, "garlic mustard occurs in small isolated populations,
never approaching densities observed in North America. Over 30 different insect species attacking
stems, leaves, and seeds of *A. petiolata* have been recorded. This assemblage of natural enemies plays
an important role in keeping garlic mustard at lower densities. No specialized natural enemies of
garlic mustard are recorded in North America."

How about grazing mammals? Alas, most animals dislike garlic, and the strong garlicky scent of this mustard's leaves, especially when young, no doubt dissuade many herbivores from chowing down. For instance, white-tailed deer—which practically own the countryside where I live and will eat almost anything green, including evergreen needles—shun garlic mustard. Nonetheless, foraging deer probably help spread the plant, picking up seeds in their fur as they amble through stands of the herbs and unknowingly dropping them elsewhere.

A member of the large and often weedy Mustard family, garlic mustard is found throughout northern Europe and northwestern Asia, where it is known by such names as hedge garlic, sauce-alone, jack-by-the-hedge, poor man's mustard, jack-in-the-bush, garlic root, garlicwort, mustard root, and penny-hedge. Some botanical historians claim to have traced its arrival in North America to 1868 on Long Island, probably brought over as a salad herb. By the year 1900, it was found from Quebec to Virginia. Its numbers then were not those of today, however, probably because the landscape a hundred years ago was much different from today's. Wide-open fields and pastures covered most of the terrain, and garlic mustard, which shuns full sunlight, kept to the edges of the then less common woods or near hedges and other sources of shade. As many farms in the Northeast shut down and their fields reverted to woods or began sprouting housing developments, trees and shade became more widespread—and so did garlic mustard.

Food and Flavoring

Because garlic mustard was a popular food and flavoring in its native lands, the plant may well have been here earlier than 1868. Its flavorful leaves, high in vitamins A and C, were often used in cooking. Maude Grieve reported that English country folk would add garlic mustard to sauces and salads. "The herb, when eaten as a salad, warms the stomach and strengthens the digestive faculties," she said. John Gerard, the 16th-century herbalist, called the plant "sauce-alone," and said the leaves were crushed and eaten as a sauce for salt fish. Edward Lewis Sturtevant reported that garlic mustard was often eaten with meat. In both cases, the strong garlic scent may have served not only to season the dish but also to hide the off-flavor of meat or fish that wasn't fresh.

Garlic mustard has been boiled and served like spinach and, in Wales, fried with herring or bacon, much the way Italians still like to sauté dandelion leaves today. It was widely used in salads especially in England and Germany—where it was known as *Sasskraut*, or "sauce herb." The Germans also call it *Knoblauchsrauke*, or "garlic cabbage."

Alliaria petiolata has spread to North Africa, India, Sri Lanka, Australia, and New Zealand, as well as North America. In the United States, garlic mustard is most abundant in New England and Midwestern states, but it's also well established as far west as North Dakota and Kansas, and south to Tennessee and North Carolina. The Nature Conservancy says populations began appearing in Oregon around 1974, and by the turn of the 21st century the plant has been identified in Washington, Utah, Colorado, and Idaho as well.

Although garlic mustard has been known over the last three centuries as *Sisymbrium alliaria*, *Alliaria alliaria*, and *Erysimum alliaria*, scientists seem to have settled on *Alliaria petiolata*. *Alliaria*

Prolific Producer

Two Boston University biologists—Richard B. Primack and Brian Drayton—demonstrated the spreading power of garlic mustard by planting 20 seeds in a controlled plot. Only four years later, they had more than 6,000 plants. "These plants were capable of producing over 100,000 new seeds," they said.

is derived from *allium*, the Latin for "garlic," while *petiolata* refers to the fact that the leaves have petioles, or stalks. *Sisymbrium*, incidentally, is an ancient Greek word for a fragrant plant and was applied to watercress, the popular salad herb; garlic mustard is closely related to the cresses.

The mustards (*Brassicaceae*) are a worldwide family of more than 200 genera and 1,800 species. More than 40 genera and 100 species are found in North America. They are distinguished by their four-petaled flowers that usually appear as a cross—the family was once known as *Cruciferae*, a word based on the Latin for "cross."

Prolific Production

Garlic mustard's small, white flowers bloom in small clusters atop a stalk that's one to three feet tall. The flowers can be insect pollinated or can self-pollinate, and produce many long, slender pods full of seeds that have a high rate of success—necessary in a biennial. In the first season of its life, garlic mustard is limited to a basal rosette of kidney-shaped leaves, which build up the strength in its roots to produce the tall, flowering "adult" in the second year.

The plant is very difficult to eradicate since it has so much working in its favor. It lacks natural enemies, can self-pollinate, and produces many seeds. What's more, the seeds—or "seed bank," as the botanists call the accumulation of several years' worth of seeds—can last years.

The simplest method of attack is to chop down garlic mustard whenever and wherever you see it. At the least, pull up the plants—which is not difficult. Your attack needs to be continuous because garlic mustard seeds can germinate many years after you've eliminated the parents. Forest and natural resource agencies resort to herbicides and controlled burning to kill them off, but even fires are ineffective unless the leaf mold, where seeds lurk, is also burned.

In 1998, the Departments of Natural Resources in Minnesota, Illinois, Indiana, and Kentucky, plus a half-dozen other agencies, commissioned a Swiss company to find a biological control for garlic mustard. Of 69 insects and seven kinds of fungi associated with the plant in Europe, six insects, including beetles and weevils, were selected for close study as possible biological agents. Five were "monophagous," meaning they feed on only one kind of food—in this case, garlic mustard. Of course, an insect that eats only one species in Europe may find, upon being introduced into North America, that other plants it has never met are equally tasty. That's why studies of this kind have to be very careful and extensive—otherwise, we may be importing a creature as damaging as the plant it's supposed to control.

Even with an invasion of garlic-gobbling insects, this plant will probably never be eradicated. However, the more we ourselves kill them—and the more we encourage others to do likewise—the more native species that will be able to survive. In the process, we might even get some nourishment. Correspondent Phil Corbett, who lives in England, where garlic mustard is not a problem, reports that while the leaves of mature plants can be bitter, young sprouts are tasty. "I've found that the seeds can be germinated to give one of the best tasting cresses you'll ever eat—sweet and mildly garlicky," he said. "Maybe mass seed collection could be a commercial solution!"

In other words, help your environment—eat its enemy!

Garlic Mustard Pesto

4 cups packed garlic mustard
    leaves
1 cup packed fresh basil
2 medium cloves garlic
¼ cup Parmesan cheese
¼ to ½ cup water
Salt and pepper to taste

Steam the garlic mustard just until tender and bright green. Put garlic mustard, basil, and garlic in a blender or food processor and puree until smooth. Transfer to a warm bowl, and add the Parmesan and enough water to thin to the desired consistency. Serve on pasta, steamed vegetables, baked potatoes, or baked fish.
—The *Columbus (Ohio) Dispatch*,
(June 18, 2000)

Trout Lily

A LILY BY ANY OTHER NAME . . .

Trout lilies make many contributions to the forest community.

The trout lily has many names and serves many uses in nature.

How can an early-spring woodland lily affect late-spring farmers' crops? How does a small wildflower help hold together the forest floor and feed many plants that inhabit it? And why does such a modest flower have such a menagerie of names? The complex interrelationships of life—and human imagination—come together in the genus *Erythronium*.

Anyone writing a book on the folk names of American plants could have a field day with *Erythronium americanum* and its siblings. Commonly called trout lily, *E. americanum* is also widely known as adder's tongue and dogtooth violet, and by a passel of other names.

The flower's blooming in mid-April, just about the time the trout season opens, probably inspired "trout lily." It's also possible that the name stems from the leaves, whose purplish blotches resemble the markings on some kinds of trout, or from the fact that the plant often grows near woodland streams in which these fish live.

"Dogtooth violet," really an inappropriate name, was inspired by a European version of the trout lily, *E. dens-canis*. That species has pointed corms shaped somewhat like a tooth.

"Adder's tongue" has confused people the most. Some authorities feel the spots on the leaves resemble the markings on certain snakes. Others liken the twin leaves that accompany the flowers to the forked tongue of a snake. Still others say the name was inspired by how the leaves look as they emerge from the soil. "Whoever sees the sharp purplish point of a young plant darting above the ground in earliest spring . . . at once sees the fitting application of 'adder's tongue,' " said a 19th-century writer. Timothy Coffey, in his *History and Folklore of North American Wildflowers*, believes the protruding stamens on the flowers are the "adder's tongue."

If you don't like any of those names, there are plenty of others to choose from: yellow lily, yellow bells, amberbell, yellow snowdrop, yellow bastard-lily, rattlesnake tooth violet, rattlesnake violet, yellow snakeleaf, lamb's tongue, deer's tongue, serpent's tongue, snakeroot, starstriker, and scrofula root. (Scrofula, the skin disease, was once treated with this plant.)

John Burroughs liked the name fawn lily, partly because he thought the leaf mottling resembles the markings on a young deer. "It is a pity that this graceful and abundant flower has no good and appropriate name," he lamented in the 1890s. "It is the earliest of the true lilies, and it has all the grace and charm that belong to this order of flowers. . . . In my spring rambles I have sometimes come upon a solitary specimen of this yellow lily growing beside a mossy stone where the sunshine fell full upon it, and have thought it one of the most beautiful of our wild flowers. Its two leaves stand up like a fawn's ears, and this feature with its recurved petals, gives it an alert, wide-awake look."

The trout lily's scientific name also seems odd. *Erythronium*, from a Greek word, is an allusion to the color red. While the trout lilies we know are hardly red, other species within the genus, including *E. dens-canis*, bear red flowers.

Good Citizen

Many trout lily species are key members of the forest community whose link in the chain of life can extend far beyond the woods. Trout lily colonies help stabilize the soil and contribute an important nutrient to woodland plant life. In addition, they provide early-spring food to queen bumblebees, helping them to establish colonies that will fertilize countless flowers of many species all season long.

A good example is *Erythronium americanum*. While many members of the lily family grow bulbs near the surface, the trout lily has deep "corms"—underground, food-storing stems—and spreads much more through an elaborate system of cloning than by seeds.

The seeds, which appear in June, don't sprout until early the next spring. A successful seed will develop a little corm that grows near the surface. Early the next season, the young corm produces several threadlike "droppers" that burrow down at an angle of about 45 degrees. (Some misguided ones may surface and then dive, which explains the white "threads" that appear in trout lily groves.) At the end of each dropper—several inches lower in the soil and up to 10 inches away from the mother—a new corm is formed from food sent down the line by the parent. Eventually the line withers away and the offspring corm sends up one leaf, which makes food to develop the new corm. This corm in turn sends droppers down even farther the next year. After four years a sprouted seed can have produced nine plants with corms as deep as seven or eight inches, even deeper if the soil is loose and loamy. When the descenders hit hard soil, they stop the dive.

Only a few corms will produce flowers—about 1 percent of the plants in a trout lily colony will bloom in a given season. While most corms produce only one leaf, flowering corms will send up two; they need more leaf-made food to produce the flowers and later, the seeds. Scientists are not certain why so few corms bloom, but it is probably because many trout lilies have come to rely more on corms than on seeds for propagation. One researcher has determined that in the white trout lily (*E. albidum*), the plant devotes nearly 60 percent of its energy to cloning and only 3 percent to seeds, many of which are not even viable. In at least one species, the endangered Minnesota fawn lily, *E. propullans*, reproduction appears to be solely via corms—the seeds don't even function. This species of southeastern Minnesota has a very limited range, covering only a few counties. This is not surprising; although seeds can travel far and wide by various methods, cloning is usually not an expansive way to reproduce.

Ear Flower?

Taking wildflower photos like the picture on page 40 can have its hazards. The shot required lying down on the ground next to the plant. While I was focusing on the flower, a small woodland fly was focusing on my ear, which it apparently mistook for a strange but plausible blossom. In it flew, buzzing around for several minutes—a loud and most uncomfortable sensation especially when it flew up against my eardrum. Finally, the fly found its way out and peace returned. The picture was worth it.

Menagerie

When casting about
For a name of this plant,
Most use the trout;
Others just can't.
Some say the flower
Looks more like a fawn.
That turns a few dour,
And others just yawn.
Some liken the root
To the tooth of a dog.
Critics will hoot:
"You've slipped your main cog."
Still others get madder
And claim that you're lame;
They believe tongue of adder
Is the very best name.
All this allusion
Is really too silly;
To avoid mass confusion,
Just call it zoo lily.
—J. S.

On the other hand, this colonial arrangement allows the trout lily to develop stable colonies in environments it likes. In fact, *E. americanum* is among the most stable of any common wild herb. Groves of trout lilies more than a century old exist, and probably there are colonies much older. These stable colonies, with a compact collection of deeply rooted plants, help to tie together the delicate forest floor, especially in wet areas, and thus prevent erosion.

Aside from humans, who've cut down too many trees and drained too many wetlands, these colonies have few enemies. While deer will eat the flowers, they and other grazing mammals shun the leaves, which contain distasteful flavorings. Perhaps the biggest animal threat to a colony, besides humans, is the black bear, which will dig up and eat the corms.

Most trout lily species produce just enough viable seeds so that some new colonies can be established. Their method of moving the seeds to new locations is similar to the technique used by many spring wildflowers. The seeds bear appendages, called elaiosomes, containing fatty food that many insects love. Usually, the insect carries the seed to a new location before dining on the elaiosomes and leaving the seed proper behind. Most spring plants seem to direct their elaiosomes toward the tastes of ants, but Professor Douglas Schemske of Michigan State University found that ground beetles and crickets also disperse trout lily seeds.

Most trout lilies bloom in the early spring. Their foliage withers away by midsummer. For a reason not fully understood, trout lily leaves amass a good deal of phosphorus, considerably more than most plants, capturing the mineral from the spring runoff that's fed by melting snow. When they die, the leaves return the phosphorus to the soil in a form that is readily usable by other plants and thus they help vegetation in the neighborhood.

Bumblebees

In his fascinating and entertaining book, *Wily Violets and Underground Orchids*, Professor Peter Bernhardt of St. Louis University describes a special relationship between bumblebees and trout lilies. Queen bumblebees emerge in early spring with the sole mission of establishing underground nests of workers. Each queen needs pollen to feed the first emerging workers. One of her primary sources is the trout lily, from which she takes both pollen and nectar. The nectar serves as an energy source for the queen as well as a glue to hold together the pollen as she carries it back to the nest. "The bumblebee larvae fed on trout lily pollen during the spring mature to pollinate clover, alfalfa and other early crops," Dr. Bernhardt says. "The trout lilies form an early but essential link in a chain of different flowers, separated in time, that use the same pollinator."

The trout lily's flowers have a faint scent, possibly more detectable by insects than by humans. They are closed at night, but open each morning, with the petal-like yellow sepals or "tepals" (a combination of petal and sepal) curving backward. As in many of the lilies, the trout lily flowers point groundward, a position that may serve two purposes. The central flower parts are protected from the rain that could wash away the pollen. The position also helps to keep certain kinds of crawling insects from robbing the nectar. An ant, for instance, is likely to slip and fall off the smooth interior of the flower before reaching its destination.

Western Species

Some 18 species of *Erythronium* live in North America, mostly in cool or mountainous states as well as most provinces of Canada. The East has two widespread species of *Erythronium. E. americanum* is found from New Brunswick to Florida and westward to the Mississippi and into Arkansas and Nebraska. White trout lily, *E. albidum*, extends more westward, to the foothills of the Rockies, and is most common in the Midwest.

The western states and provinces have more than a dozen types, some larger or more colorful than the Eastern ones. One handsome species is the yellow fawn lily (*E. grandiflorum*), also called the yellow avalanche lily, which blooms brightly from sagebrush and clearings in the mountains just as the snow recedes—when avalanches are common. The avalanche lily is apparently tastier to wildlife than other species; mule deer, cattle, and sheep graze on its leaves, and grizzly bears emerging from hibernation relish the corms.

Many western species have very limited ranges. The elegant white and yellow California fawn lily (*E. californicum*) is found in only seven or eight counties of northwestern California. The coast range fawn lily, *E. elegans*, lives only in parts of Oregon. The Tuolumne, or mother lode fawn lily (*E. tuolumnense*), grows wild only in Tuolumne County, California, in the western Sierra Nevada. The flower is so pretty, however, that a number of nurseries propagate and sell the species as a garden plant throughout North America.

Trout lilies can be grown in wildflower gardens, and some, like *E. americanum*, make pretty ground covers. Don't expect a lot of flowers, however. I once transplanted some *E. americanum* corms from a building lot. Twenty years later, a small colony of a dozen or so plants appears each spring, yet only one plant ever blooms; however, it has done so faithfully for more than 15 years.

Gardeners should always get trout lilies from reputable nurseries—taking them from the wild, especially species of limited range, may endanger colonies. A good wildflower horticulture book will provide the details on how to grow them.

Herbals

Trout lilies have seen limited use as a food or medicine. European herbalists began using *Erythronium* plants, especially *E. dens-canis*, long before the settlement of North America. Today, however, even some European herbals consider our native *E. americanum* the best of the genus for medicinal use. Its chief internal benefit is to produce vomiting.

Externally, its leaves have long been employed as a poultice to treat ulcers and tumors, as well as scrofula. American Indians used the leaves of the trout lily to brew a tea that was said to relieve stomach pains.

Some native tribes, such as the Winnebagos, ate the corms of various trout lily species. Some were more worthwhile than others to gather; *E. grandiflorum* corms, for instance, could be as big as a human fist. The corms were always boiled to remove a bitter taste, and then eaten fresh, mixed in stews, or dried for later consumption. Only an ursine stomach could handle them raw.

Ginsengs

THE MAN-PLANTS

Our woods have two ginsengs, but the valuable one is in trouble.

Dwarf ginseng is so small, it often goes unnoticed on the forest floor. Its bigger sibling is harder to find because sang diggers have removed it from most of our woods.

While wildflowers are usually valued most for lifting the spirit, a few have lifted incomes. Perhaps the most famous of the valuable native plants in North America is the American ginseng, known almost around the world for seemingly magical powers to cure any ailment and to lift the spirits of those who consume it. But fame doesn't always bring success and in the case of the ginseng, it could lead to its own downfall.

American ginseng (*Panax quinquefolius*) was once common in woodlands east of the Rockies, but by the early 1900s, wildflower writers reported that it was disappearing from the continent's forests. That's because so many people were digging it up and shipping it off to distant lands, thanks to two 18th-century Jesuits.

For centuries the Chinese had made extensive medicinal use of a closely related ginseng species, *Panax schin-seng*. By the early 1700s, however, there wasn't enough ginseng left in China to meet the demand. When a Jesuit missionary in China wrote an article on the shortage for a British publication in 1714, a Jesuit in Quebec saw the article and sent samples of American ginseng to China. The Chinese liked the root and turned to North America for plants. A new industry blossomed, and companies were formed to hire harvesters. John Jacob Astor, who became fabulously rich trading in furs, started out by shipping ginseng to China in the late 1700s. By the 1860s and 1870s, 300 tons of ginseng roots were exported annually from the United States to China. Virtually all of this was collected from the wild. Pickers decimated native populations of ginseng—or sang, as many of them called it—in much of its range.

Ginseng was so precious that several "get-rich-quick" books have been written about hunting and growing the plant. One ginseng grower, A. R. Harding, wrote in 1936 that ginseng root under cultivation was bringing between $5 and $10 a pound, amounting to thousands of dollars per acre—a tidy sum during the Depression. In 1992, a newsletter of the Illinois Department of Conservation reported that wild ginseng root was fetching $235 a pound.

In 1975, more than 100 nations signed a treaty called the Convention on International Trade in Endangered Species (CITES), agreeing to regulate international commerce in threatened or endangered plants and animals. American ginseng is among those threatened plants. Although many state, provincial, and federal agencies now regulate and monitor the harvest of American ginseng, however, collecting from the wild has continued, probably because so many generations of Americans had earned a livelihood from sang digging. In remoter parts of the eastern and central United States, such as Appalachia, harvesting wild plants provided a significant source of income for 20th-century families of limited means. "The whole economy was built up around ginseng," the resident of one small West Virginia town told a Library of Congress researcher. "They had a few eggs and chickens, but most of it was the whole crew would go out and hunt ginseng in the fall."

Some states, such as Maryland, issue permits for ginseng collecting, and the U.S. Department of Agriculture allows its export only through certain controlled ports. Many states list American ginseng on their "no-pick" and endangered lists, and the Canadian Museum of Nature considers it as "at risk." "The Chinese have as industriously rooted the plant out of their dominions as we are destroying it today," wrote Charles M. Skinner in 1911. "We being a reckless race that seldom thinks to sow where it reaps."

Although cultivating ginseng began in the 1880s, it was not as inviting then as many other crops, partly because the plant is susceptible to disease but mostly because it takes 6 to 10 years to get a mature root from seed. Today, much is grown. Steven Foster reported in *Wildflower* magazine that a total of 2.3 million pounds of cultivated American ginseng root was exported from the United States in 1989, along with 203,000 pounds harvested from the wild. The cultivated root was fetching an average of $23 a pound while the wild root was going for $93 a pound. Today, 85 percent of North America's cultivated ginseng is sent to Asia.

The size of the root affects the price. Large roots that have been growing more years are usually more valuable. Thus, one dealer in 2001 was selling a pound of "small ginseng roots" (about 360 roots) for $60, and a pound of large ginseng roots (80 roots), for $180. If ginseng roots get too big and woody, though, they can lose their value.

Aphrodisiac

The Chinese have respected and used ginseng root to treat just about every possible ailment. Roots shaped like a human being are the most prized. In fact, a particularly human-like root was said to be literally worth its weight in gold. The Chinese also found ginseng an invigorating tonic, and even a love potion. "Considering the population of China, who can quarrel with its reputation as an aphrodisiac?" asks herbalist John Lust.

Among the American Indians, the Meskwakis of Wisconsin made a love potion from ginseng. Penobscot women in Maine steeped the root to obtain a fertility drink. The Creeks of Alabama drank the same solution as a cough medicine. The Delaware and Mohegan tribes considered it a cure-all tonic. Some modern herb fans still recommend chewing the root or drinking the tea to reduce stress and tension. While some authorities seem to believe that ginseng has no real medicinal value, Steven Foster and James Duke's book, *A Field Guide to Medicinal Plants*, says: "Research suggests it may increase mental efficiency and physical performance, aid in adapting to high or low temperatures and stress (when taken over an extended period)."

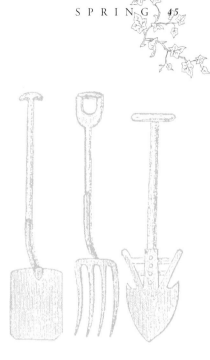

A Boon for Boone

Among the big-time sang hunters was Daniel Boone (1734–1820), who as early as 1788 was hiring Indians in Kentucky to dig ginseng roots that he would sell in New York and Philadelphia for export. He once lost two tons of roots when the barge carrying them sank in the Ohio River.

A new interest in ginseng supplements appeared in the early 1990s. The *Wall Street Journal* reported in October 1992 that sales of ginseng pills, such as Ginsana, had jumped 170 percent in the past year, far outstripping sales increases in other across-the-counter supplements, such as multivitamins, vitamin C, and vitamin A. Ginsana, made by a Swiss pharmaceutical firm, is promoted as a substance that helps build physical endurance. "Consumers tell us that they feel gradual improvements in energy, vitality, and overall mood in as early as four weeks with continuous, uninterrupted use," says Pharmaton Natural Health Products, the producer.

"Man-Plant"

The word *ginseng* is believed to be a corruption of the Chinese *schin-seng, schin-sen,* or *jin-shen,* meaning "man-like" or "man-plant." The name refers to the tendency of some of the Chinese (as well as the North American) ginseng roots to grow in the shape of the human body. Certain American Indians called it *garantoguen,* which is supposed to have had the same or a similar meaning.

The plant's scientific name, *Panax quinquefolius,* means "all-healing" or "panacea," and "five-part leaves." The specific (second) name distinguishes it from *P. trifolius,* the lesser known but also less threatened dwarf ginseng, which has three-part leaves.

American ginseng bears a cluster, or "umbel," of yellow green flowers in July. Male and female flowers appear on separate plants. Since they bloom in the forest at a time when most bees are busy in flower-filled fields, the male blossoms help attract pollinators by offering a strong, sweet scent similar to that of lily of the valley. Probably nature's expectation is that once they are drawn to the pollen-bearing flowers, they will also stop by the less exciting females, which have no scent.

The red fruits appear in late summer and early fall—years ago they were prized, the seeds inside selling for as much as $1 apiece.

The Dwarf

As its very name suggests, dwarf ginseng is not a spectacular plant. Nonetheless, its little cluster of white fluffy blossoms—an author of the last century described it as "one feathery ball of bloom"—is among the early-spring flowers that woodland trekkers delight to find amid the blanket of brown leaves. Dwarf ginseng blooms in April and May in rich woods, and produces yellow berries soon after. Its aboveground parts last only a couple of months.

The plant has probably survived better than its brother because it springs from a small round ball of a root (whence another common name, ground nut). "One must burrow deep, like the rabbits, to find its round, pungent, sweet, nut-like root, measuring about half an inch across, which few have ever seen," wrote Neltje Blanchan.

Dwarf ginseng is rarely collected. If it has the active ingredients of its big brother, they occur in too small a quantity to be of value, commercially or otherwise, and little research has been done into its constituents. American Indians, however, made some use of the plant to treat such problems as indigestion, headaches, colic, gout, and hives.

Ginsenging

"That's all my grandma used to do, years ago, she'd ginseng," recalled Shelby Estep, who now ginsengs with her daughter and granddaughter on Coal River Mountain. "That's the way she bought the kids' clothes. She had twelve."

—*Tending the Commons: Folklife and Landscape in Southern West Virginia,* American Folklife Center, Library of Congress, (1992–1999)

Ginsengs are members of the Ginseng family of plants (Araliaceae), closely related to the Parsley family and consisting of some 52 genera and more than 475 species worldwide. The family includes our two *Panax* species and several members of the *Aralia* genus, among them wild sarsaparillas and the spikenards. None of these plants is noted for its beauty, but most have histories of being used as medicines.

If you consider following the Chinese and using ginseng to spice up your life or increase your endurance, be careful with your dosages. Consider this description of the physiological actions of a sizable dose, as written by 19th-century medical writer Charles F. Millspaugh: "Ginseng causes vertigo, dryness of the mucous membranes of the mouth and throat, increased appetite, accumulation of flatus with tension of the abdomen, diarrhoea, decreased secretion of urine, sexual excitement, oppression of the chest and a dry cough, increased heart's action and irregular pulse, weakness and weariness of the limbs, increased general strength, followed by weakness and prostration, somnolence, and much chilliness." Take care!

Violets

LOVE IN THE SPRINGTIME

Napoleon so loved this springtime classic that he was long known as *Caporal Violette*—Corporal Violet.

The dog violet makes up for its small size with bright color.

Asked to name a favorite spring wildflower, few would pick the violet. Certainly, this spring classic is well loved, but it has become so common in gardens and lawns that most people don't consider it wild. Yet the forest floor and open field are the usual haunts of our most common native violets. Unlike their garden-born brethren, however, they are sometimes so small and unassuming that the woodland walker might miss their faces pushing demurely but firmly through the brown carpet of last year's leaves or brush.

Even if your careful eye does spot an early violet, you might have trouble finding its name, for the world of violets is a jumbled one. More than 75 species exist in North America, most of them natives. However, interbreeding has created numerous new forms and varieties, some of which only the most dedicated botanist could identify. Dr. Harold N. Moldenke estimated in the 1940s that about 300 violet species, varieties, and natural hybrids were living north of Mexico, with the Northeast alone being home to 132 of them. While that's enough to tax the best taxonomist, were we to go south of the border, we'd find hundreds more—some plants so big they are classified as shrubs.

The violet would seem to need no description, since even kindergartners can count it among the handful of flowers they readily recognize. Nonetheless, few admirers of any age probably take the time to look closely at the blossom, which has five petals: two upper, two lateral, and one bottom. The two pairs act as flags to attract pollinating insects while the bottom petal serves as a landing strip. In many species small veins of color—which to us are just decorations—act as arrows, directing the insect to the nectar-laden spur at the rear of the bottom petal. These guides are much more visible to the ultraviolet-sensing eyes of the bee.

Some species have hairs near the nectar opening, giving the insect something to grab onto while pushing its head inside. Functioning like our eyelashes, these "beards" also prevent rain or dew drops from getting in and diluting the nectar. (Most varieties of violets also turn toward the ground at night or when it's cloudy or raining, another defense against dilution.)

Insect Tricks

When visiting most flowers, a bee must touch the anther to pick up the pollen on it. Not so in violets. As the insect wiggles in for a drink, it jiggles loose grains from the partly hidden anthers overhead. The pollen drops and dusts the bee's back. (Various native flowers that attract smaller bees have similar, hidden anthers to prevent larger insects, such as bumblebees, from making their pollen a meal instead of a cargo.)

If few people pay close attention to the violets' pretty blossoms, even fewer notice the other flowers, the ones that never bloom. Called cleistogamous flowers, they appear lower on the plant, sometimes under the ground and often later in the season so that even if they are noticed, they are often viewed as buds, pods, or defective flowers. In fact, while they never open or bloom, they contain all the necessary parts to produce fertile seeds. This system may have developed because so many violets bloom so early in the season, when insect pollination is chancier than in the warmer, bee-filled months. Not all violets produce these nonblooming flowers. Some summer violets, such as *Viola tricolor*, bear showy blossoms, can easily attract insects, and do not appear to need backup cleistogamous flowers.

Once the seeds are ripe, another insect may stop by to do its job. Some species of ants harvest and "plant" violets and certain other spring wildflowers in a symbiotic relationship called myrmecochory—literally "ant farming." They are drawn to the seeds by small protuberances called elaiosomes that contain attractive oils and possibly sugars. The ants carry the seeds, sometimes as far as 70 yards, to their nests where they eat the treat. The shell, however, is too hard to open, so the ants discard the seed proper, often in an unused tunnel in the nest. Here, amid nutrients provided by the soil and accidentally by the housecleaning ants, the seed has a much better chance of producing a plant than does one dropped on the forest floor where it may be eaten by foraging birds and rodents. In some environments, myrmecochory also protects the seeds from wildfires. Among other spring bloomers that get a helping hand from seed-hunting ants are bloodroot, anemones, wild ginger, hepaticas, and trilliums. The phenomenon is much more common among plants of forests than those of field and meadow.

Elaiosomes are small-scale, primitive versions of what nature does more gloriously with fruiting plants. Thousands of species—from small blueberries to large apples—offer a reward for transporting the seed. In the case of fruit, the treat is a sweet while for violets and other myrmecochorous plants, it's vegetable oil or fat. And with fruit, the seed is ingested and later deposited, with fertilizer, instead of being tossed aside uneaten.

Myth and Medicine

Violets have long been important in mythology and herbalism, two traditions that often intermix. John Gerard said that the very name of the plant stems from Greek mythology. One story he relates says that *viola*, the old Latin word for the plant as well as the modern generic name, may have come from the Greek, *Ione* or *Io*. Io, one of Zeus's lovers, evidently picked the wrong god to fool around

Health Food

Whether in salads or in candies, violets have a long history as a food. And with good reason. The basal leaves of the common blue violet (*Viola papilionacea*) have, in the springtime, five times more vitamin C per 100 grams than the equivalent weight of oranges, and 2.5 times more vitamin A than spinach.

Fair as a Star

A violet by a mossy stone,
Half hidden from the eye!
Fair as a star when only one
Is shining in the sky.
—William Wordsworth
(1770–1850)

Less Bright?

Hath the pearl less whiteness
Because of its birth?
Hath the violet less brightness
For growing near earth?
—Thomas Moore (1779–1852)

with. When his wife, Hera, became jealous, he turned Io into a white heifer to protect her and provided the sweet-scented violet for her to graze on.

Greeks treasured violets, and Athenians considered them the symbols of their city. According to legend, when Ion, the founder of Athens and another possible source for *viola*, was leading his people to Attica, he was welcomed by naiads, water nymphs who could inspire men. The naiads gave him violets as signs of their good wishes, and the flower became the city's emblem. Rare was the Athenian house without violets in the garden. Violets decorated Athenian altars, decorated brides, and even decorated busts. The last could be taken as a bit of an embarrassing memorial, for violet wreaths were sometimes employed—by the Romans, at least—to relieve hangovers. (One could wonder at Aristophanes' reporting that the people of Athens were proud to be known as "violet-crowned Athenians.") On the more practical side, Greeks also used the plants to help induce sleep, to strengthen the heart, and to calm anger.

Romans acquired much of their culture from the Greeks, and with it came an appreciation of the violet. Like Greeks, they decorated banquet tables with thousands of violets in the mistaken belief that the flowers could prevent drunkenness. Ironically, Romans often also drank a wine made from violet blossoms.

The flowers were also a symbol of innocence and modesty. Romans often placed violets on the graves of small children. Even to Shakespeare's time, they were associated with death. "I would give you some violets," said Ophelia to Laertes, "but they withered all when my father died." It was also once believed that the soul leaving the body would take the form of a flower. Later in *Hamlet*, after Ophelia dies, Laertes hopes that violets will grow from her grave: "Lay her i' the earth, and from her fair and unpolluted flesh, may Violets spring."

Medieval Christians believed violets were once strong, upright flowers until one day on Mount Calvary, the shadow of the cross fell over them. After that, they bowed in shame at what mankind had done. Probably in connection with this legend, violets were often used in Good Friday ceremonies. While the violet is usually styled as being modest, however, Sir Walter Scott once characterized it as a boastful queen of the forest flowers:

> *The Violet in her greenwood bower,*
> *Where Birchen boughs with Hazels mingle,*
> *May boast itself the fairest flower*
> *In glen, in copse, or forest dingle.*

Caporal Violette

A small boy from France did much to spread the violet into modern gardens. As a child on Corsica, Napoleon Bonaparte loved the sweet-scented violets that grew there. Josephine wore them on her wedding day, and, though he was not always faithful to her and eventually married again, Napoleon gave her a bouquet of violets each year on their anniversary. She, in turn, maintained an extensive garden of violets, which, of course, became all the rage in France.

After Napoleon was banished to Elba, he declared: "I shall return with the violets in spring." As a result, the flower became the symbol of his followers, who called him Caporal Violette or Le Père Violet. After his defeat at Waterloo, Napoleon tried to relieve the boredom of his exile on St. Helena by growing violets in a garden. He is also supposed to have visited the grave of Josephine, picked a few violets, and placed them in his locket, where they were found six years later when he died.

Later Napoleon III adopted the violet as the symbol of his regime. The day he met his future wife, Eugenie, she reportedly showed she liked him by wearing a violet gown and violets in her hair at a ball he was attending. And, naturally, she carried violets at her wedding and received bouquets of them on their anniversaries.

Because of all the Napoleonic interest in violets, France became a leader in developing and cultivating new varieties of violets and pansies. *Pansy*, in fact, comes from the French, *pensée*, meaning "thought" or "sentiment," as in those anniversary bouquets. "There's rosemary, that's for remembrance; pray, love, remember; and there is pansies, that's for thoughts," said Ophelia.

Violets have charmed many others. Mohammed considered them his favorite flower. A 10th-century English herbal said the blossoms could chase away evil spirits. Ancient Britons used the flowers as a cosmetic, says Maude Grieve, adding that Celtic women mixed violets and goat's milk to concoct a beauty lotion. Writing about the violet, herbalist Gerard was almost ecstatic: "There be made of them garlands for the head, nosegaies and poesies, which are delightfull to looke on and pleasant to smel to . . . Yea, gardens themselves receive by these the greatest ornament of all, chiefest beauty, and the most excellent grace, and the recreation of the minde which is taken hereby cannot be but very good and honest; for they admonish and stirre up a man to that which is comely and honest. . . ."

Violets were extensively used as medicines from at least the 16th century on, and many herbals highly recommended them for such problems as insomnia, epilepsy, pleurisy, impetigo, ulcers, jaundice, eye inflammations, and rheumatism. Because of their ability to lubricate the linings of the alimentary canal with a soothing coating, they were widely used as a mild laxative and as a cough medicine. Among the few plants to contain salicylic acid, the chief ingredient in aspirin, certain violets have found use as pain relievers. As Nicholas Culpeper so quaintly put it, they were useful "in cooling plasters, oyles, and comfortable cataplasms or poultices. A drachm weight of the dried leaves or flowers . . . doth purge the body of choleric humours and assuageth the heat if taken in a draught of wine or other drink."

Perhaps its most interesting medicinal use, mentioned in several herbals right up to modern times, has been as a treatment for cancers, such as those of the tongue, skin, and colon. Mrs. Grieve records one case in which a man was supposedly cured of colon cancer in nine weeks, during which time he had consumed almost all the leaves from a nursery bed of violets covering an area equal to 1,600 square feet.

Violets, which contain a good deal of sugar, have found their way into the culinary world, especially in confections. The flowers have been popular crystallized and served as a candy or a

"Sirrup of Violets"

"Take a quantity of Blew Violets, clip off the whites and pound them well in a stone morter; then take as much fair running water as will sufficiently moysten them and mix with the Violets; strain them all; and to every halfe pint of the liquor put one pound of the best loafe sugar; set it on the fire, putting the sugar in as it melts, still stirring it; let it boyle but once or twice att the most; then take it from the fire, and keep it to your use. This is a daynty sirrup of Violets."

—17th-century recipe from *A Modern Herbal*, by Maude Grieve

cake decoration. Syrups and even marmalades are made from the pectin-rich flowers, which were also added to gelatins and salad dressings for both color and flavor. Gerard tells of "certaine plates called sugar violet, violet tables, or plate, which is most pleasant and wholesome, especially it comforteth the heart and the other inward parts." Violet plate (plate being a thin confection) was once carried in drugstores as a sort of cough lozenge. The flowers have also been used as a food dye, particularly in candy making. (Violet, like rose, has become so well known as a flower of a certain hue that the word is also a color.)

Though somewhat bitter when raw, the leaves were used in salads and in fritters. Added to soup they functioned as a thickener. Captain John Smith reported in 1612 that violets found in Virginia were good in salads and broths. Many birds and mammals also enjoy the seeds. The wild turkey is said to relish the roots.

Famed Europeans

Many of the uses as well as much of the lore of violets sprang up around *Viola odorata*, the sweet-scented violet. A native of the Mediterranean region, the species has been so popular it has been spread far and wide as a garden escape, and is found coast to coast in North America. The deep purple flower is so sweet that an oil from it is used in the perfume industry, though some authorities say that the scent tends to numb the olfactory sensors after a short time. Because of its scent this species was also used to grow many hybrids.

Even more widely used in hybridizing is *V. tricolor*, known by a host of names, including Johnny jumpup, heartsease, bird's eye, bullweed, pink-eyed john, godfathers and godmothers, and wild pansy. The fondness people had for it is shown in other, more colorful, folk names, including some of the most verbose names ever recorded: love-lies-bleeding, love idol, cuddle me, call-me-to-you, meet-me-in-the-entry, kiss-her-in-the-buttery, kit-run-in-the-fields, three-faces-under-a-hood, and jack-jump-up-and-kiss-me. It is the ancestor of all our garden pansies, which are nothing but overblown violets. The small blue, yellow, and white flowers, common wild in Europe and found as a garden escape here coast to coast, were revered by early Christians who saw in the three colors a symbol of the trinity; hence, it was often called herb trinity.

Symbiosis for Survival

The importance of "farming ants" to plants like violets was confirmed in 2001 by Caroline E. Christian, a student at the Center for Population Biology at the University of California, Davis. She studied shrubland in South Africa, where a third of the thousand plant species rely on ants to disperse their seeds underground. An Argentine ant that does not collect seeds has invaded the territory, pushing out some natives that do, and, as a result, certain plant species are now declining in numbers.

The name "heartsease" may have stemmed from the flower's old use as a medicine to treat heart disease; people believed God had given the plant heart-shaped leaves to mark it for that use. The name may also come from its ancient use as an aphrodisiac and a love potion. As the latter it played a major part in Shakespeare's *A Midsummer Night's Dream*, a use described by Puck:

> *Yet mark'd I where the bolt of Cupid fell:*
> *It fell upon a little western flower,*
> *Before milk-white, now purple with love's wound,*
> *And maidens call it love-in-idleness . . .*
> *The juice of it on sleeping eye-lids laid*
> *Will make or man or woman madly dote*
> *Upon the next live creature that it sees.*

Native Violets

While it might be said that Europe has the most famous and spectacular violets, North America has the greater variety, six times as many as the Old World. Ours come in purple, blue, yellow, and white, and sundry shades and combinations thereof. They also come in two forms: those whose flowers and leaves rise directly from the underground root, and those with stems bearing the leaves and flowers. And they are certainly popular; Illinois, New Jersey, Rhode Island, and Wisconsin have made them their state flowers. No other genus has been so honored so often.

Perhaps the most popular of the natives is the birdfoot violet (*V. pedata*), which inhabits woods and dry fields across the eastern half of the United States and lower Canada, bearing handsome violet and lilac-purple flowers. The namesake leaves are unusual, deeply cut like the claw of a bird and much like the buttercups called crowfoot. Often it blooms a second time in a season, surprising many an autumnal walker.

It is said that John Bartram (1699–1777), the first famous American botanist, was inspired to pursue botany instead of farming by one day finding a colony of birdfoot violets at the edge of a field. That night he dreamed of the flower, and the next day announced that he was hiring a manager for his farm and heading for Philadelphia to study botany. He mastered Latin in only three months so he could understand the nomenclature. Over the years Bartram sent more than 200 species of plants to Europe, many of them identified and named because of him. Plants whose names recall Philadelphia (*Lilium philadelphicum, Erigeron philadelphicus*) or Pennsylvania (*Polygonum pensylvanicum, Silene pensylvanica*) were probably so named by Linnaeus because he got the specimens from Bartram.

Another well-known species is the marsh blue violet (*V. cucullata*), one of the spring's earliest. It favors woodland swamps, but according to the late U.S. senator George Aiken, an expert wildflower gardener, does well in ordinary gardens or makes a good seasonal ground cover. "Royal in color as in lavish profusion, it blossoms everywhere—in woods, waysides, meadows and marshes

New but Old

Who said there's nothing new under the sun? In March 1987 Park Ranger Brent Wauer was hiking in a remote section of the 86,000-acre Guadalupe Mountains National Park on the Texas–New Mexico border when his eye caught something yellow on the side of a cliff. Investigation revealed 35 plants of a violet he'd never seen before. Experts summoned to the scene determined it was a new species, subsequently named *Viola guadalupensis*. "This odd-ball violet appears to be a sturdy survivor of the area's ancient rain forest, most other species of which disappeared at least 8,000 years ago," said the newsletter of the Flora of North America Association in 1991.

. . . from the Arctic to the Gulf," said Neltje Blanchan. This is one of the "bearded" violets that attract small bees. Another is the palm, or early blue, violet (*V. palmata*), found east of the Rockies, which is so thick with foliage that it, too, makes a good cover. A light blue, almost white species of wet woodlands is the long-blooming American dog violet (*V. conspersa*), found in the eastern half of North America. Whether the flowers or the animals should feel insulted, I don't know, but the name reportedly is a belittling reference to the flower's lack of scent.

Among the white violets, the sweet white (*V. blanda*) is known for its scent, though it is not nearly as strong as that of *V. odorata*. Its flower bears very clear markings. "The purple veinings show the stupidest visitor the path to the sweets," said Ms. Blanchan. Other white violets include the lance-leaved or bog white (*V. lanceolata*), which grows east and west of the Rockies; primrose-leaved (*V. primulifolia*), and the Canada (*V. canadensis*). The last, found coast to coast with purple-tinged petals, has been called a violet in the process of evolving from white to purple, which Sir John Lubbock and other scientists have considered the most advanced flower color.

Some scientists believe that after green, yellow was the first color developed by flowers. There are many species of yellow violets in North American woods, particularly on the West Coast, where at least a dozen yellow species are found. All the continent's yellow violets, like the downy yellow (*V. pubescens*), the prairie yellow (*V. nuttallii*), or the round-leaved yellow (*V. rotundifolia*), have at least a tad of blue, purple, or brown, usually as part of the insect guidance system. The round-leaved violet is one of our earliest wildflowers. But in the Northeast at least, it comes long after the bluebird, despite the poetry of William Cullen Bryant, who employed his profession's license when he wrote:

When beechen buds begin to swell,
And woods the blue-bird's warble know,
The yellow violet's modest bell
Peeps from the last year's leaves below.

Trilliums

DEAD MEAT

Our handsome trilliums can be cadaverous in their trickery.

Those who study and write about wildflowers have given red trillium somewhat mixed reviews. The flowers literally reek. But red trillium isn't out to draw our attention. Instead, it wants to draw flies.

Trillium erectum is one of the most recognized members of this family of two dozen or so native North American species, some of which are spectacularly beautiful. Possibly because the flowers are strange looking and showy, and the plant grows in the woods, many people believe red trillium to be a rarity. Actually the species is about as common as any forest flower, both because it is not excessively finicky about its habitat and because its odor discourages people from picking the blossoms. Found from Canada to Georgia and Alabama and westward to the Mississippi, red trillium dwells in rich, cool woodlands, preferably with some evergreens nearby. Often the plants favor hillsides. The purple red flowers of mature plants are about six inches above the ground and often tend to nod a little so that the blooms are partially hidden and may go unnoticed by the casual passerby.

Linnaeus created the name, *trillium*, to describe the "threeness" of the plant, which has three leaves, flowers with three petals, three sepals, three-celled ovaries, and berries with three ribs. Plants of the genus are also commonly called wake-robin because many bloom at about the time of the arrival of migrating robins in spring.

Another folkname, birthroot or bethroot, recalls the Indians' and early colonists' use of the powdered root to promote birth. American Indians also recognized other medicinal properties in the plant, sometimes called Indian shamrock, using it as an antiseptic, astringent, and expectorant, and to control hemorrhages and treat heart palpitations. They boiled the leaves in lard and applied them to ulcers and tumors. In Canada, people once thought chewing the root was an antidote for rattlesnake bites, despite a reported terrible taste. For skin ailments, such as sore nipples, the trillium-based medicine was often "injected" into the skin with jabs of a dog whisker. Today, herb experts debate its value as a medicine. A product called Trillium Complex, used for uterine bleeding, was commercially available until the late 1990s, when it was discontinued. Besides red trillium, it contained wild geranium, goldenseal, and ginseng.

The color and scent of the red trillium flower mimic carrion.

Scent Sign

In past ages, the appearance of many plants was used as a divine sign of what they would be useful in treating. Hepatica, with liver-like leaves, treated liver diseases, and bloodroot's red juice inspired its use as a blood purifier. With red trillium, the scent was the sign. Because the flower has a putrid smell, the plant was used to treat gangrene.

White-Faced Maid

A white-faced maid, Wake-robin,
In a tiny, three-leaved hood,
Knows many of earth's secrets
While nodding in the wood.
No longer is she sleeping,
From magic spell she's free,
Her heart with wise lore laden
Of the cabalistic Three.
This triple, ancient symbol,
The mystic, magic Three,
In leaf, whorl, seed, and flower
Odd number we can see.
Did floral sprite endow her
With nature's secrets deep,
Before the wizard winter
Placed over her spell of sleep?
—Ray Laurance

A Stinker

One of red trillium's more colorful names—one that my son Ben loved when he was young and hated when he grew older—is stinking benjamin. Benjamin, however, was not a person. The name is a corruption of the word *benzoin* or the earlier form, *benjoin,* a substance obtained from Sumatran plants and used in the manufacture of perfumes and incense. (Our native shrub, the spicebush, noted for its strong spicy scent, bears the Latin name, *Lindera benzoin.*) There is, however, no "perfume" made from red trillium, and the name was probably meant to amuse. But for apt humor, one can't beat the much more colorful moniker, "wet-dog trillium."

Words can't really describe the smell of the flower, and you need to get down on your hands and knees and stick your nose up next to a blossom to smell it. The first time I did so, my head literally jerked back with surprise. The flower really *stinks!* Some wildflower enthusiasts have seemed insulted that so showy a bloom would offer so malodorous a scent. "It repels us by its unpleasant odor," wrote one turn-of-the-20th-century author. "Altogether we are inclined to believe that the plant has too great an idea of its own importance." Neltje Blanchan described the bloom as an "unattractive, carrion-scented flower . . . resembling in color and odor raw beefsteak of uncertain age." But she did more than belittle the plant. Studying it, she found that most flying insects ignored the flower, except the common green flesh-flies that are also found around garbage and on dead animals. Attracted by the scent and probably the color, they may feed on the pollen, since the flowers have no nectar. In the process they pick up enough grains to bring to other flowers and effect pollination. Thus, trilliums look and smell like rotten meat for a good reason.

Other names for this species include Indian balm, purple trillium, beth-flower (a corruption of "birth-flower"), bumblebee root, herb trinity, lambs quarters, nosebleed (it was used to stop that condition), red benjamin, and true-love. Members of the large Lily family of plants, they have also been called trinity lily and ground lily.

Red trillium blooms in April and May and is generally easy to transplant in any season. However, care should be taken, and a good-size ball of soil should accompany the roots. Transplants may not bloom for a year or two after being moved. I once acquired some small bulbs from a lot being bulldozed for a new house, and although they grew leaves each year, they didn't blossom until three or four years later.

Trillium seeds are generally successful at producing plants but will not give flowering plants until several years after sowing. In nature, ants help the trillium sow its seeds, hauling them underground in order to eat a tasty appendage and then abandoning the seed proper to sprout. This process, which is common among spring wildflowers, is called myrmecochory, or "ant farming." The ants don't realize that they're farmers, of course, but the system works well for the trilliums.

Other Trilliums

Trilliums are found in various shapes and shades throughout much of North America, and some wildflower enthusiasts specialize in collecting the more showy white and pink varieties. The late U.S. senator George Aiken of Vermont was an expert trillium gardener. In *Pioneering with Wildflowers* he wrote that "for a beginner in growing wildflowers, there is hardly a family more satisfactory than the trilliums. They grow wonderfully well in hardwoods shade and rejoice in a plentiful supply of leafmold. All may be propagated from seed. . . ." Senator Aiken grew at least a dozen varieties, including species from California, the Rockies, and even a rare yellow variety from the mountains of Tennessee. All the plants seemed to do well.

Some nurseries carry trilliums, especially the large-flowered and the dwarf trilliums (*T. grandiflorum* and *T. nivale*), both of which are attractive and long lasting. While large-flowered trillium's range is supposed to include Connecticut, I have never seen one in the "wild" in my hilly town. However, along one of our lakes is woodland that once belonged to the large estate of a woman who was a pillar of the local garden club early in the 20th century. Each spring those woods are dotted with white trilliums that she had no doubt planted long ago. We can enjoy them today because the woman left her estate to the town as a park. There are places, particularly rural woods of beech and maple trees, where vast groves of large-flowered trillium bloom for several weeks each spring. This species is the provincial flower of Ontario.

The Pacific Coast has several native species, including the widespread western trillium (*T. ovatum*), which has pink or white flowers.

Many think painted trillium (*T. undulatum*), with white petals "painted" with red-pink near the center, is the finest-looking trillium; it was ranked as the sixth out of more than 1,000 candidates in a 1940s poll of favorite North American wildflowers. Painted trillium ranges from Nova Scotia to the mountains of Georgia but seems to be rather uncommon in the southern two-thirds of its range, probably because it has been picked or bulldozed almost into extinction in more populated areas. Like most trilliums it has a mild fetid odor. But for stinking, no trillium comes close to old Ben.

Quick Sprouts

While many authorities say it takes two or more years for trillium seeds to germinate, wild-plant propagator Penny Lee says otherwise. Writing in *Wildflower* magazine in 1995, Ms. Lee tells how to sprout *Trillium grandiflorum* or *erectum* within a few months:

Collect seeds from ripe fruit about six weeks after flowers are gone.

Put in cup of water three to six days, then clean off seeds.

Mix one part seeds to six parts damp (not wet) peat moss.

Put mixture into plastic bag, seal, and place in refrigerator (not freezer) for four months.

Spread mixture over some potting soil in pots so mixture is no more than one inch deep over several inches of soil.

Cover pots with glass or plastic and put in cool place with filtered light.

Sprouts should appear in about two months. Keep in pots as long as possible—mice seem to attack very young plants outdoors.

Speedwells

DIAMONDS IN THE ROUGH

Speedwells add color and character to a natural lawn.

Speedwells are fingernail-size wildflowers that can add color to a lawn.

The suburban yard is often the object of a strange fanaticism. People who plant fancy and expensive flowers in beds and borders collectively spend millions of dollars on chemicals to kill the flowers that grow in their grass. They classify giant, often cumbersome, and sometimes bizarre-colored hybrids as beautiful and desirable, while they attack small, delicate blossoms the size of fingernails with costly, perhaps dangerous chemicals in order to produce the putting-green lawn.

Why is an acre of sameness, of monotonous green grass, so desirable? Wouldn't an acre of green concrete or green pebbles be easier to maintain? Or why not install Astroturf?

A grass lawn, regularly mowed but otherwise left pretty much on its own, can become a wild garden dappled with different shades of green and shapes of growth, and spotted with pink, purple, yellow, blue, and white. Many varieties of pretty wildflowers will creep into an unpoisoned lawn, along with soft mosses, colorful lichens (if you have some rocks), and unusual mushrooms—all mixed with the usual grasses.

To me this variety of color and form is far preferable to a rolled, aerated, fertilized, and poisoned carpet of perfection. No matter where you walk or sit on it, a natural lawn will offer something interesting—an orchid-like gill-over-the-ground, a pastel blue speedwell, a heal-all stacked with blossoms, a star-like chickweed, a shiny buttercup, and, yes, even a bright yellow dandelion, the most dread invader for the lawn perfectionists. What's more, many of these flowers will attract butterflies, and their seeds, songbirds.

Several dozen varieties of wildflowers will do well in a yard that is regularly mowed and possesses halfway decent soil. Among my favorite fingernail lawn flowers are the speedwells, represented in North America by at least a half-dozen common species. All have the same general form: three larger petals—at each side and at the top of the blossom—and one small petal pointed groundward. Each also has a pair of stamens that protrude from the center like two stalked crab's eyes and bend outward, opposite each other.

One of the most common of the speedwells is called, suitably enough, common speedwell, *Veronica officinalis*. This spring and early-summer flower is blue with a hint of red. To Tennyson the color was special. He wrote of spring in his poem *"In Memoriam"*:

> Bring orchis, bring the foxglove spire,
> The little speedwell's darling blue,
> Deep tulips dashed with fiery dew,
> Laburnums, dropping-wells of fire.

After a visit to England where the plant is native, John Burroughs called the common speedwell "the prettiest of all humble roadside flowers I saw. It is prettier than the violet . . . a small and delicate edition of our hepatica, done in indigo blue and wonted to the grass in the fields and by the waysides . . . I saw it blooming with the daisy and buttercup upon the grave of Carlyle. The tender human and poetic element of his stern, rocky nature was well expressed by it."

A Gypsy

A native of both Europe and Asia Minor, the common speedwell is also called common gypsyweed, a name no doubt reflecting its wanderlust. It joined many other plants, common today, that made the trip across the Atlantic with settlers or later immigrants. The perennial owes its success to its ability to spread by underground runners and to produce seeds without help. While such insects as bees will effect cross-pollination, the flower can also self-fertilize as it withers and its two protruding stalks bend inward, allowing the pollen-bearing anthers or "eyes" to touch the pollen-catching stigma.

Old World herbalists employed common speedwell to treat skin diseases, scrofula, wounds, hemorrhages, and coughs, and as a diuretic and expectorant. "It wonderfully helps all those inward parts that need consolidating and strengthening," wrote Nicholas Culpeper. "It cleanses and heals all foul or old ulcers, and fretting or spreading cankers."

Leaves of common speedwell were once used in England as a substitute for tea, though one 19th-century authority said it was "more astringent and less grateful than tea."

Speedwell, a name that dates back to at least the 1500s, may have been related to a belief that the plant was quick in curing. Another theory says it reflects the fact that the colorful corollas fall off and fly away soon after the flowers are picked. In other words, *speedwell* is used in the sense of "So long!" or "Good-bye!" Botanist Willard N. Clute, who wrote *The Common Names of Plants and Their Meanings,* said simply, "The name of speedwell refers to the transitory nature of the flowers."

There are also a couple of theories about its Latin generic name, *Veronica.* The name may have stemmed from the Greek words *phero,* meaning "I bring," and *nike,* "victory," because of its supposed curative properties. However, in the more common explanation, the name comes from St.

The Celebrity Speedwell

While wild speedwells are generally considered lowly weeds, some have been cultivated into colorful garden flowers with long blooming seasons. The spiked speedwell, *Veronica spicata,* found in Europe, has been turned into a whole garden full of flowers, bearing such names as *Icicle White Veronica, Veronica Blue Charm, Veronica Red Fox,* and *Veronica Crater Lake Blue.* Some varieties reach two feet in height.

A Delight?

Scientific names are employed to be precise, but sometimes even precision can have unclear origins. Water speedwell is scientifically named *Veronica anagallis-aquatica*. Anagallis, the generic name of the scarlet pimpernel, was probably applied to water speedwell because of its leaves' resemblance to the pimpernel's leaves. But what does *anagallis* mean? David Gledhill, in *The Names of Plants*, says it means "unpretentious, without boasting, without adornment." Nancy Dale, in *Flowering Plants*, says *ana* means "again" and *agallein* "to delight in"—applied "since the flowers open each time the sun strikes them and we can enjoy them anew each day." However, Roger Hyam and Richard Pankhurst, in *Plants and Their Names*, say it's from the Greek *anagelao*, meaning "to laugh," because the pimpernels were said to chase away the blues.

A. T. Johnson and H. A. Smith, in *Plant Names Simplified*, agree that the word may relate to dispelling melancholy but also say *anagallis* may mean simply "delightful."

Veronica. As Neltje Blanchan described it, "an ancient tradition of the Roman Church relates that when Jesus was on his way to Calvary, he passed the home of a certain Jewish maiden who, when she saw the drops of agony on his brow, ran after him along the road to wipe his face with her kerchief. This linen, the monks declare, ever after bore the impress of the sacred features—*vera icona*, the 'true likeness.' When the church wished to canonize the pitying maiden, an abbreviated form of the Latin words was given to her, St. Veronica, and her kerchief became one of the most precious relics at St. Peter's where it is said to be still preserved. Medieval flower lovers, whose piety seems to have been eclipsed only by their imaginations, named this little flower from a fancied resemblance to the relic."

Other names for the common speedwell include lluellin, fluellein, Paul's betony, groundhele, gypsy weed, and upland speedwell. Lluellin and fluellein, once common names in England, were corruptions of the Welsh name of the plant, *Ilysiau Llewelyn* or "Llewelyn's herb." Llewelyn was a 13th-century Celtic prince of Wales conquered by Edward I; the event gave England control over the Welsh territory.

V. officinalis is the type species for the genus *Veronica*, a large group of some 300 species found throughout the world. About 30 species live in North America, including many small, widespready varieties, such as corn speedwell (*V. arvensis*), bird's eye speedwell (*V. chamaedrys*), slender speedwell (*V. filiformis*), and the beautiful blue-and-white thyme-leaved speedwell (*V. serpyllifolia*), listed by the U.S. Department of Agriculture as both native and introduced. Most love lawns, blooming in the spring or early summer in varying shades of blue. Various European species have become popular as border and rock garden plants, and are sold in many nurseries.

Veronicas in turn are members of the Figwort family of some 225 genera and 4,500 species worldwide, including mulleins, toadflaxes, snapdragons, turtleheads, beardtongues, and monkeyflowers.

Natives

While European speedwells are probably the most often seen here, there are native species. The American brooklime or American speedwell (*V. americana*) is a handsome, blue-flowering species that may be found in and about brooks and swamps from coast to coast. A succulent plant that grows upright to nearly a foot, it has been used as a salad food, though some think its taste is too bitter.

Also found coast to coast is the water speedwell (*V. anagallis-aquatica*; see also the sidebar on page 60), which has been described as native by some authorities and as introduced from Europe by others; it is probably circumpolar, for it is also found in both Europe and Asia. As its name suggests, water speedwell likes water, and it and the brooklime are among the few wildflowers that may be found growing in streams. To keep from washing away in the swift currents, water speedwell uses its roots to grip the streambed. And that's all it uses its roots for. Most herbs obtain water and nutrients in the soil through their roots, but water speedwell absorbs both from the stream through its leaves.

Botanists are not clear about how water speedwell reproduces—how it is able to gain a foothold in sometimes swiftly moving water—but they suspect that the plants establish themselves when the streams are fairly dry and slow.

One of the largest-flowered species is Cusick's speedwell (*V. cusickii*), a native found in alpine meadows of the Pacific Northwest and northern Rockies. The plant bears half-inch, blue violet blossoms. Most of the eastern and alien varieties have quarter-inch or smaller flowers.

A large native plant once included in the genus *Veronica* is the widespread Culver's root, long known as *Veronica virginica* and now called *Veronicastrum virginicum*—a generic name that indicates the plant bears a resemblance to *Veronica*, but not a close one. Culver's root, a plant of moist woods and thickets, was widely used in the 19th century as a purge to empty the bowels but was eventually found to be too potent. Chippewas called the plant *wisugidjibik*, or "bitter root," and treated scrofula with it—just as Europeans had done with their own species. Chippewas also used it to stop nosebleeds.

Unlike most speedwells, Culver's root is a tall plant, growing to seven feet and looking not much like the dainty lawn and field speedwells. It has also borne such colorful and unusual names as oxadaddy and quitch. *Culver* is said to recall an early-American physician who used it. It and the speedwells are closely related to digitalis, the foxglove of medicinal fame.

Speed Well!

Fair flowers, modest, shy,
In depths of billowy meadow grasses
   hiding,
And yet worn footpaths nigh
Is found the wonted place of your
   abiding,
To watch with careless gaze the
   passer-by!
Your eyes, wide open, tell
In tones of Saxon blue your heart's
   warm feeling;
As from the hermit's cell
Shines midnight lamp his piety
   revealing,
The fragrant breath of flowers bids
   me 'Speed well!'
—Isaac Bassett Choate
   (1833–1917)

Pussytoes

THE FEET IN THE LAWN

Pussytoes and everlasting offer variety—and butterflies.

Pussytoes form colonies in old lawns and fields. Kids love them.

Pussytoes are among the plants that make a yard interesting. They are also among the plants that grass fanatics attack with herbicides in their quest for the putting-green lawn. In fact, many writers on flowers ignore pussytoes or, as F. Schuyler Mathews does, disparage them. "There are great patches of straggling white seen in the meadows through April," he wrote at the turn of the 20th century, "and one wonders, from the distance of a car window in the swiftly passing train, what the 'white stuff' is—leastwise, I have been asked such a question. But it is only [pussytoes], and scarcely merits attention."

Yet, for children especially, pussytoes can be a treat. When little, my two boys were always entertained by the similarity of the clusters of flowers to a cat's paw, and even felt an affection for the colonies of pussytoes that appeared on one lawn we'd pass while walking to school together. They knew, too, that pussytoes were a sign that winter was over, and warmer days were on their way. One year, the owner of the pussytoed yard hired a lawn-care service that, among other things, laid down weed killer. The next spring, the boys searched in vain for the old colony. In the years that followed, the pussytoes never returned. The poison worked well.

Fortunately, some people would rather have a patch of pussytoes than a lawn of poisoned perfection, and there are still plenty of old lawns, as well as some fields, where pussytoes abound each spring. Their flowers usually come up and die down before the grass needs mowing, and their basal leaves stay low during the year, not minding the mower's visits.

Pussytoes are probably the best known of the Composite family "tribe" known as the everlastings. Pussytoes send up odd, whitish puffs of flowers from basal rosettes of furry green leaves that lie on the ground and seem alive all winter. They are usually found in large colonies, with the plants interconnected by underground runners, and when in bloom make patches of old lawns or field appear almost as if some of winter's snow had been left behind.

Looking like their namesake toes, the small fuzzy flowers top long downy stems. These furry heads and stems are said to entangle the legs of crawling insects, discouraging them from robbing nectar or pollen. The flower heads consist of tight clusters of tiny tubular yellowish flowers, which grow long hair like extensions that later carry away the seeds.

Pussytoes are among our few plants that have both male and female flowers, growing in separate colonies close to one another. The males, lower than the 12- to 18-inch-high females, produce the pollen that small bees and flies can transfer to the loftier females. In some species, such as smaller pussytoes (*Antennaria neodioica*), the male flowers are considered rare.

Although the floral tubes contain nectar, pussytoes don't rely on insect visits to produce seed. If the female fails to be fertilized, it can still develop seeds on its own, though their quality is said to be not as good as that of fertilized seed.

A Flower for Children

There are many plants called pussytoes in North America. The species most common in my area, and one that loves lawns and fields, is often called simply "pussytoes." However, it also goes by a dozen other names, including plantain-leaved pussytoes, early everlasting, plantain-leaf everlasting, woman's tobacco, ladies' tobacco, Indian tobacco, dog toes, four toes, love's nest, poverty weed (many plants that frequent poorer soils are so called), white plantain, and pearly mouse-eared everlasting.

To the botanist it's known as *Antennaria plantaginifolia*. *Antennaria* comes from the resemblance of the "pappus" (the hairs that carry the seeds away) to an insect's antennae, while *plantaginifolia* means that the leaves are shaped like those of plantain. The plant is found from Quebec to Florida and west to Manitoba and Texas.

The genus *Antennaria* contains about 33 North American species. Some botanists have counted as many as 85 species, but the latest thinking seems to be that about 50 of them are subspecies, not species. For instance, more than a dozen old species of *Antennaria* are now considered simply the rosy or pink pussytoes, *Antennaria rosea*, or subspecies of it. Rosy pussytoes are found in the western and northern states and many of the Canadian provinces.

Most species like colder weather and many are alpine. They belong to the Composite family, which includes such common flowers as the daisies, asters, and their frequent lawn companion, the dandelion.

Fresh Drawers

Closely related to members of the *Antennaria* genus—and once included in it—is pearly everlasting (*Anaphalis margaritacea*), a common summertime plant of the open fields from coast to coast, except in the Southeast. *Margaritacea* means "pearly," describing the shape and color of the flowers. Under a magnifying glass, the yellow-eyed, fuzzy white flowers bear a surprising resemblance to the blossoms of the much larger pond lily. *Anaphalis*, an ancient Greek word for a similar plant, has only one representative in North America, and some 35 in Europe and Asia.

Also called Indian posy, pearly everlasting was once widely used by American Indians and colonists to treat dysentery, heart diseases, paralysis, and bronchitis, and as poultices for sprains, bruises, boils, and "painful swellings." Mohegans treated colds with a tea made from the leaves. Some tribes soothed sore throats and relieved hoarseness with it, and medicine men even claimed

Butterfly Friends

Everlastings, both natural and cultivated varieties, are sold in many nurseries because they are attractive not only to gardeners but also to butterflies. The California Native Plant Society notes that the beautiful American painted lady butterfly is particularly fond of *Anaphalis margaritacea*, which it recommends for butterfly gardens. Many species of pussytoes also attract butterflies, another reason for having them in a lawn.

that chewing everlasting made the user want to sing. The dried leaves were also widely smoked, both for enjoyment and to relieve headaches and asthma.

The names "everlasting" or "live-forever" were applied first to European species. When picked, they maintained a nice scent for many months, and were used to freshen chests and drawers in Elizabethan England. Colonists also used them. "Ladies are accustomed to gather great quantities of this life-everlasting and to pick them with the stalks," wrote Peter Kalm on visiting Philadelphia in 1748. "Ladies in general are much inclined to keep flowers all summer long about or upon the chimneys, upon a table or before the windows, whether on account of their beauty or because of their scent. . . . [The plant] was one of those which they kept in their rooms during the winter because its flowers never altered."

Pearly everlasting is also called silver leaf, life-everlasting, moonshine, cottonweed, none-so-pretty, lady neverfade, silver button, and ladies' tobacco. Like pussytoes, it was once dried and used as a tobacco. It ranges across North America from the northern states to Alaska and Newfoundland.

The name "cottonweed" was probably inspired by the fuzziness of the underside of everlasting leaves. Such "fur" helps early-spring plants to retain heat, but the everlasting blooms in dry places in the heat of the summer. Its woolly leaves are designed to help protect the leaves from the heat so they won't dry out.

Incidentally, there is a species of pussytoes that so much resembles the everlasting that both its English and Latin names reflect the similarity. Pearly pussytoes (*Antennaria anaphaloides*) is an alpine species of the northwestern states and western Canada. *Anaphaloides* means it is like an everlasting.

Both plantain-leafed pussytoes and pearly everlasting favor poorer soils, and the pussytoes are most often found in old lawns that have not been fattened with expensive fertilizers. Transplanting is easy; just dig up a wad in May and plant them—with a shot of water—where they won't be overnourished or too wet, and where it's sunny, particularly in the spring.

Most people who have everlastings don't mind sharing them. In fact, fans of the putting-green lawn would love you to haul them all away. *De gustibus non est disputandum*—there's no accounting for taste.

Ouch!

Look at those cats, all in rows
Lying on their backs, showing
*   their toes.*
With the sun burning bright,
*   that's bad because*
Cats on their backs will get
*   sunburned paws.*
—J. S.

Buttercups

BITTER BEAUTIES

Buttercups are among our most ancient
and most popular flowers.

Buttercups are famous flowers. Like daisies and dandelions, almost everyone recognizes them, even children. Natives of both Europe and North America, they can be found across the continent, and most are common and colorful additions to our landscape. But few people realize that buttercups can be dangerous as well as beautiful.

Also called crowfoots, buttercups are a large genus of relatively primitive herb, most of which bear yellow flowers from May through September. Occasionally you will see half-white and half-yellow blossoms and, rarely, all white ones. More than 80 species live in North America and more than 300 worldwide, though botanists disagree on whether some are species or just varieties of species.

The genus, called *Ranunculus*, is sizable and significant enough to have lent its name to *Ranunculaceae*, the Crowfoot, or Buttercup, family of about 60 genera and 1,800 species around the world. These include the anemones, hepaticas, delphiniums or larkspurs, snakeroots, columbines, wolfbanes, and bugbanes. *Ranunculus* is Latin for "little frog." Some say the name comes from the fact that, like most frogs, buttercups favor moist places. Others believe it reflects a froglike shape of the achenes or seeds in some species.

Buttercups, like this swamp buttercup (Ranunculus hispidus), *have shiny, bright petals to attract bees and flies.*

A Basic Flower

Botanists consider buttercup flowers to be one of the simplest designs on the evolutionary scale. Flowers started out as modified leaves, and most early ones were green, greenish white, or greenish yellow. Many of the first flowers were merely petals or sepals emanating from a collection of male stamens and female pistils. Most modern flowers evolved side by side with insects, developing specialized forms that best suited the most compatible insects. The Composites, among the most highly evolved, developed blossoms that are attractive, compact, sweet, efficient, and convenient. Some orchids developed elaborate methods of directing visitors through passages and past pollen-giving and -receiving devices. The milkweeds employ outright trickery to gain fertilization.

But like magnolias, also primitive flowering plants, buttercups retained an ancient and basic collection of bright sepals, pistils, and stamens, with no special position or shape to manage pollinators. The flowers attract all sorts of insects, including bees, flies, wasps, and even beetles. One German scientist found 62 different species on buttercup flowers in his neighborhood. Both yellow and white are "the democratic colors," wrote Clarence Moores Weed. "Blossoms of these colors—except those pollinated by night-flying moths—generally have nectar which is easily accessible and are visited by a great variety of insects." Thus, buttercup blossoms, sometimes mounted singly on tall plants, other times appearing in great numbers, get their share of the action and, as is obvious from their numbers, are quite successful at not only surviving but also multiplying.

Bitter History

Among the most common of our buttercups is the tall, common, showy, or meadow buttercup (*Ranunculus acris*), an import from Europe that now ranges from coast to coast. Growing six or more feet high at times, the tall buttercup is found in moist fields, along roadsides, and in lawns (where mowers may limit its height, but not its ability to thrive and blossom). The plant's leaves have many slender, pointy lobes, and the design looks somewhat like a large bird's foot—whence the name, crowfoot. It's quite possible that this is the same flower Shakespeare wrote of in *Love's Labor's Lost*:

> When daisies pied and violets blue,
> And lady-smocks all silver-white,
> And cuckoo-buds of yellow hue
> Do paint the meadows with delight.

As delightful as the flowers may look, the plant's specific name, *acris*, means "bitter." Herein lies much of the buttercup's fame in folklore and folk medicine, for nearly all species are acrid, sometimes painfully so. Some have been known as "blister plant" for centuries. European beggars used to rub buttercup juice on their skin to grow sores so that passersby would take pity on them and give them food or money. Anne Pratt, a 19th-century British writer on wildflowers, reported that "instances are common in which the wanderer has lain down to sleep with a handful of these flowers beside him, and has awakened to find the skin of his cheek pained and irritated to a high degree by the acrid blossoms' having lain near it." Maude Grieve wrote, "Even pulling it up and carrying it some little distance has produced considerable inflammation in the palm of the hand." She added, "Cattle will not readily eat it in the green state and if driven from hunger to feed on it, their mouths become sore and blistered." Nonetheless, sneaky farmers in ages past fed buttercup blossoms to cows to add a golden tint to the cream and butter produced from the milk, just as today marigold petals are fed to chickens to give their flesh a more marketable golden hue.

As an experiment, a 19th-century scientist placed a slice of the rootstock of the bulbous buttercup or St. Anthony's turnip (*R. bulbosus*) on a person's palm. It began to cause pain within two minutes. The sample was removed, but by 10 hours later, a sizable blister had appeared. It eventually became an ulcer that took some time to heal. In his *American Medicinal Plants*, Charles F.

Holey Plant

Mohawks believed that too much water in the blood was unhealthy. They'd remedy the situation by mixing buttercup, poison ivy, and water, and place a bit of the mixture on the skin. A sore would form and from it would run "surplus water." The practice explains why Mohawks called buttercups by a word that meant "the plant that makes a hole."

Millspaugh had a more entertaining description of buttercup's effects: "A lady who applied the bruised plant to the chest as a counter-irritant, became ill-humored, fretful, cross, and disposed to quarrel, and suffered from soreness and smarting of the eyelashes some time before its action was felt at the region nearest the application."

The buttercups' bitterness probably evolved as a defense against being eaten by the creatures that graze in meadows and swamps. This defense mechanism apparently extends beyond the plant itself, for buttercups reputedly poison the soil near their roots, killing the nitrogen-fixing bacteria. This prevents other plants from growing too close to the buttercup. Even a weed lover like Audrey Wynne Hatfield, who wrote *How to Enjoy Your Weeds*, called buttercups and their close relations "the worst villains in any garden" and something to be avoided even in lawns. I disagree, and have enjoyed colorful patches of buttercups in my yard for 30 years.

Speaking of lawns, another common species is the creeping buttercup (*R. repens*, or "creeping"). This plant spreads by means of both seeds and stolons. A "stolon" is an aboveground, stemlike arm that reaches out until it finds a spot several inches from the parent plant. The tip of the stolon then sinks roots to start a new plant. Eventually the connection between mother and offspring withers away, and the new plant is on its own, ready to send out its own stolons. The technique is obviously successful, since the European import has crept its way across fields and meadows of almost every state and province in North America. While the plants are moderately toxic, a variety of grazing animals feed on them.

Accursed

Perhaps the most powerful of our buttercups is *R. sceleratus*, a circumboreal species found coast to coast in North America. This plant bears the ominous name "cursed crowfoot," and was used by ancient Greeks to remove tumors and other growths. Swallowing just two drops of the juice is said to be enough to kill a person by severely inflaming the alimentary canal. *Sceleratus* is a Latin word with a variety of meanings, none of them too friendly. While it meant "ungodly," "irreligious," "wicked," or "unnatural," the word was also used in the sense of "sharp," "nipping," or "biting," which is probably how it came to be attached to this buttercup and not through some sinister employment of the past.

While the buttercup is an attractive flower, especially in large numbers, you need not bother risking blistered hands to gather them—when picked, the petal-like sepals of most species soon fall off, making them ill-suited for bouquets. Yet despite their many shortcomings, buttercups have endeared themselves to people through the centuries. During the Middle Ages, lovers wore buttercups at betrothal time. In many cultures, sighting buttercups was said to be good luck. And what child has never picked a buttercup and placed the blossom under a playmate's chin to see whether the companion likes butter?

The shiny, waxy surface that is able to reflect light onto chins is the result of a high starch content in the cells on the sepal surface. This flashy outfit is undoubtedly aimed at catching

Pledge to Sun

The rich, milk-tinging buttercup
Its tiny polished urn holds up,
Filled with ripe sunshine to the edge,
The sun in his own wine to pledge.
—*James Russell Lowell*
(1819–1891)

the eye of passing insects and drawing them to its plentiful supply of nectar. Probably because of the starch and the sweets, early settlers used to pickle the flowers. American Indians of the West ground seeds of certain species as an ingredient in flour and used roots to create a yellow dye.

Poison for Poisons

In medicine, buttercups were chiefly used to remove warts and other unwanted growths. The *Ladies' Indispensable Assistant*, a guide to the housewife published in 1852, said the buttercup is good "for corns on the feet." But it was also employed as an external relief from headaches. (Perhaps its pain, worse than the ache, diverted attention from the head!) Europeans used to bind buttercup leaves to the wrists of people suffering from fevers and pneumonia, and one Englishman in the 1790s claimed to cure cancer with it. Certain buttercups were used in Europe to treat lunacy and cure the plague. In the United States during the 1800s, a tea made from the plant was a folk treatment for asthma.

Ironically, buttercups were once used as an emetic on people who had swallowed a poison; the effect on the stomach was so quick and violent that it would cause people to vomit instantly. Said one 19th-century writer, "It is . . . as if Nature had furnished an antidote to poisons from among poisons of its own tribe."

Modern herbalists usually recommend against use of buttercups as any kind of medicine, considering the plants to be too dangerous. Even John Gerard warned about them in the 16th century: "There be divers sorts or kinds of these pernitious herbes comprehended under the name of Ranunculus or Crowfoote, whereof most are very dangerous to be taken into the body, and therefore they require a very exquisite moderation, with a most exact and due manner of tempering; not any of them are to be taken alone by themselves, because they are of a most violent force, and therefore have the great nede of correction."

But if you're a fisherman who favors live bait, some of that "violent force" may be harnessed to help you. According to an early-19th-century herbalist, if you pour some buttercup tea on ground containing worms, "they will be forced to rise from their concealment." That's probably more practical than using it for headaches, fevers, or asthma.

Forecaster

Among English lower classes butter was a luxury only the wealthy could afford. Thus, when a peasant held a buttercup under a friend's chin, he didn't interpret the yellow glow as "You like butter." Instead, he proclaimed, "You're going to be rich!"

Celandine

A GOLDEN POPPY

Celandine has treated ailments from head to foot.

You walk into the doctor's modern office. He inspects your problem—a wart on the sole of your foot. Then, instead of scratching out a $50 prescription to be filled by the local pharmacy, he writes down the word *celandine* and tells you to go pick some. Frequently squeeze its orange yellow juice on your wart, he says.

This treatment seems strange, something from another century and not the recommendation of a modern physician. Yet there are doctors today—at least one in my neighborhood—who prescribe celandine to treat warts, just as herbalists did in ancient Greece and Rome, and during the Middle Ages. For 20 centuries, celandine was considered one of a few dozen herbs essential to the basic collection of any practitioner of botanic medicine, and was used to treat nearly two dozen major kinds of disease. It is also a widespread and colorful spring wildflower whose greens are among the first to appear each spring.

Colorful Medicine

Celandine is famous for its plentiful and brightly colored juice, which can irritate the skin and should be handled with care. The juice's odor has been described as strong and disagreeable, and its taste persistent and nauseating. "A drop of this acrid fluid on the tip of the tongue is not soon forgotten," wrote Neltje Blanchan. No doubt, this bitterness helps prevent the plant from being consumed by grazers, be they mammal or insect.

Celandine's potent juice includes several alkaloids, one of which is narcotic and quite poisonous in its pure state. The juice found many medicinal uses in the past, especially as a treatment for ocular problems. John Gerard, the 16th-century English herbalist, wrote, "the juice of this herbe is good to sharpen the sight, for it cleanseth and consumeth away slimie things that cleave about the ball of the eye and hinder the sight. . . ." Seventeenth-century herbalist Nicholas Culpeper added that it's "one of the best cures for the eyes. . . . Dropped into the eyes the juice cleanseth them from films and cloudiness that darken the sight, but it is best to allay the sharpness of the juice with a little breast-milk." Nicholas Culpeper added, "most desperate sore eyes have been cured by this only medicine" and posed a question that seems easy to answer: "Is not this far

The leaf of this celandine has been torn to show the distinctive orange yellow juice inside.

Whoops!

In the poem, "To the Small Celandine," William Wordsworth wrote:
There's a flower that shall be mine,
'tis the little celandine.
Wordsworth was celebrating a buttercup called lesser celandine (*Ranunculus ficaria*). The sculptor of the Wordsworth memorial in Grasmere Church in the Lakes District of England knew the poem but not the plant. Meaning to recall Wordworth's favorite flower, he mistakenly portrayed the greater celandine poppy (*Chelidonium majus*) on the monument.

Felon Fighter

Celandine is a plant of yellow
From its flower to its juice;
Tis a very potent fellow
With a very special use.
Be it felon, wart or tetter,
Celandine may save the day.
Herbals say you can't find better
To send these ailments on their way.
—J. S.

better than endangering the eyes by the art of the needle?" (Despite these glowing ancient endorsements, never put *anything* into your eye without a modern physician's approval!)

Because its orange juice looks like bile, herbalists of old treated liver ailments with it. The plant was used to improve the blood, cure wounds, promote perspiration (to cleanse the body of poisons or "bad humors"), and to treat jaundice, eczema, scrofula, piles, toothaches, corns, itches, and ringworm. The powdered root was placed on a decayed or loose tooth to make it fall out.

By the 20th century, celandine had become "a very popular medicine in Russia where it is said to have proved effective in cases of cancer," reported Maude Grieve in the 1920s. By the 1990s, a Viennese company was selling Ukrain, a drug that is injected directly into the tumor mass and uses alkaloid extracts of celandine along with a veteran tumor-toxic drug, thiotepa. While Ukrain is available by prescription in some European countries, such as the United Kingdom, neither the U.S. Food and Drug Administration nor the American Cancer Society has approved the treatment; in fact, the FDA has issued warnings against its use and has ordered that the drug not be allowed to be imported into the United States.

Donald Law, a modern British herbalist, said gypsies used to put celandine in their shoes and keep it there when they walked, claiming that it not only kept the feet fresh but also cured jaundice. Dr. Law, who is very enthusiastic about herb and folk medicine, connects the gypsy practice to a theory that every part of the human body has a corresponding "pressure point" on one of the feet. He notes that gypsies are descended from the Chinese and that the Chinese practice acupuncture. "The gypsy remedy may be wiser than we think," he says.

A Gypsy

Celandine itself is a gypsy. A native of Europe and Eastern Asia, it was probably brought to North America for use as a medicine and as a yellow dye. The Rev. Cotton Mather of Massachusetts witch trial fame knew it and perhaps used it in the late 1600s. By the turn of the 20th century, celandine was found only locally along the East Coast. While Ms. Blanchan predicted that "doubtless it will one day overrun our fields, as so many other European immigrants have," celandine has extended its territory without becoming a pest. The plant has now traveled to and across the Mississippi and is found locally in some cooler western states, including Washington. However, none of the many states or provinces it inhabits lists it as a troublesome invasive plant.

Celandine can be found in almost any situation, from poor to rich soils, from open fields to woods, from fairly dry to moist ground. However, the plant seems to prefer shaded rich soils; a favorite haunt is a wooded roadside. Along a country road near my home, several celandine plants live 15 feet off the ground, rooted in the rot of a limb-hole in a living tree.

Celandine also has a long blooming season; I've seen its yellow, four-petaled flowers as early as May 1, and plants will bloom throughout the summer and into the fall. Its leaves are among the last to fold up and die in late fall and early winter—they've been spotted healthy in late December in Connecticut. And it is among the earliest herbs to come to life in late winter or early

spring. I've found them, juice flowing, in late February, and one observer has seen their green leaves coming up under the ice in late January.

Like some other spring plants, such as violets, celandine has evolved a system of making use of ants. The seeds bear a tasty, whitish appendage, called an elaiosome. The ants carry the seed to their nests, eat the elaiosome, and then toss aside the seed proper, which can then sprout—far from the parent plant—even high up in a tree. (This process is described in more detail in the chapter on violets.)

Seeds aren't celandine's only method of reproduction. Most plants have more than one way of ensuring survival of the species, and in the case of celandine, it's an uncommon form of "vegetative reproduction." If you place a celandine leaf in soil, roots and stems will sprout from the leaf edges. Why would a plant evolve a system that seems to rely on another agent to connect its leaves with soil? The stems are known for being weak and easy to break or bend. Perhaps celandine has historically favored habitats that make the weakling plants susceptible to being flattened or crushed, by the effects of weather or maybe even by hoofs or paws of wild animals. This system of propagation may be useful for establishing and preserving small colonies of celandine. It's not effective for spreading the species over wide areas, however; if celandine had to move across the continent leaf by leaf, the march would be exceedingly slow. Seeds remain the method of establishing new colonies away from the mother plants.

The Swallows

Celandine is a word of peculiar etymology, with at least two theories for its origin. The word comes from the Greek, *chelidon*, meaning "a swallow." Pliny, the Roman writer, traced it to the tradition that the flowers bloomed when the swallows (of Europe) arrived and that the blossoms faded at their departure. Gerard disputed this, maintaining that in southern Europe, celandine blooms year-round. He said that the name stemmed from the mistaken belief that swallows used the plant as an eyewash for their young.

Among celandine's many folk names are swallowwort, felonwort, wartweed, sightwort, kenningwart, tetterwort, killwort, and garden celandine. A "tetter" was a skin disease. A "felon" is a finger or toe infection, not a criminal. *Kenning* is an old word for "sight."

To the botanist, the plant is *Chelidonium majus*, meaning simply "greater celandine," to differentiate it from lesser celandine, which is, in fact, not a *Chelidonium* at all, but *Ranunculus ficaria*, which belongs to the unrelated Buttercup family.

Actually, *C. majus* has no brothers and sisters in the entire world and is what is called monotypic, with only one species in its genus. Celandine in turn is a member of the small Poppy family of 23 genera and about 210 species worldwide. It is one of only a few poppies found wild in the eastern United States. Another is the bloodroot (see page 22), also a monotypic plant, whose juice is red orange instead of yellow orange.

How's That?

Wort is an Old English word for "plant." Thus, it's not surprising that celandine, an herb widely used to treat warts, would be called by one of the more entertaining accidents of plant nomenclature, wartwort.

Eye Friend

"Ask now the fouls of the air, and they shall tell thee. The swallows will carry thee to the Celandine. Feeble Eyes will not find a greater friend in the whole of the vegetable kingdom."
—*The Rev. Cotton Mather*
(1663–1728)

Marsh Marigold

FRIEND OF THE FARMER

Marsh marigolds opened many hearts—and swamps.

To the old New England farmer, the blooming of the marsh marigolds was a noteworthy event several times over. The yellow flowers, which appear from mid-April through mid-May, are the first bright sign that the growing season has finally arrived. Swamps, woodland streams, and moist fields light up with their abundant blossoms. As John Burroughs described it, they give "a golden lining to many a dark, marshy place in the leafless April woods, or [mark] a little water-course through a greening meadow with a broad line of new gold. One glances up from his walk, and his eye falls upon something like fixed and heaped up sunshine there beneath the alders, or yonder in the freshening field." To some Indian tribes, the plant was called by a name that translates almost poetically as "opens the swamps."

The marsh marigold, also called a cowslip, has long been a symbol of spring. Centuries ago English peasants would pick marsh marigolds on April 30 and throw the flowers on the thresholds of cottages and farmhouses the next day in celebration of May Day. They were said to protect homes against witches. The flowers were also woven into garlands for May 1 celebrations.

To many a woods-wise farmer, however, the marsh marigold had more practical value. The shiny, kidney-shaped leaves were gathered young and boiled in a couple of changes of water, producing greens that some New Englanders would insist are better than spinach and that American Indians had long enjoyed as a vegetable.

Boiling, incidentally, removes acrid irritants that could be poisonous and that cause grazing livestock and wildlife—except moose—to avoid the plant. In this respect, marsh marigold is much like its close cousin, the buttercup, and indeed the acrid chemical may be the same as that found in so many *Ranunculus* species. Some say very young plants have less or none of the poisonous constituent.

The penny-wise farmer would grab not only the leaves but also the blossoms, which years ago were peddled on city street corners. They were, after all, the first big and bright wildflower of the season, and they were common and free to any who would risk wet feet to pick them. Farmhouse rooms, too, were decorated with lush bouquets of the blossoms.

Marsh marigolds, related to buttercups, thrive in swamps.

In some areas, including Virginia, people picked and pickled the buds as a substitute for capers. Herbalists used the plant to treat several maladies, such as warts, anemia, and fits. Some herbals mention its use for clearing the throat and bronchial passages, but Charles F. Millspaugh, in his *American Medicinal Plants*, said, "the medical history of this herb is very sparse and of no consequence; it has been used in cough syrups which would, without doubt, have been fully as efficacious without it." Some American Indians treated scrofulous sores with the plant, and Chippewas used it as a postpartum medication for mothers.

One 19th-century physician even maintained that "it would appear medicinal properties may be evolved in the gaseous exhalations of plants and flowers, for on a large quantity of the flowers' . . . being put into the bedroom of a girl subject to fits, the fits ceased."

Whose Gold?

Commonly called either marsh marigold or cowslip, the plant is neither a marigold (as in the garden *Calendula*) nor a true cowslip (an English primrose). The origins of both names, however, are interesting and still being debated.

There are several theories about "marigold." Some authorities say it's derived from the church festivals in the Middle Ages when the flower was one of several devoted to the Virgin Mary; hence, "Mary-gold." Mrs. William Starr Dana, however, noted that the Anglo-Saxon word for marsh is *mere* (pronounced with two syllables) and suggests that the word is a modern English equivalent of "marsh-gold." As reasonable as that may sound, The *Oxford English Dictionary* favors the Mary derivation.

Yet another theory proposes that marigold is from a misunderstanding of an Anglo-Saxon name, *mear-gealla*, meaning "horse-blister," because the flower buds look like blisters. This seems a stretch.

Cowslip has also been misunderstood. The word literally means "cow slop," which is to say, cow dung. The English cowslip frequents meadows and pastures, as does its bovine namesake. And if the ground's moist enough, so does our marsh marigold.

A flower so early, common, bright, and widespread is bound to be well known and consequently picks up many names. Among people here and in Europe—it is native to both continents as well as to Asia—the plant had been known as king cups, water blobs, May blobs, mollyblobs, horse blobs, bull's eyes, leopard's foot, water gowan, meadow gowan, Marybuds, *verrucaria*, *solsequia*, water dragon, capers, cowlily, cowbloom, soldier buttons, palsywort, great bitterflower, meadowbouts, crazy bet, gools, drunkards, water crowfoot, and meadow buttercups.

Blob is a word that originally meant just "bubble," but because bubbles are round, it came to be used for other things that are round, such as drops, fruit, flowers, blisters, and even a science fiction movie monster. *Gowan* is based on the Old Norse word for gold. *Verrucaria* is Latin, meaning "cure for warts," while *solsequia*, also from the Latin, means sun-follower because the flowers open in the morning and close at night—"Winking Marybuds begin to ope their golden eyes," wrote

Cow's Lip

Through the years, people have misunderstood or at least had fun with the word *cowslip*. Even as notable a naturalist as Thoreau called the marsh marigolds cow's lips. Many people believed the yellow color in butter came from cows' having eaten the cowslip flower. This is not true and cows, in fact, avoid the acrid-tasting plant, considered poisonous to livestock.

Shakespeare. Drunkards, an old Devonshire name, stems from a belief, especially among children, that the scent of the flower encouraged drunkenness because the wetland-loving plant seems to drink so much water.

Water crowfoot and meadow buttercups are technically more fitting than the two commonly used names, for the plant is a member of the Crowfoot, or Buttercup, family. The flowers, bearing five to nine petal-like sepals or tepals, are quite similar to those of the common buttercups. The sepals bear a yellow, waxy coating that gives the flower its color—scratch it off and the sepal becomes transparent. And like buttercups, as well as the related anemones and hepaticas, they are early bloomers that don't mind chilly northern climates.

Swamp Cups

To the scientist, the marsh marigold has but one name, *Caltha palustris*. *Caltha* is from the Greek for "cup" or "goblet." Caltha was also a character in German lore. As folklorist Charles M. Skinner tells it, Caltha was a maiden who fell so deeply in love with the sun god that she lived in the fields, day and night, so that she could see him as much as possible. She eventually wasted away and from the spot where she had stood, the first marsh marigold appeared, in a form and color that reflects the sun. "And on its petals [was] a drop that might have been dew or a tear of happiness at the maid's translation," Skinner said.

Palustris is from the Latin for "marsh" or "swamp." Thus, observed Frederic William Stack in 1909, the plant is a "marsh cup"—"a name which has some real significance, and is aptly applied."

C. palustris is the type species of a small genus of temperate and arctic plants, 3 of which can be found in North America and about 15 worldwide. The other two natives are white marsh marigold, *C. leptosepala*, found from the Rockies west to the Pacific, and floating marsh marigold, *C. natans*, which is found in Minnesota, in one county in Wisconsin, and in limited regions of the central and western provinces of Canada up into Alaska. Both bear white tepals.

The marsh marigold grows from Labrador to Alaska, and south into the Carolinas and Nebraska, and along the Pacific Coast from British Columbia to California.

Marsh marigolds, incidentally, are among the few wildflowers that can be found in the middle of a stream. They probably manage to gain a foothold when the water is low, but they are certainly an unusual sight blooming away from stalks that are standing in a swift spring current. They are also among the few cold-climate wildflowers that, like forsythia, may bloom in the fall if conditions are right.

The marsh marigold is ideal for anyone who happens to have a moist, swampy spot that's sunny in springtime. The soil may be wet only in the spring, for the roots of the plant, whose leaves disappear by summer, can survive in places that become fairly dry later in the year. However, the location must be quite moist, at least from March through May, and it's best if the ground is damp year-round. Marsh marigold can be introduced with seed obtained from healthy flowers, though it will take a couple of years to get mature, blooming plants. They self-sow and

Rich and Yellow

O velvet bee! You're a dusty fellow!
You've powdered your legs with gold.
O brave marsh marybuds, rich and
*   yellow,*
Give me your money to hold!
—Jean Ingelow (1820–1897)

multiply fairly rapidly from seed. If you have access to a large colony of them, the plants can be transplanted at any time or divided before or after blooming. (Don't take plants from swamps where they are not common and should be encouraged to spread.) Marsh marigolds are susceptible to winter kill, especially if they are unsheltered, so mulching the planted area in late fall or sticking a pail or basket over the crown of a plant for the winter helps assure survival.

Survival is naturally encouraged by the design of the flower itself. Unlike most blossoms of its family and of similar shape, the marsh marigold has not one but many sources of nectar— one on the side of each of the many pistils around the flower center. Consequently, the more than 40 kinds of bees and early flies drawn to the flower will wander all around the fountain of sweets, in the process carrying pollen to most or all of the stigmas. The flower is also said to have a scent that few human noses can detect, but that apparently attracts insects. The flower reflects light in the ultraviolet range and is one of many flowers that look yellow to us but purple to bees.

John Moore, a 20th-century British novelist and naturalist, appreciated the image of bees buzzing around marsh marigolds. Describing in a novel an English soldier in Korea sentimentally remembering what springtime is like in his homeland, he included finding "kingcups by the river so shiny you'd think the bees could see their faces in them."

Peter Rabbit's Gold

"Peter laughed happily. 'They are my gold!' cried he. 'See how they shine! And they are full of golden meaning, for now I know that truly Mistress Spring is here to stay. I hoped I would find the very first one, and I guess I have.' Once more Peter kicked up his heels for pure joy."
—Thornton W. Burgess, *The Burgess Flower Book for Children* (1923)

Blue Flag

BORN TO THE PURPLE

The blue flag is a colorful iris in a regal family.

Here's a bee's-eye view of a blue flag, an iris whose markings direct insects to the store of nectar.

Blue flag, one of our more majestic and unusual midspring wildflowers, is a member of the regal Iris family that has impressed both naturalists and gardeners through the ages. Yet the plant received only a mediocre review from none other than Henry David Thoreau. "How completely all character is expressed by flowers," the essayist wrote. "This is a little too showy and gaudy, like some women's bonnets."

Without doubt, the blue flag is showy, but that's part of its means of survival. At a time of year when many blossoms vie for the attention of nectar-hunting pollinators, its big, showy blossoms are able to flag down many passing bees. The flowers offer plenty of room to land and ample veining to act as a guide to the sweets inside.

Blue flag's blossom has evolved to move pollen very efficiently from flower to flower. Bees can't help rubbing against the pollen-bearing anther, located overhead and positioned so that the grains can't fall onto the stigma, self-fertilize, and lead to poor-quality seeds. The sticky stigma is situated such that the visiting bee will deposit pollen from other flowers.

A-turn-of-the-century plant naturalist, appropriately named Clarence M. Weed, found that irises like the blue flag are particularly susceptible to thievery. While the flowers are adapted to large bumblebees, many flies, skipper butterflies, moths, and other insects are also attracted to them and usually don't transfer pollen. Nevertheless, the iris has plenty of nectar to go around, and it's perhaps no accident that the blue flag is a denizen of wet places—swamps and moist fields—making production of large amounts of nectar easy.

The leaves, too, are specially designed. Grasslike and vertical, they allow the sunlight to penetrate through the mass of vegetation in a tightly packed colony of plants. What's more, unlike broad-leafed plants, the iris can assimilate light on both sides of its leaf, not just the upper surface.

Larger blue flag (*Iris versicolor*) is one of the most visible and most representative of the wild irises east of the Mississippi. Although not rare today, the species was more plentiful in the days when there were more pastures and swamps, so many of which have been drained, filled, or bulldozed for fields and, more recently, subdivisions and shopping centers. Their blooming season in the Northeast runs from late May through June. When they've been left undisturbed, these irises often form impressive colonies, which may be in shaded swamps or open meadows, but almost always where their roots can remain moist most of the year.

Wild irises are not overly common and the flowers shouldn't be picked, no matter how tempting. Although blue flags are perennials and spread from their rhizomes, they also depend on their seeds for propagation. Besides, said Mabel Osgood Wright, "this iris must surely be seen in its home to be known in anything but outline. If many flowers of wood and field lose quality away from their surroundings, the herbaceous flowers of moist lands and waterways do so in far greater degree." Even the critical Thoreau admitted, "It belongs to the meadow and ornaments it much."

Regal History

The iris has had a lofty and regal history. Henry Wadsworth Longfellow wrote of the flower:

> Born in the purple, born to joy and pleasance
> Thou dost not toil nor spin
> But makest glad and radiant with thy presence
> The meadow and the lin.

The name comes from the Greek goddess Iris, who was a messenger between humans and the gods atop Mount Olympus. Wherever she went, a rainbow followed her. Whenever the ancient Greeks saw a rainbow in the sky, it was a sign that Iris was delivering a message to someone. Thus, *iris* came to mean "rainbow" and, used as the generic name of these plants, reflects the variety of colors sported by many species. One of the goddess Iris's duties was to guide the souls of dead women to the afterworld, and so Greeks often planted the flowers next to graves.

The ancients consider the iris a symbol of power and majesty. Egyptian kings used the design of the blossom on their scepters and placed it on the brow of the Sphinx, believing its three major petals to be symbols of faith, wisdom, and valor. Modern use of the iris as a royal symbol may trace back to Clovis, a sixth-century king of the Franks. According to one legend, a large force of Goths trapped his army, with his back up against the Rhine River near Cologne. As he searched for a way to escape, Clovis noticed in the distance a large colony of golden irises extending far out into the river. He realized this was a sign that the water was shallow enough there for his troops to cross. In another version of the tale, Clovis was able to sneak across the river and attack the rear guard of the Goths by finding flags growing in a shallow area. Yet another legend involving Clovis is more colorful, if not believable. The king was having a hard time at war, constantly losing battles. One day an angel appeared to a holy man, explaining that Clovis needed to get rid of his coat of arms—three black toads—and replace it with three irises. The angel gave the man a shield with the irises on a bright blue background. The holy man brought the shield to Clovis's wife, Queen Clotilde, who gave it to the king. Clovis got rid of the toads, used the new symbol, and began to win battles. Whatever the reason, angelic or riparian, Clovis adopted the iris as his family's badge.

Perhaps knowing this tradition, King Louis VII of France selected the iris as his house emblem when he was a young Crusader. It thus became the *fleur-de-lis*, *fleur-de-lys*, or *fleur-de-luce*, all

Iris Pasta

A famous Italian dish may have gotten its name—via the Greeks—from the iris. According to the story, a Greek name for one type of iris was *machaironion*, and the root of this species was ground with flour to create a variety of pasta, later called simply "macaroni."

The Enemy

Blue flags and other irises are the targets of a moth whose larvae can kill them. The iris borer moth (*Macronoctua onusta*) flies at night and in the fall lays up to 1,000 eggs on the dried iris leaves. Pinkish caterpillars, called borers, hatch in the spring, begin eating the leaves, and work their way down to the rhizome, which they can completely consume, except for the shell. And if the borer doesn't kill the plant, bacteria introduced through the wound leads to rot that does. The best solution to ridding infected plants appears to be biological: commercially available worm-like nematodes that enter the borer and release a bacterium that kills the caterpillar, whose corpse the nematodes then eat.

corruptions of *fleur-de-Louis*, "flower of Louis." (Another theory has it that the fleur-de-lis is a lily—*lis*, the French word for "lily"; and in *The Winter's Tale*, Shakespeare spoke of "lilies of all kinds, the fleur-de-luce being one.") Our blue flag, a different species from the white iris of Louis, is sometimes called the American fleur-de-lis. Some authorities claim the flowers are commonly called flags because Louis, Clovis, and some other rulers in Europe frequently employed the design on flags and banners. A simpler and more probable explanation, however, is that iris leaves look like reeds, the Middle English word for which was *flagge*.

Less regal are some of the other folk names for our own *Iris versicolor*: poison flag, liver lily, snake lily, dragon flower, and dagger flower. Some of these refer to the shape of the blossom (dragon) or the leaf (dagger); the Old English word for the plant was *segg*, which was a small sword. Others reflect the plant's long history as a medicinal herb.

Food and Drug

Iris versicolor has probably been used in medicine more extensively than any other member of its clan. American Indians dug the roots from wild plants and even cultivated colonies near ponds. They used the root to treat stomach problems and dropsy, and as an emetic, a laxative, and a poultice. Members of some western tribes carried the root of another species to prevent snakebites.

"It is excellent in removing humor from the system, much more so than the outrageous mercury and much more safe," said the *Ladies' Indispensable Assistant* in 1852. This advice did not suggest that a clown would turn dour from consuming it; this "humor" was a bodily fluid, and the writer presumably meant a "bad humor" that would cause sickness.

The "rhizome," or creeping rootstock, contains a powerful, acrid resin so strong that many modern authorities warn against its internal use. This may be why the plant is also called poison flag. Some herbalists in the past, however, considered the plant valuable in treating chronic vomiting, heartburn, liver and gall bladder ailments, sinus problems, colic, gastritis, enteritis, syphilis, scrofula, skin diseases, and even migraines. Drugs called Iridin or Irisin, used as diuretics, were once produced from the plant, which was long listed in the *U.S. Pharmacopoeia*, a catalogue of accepted drugs. Modern research indicates the root may have the ability to increase the rate at which fat is converted into waste, and an iris has been used in India as a treatment for obesity.

Mixed with water, blue flag flowers can produce a blue dye that acts like litmus paper, turning red when exposed to an acid, or back to blue if the substance is alkaline.

Various species, particularly European ones, are known as orris root—*orris* being a corruption of the word *iris*. After drying a few months, their roots gain a sweet scent, not unlike that of violets. Ground into powder, these roots were once made into little pomander balls that were carried by the wealthy as a perfume. This same powder was also carried by witches who, it was said, induced abortions with it.

In the 19th century, growing *Iris florentina* was a major industry in parts of Italy, particularly the Chianti region of Tuscany, which shipped the dried rootstock to Florentine perfumeries. Florence, whose city seal bears the likeness of an iris, is still a center of interest in the plants and hosts the International Iris Trials, a competition for growers. Iris roots are still used as fragrances in fancy soaps, cosmetics, and liquid perfumes.

The French, who enjoy all sorts of drinks made from plants, once used roasted iris seeds as a coffee. The leaves have been used to make a green dye, and the root to make black dye and ink.

Many Varieties

Throughout North America at least 47 species of iris exist, some of them garden escapes native to other continents. One botanist claimed that just in the southeastern United States, nearly 100 different species can be found, many of them in southern Florida. However, current taxonomical researchers have reclassified about 65 previously defined species into one, the Dixie iris (*I. hexagona*). Worldwide, more than 150 species grow in the north temperate zone, much to the pleasure of gardeners specializing in this handsome genus.

I. versicolor, also called the harlequin blue flag, ranges wild from the East Coast to Wisconsin and from Canada south to Virginia. It is also found in Idaho. Of several beautiful western species, the most widespread is the western blue flag (*I. missouriensis*), found from British Columbia to southern California and eastward to the Mississippi. American Indians used fibers from the outer edges of the leaves to make surprisingly strong rope, string, and netting, as well as fabric for bags. Weaving the fibers into rope was a tedious task. The U.S. Department of Agriculture's National Plant Data Center reports that it took an Indian nearly six weeks to make 12 feet of iris rope.

Almost all irises are showy and colorful. Some are actually shocking to encounter in a verdant wooded wetland. Blue, purple, lilac, orange, white, and yellow kinds are known in North America. The yellow iris (*I. pseudacorus*), an introduced species from Europe now found as an escape in most states and provinces, was used in ancient herbal medicines.

Irises are in turn members of the Iris family (Iridaceae), which consists of more than 90 genera and 1,800 species worldwide, most of them growing in Africa. The Iris family includes the modest little blue-eyed grasses of our spring fields, and the springtime favorites of gardeners, the crocuses. Many irises bear a resemblance to many orchids, and so it's not surprising that the Iris family is classified as fairly closely related to the Orchid family (Orchidaceae).

It's Official

Nashville may be known for its country music, but among flower fans it's the Iris City. The iris is the official Tennessee state *cultivated* flower (the passion flower is the official wildflower). The wild blue flag (*Iris versicolor*) is the official provincial flower of Quebec.

Sailboats

Kings may have used irises to save armies, but some kids used them as toys. A man from the Shetland Islands told British naturalist Roy Vickery about making childhood sailboats from the leaves of yellow iris in the 1940s. He'd pick an iris leaf and make a small lengthwise slit about halfway down. "The tip of the leaf was then bent up and over until its apex would be pushed a little way through the slit, thus forming a 'sail' and a 'keel' at the same time," the man said. With a little breeze the "boats" would sail far enough to disappear from sight.

Solomon's Seals

THE SEVERAL SEALS OF SOLOMON

Who's true and who's false among these prehistoric-looking lilies?

The flowers of great Solomon's seal dangle beneath the leaves.

In the cool air of a shaded wood, amid the fresh spring ferns and the shoots of summer's plants, we often find the Solomon's seals, both true and false. Sometimes growing side by side, they are as much a part of spring in eastern and central North America as asters are of fall. They are odd, primitive-looking plants that would seem more at home with dinosaurs than with the automobiles whose woodland roads they frequently line. They rise straight from the soil, and then lean over almost parallel with the ground, with leaves spread out like the fronds of uncut ferns.

While the true and false Solomon's seals bear a general resemblance in leaf form and placement, and both are members of the Lily family, they belong to separate genera and bear very different flowers.

Our most common "true" Solomon's seal is the smooth Solomon's seal, *Polygonatum biflorum*, whose tubular, yellow green flowers hang singly or, more often, in pairs from under the stem. Their dangling is no accident. The position makes it difficult for rain or for many types of crawling insects to invade the store of nectar. Yet higher species of bees, which pollinate the flowers, have no difficulty landing on the blossoms and gathering sweets and pollen.

In the summer, *P. biflorum* forms dark blue berries that, like the flowers, dangle from the stem. By planting these berries, either whole or mashed, in rich, slightly acid, dry soil, you can easily introduce the plant to shaded spots around your yard. Solomon's seals can also be transplanted in the spring, but only from places where they are common or threatened. Once established *Polygonatum* enlarge into great clumps and also multiply from seed. A wildflower gardener reported that she once acquired about a dozen roots of Solomon's seal and within about five years had more than 500 shoots coming up in her garden.

For a couple of centuries, botanists recognized a species called great Solomon's seal and officially labeled it *P. commutatum*. Recently, however, scientists have decided that great Solomon's seal is merely a subspecies of *P. biflorum*. The statelier version, now called *P. biflorum commutatum*, can reach a height of five or more feet, and instead of having only single or pairs of flowers has up to eight blossoms dangling in clusters. It tends to bloom in June instead of May in my neck of the

woods. Species and subspecies are found from southern Canada to Florida, and out to Texas and the eastern slopes of the Rocky Mountains.

The only other North American Solomon's seals are the hairy Solomon's seal (*P. pubescens*), found in eastern North America; the rare broadleaf Solomon's seal (*P. hirsutum*), found only around New Hampshire, Vermont, and Massachusetts; and McKittrick's Solomon's seal (*P. cobrense*), a native of Texas, New Mexico, and Arizona.

The Seal

Those who research such things have much debated the origin of the name Solomon's seal. In one common explanation, the name is derived from the fact that the rootstock bears indentations that look like the impressions of a signet ring, as if it had been pressed into hot wax. These scars occur when the previous year's aboveground growth dies off the roots; the approximate age of the plant can be determined by counting the number of scars. It is said that the depressions resemble Hebrew letters and were originally set in the rootstock by King Solomon as testimony to its medicinal values. Another theory is that slicing the root transversely reveals a shape similar to that of the Hebrew alphabet character employed as a seal of approval by King Solomon.

Still another explanation is that *seal* refers not so much to the scars as to the fact that the root was used to heal up or "seal" fresh wounds or broken bones.

Mary Durant, in her book *Who Named the Daisy? Who Named the Rose?*, has her own theory. The name was introduced to Europe in the early Christian era, when the desire to see symbols in wild things was strong. The six-pointed Star of David was commonly called Solomon's seal, so the six-pointed flower picked up the same name. However, while the name survived, its origin based in the flower design was forgotten. And, she says, when people in more modern times tried to figure out where the name came from, they turned to the roots, using the marks on them or their use in treating wounds as the explanation.

Polygonatum is Greek for "many kneed," referring to the joints of the zigzag stem. *Biflorum* refers to the two-flowered characteristic of the small Solomon's seal, while *commutatum* means "changes" or "changing," probably because great Solomon's seal was considered a rather variable plant, growing sometimes only a foot tall and other times nearly as tall as a man, and bearing from two to eight flowers per cluster. Now it works as a subspecies name, suggesting that *biflorum* is variable—which it is.

The English folk names for the smaller Solomon's seal include sealwort, conquer-john, hairy Solomon's seal, and dwarf Solomon's seal. The larger species is called sealwort and smooth or giant Solomon's seal.

Hastie Fists

Europe has several species of Solomon's seals, including *P. multiflorum*, which is similar in chemical composition to our species. Its root has been used for treating lung ailments, "female complaints," stomach inflammations, broken bones, piles, and poor complexions (for a long time it was an

Snake Corn

"Reached the Highland Light about 2 P.M. The *Smilacina* is just out of bloom on the bank. They call it the 'wood lily' there. Uncle Sam called it 'snake corn,' and said it looked like corn when it first came up."
—*Henry David Thoreau, Cape Cod* (June 18, 1857)

True or False

Now here's the deal
With Solomon's seal:
Two kinds of plants exist.
One seal is real,
Some people feel,
And the other they dismiss.
"False," they say,
Is the way
To label this pretty flower.
But how'd they know
To name it so?
Where did they get the power?
False isn't true,
It's a name to eschew
And give to some legislature
That can declare
A name more fair,
For veritable nomenclature.
—J. S.

Big John

"I knowed a man whose daughter was foolin' wit' a married fellow, so he got a Big John [*Polygonatum biflorum*] and mixed it wit' goofer dust and red brick dust and put it under the married man's front steps. He say, 'Johnny, do your stuff!' and went away. It wasn't two days before that man come to him and broke down and say he was sorry he had gone wit' his daughter. Well, that fixed that, but the girl start grievin' and that worried her pa. He got him another Big John and soaked it in olive oil and placed it under the front steps of a fine young man in his block. A week later that young man was hangin' 'round wit' the gal and they got married. If you have any trouble wit' women use Johnny. He's a woman-fixer."

—Abner Thomas, quoted in
Voodoo in New Orleans
by Robert Tallant (New York: Macdonald, 1946)

ingredient in beauty creams). Because they used it to heal or "seal" wounds, the French called it *l'herbe de la rupture*. Like jewelweed, our native Solomon's seal was employed to wash skin that had come in contact with poison ivy. American Indians mashed the root and, warming it with water, made a poultice with it. Midwestern Indians used it to relieve headaches. Practitioners of voodoo in Louisiana prized the root for many uses.

Besides treating bruises, Solomon's seal was supposed to be handy for black eyes. John Gerard noted in his 1597 *Herball*: "The roots of Solomon's seal, stamped while it is fresh and greene and applied, taketh away in one night or two at the most, any bruse, blacke or blew spots, gotten by falls or women's wilfulness in stumbling upin their hastie husband's fists, or such like."

Why False?

Solomon's seals are members of the large Lily family, within which is the genus *Maianthemum* and the species *M. racemosa*, the false Solomon's seal. Long known as *Smilacina racemosa*, the genus is found coast to coast and has eastern and western subspecies: *M. racemosa racemosa* and *M. racemosa amplexicaule*, respectively. Instead of flowers dangling from beneath its leaves, it bears clusters, or "racemes," of small white flowers at the ends of its leaves.

False Solomon's seal has seen limited use as a medicine and as a source of starchy food, obtained from the root. The young shoots of both false and true Solomon's seals have long been cooked like asparagus, not surprising since both plants are closely related to asparagus, another lily.

"The false Solomon's seal is, in my estimation, even more beautiful than the true," writes F. Schuyler Mathews in *Familiar Flowers of Field and Garden*. "Its spike of fine white flowers is like the *Spiraea japonica*; besides, its wavy bright green leaf with the parallel veining is particularly graceful. Most wildflowers, like the true Solomon's seals, have rather insignificant blossoms; but there is nothing meager about the bloom of this little plant. It deserves cultivation and, in truth, if it is transplanted to a position in the garden similar to its natural environment, it will flourish most satisfactorily."

Perhaps its name has helped prevent it from being popular with gardeners. "It is a shame that any aspersion of falsity should attach to it," said Mathews. "Why should not a plant so deserving have its own good name? We might as well call a Frenchman a false Englishman."

Neltje Blanchan wrote: "As if to offer opportunities for comparison to the confused novice, the true Solomon's seal and the so-called false species—quite as honest a plant—usually grow near each other. Grace of line, rather than beauty of blossom, gives them both their chief charm."

The "false" name purportedly stems from the belief that this plant, while looking like a "true" Solomon's seal, does not have *Polygonatum*'s medicinal qualities. However, the plant's false reputation doesn't end with Solomon's seal; it's also called false spikenard and false lily of the valley. Other names include Job's tears, goldenseal, and—my favorite—Solomon's plume. *Maianthemum*, incidentally, is from the Greek, meaning "May blossom."

The red-speckled berries of this false Solomon's seal are food for some woodland birds, as are the fruits of "true" Solomon's seal. And the birds, after all, don't discriminate on the basis of our poorly chosen names.

Wild Ginger

AN OVERLOOKED CRANK

Wild ginger hides its head, much to the delight of some creatures.

"Certain flowers might be grouped under the head of 'vegetable cranks,'" wrote Mrs. William Starr Dana. "Here would be classed the evening-primrose, which opens only at night; the closed (bottle) gentian, which never opens at all; and the wild ginger, whose odd unlovely flower seeks protection beneath its long-stemmed fuzzy leaves, and hides its head upon the ground as if unwilling to challenge comparison with its more brilliant brethren."

Wild ginger flowers do indeed grow from the base of the plant, prostrate on the ground under the heart-shaped leaves—springtime hikers may pass a hundred of them in the woods and never know it. But the plant's posture has purpose: The flower stays low because the ground is the source of the insects that visit and pollinate it.

The three-pointed purple flower of the wild ginger is hidden at the base of the leaf stalks.

Insect Friends

As an early bloomer, wild ginger attracts the types of early-spring flies and gnats that come out of the ground, looking for the thawing carcasses of animals that died over the winter. These flies are probably drawn to the flower by the dull red color, similar to carrion, and to the pollen, much of which they eat but some of which they transfer to other blossoms. The cuplike shape of the flower also provides insects with shelter from the cold winds of April and early May. And while in their shelter, the insects may just pick up some pollen to pass on to other flowers, increasing the chances of fertilization.

Later, when the plant produces seeds, wild ginger uses ants to help disperse them. Like the seeds of many other spring wildflowers, wild ginger's have oily "elaiosomes," appendages that ants find tasty. They haul the seeds to their underground chambers, eat the elaiosomes, and discard the seed proper to sprout safe from predators.

Sprinkle of Flavor

Wild ginger is a native North American plant and is not related to the common flavoring herb of the tropics. Its rootstock, however, does have a similar taste. In fact, the powdered root was widely used as a flavoring substitute for real ginger in the late 1700s and early 1800s, and Canadians used it as a spice throughout the 19th century.

"I know one person who will not drink a cup of tea without a sprinkle of wild ginger on it," wrote George Washington Carver, whose research into uses for the tropical peanut is famous, but who was also interested in many native wild foods. He not only used the powdered root as a flavoring but also considered the leaf the "acme of delicious, appetizing, and nourishing salads."

For woodsmen of the 19th century, wild ginger provided a rare sweet treat. Pieces of the root were cooked in thick sugar water for long periods—some recipes call for simmering it off and on over three or four days. The resulting candied root is said to be delicious, and the leftover gingery syrup was a treat on flapjacks and fruits. The root was used as a fragrance; an oil obtained from it was once an ingredient in expensive perfumes.

Chippewas called the wild ginger *namepin*, which translates as "sturgeon plant," possibly because the lake sturgeon (*Acipenser fulvescens*) is dark olive in color above, and reddish below, similar to the combination of colors found on the flower. The plant is sometimes called sturgeon potato. And these fishy names may be connected with a recipe rather than coloring. For instance, Meskwakis cooked mud catfish with wild ginger root to improve its flavor.

The Montagnais Indians of Newfoundland called the plant by a name meaning "beaver his food," suggesting that these rodents also enjoyed the plant.

Antibiotic

American Indians, who rarely overlooked a plant of possible value, made use of the wild ginger as a medicine as well as a food flavoring. According to one authority, the women of a certain tribe drank a strong asarum root tea as a contraceptive. Others used it as a heart medication. But its most common uses among Indians and early settlers were more to be expected. It was a popular "carminative"—something that removes flatulence—and was used to relieve stomach and intestinal cramps, colic, and, generally, upset stomachs. Many tribes also used it as an appetite stimulant.

In his journal of the Lewis and Clark expedition in 1806, Meriwether Lewis reported its use as a poultice to treat open wounds. Since two antibiotic substances have been found in its roots, that may have been a most appropriate use of the plant. According to a 1970 study, wild ginger is an active agent against a broad spectrum of bacteria and fungi. This may also explain why many tribes of American and Canadian Indians employed the root as a seasoning that was supposed to render food safe for consumption. Potawatomis used wild ginger on older meat, as well as on foods being preserved for later use.

Wild ginger also contains aristolochic acid, a substance that had been touted as a treatment for tumors and that was used in a variety of over-the-counter medicines and dietary supplements. However, the Food and Drug Administration in 2001 issued a warning that aristolochic acid may cause serious renal diseases, including cancer.

Fading Flowers

Ginger is one of many plants whose names were once popular as names for girls. No more. A Social Security Administration survey of nearly two million girls born in the year 2000 revealed that among the top 1,000 given names, the most popular plant name (28th) was Jasmine (not counting such variations as Jasmin, Jasmyn, Jazmine, Jazmyn, or Jazmyne). Lily ranked 126th (Lilly was 434), Heather, 129; Veronica, 138; Daisy, 143; Rose, 294; Ivy, 352; Iris, 406; Sage, 494; Aspen, 572; Violet, 754; Willow, 772; and Hazel, 884. But no Gingers.

A Birthwort

Wild ginger, *Asarum canadense*, belongs to a small genus of some 100 species found in the north temperate zone worldwide. The plant ranges throughout the northern states and the provinces, from the Atlantic to the Plains. A dozen other species may be found in North America, including three in the far West, among them the exotic-looking long-tailed wild ginger (*A. caudatum*), found from British Columbia and western Montana south to central California. Each of its three purple "petals" tapers to a long, whiplike end.

The genus *Asarum*, in turn, is a member of the small Birthwort family, with only a half-dozen genera and several hundred species worldwide—mostly tropical and subtropical. It is a rather independent clan, not closely related to any other in the plant world. That is not surprising, in view of the wild ginger flowers, which are unlike any other you are apt to see in North America.

Asarum, incidentally, is an ancient Latin word whose original meaning is unknown. An old Latin dictionary, published in 1835, defines the word as "the wild foalsfoot or wild spikenard," giving Pliny as the source of this information. The botanical name of the Birthwort family, Aristolochiaceae, comes from the Greek words for "best," *aristos*, and "childbirth," *lochia*, because the curved flowers of European species are said to look like a fetus in the correct position for birth. The European birthwort, *Aristolochia longa*, was used as a post-childbirth treatment for women.

Eastern wild ginger is a curious, rather attractive, herb. Growing up to a foot in height, the plant bears pairs of large heart-shaped leaves, designed to capture what sunlight makes its way through the forest canopy. The plant likes slightly moist, rich soil and spreads slowly, eventually producing a handsome and full woodland ground cover. Wild ginger was once common and widespread, but unfortunately this is no longer so; some states include it on their protected plants lists. While it transplants easily, wild ginger should not be taken from natural habitats unless threatened with destruction. It is preferable to buy the plants from a reputable wildflower nursery—one that doesn't sell plants stolen from the wild.

The leaves begin to come up in late March and by mid- to late April, the flowers are usually out. Blossoms generally last until mid-May or later. Unlike some other spring flowers, the foliage does not die down in midsummer and remains lush until well into the fall, as the plant processes and stores food to send up next spring's growth. The leaves remain green in winter and don't die away until new leaves appear in spring.

Other names for wild ginger include Indian ginger, colic root, heart-leaf, heart-snake-root, Vermont snakeroot, Canada snakeroot, false coltsfoot, and asarabacco (an old European name for another, apparently similar, plant). *Ginger*, incidentally, is a word of ancient origin. The *Oxford English Dictionary* traces it back to *srngavera*, a Sanskrit word that may have meant "horn body," referring to the shape, color, texture, and arrangements of the root of the true ginger. Over many centuries and through several languages, it became *ginger*.

Bait Enhancer

American Indians used wild ginger to flavor not only fish but also fish bait. Fishermen among certain tribes, including the Meskwakis, would chew the root, spit the resulting juice on bait, and use it to help improve its ability to catch catfish.

Great Relief

"Joe Potts's leg, which had been much swollen and inflamed for several days, is much better this evening and gives him but little pain. We applied the pounded root and leaves of wild ginger, from which he found great relief."
—Meriwether Lewis (1806)

Jack-in-the-Pulpit

THE SILENT PREACHER

When should Jack really be Jill?

The overhanging jack-in-the-pulpit spathe keeps the rain off the spadix, which bears tiny flowers.

He is found where the ground is damp and shady. He stands short or tall, depending on his food. He was a friend of many Indians and is a foe of certain insects. He may become a she, and then a he again. He might even kill you. His name is common, but his stage makes him famous.

He is Jack-in-the-pulpit, one of our strangest-looking flowering plants, common from Nova Scotia and New England to Texas. The plant is well known, although some mistake it for a pitcher plant. And while it is shaped somewhat like that insectivorous species, Jack-in-the-pulpit lives off nutrients in the ground, not on the corpses of insects.

The common name is perfect. The long spathe looks like an old-fashioned pulpit, complete with overhead baffle to reflect and spread sermons throughout the church in the days before public address systems. For the plant, however, the hood is simply an umbrella, preventing the vertical, tube-like spathe from filling with rainwater that could drown the flowers deep down inside or wash away their pollen.

"Jack" is the spadix, the clublike, flower-bearing stick that stands erect in the pulpit with just his head protruding to survey his "congregation." *Jack* has long been a common colloquialism for "fellow" or "guy," especially in England.

Hot Stuff

Jack-in-the-pulpit is a member of the Arum family, a small group of primitive flowering plants whose name comes from the Arabic word for "fire." Anyone who has tasted the raw root quickly understands the meaning. The root contains crystalline calcium oxalate, a powerfully bitter substance that burns so badly it can cause blisters (see also sidebar on page 87). Schoolboys used to dare their comrades to take a bite of the root, with results the taster would long remember. What was a joke among pupils was serious business for young men of certain American Indian tribes, however; without complaint or hesitation, they had to eat one of the fiery roots before they could officially enter manhood. Both trick and ritual were dangerous; a calcium oxalate crystal bears many microscopically small but sharp needles that cut and poison the flesh. If the root gets to the back of the mouth, it can cause enough swelling in the throat to suffocate the victim.

Jack-in-the-pulpit is what one herbalist calls "violently acrid" in taste. "In its fresh state, it is a violent irritant to the mucous membrane, when chewed burning the mouth and throat," said English herbalist Maude Grieve. "If taken internally, the plant causes violent gastro-enteritis, which may end in death." Despite this ability to burn and poison, the dried and powdered root has been used in small doses to treat such maladies as croup, whooping cough, malaria, bronchitis, and asthma. Chippewas employed it for sore eyes, and Mohegans of Connecticut concocted a liniment and a throat gargle from it. For Osages and Shawnees it was a cough medicine, while Pawnees applied the powdered root to their heads to relieve headaches—or at least provide a real reason for the pain.

American Indians long ago discovered that one of the chief constituents of the root is starch. They also found that roasting the roots (or corms), or drying them for at least six months, removed the acridity. ("How can men have learned that plants so extremely opposite to our nature were eatable and that their poison, which burns the tongue, can be conquered by fire?" wondered explorer-naturalist Peter Kalm in 1749.) The roots were peeled and then ground into a powder from which a kind of bread was made. The chocolate flavor is nice, said Adrienne Crowhurst in *The Weed Cookbook*, but she wondered whether it was worth all the bother to prepare. Shredded root that had been boiled along with berries was mixed with venison by certain Indian tribes. Bradford Angier, in his *Feasting Free on Wild Edibles*, tells how to make Jack-in-the-pulpit cookies, flavored with hazelnuts. Lee Allen Peterson's *A Field Guide to Edible Wild Plants* mentions potato chips made from the roasted root.

Because of its popularity among the American Indians, Jack-in-the-pulpit is also called Indian turnip, the rootstock being shaped somewhat like that of the turnip. The plant's generic name is *Arisaema*, a Greek word that refers to the red-blotched leaves of some European species, or perhaps to the purple stripes on the native plant's pulpit. Our most common species of Jack-in-the-pulpit is *Arisaema triphyllum*, *triphyllum* referring to the three-leaved clusters, one or two of which accompany each flower.

Jack-in-the-pulpit is found in moist woods or wood edges, frequently inhabiting the borders of wetlands, and is sometimes used by those who study soil conditions as a sign of nearby wetlands or swampland. As the soil becomes wetter or more poorly drained, you are apt to find Jack-in-the-pulpit's cousin, skunk cabbage, another member of the Arum clan (see page 3). Jack-in-the-pulpit grows from less than a foot to three feet tall, depending on the nutrients and water supply available to it.

Visitors

The plant is so constructed and colored that insects, especially fungus gnats, are drawn down the spathe to the base of the spadix, which bears the tiny flowers. The floor of a chamber at the base of the tube is covered with pollen. After it has descended and picked up the pollen, an insect has a hard time leaving. It cannot easily climb back up the slippery tube, nor up the spadix because of a projecting ledge. The only exit is a small flap at the base, where the two sides of the pulpit join

Jack as Art

Some of artist Georgia O'Keeffe's most famous paintings are a 1930 series of oils portraying the Jack-in-the-pulpit at various angles. The National Gallery of Art in Washington, D.C., owns at least one, *Jack-in-the-Pulpit IV*.

Watch That Dose

Some American Indians believed Jack-in-the-pulpit was a contraceptive. One dose of about a teaspoon of the dried powder in cold water was enough to last for a couple of weeks. But care was called for; twice that dose in hot water was believed to cause permanent sterility.

together. Insects that are small or strong enough can find and squeeze through this "door" to move on to other plants. Larger flies may not fit through and are sometimes trapped. The bottoms of the pulpits often contain insect corpses, leading some scientific observers to wonder whether the Jack-in-the-pulpit is evolving slowly over the eons into an insect-eating variety like the pitcher plant or the Venus flytrap.

The spathes vary in color. Some are deep purple, vertically striped white or greenish. Others are almost pure green. Some authorities say the males are green while the females are purple. Others say green plants are simply sterile, which makes sense if the purplish "meaty" color is designed to draw flies as it is in the related skunk cabbage. An old legend that the purple color comes from the blood of Christ at the crucifixion, inspired an unknown 19th-century poet:

> *Beneath the cross it grew:*
> *And in the vase-like hollow of the leaf*
> *Catching from that dread shower of agony*
> *A few mysterious drops, transmitted thus*
> *Unto the groves and hills their healing stains*
> *A heritage, for storm or vernal shower*
> *Never to blow away.*

Sex Changes

Dr. Harold N. Moldenke of the New York Botanical Garden reported in his 1949 book, *American Wildflowers*, that Jack-in-the-pulpits start out life as males, then become females, and may revert to the male state. The young plant stays male for a couple of years or until it has gained enough strength and food-storage capacity to take on the tougher job of being a female. As in mammals, where the task of feeding young before and after birth requires a special ability and good health, the job of producing seeds requires strength and sound health in the plant, which must put aside food, not just for itself but also for its offspring. (Seeds are, after all, largely stored food or "meat." That's why many are so nutritious and we eat grains like wheat, corn, and rye, and all sorts of nuts.)

Sometimes a plant will remain male for many years because it lacks the proper food, moisture, or light to develop into a strong female. Or, a female may revert to the male state if conditions suddenly change. For example, a transplanted female might need all its strength to heal whatever wounds may have occurred in the move and to adapt to its new surroundings.

The unusual characteristics of this plant have generated most of its folk names: marsh turnip, pepper turnip, wild turnip, bog onion, brown dragon, starchwort, dragon root, devil's ear, cuckoo plant, priest's pintle, and wake-robin. The last name, also applied to the red trillium (see page 55), refers to the fact that in some areas the plants bloom at about the time that the robins return.

His Reverence

Jack-in the pulpit preaches to-day
Under the green trees just over the
*   way.*
Squirrel and song sparrow high on
*   their perch,*
Hear the sweet lily-bells ringing to
*   church.*
Come hear what his Reverence rises
*   to say,*
* In his painted pulpit, this calm*
*   Sabbath day.*
Fair is the canopy over him seen,
Pencilled by nature's hand, black,
*   brown, and green.*
—John Greenleaf Whittier
(1807–1892)

Some authorities used to list three Eastern Jack-in-the-pulpits: *A. triphyllum* was the swamp Jack-in-the-pulpit; *A. atrorubens*—"dark red"—was woodland Jack-in-the-pulpit; and *A. stewardsonii*, northern Jack-in-the-pulpit. Each had minor differences of appearance and habitat. However, today the last two are classified among the half-dozen variants of *A. triphyllum*.

Also in the genus is the distinctive green dragon (*A. dracontium*), readily recognized by its long spadix or tongue that extends way beyond the spathe. Green dragon is found east of the Rockies but is not as common as Jack-in-the-pulpit. It was once used to poison vermin.

Jack-in-the-pulpit is easily grown in a rich, shady spot. You can dig up and move whole plants or, better yet (and to avoid unnecessary sex changes), find some of the bright red berries that appear on the spatheless spadix by August and September, and plant them about an inch under the surface. The berries, which come in clusters and are at first bright green, are delicacies for pheasants and other woodland birds, but may be somewhat toxic for humans.

Jack-in-the-pulpit's germination rate is good—the hard-working mothers do their job well. Flowering plants usually appear the next year, occasionally in two years. The plants are hardy as well as long lasting and, while not colorfully showy, they add a touch of the exotic to any spring wildflower garden.

Oxalate Veggies

Calcium oxalate, which causes Jack-in-the-pulpit roots to be so acrid, is also found to a lesser degree in such vegetables as spinach, parsley, broccoli, beets, and Brussels sprouts. Calcium oxalate is also the chief constituent of most kidney stones, which is why health officials often recommend that patients with the affliction avoid these vegetables. Chocolate and peanuts, too, are high in oxalates, alas.

Saxifrages

ROCK CRUSHERS?

Though this dainty flower thrives in tough environments, the saxifrages don't do what the name suggests.

Colonies of early saxifrage are often found in rocky places.

Saxifrage is a name that seems at once ridiculous and appropriate. Many of the most common native species are small, their flowers tiny, and their aspect rather delicate. Yet, saxifrages thrive on high mountains and in the Arctic harshness, and its name means "stone breaker." The little plants don't possess amazing powers of strength; the stones were broken before the "breaker" arrived. They are so called because people thought that the plants, which often make their home in rock outcroppings, caused the cracks and crevices in which they live.

Tiny but Many

Early saxifrage (*Saxifraga virginiensis*), common on hills and mountains of the cooler states east of the Mississippi, bears among the smallest early-spring blossoms. Each five-petaled flower is only a quarter of an inch across. Years ago, some botanists used the generic name, *Micranthes*, or "small flower," instead of *Saxifraga*.

But what it doesn't have in size, the early saxifrage makes up for in numbers. Each stalk bears a cluster of from 6 to 12 or more blossoms, and the plants in turn form colonies, whose thousands of blossoms create a white blush. Its colonizing and love of rocky places make saxifrage a favorite among rock flower gardeners who specialize in native species. The flowers appear as buds before the stem is much above the basal rosette of roundish leaves. As the stalk grows, the flowers bloom and continue blossoming as the stem gets taller, as high as nine inches.

Saxifrage is one of the many wildflowers that uses hairy, sticky stalks to protect its nectar and pollen from hungry ants and other wingless critters. The feet of ants become entangled in the fuzz, encouraging the creature to look elsewhere for nourishment.

Other names for our *S. virginiensis* include spring saxifrage, may-flower, rockfoil, and everlasting—the latter, apparently, because the flowers bloom for up to three weeks or longer.

S. virginiensis is one of 70 or so members of the genus found in North America, and 250 worldwide. The Rocky Mountains are a favorite haunt of the genus, and about 25 species can be found there. Purple mountain saxifrage (*S. oppositifolia*) is native to the Rockies above 9,000 feet, the Adirondacks, and northern Vermont, and is also found more than 5,000 miles away in the

European Alps. Scientists suspect that glaciers carried the plant from common Arctic ground south to these disparate places.

Saxifrages are in turn members of a sizable family—like the genus, it's called Saxifrage (*Saxifragaceae*)—that is closely related to the roses. Some 25 genera in North America include the mitreworts, stonecrops, heucheras, grass-of-Parnassus, currants, gooseberries, and even yard shrubs like mock orange and hydrangeas.

Cold Climates

Many North American saxifrages favor cool or downright cold climates. In the summer of 1899, naturalist John Burroughs visited Alaska and found many specimens there. At Port Clarence, on the Bering Strait, he stood with excitement on the flower-covered tundra:

> In a few moments, our hands were full of wild flowers, which we kept dropping to gather others more attractive, these, in turn, to be discarded as still more novel ones appeared. . . . Soon I came upon a bank by the little creek covered with a low, nodding purple primrose; then masses of shooting-star attracted me; then several species of pedicularis, a yellow anemone, and many saxifrages. A complete list of flowers blooming here within 60 miles of the Arctic Circle, in a thin layer of soil resting upon perpetual frost, would be a long one.

Saxifrages are among the few native plants that seem to have little history of special uses. The plants were not widely employed as a medicine, a dye, or a scent source. However, the greens of various species—such as the lettuce saxifrage (*Saxifraga micranthidifolia* or *Micranthes micranthidifolia*) of eastern mountains and swamp saxifrage (*S. pensylvanica*) of eastern and midwestern wetlands—have seen some use as salad ingredients or as boiled vegetables.

Several unrelated British plants are called saxifrages, not because they are similar to the genus, but because they are said to have the ability to "break up stone in the bladder." Some authorities say that *Saxifraga* was similarly derived. The roots of some species bear pebble-like tubers, a divine sign that they could treat bladder stones.

A perennial, early saxifrage is easy to grow in dry woodland soils, in sun or in shade. In the wild, the plant is often found near rocks that are wet in the spring. Seeds collected in July and planted any time can be used to start saxifrage near rocks. Dozens of saxifrages, both from the wild and hybridized, are for sale at nurseries, especially those specializing in rock gardens. A double form of the European meadow saxifrage (*S. granulata*) is known as pretty maids and figures in the popular nursery rhyme:

> Mary, Mary, quite contrary
> How does your garden grow?
> With silver bells and cockleshells
> And Pretty Maids, all in a row.

Sweet Wilson

Saxifrage has also been known as "sweet Wilson." Fanny Bergen, who wrote about plant folklore in the 1890s, said the name was coined around 1850 by a Mrs. Ward to please her husband, Wilson Ward, "who complained there was a sweet William, but no sweet Wilson."

Pale Nurslings

Pale nurslings of the early waking
     year,
Forerunner of the coming spring,
Shy creeping round the edge
Of broken granite ledge
Soon as the drifts of winter disap-
     pear;
Your tender rootlets fondly cling
Close in the frost-made rifts,
Your slender stalk uplifts
Sweet clustering flowers of hope our
     waiting hearts to cheer.
—Isaac Bassett Choate
(1833–1917)

Lady's Slippers

THE SECRETIVE SLIPPERS

Hard to find and harder to grow, lady's slippers
survive amazing odds.

*Lady's slipper orchids, like this yellow
species, attract bees into their chambers in a
complex pollination process.*

Lady's slippers are among those special wildflowers whose locations are whispered only to trusted people. It's not only that they might be rare and exotic, but also that they *look* rare and exotic.

Indeed, wildflower enthusiasts are usually careful to catalogue, mentally at least, the locations of these largest of our wild orchids. One May, when I was looking for some yellows and pinks to photograph, I asked a couple of knowledgeable friends who immediately remembered where they had seen yellow lady's slippers 20 years earlier. We went to the spot in deep moist woods and, sure enough, they were still there.

The pink lady's slipper proved more elusive. The friends recalled a favorite colony from a decade or two earlier, but when we drove to the place, we found not flowers, but houses had sprung up. We checked several other localities without success. Then another flower watcher told me they were blooming in a somewhat remote, hilly section of the town. We drove up and—lo and behold!—several fine plants were standing, not in deep, distant woods, but in a clearing four feet from the pavement of the road.

But that was far from my strangest sighting of pink lady's slippers. Some years ago I was invited to lead a wildflower walk at a nature preserve in Connecticut. As I prepared for the walk by scouting the territory, I came across a straight line of pink lady's slippers, stretching for some 20 feet. At one end was a very rotten, barely visible stump. When I asked the local naturalist about what I'd seen, she said that years ago a tree had fallen there and had been left to rot. Along the path when the trunk decayed into the ground, pink lady's slippers had appeared.

W. T. Baldwin, author of a 19th-century book on New England orchids, quotes an Adirondacks resident as saying that lady's slippers have a "great fondness for decaying wood, and I often see a whole row perched like birds along a crumbling log."

Where?

Searchers have found lady's slippers in various habitats. Mr. Baldwin said that "the finest specimens

I ever saw sprang out of cushions of crisp reindeer moss high up among the rocks of an exposed hillside, and again I have found it growing vigorously in almost open swamps, but nearly colorless from excessive moisture." Asa Gray, the noted botanist, said the pinks are found in "dry or moist woods," particularly near evergreens. F. Schuyler Mathews usually saw them "among withered leaves that lie under birch, beech, poplar, and maple," but admitted that "Nature is not always regular in her habits." Mrs. William Starr Dana had seen them in little shelves on cliffs. "It has a roving fancy and grows up hill and down dale," concluded William Hamilton Gibson.

That "fancy" depends to a great extent upon the nature of the soil, which must be acidic and which must contain a certain type of fungus, with which the lady's slipper species have an unusual but vital symbiotic relationship. Unlike most seeds, the minute and dustlike lady's slipper seeds contain no food to allow them to grow. However, the outside of the seed is susceptible to attack by Rhizoctonia fungi, which digest the outer cells. If things balance out just right, the inner cells escape digestion and absorb some of the nutrients the fungus obtained from the soil. Not until this happens can the seed germinate and begin growing.

The symbiosis with the fungus doesn't end there. In order for the infant corm (or "protocorm") to obtain minerals and other soil foods, it must use the "go-between" services of Rhizoctonia fungi. The fungi, in turn, take from the seedling lady's slipper foods that are photosynthetically manufactured. These sensitive and complex relationships make native orchids of all kinds relatively uncommon, and make growing them from seed virtually impossible outside a laboratory. What's more, in the wild, it takes from 10 to 17 years for a lady's slipper seed to become a mature plant capable of blooming.

About 10 species of lady's slippers live in North America, and some two dozen are found worldwide. They belong to the genus *Cypripedium*, Greek for "Venus's shoe" or "sock." In medieval Europe, the plant was called the Virgin's shoe or the shoe of Mary (*Calceolus marianus*). The French still sometimes call it *soulier de Notre Dame*, "shoe of Our Lady." In North America, the plant is widely known as moccasin flower.

The Labellum

These and other names suitably describe the main part of the flower, called the lip or labellum. This sac-like structure is designed to attract insects, particularly bees. Vein-like lines that attract and direct the insect's eye surround the roundish opening at the top. In many species, long sepals or wings also help the insects find the opening. The flower's scent, described by some as heavy and oily, also draws in passing bees.

The edge of the circular hole is inflected or lipped downward. Once inside, a bee finds it difficult to escape through the entrance. The chamber is lined with hairs—many secreting a sweet nectar—that lean toward an opening at the rear. Directed by the hairs, the trapped bee works its way through the nectar toward the beckoning light from the opening. To escape, the bee must rub against first the stigma, built like a comb to remove pollen, and then against the anthers, which spread on the pollen in a semiliquid, but quick-drying form. If the bee visits another lady's slipper,

Hard Work

Bearing a flower and seeds takes a lot of work. Richard Primack and Pamela Hall of Boston University studied pink lady's slippers and found that if a plant bloomed and bore seeds one year, its leaf area would be 10 to 13 % smaller the next season because of the effort spent on flowering and fruiting the year before. In fact, it can take up to four years for a pink lady's slipper to fully recover from producing a flower.

the stigma rakes off the previous deposit of pollen, thus fertilizing the flower, and the anther pastes on a new load. Big bumblebees, which have difficulty squeezing through the narrow exit, will sometimes give up and simply chew their way out of the sac, defeating the ingenious mechanism. Some bees simply die, entombed.

In hunting for nectar, bees must be careful not to waste energy, for part of what they collect is used for their own fuel; beating those wings so rapidly is a high-energy task. If the search requires too much time, the bee will consume most or all of what it collects, and fail to support its colony. Consequently, bees are usually most attracted to flowers in which pollen collection is easiest. For example, members of the Composite family, like daisies and sunflowers, and of the Pea family, such as the clovers, draw bees with close-packed, nectar-filled tubes. Some flowers, like the lady's slippers, monkshoods, lobelias, and certain gentians, are difficult to get in or out of, so they must offer an extra-rich store of nectar as a reward for all the work. Otherwise, they would fail in the competition with more open flowers to attract pollinating insects, and the species might not survive.

Dr. Douglas E. Gill, a University of Maryland zoologist, spent 16 years studying 3,000 pink lady's slippers in a national forest and found that over that time only about 1,000 of the plants flowered. Of those, only 23 were successfully pollinated. In other words, once a bee has gone through the ordeal of visiting one flower, it's not likely to visit another.

How can the species survive with so few "successful" flowers? Since the average life span of a plant is 20 years, and some may live for 150 years, lady's slippers have a long time to turn out one fruitful flower. And once pollinated, that flower could generate up to 60,000 seeds.

Pink and Yellow

Most lady's slippers bloom in May and June with the greater yellow lady's slipper (*Cypripedium pubescens*, previously known as *C. calceolus pubescens*) or the lesser yellow (*C. parviflorum*, previously *C. calceolus parviflorum*) usually a week or so earlier than the pink (*C. acaule*). The two differ not only in color but also in leaf positioning. The pink lady's slipper has leaves that rise from the base while the yellow species have clasping leaves right up their stalks. The pink has brown sepals—sometimes called the "shoestrings" of the slipper; the yellows have purplish sepals.

It's difficult to say which is the less common of the two; I have seen more of the yellow than of the pink, while others maintain that the pink is easier to find. It undoubtedly depends on where you live. None should be picked, of course, and unless they are in certain danger from the likes of bulldozers, you shouldn't attempt to transplant them, especially the pinks. While they may survive for a season or two, more often than not lady's slippers will die because of some imperfection in their new surroundings.

Cinderella's Shoe

Where Cinderella dropped her shoe,
'Tis said in fairy tales of yore,
'Twas first the lady's slipper grew
And there its rosy blossom bore.
And ever since, in woodlands gray,
It marks where spring retreating flew,
Where speeding on her eager way,
She left behind her dainty shoe.
—Elaine Goodale Eastman
(1863–1953)

Even buying from nurseries may be a mistake, not only because the plants may die, but also because they may be "stolen" stock. Countless thousands of lady's slippers have been taken illegally from the wild, often from parks and preserves, for resale to nurseries. The reason is simple: They are difficult and time-consuming to grow "in captivity."

Nonetheless, reputable growers of lady's slipper orchids exist. They have developed a system that bypasses the need for micro-fungus. For instance, Vermont Ladyslipper Company grows the seeds in a laboratory, using a sterile agar culture that includes nutrients and sugars. Once the lab-grown plant is mature, a process taking four to six years, the company maintains that the plant does not require the services of the fungus. It does require having the right soil conditions, pH, and climate, though.

Not everyone would want them in the garden. Alice Morse Earle, who wrote books on life in colonial times, said that "I have never found the lady's slipper as beautiful a flower as do nearly all of my friends, as did my father and mother, and I was pleased by Ruskin's sharp comment that such a slipper was fit only for very gouty old toes."

Bounty Hunters

Most writers, however, have found the lady's slippers attractive, probably in part because they are so exotic and unusual. In the 19th century, Europeans went wild over orchids, sometimes offering thousands of dollars for new species. That encouraged botanical bounty hunters to comb the jungles and mountains of the world in search of elusive species that might be cultivated in European hothouses. New discoveries would be sent from some far-off land to England, France, or Germany, only to spark new searches. One lady's slipper, C. fairrieanum, arrived in England from the Himalayas in the 1850s, but soon disappeared from the flower show scene, prompting someone to offer a $5,000 reward for a new specimen. Expedition after expedition over the next half century searched in vain for the "Lost Orchid." According to A. W. Anderson in How We Got Our Flowers, a surveying crew accidentally rediscovered it near the Bhutan–Sikkim border in 1904.

In North America, the rose-and-white showy lady's slipper usually wins the most praise for beauty. Once ranked second in a poll on the most beautiful flowers of the continent, C. reginae has suffered not only from being fussy in choosing habitats but also from being overpicked and overdug. Predicting a century ago that they would eventually be extinct, Mrs. Dana told of a secret place near Lenox, Massachusetts, where showy lady's slipper was growing. To her dismay a local boy discovered the spot, and proceeded to uproot the flowers and sell them by the dozens in nearby towns.

C. reginae tends to favor colder locales in southern Canada and the northern states, especially around the Great Lakes, and high up in the eastern mountains. It is the largest and most colorful of the lady's slippers, and its Latin name suggests that it is the "queen" of the clan.

Plant Genocide

In an amazing case of plant genocide, a German who bought specimens of the newly discovered Cypripedium spicerianum around 1870 then paid to have the species eradicated in its native territory in northeastern India so that he could sew up the market!

Many Feet

Yellow lady's slippers have acquired many names, including whippoorwill's shoe, yellows, slipper root, Indian shoe, Noah's ark, duck, nerve root, and American valerian (the European valerian, no relation to *Cypripedium*, is also and more commonly used to treat nerve disorders). Both yellow lady's slippers range from coast to coast and as far south as Georgia and Texas in higher elevations. The greater yellow is found in all but 7 of the lower 48 states.

The pink lady's slipper was once considered a monotypic North American species of its own genus, and was called *Fissipes acaulis*. The generic name means roughly "split-lip." Now just another *Cypripedium*, pink lady's slipper has also been called some of the above names as well as camel's foot, squirrel's foot, two-lips, Indian moccasin, and old goose. It is more eastern, and doesn't range beyond the Mississippi River.

The several West Coast species include the yellow-green-flowered California lady's slipper (*C. californicum*), the mountain lady's slipper (*C. montanum*) with dull purple flowers, and the clustered lady's slipper (*C. fasciculatum*), which blooms as early as April.

Tranquilizer

Lady's slippers have had their practical side. A resinoid substance called Cypripedin, obtained from the greater yellow lady's slipper rhizome, has been listed in the *U.S. Pharmacopoeia* and was used in the treatment of hysteria because it was believed to be a gentle tranquilizer. Lady's slipper tea is still recommended in some modern herbals for nervous headaches. American Indians treated toothaches with the plants. Too much of it, however, can cause hallucinations.

The overpopulation of both white-tailed and mule deer in parts of the country is killing off many colonies of lady's slippers. The deer were not a problem in the past, probably because they would shun lady's slippers under normal circumstances. Many species of *Cypripedium* bear tiny hairs on the leaves and stems that are mildly toxic and can give molesters a poison ivy-like rash. Today, however, deer will consume many plants they once disdained because so many of them are foraging for a finite supply of food.

Sometimes deer get desperate enough to venture across bodies of water. A few years ago at a preserve near me that surrounds a lake, naturalists thought they could create a refuge for prized wildflowers, including lady's slippers, on an island in the lake. They linked the island to the shore by a bridge that was gated to prevent deer from crossing. All went well until the deer became so hungry one year, they swam out to the island and decimated many species, including the rare lady's slippers.

White-tailed deer may be a friend to certain species, however. In *The Book of Forest and Thicket*, John Eastman says that in white cedar woodlands, colonies of showy lady's slippers often develop in old "deer yards," places where herds hang out in winter. The hooves of the milling deer both aerate the soil and mix the seeds into it.

No Blues

Orchids wear many colors, but among the more than 5,000 known species worldwide, you'll never find a blue one.

May Apples

THE GREEN UMBRELLAS

Once a favorite of pigs and boys, May apple is now a favorite of cancer researchers.

Years ago, children used to say the "green umbrellas" were out. They meant the colonies of May apples, sometimes vast in size, that would unfold their pairs of large leaves and, later in the season, yield tasty treats. Though not as common as they once were, May apple colonies can still be found each spring in rich, open woods from Texas, Kansas, Minnesota, and Ontario eastward. However, modern scientists want to expand their numbers and perhaps their range because this 19th-century treat for farm boys may be an important cancer fighter in the 21st century.

May apple is a large wildflower with an elegant blossom of six to nine waxy white petals. The flower springs from the crotch of the leafstalks but is often downturned and hidden from view by the large leaves. Its scent is usually described as unpleasant; John Burroughs called it "sickly sweet." The fragrance attracts bumblebees and other insects, which provide pollination services. The flowers have no nectar but do offer plenty of pollen, which bees use for food.

Despite the plant's name, the "apple" doesn't appear until August or September. And it is the fruit, not the flower, that once attracted the most interest in the plant. The large, egg-shaped yellow berry has always fascinated people, especially children. The "apple" is edible, and farmers' boys used to relish its taste, variously described as sweet to mawkish to insipid.

The fruit's scent is also so strong that Charles F. Saunders, in *Edible and Useful Wild Plants of the United States and Canada*, observed, "when green it exhales a rank, rather repulsive odor, but when fully matured, all that is changed into an agreeable fragrance, hard to define—sort of a composite of cantaloupe, summer apples, and fox grapes. Brought indoors, two or three will perfume a whole room."

Captain John Smith tasted May apple in Virginia in 1612, describing it as "a fruit that the Inhabitants call Maracocks, which is a pleasant wholesome fruit much like a lemond." Explorer Samuel Champlain, introduced to it by the Hurons in 1619, said it "tasted more like a fig." Early settlers of Rhode Island found it "a pleasant fruite" and many, despite a well-recognized laxative effect, ate it. Naturalist Euell Gibbons was fond of the May apple. In *Stalking the Wild Asparagus*, he

The flower of the May apple appears beneath the "umbrellas" and later turns into a sweet fruit.

Pigs and Boys

In a botany book, Asa Gray once described the May apple fruit as "eaten by pigs and boys." Writer William Hamilton Gibson used the comment to tease the eminent 19th-century scientist. "Think of it, boys!" Gibson exclaimed, "and think of what else he says of it: 'ovary void, stigma sessile, undulate, seeds covered with lateral placenta each enclosed in an aril.' Now, it may be safe for pigs and billygoats to tackle such a compound as that, but we boys like to know what we are eating, and I cannot but feel that the public health officials of every township should require this formula of Dr. Gray's to be printed on every one of these big loaded pills, if that is what they are really made of!"

tells how to make May apple marmalade, which he calls ambrosia, and says a shot of May apple juice in lemonade does wonders for the flavor.

Suicide Plant

Despite its use as a food, every part of the May apple is poisonous—except the ripe fruit. Until it is mature, however, the berry is also poisonous. This is May apple's self-defense mechanism, protecting even the fruit until it's at the appropriate stage of development. Then, for the sake of propagation, the poisonous quality disappears so the berry *will be* eaten. Many mammals, birds, and especially box turtles eat the ripe fruit; one study showed that seeds that had gone through the digestive tract of a turtle stood a much better chance of germinating than those that simply fell to the ground.

The poisonous quality of May apple has led to some sad uses. Certain tribes of American Indians employed it to commit suicide. "The root is a very effective poison which the Savages use when they cannot bear their troubles," wrote botanist Michel Sarrazin in 1708. Two years later, A. T. Raudot reported that Huron women "are very subject to poisoning themselves at the least grief that betakes them; the men also poison themselves sometimes. To leave this life they use a root of hemlock or of citron [May apple], which they swallow."

Menominees and Iroquois made more positive use of the poison: They turned it into an insecticide to kill potato bugs and corn worms on their crops.

Modern herbals recommend May apple's use only under medical supervision, or they suggest avoiding it altogether. It is a potent plant; even touching the leaves can give rashes to people whose skin is sensitive to it.

Despite its toxicity, herbalists and physicians have long used extracts of the tuberous root, probably the same substances that are so toxic. Its main use was as a "cathartic"—a vigorous laxative. "Its greatest power lies in its action upon the liver and bowels," said Maude Grieve. It "is a powerful medicine exercising an influence on every part of the system, stimulating the glands to healthy action. It is highly valuable in dropsy, biliousness, dyspepsia, liver, and other disorders." In the 1950s American scientists experimented with using May apple extracts, including podophyllin, to treat paralysis.

May apple is still an ingredient in purgative medicines and for treatment of intestinal worms. Some years ago, Abbott Laboratories had a hard time getting the 300,000 pounds of the plant it needed yearly because few people were growing it as a crop.

Today, May apple extracts are used to treat skin cancers and genital warts. However, more exciting possibilities may lie in stopping cancers. Podophyllotoxin, a chemical from the plant, is a source of the anticancer drugs etoposide and teniposide. Etoposide is used to treat lung and testicular cancers, while teniposide is reputed to be effective against certain kinds of leukemia. Both drugs prevent the spread of cancer by blocking the division of diseased cells.

Big Foot and Mandrake

Botanists call May apple *Podophyllum peltatum*. The generic name comes from the Greek, *podos*, "foot," and *phyllon*, "leaf," and is said to be ultimately derived from *anapodophyllum*, which means "duck-foot-leaf." In some places, the plant is called duck's foot. *Peltatum*, the specific name, also describes the leaf, and means "shield-shaped." It's as if the taxonomists couldn't agree on just what shape it really has. Incidentally, first-year plants arise with only single leaves, and no flower appears.

The plant's second most common name is American mandrake, though it is not related to the true mandrake. (A southern European plant with purplish flowers, true mandrake was believed to possess magical properties—hence, "Mandrake the Magician," once a well-known comic strip. Homer D. House wrote that the name "mandrake relates in no way to the mandrake or mandrago-ra of the ancients and, not withstanding its poisonous character, it is a very respectable herb in comparison with the traditions of the mandrake of the ancients, described as flourishing best under a gallows with a root resembling a man in shape, uttering terrible shrieks when it was torn from the ground, and possessing the power to transform men and beasts.")

May apple's folk names, mostly referring to fruit, include Indian apple, hog apple, devil's apple, vegetable mercury, vegetable calomel (calomel was a cathartic chemical), wild lemon, wild jalop (jalop is a Mexican morning glory used as a purgative, a medicine more drastic in its effects than even a cathartic), ground lemon, Puck's foot (a reference to the forest fairy in *A Midsummer Night's Dream*), and raccoon berry.

A native in North America, May apple is a member of a tiny genus of only four species worldwide; the other three species are Asian, indicating that our May apple must have descended from an Asian species that moved from across the Bering Strait, into Alaska, and down. The genus in turn is a member of the small Barberry family, which includes the well-known and often-cursed weedy shrub.

May apples may be grown in the wildflower garden (the French imported them for their gardens in the 18th and 19th centuries), and they make a good seasonal woodland ground cover, as well as a curiosity, especially if you have some slightly acid soil (pH 4 to 7). They may be trans-planted from root divisions lifted in summer—take divisions only from colonies where plants are numerous. Seeds can be removed from the pulp of the ripe berry in early fall and sown then. However, don't place May apples where there are smaller, delicate woodland species; spreading not only by seed but also by creeping roots, they could blanket your woods, choking out anemones, hepaticas, and violets. If you do introduce May apples, also keep in mind that young children may be attracted to the berries before they ripen, when they may be harmful to eat.

Various nurseries sell May apple as well as its sibling, Himalayan May apple (*P. hexandrum*), which has a more prominent flower and more ornate leaves. In its native mountains of central Asia, Himalayan May apple is declining in numbers because of overpicking for medicinal use.

Our own native May apple suffers from both picking and declining habitat. Because of the increasing demand for the plant in the medical field, researchers at the University of

Mandrakes

Down in the shady woodland
Where fern-fronds are uncurled,
A host of green umbrellas
Are swiftly now unfurled.
Do they shelter fairy people
From sudden pelting showers?
Or are the leaves but sunshades
To shield the waxen flowers?
Perhaps they're dainty canopies
'Neath which the fairies wed,
The blossoms, fragrant marriage
*   bells,*
That softly swing o'erhead.
—Minnie Curtis Wait, (1901)

Mississippi have been studying ways to cultivate May apple. They have discovered that specimens from certain locations in the South contain more of the prized podophyllotoxin than others. In fact, they have found colonies of *P. peltatum* that have more podophyllotoxin than does *P. emodii,* a rare species from India that had long been the chief source of the chemical.

Old Miss scientists are also trying to figure out how to cultivate plants that produce even more podophyllotoxin and make a profitable agricultural crop. "Cultivating the May apple leads to greater availability of the compound," said Dr. Camilo Canel, a U.S. Department of Agriculture molecular biologist at the university, in 2000. "It also means we'd no longer need to extract the compound from the endangered Indian species, so it has ecological value as well. And, finally, it provides our small farmers with a high-value crop. So this project offers many benefits to many different people."

Daisy

A FLOWER LOVED AND HATED

Some farmers despised daisies, others liked them, but lovers have always counted on them.

Scores of official plant names have changed in the past 15 to 20 years as botanists have discovered new similarities or new differences in species, or identified older names that should have been used in the first place. For the casual observer most changes are of the "who-cares" variety, but I must confess to being saddened by what happened to our plain, old daisy. For two centuries botanists called the ox-eye daisy *Chrysanthemum leucanthemum.* Though bulky and seemingly overburdened with syllables, the name was one of the most mellifluent that botanists have devised. Try saying it aloud.

Alas, someone discovered the daisy wasn't really a *Chrysanthemum* and belonged in a new genus. *Chrysanthemum leucanthemum* is now *Leucanthemum vulgare.*

Vulgar, it is, of course, but in the original sense of the word— that is, the plant is common, everyday, ordinary. Hundreds of plant genera have species labeled *vulgare* or *vulgaris,* but it doesn't mean they are crude or indecent. They are just common, often the most common example of the genus.

That certainly must be true of the daisy. In fact, 19th-century poets wrote of the snows of June, referring to daisy-filled spring fields as white as after a midwinter's blizzard. The plant arrived with the colonists and peaked during the height of the American agricultural era; today it is seen in not nearly the numbers for which it was once known.

In fact, "whiteweed" was once feared and hated for its tendency to take over whole crop fields and gardens. Prolific and difficult to eradicate, the daisy was as much an abomination to many farmers as it was and still is a favorite of children and lovers. So despised was this plant among the Scots, who called them gools, that they appointed goolriders to see that the daisies were removed from wheat fields. The farmer found to have the biggest crop of gools had to pay a fine of a castrated ram. Yet many American farmers discovered that their livestock loved daisies, and wound up growing it as hay for cattle, horses, and sheep.

In North America the love-hate relationship with the daisy began sometime after the Europeans arrived. After the first settlers cleared off the valleys and ridges in New England, the

The petals of the ox-eye daisy both attract insects and serve as landing pads. The yellow "eye" is actually a cluster of more than 100 florets, each a fully functioning flower.

Daisy Hay

"No man can have a worse opinion of daisies than I had from my childhood, till I was more than 40 years old; but for more than 15 years, they have grown in my pastures and meadows unmolested (except when greedily eaten by my cows, horses and sheep), and now I would as soon part with any grass I have as with them . . . I have fed my horse on it since haying and never had a horse eat hay cleaner or do better than he has."
—Calvin Butler, farmer,
    Plymouth, Connecticut
    in the *Cultivator*,
    (November 1841)

Atlantic states, and Canada, their fields were relatively free of weeds. Eventually, however, sun lovers arrived from Europe, which had relatively few forests and was home to many species that favored open lands. Later, natives from the treeless plains came eastward to join the transoceanic immigrants.

Together they created many backaches for the farmers, who had no fancy weed killers and were forced to fight the invaders by hand. Most of the aliens came mixed with crop seeds from the old homelands in Europe while some snuck rides in ballast, in the hay used in packing, or on the bottoms of muddy boots. Still others were invited, to fill gardens that would supply kitchens or medicinal concoctions. One source of the daisy, it is said, was the German fodder used to feed the horses of British troops during the Revolution.

Now the farms are disappearing from parts of our continent, especially the East. Their fields have turned into subdivisions or returned to woodland. The sun-loving daisy has lost many of the haunts where it once thrived. A field full of them as white as snow is becoming a rare sight, in my part of Connecticut at least.

A plant as persistent and as hardy as the ox-eye daisy, however, could hardly be wiped out, even by the monumental changes in human society during the past half century, or even by the invention of powerful herbicides. In many places clumps of daisies still appear each June with such fellows as black-eyed Susans, St. Johnsworts, hawkweeds, evening-primroses, and other denizens of poor and mediocre soils. That, in fact, is an admirable attribute of the daisy: It beautifies waste places where few plants can survive and that might otherwise be rather drab or ugly.

The love-hate relationship with daisies extends to government. Some states, such as Ohio, list the ox-eye daisy as a noxious weed, to be avoided because it pushes out native species; other states actually recommend them for decorative planting in fields and along roadsides.

Contradiction

The ox-eye daisy may seem a simple flower, but it is actually rather complex and even contradictory. Its common name is not even its own. *Daisy* means "day's eye" and was coined to refer to a pinkish English flower that closes at night and opens in the sunlight. (That British flower, *Bellis perennis*, is mentioned in several of Shakespeare's plays; in *Hamlet*, it was one of the blossoms worn by Ophelia in her garland.) Our ox-eye daisy remains open around the clock, and isn't just the "day's eye." In fact, it has been better called the moon daisy. As the English naturalist Marcus Woodward wrote, "the flower, with its white rays and golden disc, has small resemblance to an ox's eye, but at dusk it shines out from the mowing-grass like a fallen moon."

Then there is its former scientific name, *Chrysanthemum leucanthemum*, which literally translates as "golden flower, white flower." The type species for the *Chrysanthemum* genus is an all yellow flower, which explains the generic name, "golden flower." And while our daisy is better known as a white flower, "golden flower, white flower" was most appropriate, for each daisy blossom is really a bouquet of flowers of both colors. The deep yellow center disc is composed of hundreds of tiny

fertile yellow florets, while the 20 to 30 white rays or "petals" are actually sterile flowers. The rays have, in evolution, given up their reproductive function and parts in order to serve as decorations to draw insects to the pollen-bearing center flowers, an arrangement common in the Composite family. The rays also serve as handy landing pads for arriving insects.

"Because daisies are among the most conspicuous of flowers and have facilitated dining for their visitors by offering them countless cups of refreshment that may be drained with a minimum loss of time, almost every insect on wings alights on them sooner or later," observed Neltje Blanchan in *Nature's Garden*. Watching a daisy plant affords an opportunity to view many kinds of insects. One tiny black centipede-like creature appears to live full time on the flower heads. To feast on the nectar, it inserts almost the full length of its narrow body into the tubes. It is unusual to find daisies without these creatures crawling around the discs, and they may be adapted by nature to live only on these plants.

Right Conditions

With all of their florets per blossom, each daisy plant produces a huge number of seeds, one reason why they have survived so well since being brought to North America. The daisy seems also to like our environment better than that of its native soil in Europe, where the plants are said to be not as numerous.

Daisies will thrive, however, only if conditions are right. Twenty years ago I transplanted several daisies to the yard. Although most survived for one season, none came up the next year. It seemed that I had placed them in soil that was too rich with not enough exposure to the sun. Yet, two years later, in another part of the yard with poorer soil and more sun, a daisy appeared. By the natural spread of seeds and the survival of those that found a fit place, daisies began to establish themselves. Today, the ancestors of those original misplaced plants are still thriving each spring.

The daisy blooms primarily in late May and June, although healthy plants in ideal conditions will produce blossoms throughout July and August, and into September. The flowers are long lasting, and fine for picking for bouquets.

A Bane of Bugs

A native of both Europe and Asia, the ox-eye daisy is closely related to the popular garden chrysanthemums, which are descended from Chinese and Japanese members of the genus *Chrysanthemum*. Certain Oriental members of the genus, called the pyrethrum daisies, have been found to be displeasing to insects and are used as a commercial source of pyrethrum, a popular natural insecticide. Even our daisy appears to have built-in protection from herbivorous insects, most of which seem to shun its juice. English country folk knew this. They mixed the plant with the straw bedding of farm animals, then hung it from the ceilings of their homes to chase away insects, including fleas.

Bossy and the Daisy

Right up in the Bossy's eyes,
Looked the daisy, boldly,
But, alas! To his surprise,
Bossy ate him, coldly.
Listen! daisies in the fields,
Hide away from Bossy!
Daisies make the milk she yields
And her coat grow glossy!
So, each day, she tries to find
Daisies nodding sweetly,
And, although it's most unkind,
Bites their heads off neatly!
—Margaret Deland, (1857-1945)

A dozen or so species of *Leucanthemum* and *Chrysanthemum* are found in North America. Few are native. The ox-eye daisy is by far the most widespread, found in every state and province.

A plant as widespread and as well known as this is bound to generate a good deal of folklore and folk names. Almost everyone knows the "he loves me, he loves me not" litany with which one learns the fate of a romance by plucking a daisy's petals. However, it is also said that dreaming of daisies in spring or summer will bring good luck, but such dreams at other times of the year foretell bad fortune. Eating the roots is supposed to stunt a child's growth, but eating three of the blossoms after a tooth extraction means one will never have another toothache. Children used to construct something called "white-capped old women" out of them and to make daisy chains (some college students still do at commencement—at least, they did a few years ago). English children used to pluck the flower heads, slide them onto pieces of straw, and wear them in hats like the plumes that garnished helmets of knights of old.

In folk medicine, the plant has had many uses. "The ancients dedicated it to Artemis, the goddess of women, considering it useful in women's complaints," said Maude Grieve. After the establishment of Christianity, the ox-eye daisy became the plant of St. Mary Magdalen and was called the "Maudelyn" or "Maudlin daisy." It has served as an antispasmodic, diuretic, and tonic (such as for night sweats) and in the treatment of whooping cough and asthma. Externally, the daisy was used for soothing bruises, wounds, and ulcers. "An ointment made thereof doth wonderfully help all wounds that have inflammations about them, or by reason of moist humours having access unto them are kept long from healing," wrote herbalist Nicholas Culpeper. English country folk also added extract of daisy to ale to treat jaundice.

In Italy, the young leaves, though small, were eaten in salads. Linnaeus, who gave the plant its former scientific name, *Chrysanthemum leucanthemum*, reported that sheep, horses, and goats eat it, but cows and pigs avoid it as bitter. However, perhaps when desperate, cows have been known to eat them, and some dairy farmers are said to dislike the taste of milk from cows that have consumed daisies. John Burroughs, the naturalist and essayist, wrote, "the ox-eye daisy makes a fair quality hay if cut before it gets ripe."

Among its many folk names are great ox-eye, golden marguerites, daisy, horse gowan, butter daisy, field daisy, dun daisy, button daisy, horse daisy, bull daisy, midsummer daisy, poorland daisy, maudlinwort, Dutch morgan, moon flower, moon penny, poverty weed, white man's weed, herb margaret, and dog blow.

Wild Geranium

THE CATAPULTED CRAWLER

First they're fired, then wild geranium seeds crawl.

In the wildflower world, May seems to be a month of whites, yellows, and greens. Few purples or blues color the flowers, especially among the medium- to large-blossomed herbs. A common and beautiful exception is wild geranium, whose varying hues of light rosy purple enliven many semishaded, moist places throughout much of North America.

Wild geranium is a true geranium, much different from pelargoniums, those showy plants of summer flower boxes. The miscasting occurred in the 18th century when pelargoniums were first imported as garden flowers to Europe from South Africa. Thus, "wild geranium," the common name of our common geranium (*Geranium maculatum*), is a rather silly name, meant to distinguish our native and true geranium from false "geraniums" from another continent. Perhaps wild geranium would be better called by one of its other names, such as cranesbill or alumroot.

Known from New England to Alabama and west into Nebraska, wild geranium is found growing, often luxuriantly, in open woods and along shaded roadsides where there is at least some seasonal moisture. Plants are a foot or two tall, and usually grow in groups so that they take on a shrubby appearance, sometimes creating low hedges. The fairly large, toothed, five-part leaves are somewhat mottled with brown, hence the specific name, *maculatum*, meaning "spotted" or "mottled."

Wild geranium is a true geranium, unlike the garden flowers of that name.

Geranium means "crane." Both the generic and the common name, cranesbill, refer to the plant's seed case, which has been likened in shape to the crane's long beak. This shape serves a function. When the fruit is ripe, the long pod pops and catapults seeds into the air. The mechanism that propels the seeds consists of the five sides of the beak. As the pods dry, they become tense, stretched springs. When the time is right, they simultaneously uncoil, hurling the seeds and leaving behind a whorl of five curls. Naturalist William H. Gibson calculated that some of the tiny seeds may be fired more than 30 feet. Perhaps it's not surprising that geraniums are fairly closely related to jewelweeds (page 150), which have a similar seed-shooting technique, though a totally different flower shape. Such propulsion, of course, helps to ensure the spread of the plant into new territories.

When it lands, the geranium seed continues to move. It has a tail, called an awn, which curls when it is dry and straightens when it is wet. Botanists suspect this tail-twisting motion allows the seed to "creep" very slowly a short distance along the ground until it becomes stuck in a small

Curious Pollen

Wild geranium pollen has a rather unusual color. While pollen grains of most plants are orangish, wild geranium's are bright blue. "Seen through the microscope, this blue pollen is quite a curiosity," wrote F. Schuyler Mathews in 1895.

Adventurers

Geranium seeds are a traveling lot,
First they fly, fired like a shot,
Then they crawl in search of a spot,
A nook or a cranny in which to
    squat
And settle a new geranium plot.
    —J. S.

hole or crack. At that point, the motion may help push the seed into the soil. This amazing ability to "crawl" into a protected spot helps the seed find a suitable place to germinate and to escape the mourning doves, quail, chipmunks, and other small mammals and birds that would eat it.

A Discovery

A European geranium, very similar to *G. maculatum*, alerted German scientist Christian Sprengel to the fact that insects are responsible for pollination in many kinds of flowers—shocking news in the 1780s. Sprengel advanced the theory, also novel at that time, that every part of a flower has a distinct purpose. He determined, for instance, that the hairs around the inside of the geranium's corolla serve to block raindrops and dew, preventing them from watering down the nectar that attracts pollinating insects. He also figured out that the little, deeper-purple veins in the petals help, like arrows, to guide the insects to the nectary.

Tannic Medicine

Wild geranium has long been valued as a medicine. Because of the large amount of tannin in its roots, it has been extensively used as an astringent and styptic. Leaves and roots have been used to treat diarrhea, cholera, gonorrhea, neuralgia, toothaches, hemorrhages, sore throats, and gum diseases. Certain American Indians mixed it with grape juice as a mouthwash for youngsters with thrush, a mouth disease. Added to a mixture of milk and sugar, wild geranium was a popular gargle for children. Indians also valued it for "looseness of the bowels," though more modern authors warn that the plant's use can cause just the opposite problem, constipation.

Its medicinal uses as well as its shape and color have led to many folk names for wild geranium here and in Europe, to which it was exported as a medicinal herb. It has been called storksbill, alum bloom (alum was a common styptic chemical), chocolate flower (the color of the dried medicinal root powder), crowfoot, old maid's nightcap (flower shape), shameface (presumably the color of the flower, like an embarrassed face), rockweed (it's often found near stone walls), and sailor's knot (probably the seed pod's shape).

Geraniums are members of the Geranium family of about 15 genera and more than 700 species worldwide. *G. maculatum* is one of 30 or so species of geraniums found in North America. Carolina geranium (*G. carolinianum*), found coast to coast. a bushy, white-flowered native is considered a pest in some areas. Several geraniums are imports. The smaller, deeper-purple dove's foot geranium (*G. molle*), named for its leaf shape, has become widespread, found coast to coast and even in Hawaii.

Some species are circumboreal. Herb Robert (*G. robertianum*), long used as an astringent, is a native of Europe, Asia, and North America. The origin of its name has been debated for ages. According to various sources, the plant honors St. Robert, founder of the Cistercian order of monks, whose birthday on April 29 is about when this plant begins flowering; St. Rupert, the first archbishop of Salzburg; or Robert, Duke of Normandy, who died in 1135. Some claim the plant was named for Robin Hood, the Sherwood Forest outlaw. Still others believe the origin is much simpler. The flowers are red, a Latin word for which is *rubor*.

Baneberries

TWO-SEASON TREATS

Just don't eat the eyes of the doll.

Although wildflower enthusiasts often overlook the baneberry, this plant is among the few whose ornaments can be enjoyed in two seasons for two reasons: It bears attractive flowers and, later, even more attractive berries.

Probably because the flowers are not big or plentiful, they have been almost ignored by many writers. F. Schuyler Mathews called the blossoms "not particularly interesting," and Neltje Blanchan dismissed them as "insignificant." Many books on wildflowers, including at least one modern field guide, do not even mention baneberries. Mrs. William Starr Dana, however, talked of gathering "the feathery clusters of white baneberry . . . when we go in the woods for the columbine, the wild ginger, the Jack-in-the-pulpit, and Solomon's seal."

Baneberry's flowers are delicately beautiful. During most of their appearance in May and June, the fluffy clusters are little more than stamens and stigmas, parts of flowers usually unnoticed in the fancier blossoms of other species. Like those of the closely related black cohosh or "fairy candles" (see page 154), baneberry's petal-like sepals fall off soon after opening, leaving bunches of the bright, white fuzzies. Baneberries grow, bushlike, from one to three feet high and are fairly common in and around the rich woods of the East.

White baneberry in the spring becomes . . .

. . . doll's eyes in the summer.

Natural History

Like May apple and goatsbeard, baneberry is better known for its fruits than for its flowers. The fruits, which appear in late summer or early autumn, have inspired the plant's name and provided its fame, as limited as that may be. Each white berry, which has a purple black dot at the tip, sits at the end of a short, bright red stalk. They look "strikingly like the china eyes that small children occasionally manage to gouge from their dolls," wrote Mrs. Dana at the turn of the 20th century, and thus another common name for them is doll's eyes.

The clusters of berries are striking and attractive. Inside each waxy berry is a tightly packed and finely fitted set of seeds, which, if planted in rich, humusy, shaded soil that won't dry out, should yield flowering baneberry plants in two years. If you are not patient enough to wait

that long, try dividing the roots in late fall—or early spring if you know where some live. The perennial species is not exceedingly common, so avoid transplanting whole plants.

Bane is an ancient English word that appears as early as Beowulf as *bona* or *bana*, which means "slayer" or "murderer." The berries are said to be poisonous. Just how poisonous they are probably depends on the person and the plant. Walter Conrad Muenscher's 1939 book, *Poisonous Plants of the United States*, reports children have died from eating the berries of the similar European baneberry (*Actaea spicata*), which John Gerard described as having "a venomous and deadly qualitie." And with our native red baneberry (*A. rubra*), "eating six berries was sufficient to produce increased pulse, dizziness, burning in the stomach, and colicky pains," Professor Muenscher said. Yet Professor John M. Kingsbury's 1965 book, *Deadly Harvest: A Guide to Common Poisonous Plants*, doesn't even mention baneberries, and 18th-century French Canadian herbalist Michel Sarrazin observed, "it is thought that the fruit is a poison, which I don't believe, at least I know of no bad effects."

"The question of baneberry toxicity was settled in 1903 by Alice E. Bacon of Bradford, Vermont, in a curious experiment with the fruit," say Randy Westbrooks and James Preacher in their *Poisonous Plants of Eastern North America*. Mrs. Bacon, it seems, deliberately took increasingly greater doses of the berries over a period of several days, the last batch causing "intense hallucinogenic displays with various blue shapes followed by confusion, incoherency, and dizziness. Other symptoms she reported were parched throat, difficult swallowing, an intense burning in the stomach with gaseous belches. . . ." She recovered in a few hours, and presumably ended her experiment.

Whatever their effect on humans, big or little, clearly it's best to keep baneberries away from tots who are apt to eat them, thinking they might taste as good as they look. Always make it clear to children that *any* wild berries could be dangerous and must be left alone.

Medicinal Uses

North American Indians considered baneberries an important medicine, but use of it varied with season and aspect. Among the Ojibwas, for instance, red baneberry was considered "a male plant"—that is, good for men's ailments—at certain times of the year, and a "female plant" at other times, depending perhaps on the size of the plant or the color of the berries. Chippewa women used white baneberry for menstrual difficulties while the men used red baneberry for diseases peculiar to them. Many Indians, such as Ojibwas and Potawatomis, took baneberry extracts to help with childbirth. Probably because it is said to affect the heart, the plant was also used as a substitute for digitalis. "It is said to revive and rally a patient when he is at the point of death," said a writer on Meskwaki medicines.

Maude Grieve reported that the Indians considered the plants "a valuable remedy against snakebite, especially of the rattlesnake. Hence, it is—with several other plants—sometimes known as one of the 'rattlesnake herbs.' " Its use for this purpose was not widespread, probably because the plant may be as bad for you as the snakebite.

A Rabbit Sniffs

Peter hopped over to smell of them. Then he made a wry face. They didn't smell good. No sir, he didn't like the smell of them.

Mrs. Grouse chuckled. "Those flowers are much like the berries they will turn into later—good to look at only," she said.

"Aren't the berries good to eat?" demanded Peter.

Mrs. Grouse shook her head in a very decided way. "They are poisonous," she said. "I advise you never to try one of them."
—Thornton W. Burgess,
*The Burgess Flower Book
for Children* (1923)

Names

White baneberry, known as *Actaea pachypoda*, is a member of the Crowfoot, or Buttercup, family. *Actaea* is a genus of only a half-dozen or so species worldwide. Some authorities say the word means "elder" (others say "alder") because the leaves of some species resemble those of the elder or the alder tree—take your pick. *Pachypoda* means "thick-footed" or "thick-stalked" (just as *pachyderm* means "thick skinned"). White baneberry was formerly known as *A. alba.*

Among its folk names are cohosh, white cohosh, blue cohosh, whiteheads, necklace weed, whiteberry snakeroot, grapewort, and herb-Christopher, the last referring to St. Christopher who was somehow associated with a similar plant in ancient times. Perhaps he used Britain's baneberry, the rather rare *A. spicata* found on limestone banks and called herb-Christopher, bugbane, and toadroot. Except for the fact that it has black berries, it is similar to *A. pachypoda*. In fact, Linnaeus originally classified the American species as *Actaea spicata alba*, meaning *alba* was a white variety of the species *A. spicata.*

Toadroot, incidentally, refers to a phenomenon mentioned by several authors: Toads are said to be attracted to baneberry plants. Baneberry flowers have a fetid odor, apparently more attractive to pollen-collecting halictid bees than to honeybees. Baneberry flowers are rich in pollen but have no nectar. (Halictids include the so-called sweat bees that often hover around humans on hot, humid days. Perhaps the toads are right behind, though I've never noticed them following me around while I'm working in the yard.)

The berries attract a number of songbirds, including yellow-bellied sapsucker, American robin, wood thrush, brown thrasher, gray catbird, and ruffed grouse.

Our white baneberry's close relative, the red baneberry, bears berries of bright scarlet or crimson—as its name suggests. *A. rubra* favors cooler climates, ranging from the upper East Coast as far south as Pennsylvania and west to the Pacific states; the white baneberry has been found in Georgia, though only to Missouri and Minnesota. Both have handsome berries, but the whites seem more striking because, for berries at least, white seems to be an unusual color.

Whose Eyes?

In New England white baneberry is still commonly called doll's eyes or dolls' eyes. No one seems quite certain where to stick the apostrophe. Is there one doll or are there many? One botanist avoids the problem, spelling it "dollseyes."

Summer

Goatsbeard

THE GEODESIC CLOCK

Watch the goatsbeard—it has two kinds of clocks.

When are the seeds more beautiful than the flowers that begat them? When they're the seeds of goatsbeard, a late-spring and summer import that offers not only handsome flowers but also a seed display that is one of the most stunning among our wildflowers.

At a quick glance you might mistake this yellow, many-petaled flower for a common dandelion. Although related to that ubiquitous weed, goatsbeard is different and not nearly as common. The biennial looks like blades of grass in its first year. In its second year, goatsbeard can rise as high as four feet, carrying its single blossoms on stems with grass-like leaves. Unlike the lion-hearted dandelion, they rarely appear in lawns and are instead found mostly along the edges of moist woods and fields, frequently near roadsides.

The old flower head forms a blowball or "clock" of fuzz-topped seeds, larger and more like a ball than the blowball of a dandelion and having the appearance of a geodesic dome. This stunning puffball is the source of the plant's name. "The pappus, or feathery down crowning each seed, is very beautiful, being raised on a long stalk and interlaced, so as to form a shallow cup," wrote Maude Grieve. "By means of the pappus, the seeds are wafted by the wind and freely scattered."

Why should a plant produce such a large and elaborate display of seeds? The arrangement very effectively offers the pappi, or "parachutes," to the breezes that will carry them off. The interlaced display keeps the seeds sufficiently separated so that they are dispatched separately, not in clumps (which wouldn't travel as far). Such a sizable clock may also be designed to catch the eye of passing seed-eating birds, such as finches, who provide seed dispersal in a different way.

Lunch Alarm

For goatsbeard, *clock* has more than one meaning. In its native England, goatsbeard is often called noonflower or jack-go-to-bed-at-noon, describing the blossoms' habit of closing by noon. "The promptness with which the goatsbeard shuts its flowers when the sun has reached the meridian is astonishing," wrote Willard N. Clute, "One might almost set his watch by it." Indeed, farmers in England and France watched the flowers to tell when it was time for lunch.

The pretty goatsbeard flower turns into . . .

. . . the namesake "clock" of seeds.

Early to Bed

"It shutteth itself at twelve of the clock and sheweth not his face open until the next dayes sunne do make it flour anew, wherefore it was called go-to-bed-at-noon."
—*John Gerard* (1597)

Peep

The goats beard, which each morn abroad goes peep.
But shuts its flower at noon, and goes to sleep.
—Abraham Cowley (1618–1667)

Its habit of closing early may be protection against the hot and desiccating rays of the sun. However, Sir John Lubbock, in his book on British wildflowers and their relation to insects, suggests the noontime closing may also have evolved because the types of bees that pollinate the plant aren't active in the midday sun. Like the chicory, a related flower that fades in the sun by midday, goatsbeard may stay open all day if the weather is cloudy—and presumably, the bees are about. But unlike chicory, the blossom will reopen the next day.

Other names include buck's beard, star of Jerusalem, and Joseph's flower. The last name may stem from the common depiction of St. Joseph, husband of Mary, as being a bearded, older man.

Tragopogon pratensis, its botanic name, means "goat's beard" and "of the meadow." The species was introduced into the United States around 1900 as a garden flower and, thanks to its aeronautical seeds, quickly spread. The plant can be found coast to coast in the United States and Canada, though not in some states of the Deep South. No state lists it as an agricultural problem; thus, while it is widespread, goatsbeard does not overpopulate and make a pest of itself.

Tragopogon is a small genus of about 25 Old World species, three of which have made their way across the Atlantic and can be found in most of the United States and southern Canada. Salsify (*T. porrifolius*) is a purple garden escape, found locally throughout the United States and southern Canada; it is said to taste like oysters. Two additional species that have appeared in the Pacific Northwest may be hybrids of the European imports. For instance, yellow salsify (*T. dubius*), found in most states but particularly common on the Pacific Coast, has a name that may reflect its uncertain origin. Dandelions, hawkweeds, and chicory—all members of the Composite family—are closely related to tragopogons.

Old Medicine

In medieval Europe, goatsbeard was used as a medicinal plant, to treat—among other things—stomach disorders, breast ailments, and liver ailments. The milky juice was once a popular remedy for heartburn, a sort of liquid Tums. "A decoction of the roots is good for the heart-burn, loss of appetite, disorders of the breast and liver; expels sand and gravel, slime, and even small stones," wrote Nicholas Culpeper. "The roots of Goats-beard, boiled in wine and drunk, asswageth the pain and pricking stitches of the sides," added John Gerard.

The roots were once eaten. "Buttered as parseneps and carrots [they] are a most pleasant and wholesome meate, in delicate taste far surpassing either parsenep or carrot," wrote Gerard. They've also been roasted and, like chicory roots, ground into a coffee substitute. Young stalks were cut up and boiled, like asparagus; in fact, they are said to have an asparagus-like flavor. The young basal leaves can be eaten either raw or boiled like spinach. Older raw leaves are not so tasty. In fact, the plant's bitter milky juice, disliked by grazing animals, is a self-defense mechanism.

Transplanting goatsbeard is not easy. Care must be taken not to break its rather deep taproot. It's better to try planting from seed. Since goatsbeard is a biennial, the effort is probably not worth it. Instead, the next time you see one of those handsome domes, admire it, then grab it and plant the seeds in a semishaded to sunny setting with moist, neutral soil.

Bedstraws

CREEPERS FOR RUNNERS

Many bedstraws have hitchhiked around the world.

Some wildflowers are more noted—and appreciated—for their foliage than for their flowers. Such are the bedstraws, common summer plants whose tiny blossoms often go unnoticed but whose seeds can be all too noticeable and annoying.

Creeping, low, whorled-leafed plants whose favorite haunt is open fields, bedstraws are a large clan found worldwide. Some species, like fragrant bedstraw (*Galium triflorum*), range across North America, Europe, and Asia—from the Himalayas to Japan. Few plant species can be found in so many parts of the planet, but many that are so widespread owe it to their exceptionally functional seeds.

"The most extraordinary thing about bedstraw is the way it catches on everything it touches," wrote F. Schuyler Mathews. The oval seedpods, covered with little hook-shaped hairs, have managed to hitchhike across three continents. In some species, such as the aptly named "cleavers" (*Galium aparine*), it is the hook-haired stems that are more likely to grab hold of you, carrying the pods with them. In fact, *aparine* is from the Greek, "to seize." These hairs serve also to discourage some plant eaters, such as snails, from nibbling the leaves and stems.

Through the ages and around the world, people have used different species of bedstraw for such varied purposes as medicine, cheese making, clothes dyeing, and—apparently—mattress stuffing. For example, yellow bedstraw (*G. verum*) was a popular remedy for gallstones and urinary diseases, and was once used to treat epilepsy, hysteria, and internal bleeding. "An ointment is prepared which is good for anointing the weary traveler," said herbalist John Gerard.

The four-petaled flowers of the bedstraws, or madders, often appear in lacy displays.

Old Dye and Odd Name

Although maidens in Henry VIII's time believed wearing yellow bedstraw would turn their hair blond, the plant was extensively used to create a red dye. American Indians employed the closely related wild madder, or stiff marsh bedstraw (*G. tinctorium*), to redden their feathers, porcupine quills, and other ornaments. French Canadians dyed clothing with the plant.

One of the yellow bedstraw's chief uses was in the production of cheese. The plant not only curdled the milk in preparation for cheese making, but also, in some places, added color and

Wide but Spotty

Boreal bedstraw (*Galium kamtschaticum*) is one of the rarest bedstraws but also one of the most widespread. This environmentally sensitive species, named for the Siberian peninsula, is found in Russia and in such far-flung places as Alaska, Finland, the White Mountains of New Hampshire, the Adirondacks of New York, and the Cascades of Washington state. Like other bedstraws, it bears seeds with hooked barbs. Thus, roaming boreal animals such as wolves and bears are probably responsible for its wide but spotty range.

Hard Seeds

Galium aparine has "the toughest of all seeds, and hence millers may well object to them, for if they be numerous, 'they will almost make the stones whistle.' In samples of oats, they are abominable; horses can scarcely grind them."

—The *Cultivator,* (August 1842)

sweetness to the product. Some hairy-stemmed varieties, like cleavers, were matted together and used as sieves to strain milk. *Galium,* the generic name, means "milk."

Bedstraw itself is an odd name whose origin has been traced to two possible sources: the old use of the dried plant to stuff beds or the belief that the plant was one of the "cradle herbs," mixed in the hay of the manger when Jesus was born in Bethlehem.

Freshening was a popular use for fragrant, or sweet-scented, bedstraw, a plant whose bouquet gets sweeter as it dries. Mathews, however, was no fan of the scent, at least that of the fresh rough bedstraw, *G. asprellum,* He maintained that their flowers have "a sickening-sweet odor which is unpleasant." Nonetheless, he added that "the vine is a pretty little thing, whose circularly arranged leaves give it a decorative look."

The genus *Galium* consists of about 250 species around the world, with some 75 in North America. Besides bedstraws, they include some species called madders, a couple called wild licorice, and several "cleavers." *Galium* species bear tiny white, greenish, purple, or yellow flowers with pointed petals. Leaves appear in whorls, usually of four, six, or eight. In general, the plants lie close to the ground, often forming mats.

Many Names

Bedstraws are members of the Madder family (Rubiaceae) of about 340 genera and 6,000 species worldwide, mostly tropical. About the only other well-known genera within the family are the bluets (*Houstonia*) of spring and the imported woodruffs (*Aperula*), some of which are used to flavor wines and some as ground covers.

Over the years the bedstraws have picked up many names. Cleavers (*G. aparine*) have at least 70, including goosegrass, grip-grass, beggar-lice, cling-rascal, scratch-grass, stick-a-back, pig-tail, liveman, stickywilly, sweethearts, and poorweed. The seeds were once roasted as a coffee substitute; the fact that true coffee is a related plant may explain why. The boiled young shoots, served with butter, have been eaten as a vegetable or, chilled, as a salad ingredient. Just about all grazing mammals and fowl eat the plant. Indians widely used it as a medicine. While their clinging nature has made cleavers unpopular with most people, mischievous youngsters loved to attach sprigs of them to the backs of unsuspecting comrades. The plant also had romantic associations, whence its name "sweethearts." People in the south of England believed that if they threw a cleaver at a maiden's back and it stuck without her being aware of it, she had a sweetheart. If it fell off or she pulled it off, the bent sprig would form the initial of her future sweetheart.

Yellow bedstraw has been called cheese-rennet, curdworts, bedflower, fleawort, yellow cleavers, and maidshair. In England, the flower heads were distilled into a refreshing drink. Perhaps the best use of the plant was reported by Nicholas Culpeper 400 years ago and might be noted by the recreational runners of today. "The decoction of the herb or flower," he wrote, "is good to bathe the feet of travellers and lacqueys, whose long running causeth weariness and stiffness in their sinews and joints."

So if you happen to have a lackey in your service, be kind and offer him a bedstraw bath.

Cinquefoil

A ROSE BY ANOTHER NAME

Cinquefoils are lowly but lovely flowers.

It is odd how some plants not only survive but also thrive in parched or poisoned soil, and how they can produce some of our most attractive wildflowers. Dwarf cinquefoil is just such a plant. A creeping, thornless rose that many people see but few notice, *Potentilla canadensis* is a tiny wildflower that can grow in destitute areas. I have seen it creeping right up to the edge of highways from whose pavement drains salt, oil, gasoline, and other unpleasant substances. It also grows in dry fields and lawns.

In her column "The Excellence of Little" in the *West Hartford (Connecticut) News* some years ago, Jane B. Cheney noted, "The occurrence of this plant in waste places from Newfoundland down to the Carolinas is diagnostic of poor soil and dry soil. It does not take well to competition and itself dies out when soil is enriched. This characteristic is evidently particular to [dwarf cinquefoil] because many of the other species are large and reliable garden plants."

These dry-earth cinquefoils are nature's way of covering, even decorating, the more barren parts of our landscape. Like cacti, they spring from harsh, barren soils. As we allow more of the good topsoil to be eroded or scraped away, the cinquefoils are bound to become even more common. They are among those opportunistic creatures of nature that thrive on our inability to handle our environment carefully.

Dwarf cinquefoil is a low, creeping rose often mistaken for a buttercup.

Flower of Fives

Cinquefoil is a French-based word meaning "five-leaved" and is pronounced either "sink-foil" or "sank-foil," depending, I suppose, on whether you got an A in French. Modern Europeans call them five-leaf grass, *Fünffingerkraut*, *cinco en rama*, *quintefueille*, or *cinquefoglio*. To ancient Greeks they were *pentaphyllon*, while the Romans labeled them *quinquefolium*. None of these names of five should be taken too literally, however, because the plant actually has single leaves deeply cut into five parts. The theme of five continues in the flowers: Each has five rounded, yellow petals.

The casual observer is apt to think cinquefoils are buttercups creeping along the ground. Those who know their flowers, however, will readily recognize the resemblance of the blossoms to those of wild roses. The flowers are flat, not cuplike as in the buttercups, and the petals lack the shiny surface of common buttercups.

Lofty Rarity

While most cinquefoils are weedy and widespread, odds are you won't find *Potenilla robbinsiana* creeping across your lawn. Dwarf mountain cinquefoil is so rare that, in the summer of 1985, only 200 plants were known to exist. All were growing among granite cracks near the windswept summit of Mount Washington in northern New Hampshire, 5,000 or 6,000 feet in the air, and in a couple of nearby locations.

Tanning Flower

Tannin, the substance used in tanning hides in the leather-making process, is usually obtained from tree bark. In Ireland, however, there were few trees. In 1727, the Irish Parliament awarded 200 pounds to one William Maple for discovering that the root of tormentil (*Potentilla reptans*) was so rich in tannin, it could be used to tan leather.

Almost all cinquefoils bear yellow flowers. At least, to our eyes, they are yellow. To a bee, however, the scene is quite different. The insect sees the yellow but also a great deal of purple, the result of its eyes' ability to detect the ultraviolet spectrum. If we were to shine an ultraviolet light on a cinquefoil or on certain other yellow flowers, such as evening-primrose, we would see purple lines on the petals radiating from the center of the flower. These lines serve as guides, directing the bee to the nectar.

Dwarf cinquefoil is found from Nova Scotia to Texas. It is also called five-finger, finger leaf, barren strawberry, sinkfield (based on a misunderstanding of *cinque*), starflower, and running buttercups. The last name reflects the tendency for the low-lying plant to spread by slender runners.

Dwarf cinquefoil begins blooming at my Connecticut home as early as May 1, but the leaves spring from the ground long before that. I've seen them sprouting in February, just after a thaw. The plants bloom until midsummer.

Many Varieties

North America is home to more than 100 cinquefoils, many of which are common and widespread. Common cinquefoil (*P. simplex*) is another creeper, somewhat larger than *P. canadensis*. This native is found throughout eastern North America. Unlike the latter, which has leaf sections with flattish tops, common cinquefoil has pointed leaf tips. It's also called old-field cinquefoil because worn-out fields are a favorite haunt.

Silverweed cinquefoil is a circumboreal creeper found along shores and streamsides in New England, the Great Lakes, and the West Coast from Mexico up to Alaska. This plant has been used for centuries as a medicine and food—the boiled roots are said to taste like parsnips. Its feathery leaves with silvery hairs underneath have also been much admired for their beauty. "If silverweed were less invasive, it would merit itself a place on the edge of the most elegant flower bed, by virtue of its exquisite foliage," wrote Audrey Wynne Hatfield in *How to Enjoy Your Weeds*. Silverweed has long been known as *P. anserina*, but more recently, has been given the name *Argentina anserina*. *Argentina* does not refer to the country, but to the Latin, *argentium*, meaning "silver." *Anserina* comes from the Latin for "goose," suggesting that either these waterfowl enjoy eating the leaves or that the leaves looked like goose feathers to the namer.

Shrubby cinquefoil, a sizable native up to three feet tall, blooms coast to coast in the summer, favoring meadows and shores of streams and ponds. Its many leaves give it the appearance of a shrub, and it has been used as the parent for various garden plants, often with yellow orange flowers. Shrubby cinquefoil was once popular for a tea made from its leaves. Until recently it was known as *P. fruticosa* but has now been reclassified as *Dasiphora floribunda*.

Another import called tormentil, or creeping cinquefoil (*P. reptans*), is found scattered throughout North America but is better known in its native Europe where it has been a medicinal plant for centuries. Its name is a diminutive form of the Latin for "torment," because the plant was widely used as a pain reliever or analgesic. In fact, it is the type species for the genus *Potentilla*, a name that reflects Europeans' belief that this and other members of the genus were "potent" treatments for many ailments. Cinquefoils had been used since the time of Hippocrates for fevers and toothaches. Because of the high tannin content of the roots, cinquefoil was frequently used as an astringent on wounds, ulcers, and cancers.

Herbalist John Gerard wrote 400 years ago that *P. reptans* "is used in all inflammations and fevers, whether infectious or pestilential, and in lotions, gargles and the like, for sore mouths, ulcers, cancers, fistulas, and other corrupt, foul, or running sores." Nicholas Culpeper maintained that the flowers "fasten loose teeth, and help the falling of the uvula."

Tormentil has had good and evil associated with it. Sir Francis Bacon reported that the plant was a chief ingredient in Witches' Ointment, which also included the "fat of children digged out of their graves." But because its five-part leaves looked like the outstretched hand of a priest giving a blessing, tormentil was also used to ward off evil spirits.

On this continent *P. canadensis* has seen limited use in folk medicine. Herbalist John Lust says it makes a good gargle and mouthwash, and a remedy for diarrhea. The bark of the root has been used to stop nosebleeds and other internal bleeding.

"Every time I see this humble poor-soil plant, I am amazed at the amount of experimentation which has gone on in the past to heal and cure people," wrote Ms. Cheney. "It is an impressive record of work, though I had rather have the science of today!"

Mysteries

The lowly cinquefoil is a rose,
A fact that any botanist knows,
Though it seems to me a mystery
How such a lowly plant can be
Sibling to a flower that grows
As glorious as a garden rose.
The bigger question does remain:
How you pronounce that funny
    name?
Does it "sink" or does it "sank"
As it wanders up the bank?
And as it creeps across the soil
What, pray tell, does it foil?
    —J. S.

Forget-Me-Nots

LEGENDARY FLOWERS

Forget-me-nots have inspired a storybook full of tales.

The yellow ring in the center of the forget-me-not flower helped a famous German botanist discover Saftmal.

If any flower could be considered a living legend, it would be the forget-me-not. In almost every major language, one can find a tale connected with the plant, and usually with the origin of its unusual name.

Denizens of lawns, meadows, pond shores, and brooksides—even brooks themselves—forget-me-nots are known to almost everyone as those pretty little blue flowers with the white-and-yellow-ringed eyes. Their five rounded petals and small stem-top clusters have long symbolized friendship and loyalty but have represented even more to many who have exchanged them over the centuries. They are "the sweet forget-me-nots that grow for happy lovers," wrote Tennyson.

The plant is called forget-me-not in many tongues: *Vergissmeinnicht, nezaboravak, ne-m'oubliez-pas, forglemmegie*, etc. There are almost as many stories of the name's origin as there are languages. In one widely told tale, a knight was walking with his sweetheart alongside a pond when he saw some of these flowers growing on an island in the middle of the water. Foolish with love, he jumped into the water, armor and all, and managed to grab a bunch of flowers and toss them to his lover before sinking below the surface. His last words were: "Forget me not!" This story is also told in a version that has an armorless hero falling into the Danube and being swept away by the current.

In an equally depressing German legend, a fairy guides a young man in search of treasure to a mountain cave. He found the cave marked by forget-me-nots and began filling his pockets with the gold within. Pointing to the flowers at the cave's entrance, the fairy warned the boy to "forget not the best." The youngster ignored the fairy, continued to gather only gold, and was crushed in a cave-in. Related fables attribute to forget-me-nots the power to open caves with treasure inside.

One of the more sentimental tales tells of a boy and girl who as children often played in the woods and fields together. When the boy grew up, he went off to make his fortune. As the two met to say good-bye, they promised to think of each other whenever they found one of the blue flowers that had been so common where they played as children. Years later the boy, now an old man, returned to the woods near his native village and ran into his childhood friend. Neither recognized the other till suddenly both spotted one of the blue flowers, both bent down to pick it, and their hands met. Thereafter, they called it forget-me-not.

The Persian poet Shiraz tells of a "golden morning of the early world, when an angel sat weeping outside the closed gates of Paradise. He had fallen from his high estate through loving a daughter of earth, nor was he permitted to enter again until she whom he loved had planted the flowers of the forget-me-not in every corner of the world. He returned to earth and assisted her, and together they went hand in hand. When their task was ended, they entered Paradise together, for one fair woman, without tasting the bitterness of death, became immortal like the angel whose love her beauty had won when she sat by the river twining forget-me-nots in her hair."

In a Christian legend, God named all the plants during the six days of creation, but one small blue flower could never remember what it was called. God forgave the flower's absentmindedness and named it "Forget-me-not." In a German version, God was handing out names to all the animals and plants after the creation. When he was nearly finished, he heard a little voice call out, "Forget me not, O Lord!" "That shall be your name," God replied.

In another Christian tale, Adam and Eve were leaving the Garden of Eden after their apple-eating escapade, and all the plants and animals were backing off in disapproval as they went by. All, that is, except a little blue flower that called out in a tiny voice, "Forget me not," the only friendly words spoken to them as they departed.

The ancient Egyptians believed that anointing one's eyes with forget-me-nots during the month of Thoth, the ibis-headed god, would create visions. A folk tale also maintained that the name of the plant was derived from the awful-tasting leaves—once sampled, they would not be forgotten. The flower has also served as a sort of good luck charm, and was given to people starting a journey on February 29. Friends also exchanged it on that day.

Poets have put the plant to good use, but none with quite as much license as Henry Wadsworth Longfellow. In "Evangeline," he wrote:

> Silently, one by one, in the infinite meadows of heaven,
> Blossom the lovely stars, the forget-me-nots of the angels.

That prompted the Rev. E. Cobham Brewer, in his *Dictionary of Phrase and Fable*, to comment dryly: "The similitude between a little light-blue flower and the yellow stars is very remote. Stars are more like buttercups than forget-me-nots."

Many Kinds

Eleven kinds of forget-me-nots inhabit North America, and among the most common are two species usually called simply "forget-me-nots," though one is native and the other a European immigrant. Probably most common is the "true" forget-me-not (*Myosotis scorpioides*), whose blossoms run from one-quarter to one-third inch in width on stems up to 24 inches high. A garden escape and native of both Europe and Asia, it is found locally from coast to coast along streams, in wet places, and even in fairly shady wood edges not noted for moisture. Other names for the plant include water forget-me-not, mouse-ear scorpion grass, marsh scorpion-grass, snake grass, and love-me.

Henry's Flower

Flowers have often been associated with leaders. Violets were Napoleon's favorite, and Louis VII liked irises. But for Henry IV of England, forget-me-not was the flower of choice. During his exile in 1398, he purportedly adopted it as his symbol. He didn't want his people to forget him. When he returned a year later, he continued to use it as an emblem.

Sky after Rain

"The Chinese ceramic artists have introduced in some of their vases a highly prized colour, which, in their treatises, they call 'the sky after rain.' The flowers of the forget-me-not are of this pure and delicate tint— the clear azure of the sky, the delicate colour of the turquoise."
—*F. Edward Hulme* (1881)

The bay forget-me-not (*M. laxa*), a native, has one-fifth-inch blossoms, is somewhat less tall (about 20 inches), and likes very wet situations. It can be found growing in the middle of shallow brooks, sometimes choking them. It ranges from southern Canada to Georgia and west into the Rocky Mountains and along the Pacific Coast. Both are perennials that bloom from May through July and are easily transplanted or acquired from nurseries.

The Asian forget-me-not (*M. alpestris*) is found in the Rockies from New Mexico into Canada. *A Field Guide to Rocky Mountain Wildflowers* observes that this plant blooms from late June through early August when the cow elk are migrating with their spring-born calves to higher summer ranges. *Alpestris* means "alpine."

Forget-me-nots are members of the Borage family, a clan of some 2,500 species in about 150 genera, including heliotropes, cowslips (mertensia), puccoons, and buglosses. The genus *Myosotis* consists of about 35 species around the world. Not all have the typical blue flowers; the spring forget-me-not (*M. verna*), found coast to coast, has white flowers—perhaps they are Longfellow's stars.

Myosotis means "mouse-ear," descriptive of the plant's leaves. *Laxa* is "open," referring to the looser racemes of flowers. *Scorpioides* reflects the fact that the raceme of blossoms tends to curl over in the fashion of a scorpion's tail. Employing the Doctrine of Signatures, ancient herbalists decided that since forget-me-nots are shaped like scorpions, they must be good for treating scorpion bites, and for centuries the herb was used for that purpose. People then reasoned that if it was good enough for scorpion bites, it was probably good enough for any bite, and, eventually, any wound. John Gerard, the herbalist, reported Greek pharmacologist Dioscorides (ca. A.D. 40–90) as saying, "the leaves of scorpion grasse applied to the place, are a present remedy against the stinging of scorpions; and likewise boyled in wine and drunke, prevaile against the said bitings, as also of addars, snakes, and such venomous beasts. Being made in an unguent with oile, wax, and a little gum Elemni, they are profitable against such hurts as require an healing medicine."

Yellow and Blue

The yellow ring around the center of the forget-me-not helped lead Christian Konrad Sprengel (1750–1816), a German botanist, to conclude that outstanding markings on many kinds of flowers were signposts to lead bees and other insects to the nectar and pollen. He called these markings *Saftmal*, or "honey guides." The yellow ring also forms a ridge around the opening that helps keep rainwater from getting into the flower's center tube, where it would dilute the nectar and damage the pollen.

Even though forget-me-nots have brilliant color, effective design, and large numbers of flowers to attract bees, they are nonetheless small flowers. A pollinator may never visit many of them, and if this should happen, a flower can fertilize itself. When the flowers first open, the pollen-catching pistils project out of the opening of the corolla, or flower tube. The pollen-bearing stamens are below. With this arrangement, a bee that has visited other forget-me-nots will brush

Forget-me-not

When to the flower so beautiful
The Father gave a name,
Back came a little blue-eyed one—
All timidly it came;
And, standing at the Father's feet,
And gazing in his face,
It said with meek and gentle voice,
Yet with a timid grace,
"Dear Lord, the name thou gavest me,
Alas! I have forgot."
The Father kindly looked on it,
And said, "Forget-me-not."
—Emily Bruce Roelofson

off the pollen on the pistil before dipping into the new flower. Sir John Lubbock, an entomologist and naturalist who studied the relationship of flowers and insects, found that eventually, the corolla elongates, in the process pushing up the stamens to a point where they can touch the pistil, effecting self-fertilization.

The pollen, incidentally, is amazingly tiny. Six thousand grains of it lined up would measure only an inch. In comparison, about 125 pumpkin pollen grains would measure an inch. The seeds, too, are minuscule; 225,000 of them weigh one pound.

Forget-me-nots have always been admired for their color. Although the petal shades will vary, the best blues of these flowers are said to come the closest of any flower to true blue. Says F. Schuyler Mathews: "Blue in a pure state does not exist on the petal of any flower, wild or cultivated. I might with justice except the familiar forget-me-not, whose quality of color is very nearly a pure blue."

A couple of naturalists remarked on seeing this color in the wilds of Alaska early in the 20th century. John Burroughs, hiking there, observed, "the prettiest flower we found was a forget-me-not, scarcely an inch high, of deep ultramarine blue—the deepest, most intense blue I ever saw in a wild flower."

John Muir, in *Travels in Alaska* (1915), described the reverence with which an Alaska native held this flower. "[He] proudly handed it to me with the finest respect and telling its many charms and lifelong associations, showed in every endearing look and touch and gesture that the tender little plant of the mountain wilderness was truly his best-loved darling."

No wonder a forget-me-not is the state flower of Alaska.

Chickweeds

FOR THE BIRDS

Chickweeds have also followed humans around the world.

Common chickweed is a tiny flower—note the dime for comparison — that has traveled the world.

The normally staid, conservative Maude Grieve became expansive when describing the range of the common chickweed in *A Modern Herbal*: "It has been said that there is no part of the world where the chickweed is not to be found," she wrote. "It is a native of all temperate and north Arctic regions, and has naturalized itself wherever the white man has settled, becoming one of the commonest weeds." Some authorities say it may be the most common flowering weed in the world.

The common chickweed is indeed a nearly ubiquitous plant, blooming in lawns, gardens, and even from cracks in sidewalks and parking lots. It is a survivalist, employing techniques like long blooming seasons, prodigious seed output, and a taste for disturbed soils to make itself at home on every continent—and seemingly in almost every lawn.

The white flower of the common chickweed (*Stellaria media*) is distinctive. Its five petals are so deeply cleft that it almost seems as if there are 10 narrow petals. This is typical of several chickweeds and "stitchwort" species of the genus *Stellaria* that inhabit North America, mostly in lawns, fields, and the ever popular "waste places." Chickweeds, like dandelions, are a scourge for those who want a putting-green lawn. Even television commercials for weed killers mention chickweed by name as a major target for poisoning.

Bird Food

Though lawn fanatics hate chickweeds, birds love them. Four centuries ago, John Gerard wrote in his *Herbal*: "Little birds in cadges (especially Linnets) are refreshed with the lesser chickweed when they loath their meat." Mrs. Grieve wrote, "Both wild and caged birds eat the seeds as well as the young tops and leaves." Indeed, canary owners have been known to crawl around on hands and knees, gathering the papery, seed-filled pods for their pets. One study of wildlife eating habits lists more than 30 common North American birds that eat *S. media*, but adds that a complete inventory would be too long to publish. Thus, chickweed—like thistles, sunflowers, and berry-bearing plants—is good to have in the yard if you want to attract wild birds. Not surprisingly, the plant has acquired many avian names, including birdweed, chickenweed, chick wittles, cluckweed, and chicken's meat in England and America, *mouron des oiseaux* ("morsel for the birds") in France, and *Vogelkraut* ("bird plant") in Germany. An old Latin name, *morus gallinae*, meant "morsel for the hens."

Another set of names reflects the flowers' shape; *Stellaria* means "star." *S. media* has also been called starweed, starwort, star chickweed, and, in France, *stellaire*. Perhaps to give it a more native flavor over here, it is sometimes called Indian chickweed (though Chippewas, who used this import in an eyewash, called it by a word meaning "tooth plant"). Other names picked up over the centuries include satinflower, skirt and buttons, white bird's eye, adder's mouth, and tongue grass (it looks like a snake's open mouth, complete with tongue).

Because of its long blooming season, chickweed is also called winterweed. British naturalist William H. Gibson tells of digging under snow and ice in midwinter and finding it blooming, and Neltje Blanchan says that "except during the most cruel frosts, there is scarcely a day in the year when we may not find the little starlike chickweed flowers."

Food and Medicine

For a lowly lawn pest, chickweed has had quite a history of popular uses. C. P. Johnson, in *Useful Plants of Great Britain* (1862), found it "an excellent green vegetable, much resembling spinach in flavor and is very wholesome." Mrs. Grieve wrote, "The young leaves when boiled can hardly be distinguished from spring spinach, and are equally wholesome." Bradford Angier said the flavor is, to many people, "less disagreeable" than that of spinach. Herbalist John Lust reports that the plant contains significant quantities of vitamin C and is a good source of phosphorus. It's also one of the few edible plants that are a good source of copper. However, because of its high nitrate content, says Barrie Kavasch, it should be eaten in moderation. Dr. E. Lewis Sturtevant, who headed the New York Agricultural Experiment Station in the late 19th century, noted that "this plant is found in every garden as a weed." Perhaps chickweed *belongs* in every garden.

As an herb medicine, chickweed has been used to treat ulcers, constipation, carbuncles, coughs, and hydrophobia. The crushed leaves were a popular poultice for wounds and insect stings. If you believe the 17th-century herbalist Nicholas Culpeper, chickweed can cure a whole slew of things. "The herb bruised, or the juice applied, with cloths or sponges dipped therein, to the region of the liver, doth wonderfully temper the heat of the liver, and is effectual for all impostumes and swellings whatsoever for all redness in the face, wheals, pushes, itch, or scabs, the juice being either simply used, or boiled in hog's grease; the juice of distilled water is of good use for all heat and redness in the eyes . . . as also into ears. . . . It helpeth the sinews when they are shrunk by cramps or otherwise, and extends and makes them pliable again." No wonder ancient herbalists lost many patients to the grave!

McChick?

In her book *How to Enjoy Your Weeds*, Audrey Wynne Hatfield recommends a chickweed sandwich, consisting of fresh greens flavored with a squeeze of lemon juice, a bit of salt and pepper, and a few drops of Worcestershire sauce between two slices of buttered bread. "Like any cress, this one goes well with tomato or any other sandwich filling," she adds.

Humble Chickweed

Dearest but humblest born
Of nature's blameless brood,
Creeping among the grass,
Among the corn,
Keeping well out of sight
Beneath the dock and plantain
    hidden quite,
Around the glow-worm's light,
Poor gypsy vagabond of road
    and lane,
Thou has of men their coldness
    and disdain,
Contempt and bitter scorn.
Yet Mother Nature good
To all her children with unstinted
    love,
Holds thy form closely pressed
To her warm loving breast
And smiles in sunshine on thy
    frequent bloom.
—Isaac Bassett Choate
    (1833–1917)

According to an old wives' tale, chickweed water was a remedy for obesity. But the good-humored Professor Lawrence J. Crockett observes that if that tale were true, chickweed would quickly disappear from overweight America.

In modern herbals, chickweed's medicinal uses are limited. Mr. Lust offers a chickweed recipe for constipation and says it's good mixed with petroleum jelly to treat skin irritations. Joseph and Clarence Meyer recommend it only for external ailments.

Range and Survival

Chickweed's range is remarkable. It is found in both hemispheres around the world, including north of the Arctic Circle. Describing exploration of southern New Zealand islands, Joseph Hooker (1817–1911) wrote: "On one occasion, landing on a small, uninhabited island nearly at the Antipodes, the first evidence I met with of its having been previously visited was the English chickweed; and this I traced to a mount that marked the grave of a British sailor, and that was covered with the plant, doubtless the offspring of seed that had adhered to the spade or mattock with which the grave had been dug."

The plant has clever ways to assure survival. In cold months, when few flying insects are available for pollination, it produces "cleistogamous" flowers, which never open yet make seed. In warmer months, when its normal flowers compete with numerous larger and showier blossoms for the attention of insects, it produces nectar in great (for its size) quantities. These flowers are pollinated by cross-fertilization, which produces a better quality of seed. As an annual *S. media* needs seeds in considerable numbers, and with an excellent germination rate. That the species is so common and widespread is testimony to both the quantity and quality of seed.

The stem is from 4 to 16 inches in length, but is weak; the taller stems flop over, making the plant look like a creeper. When it flops, the plant sinks new roots, helping it to spread into dense carpets.

Dr. John Hutchinson, once head of the Botanical Museums at the Royal Botanical Gardens, found *S. media* "of considerable economic and biological interest, representing a high stage of evolution." As an example of its highly evolved systems, he cited the line of hairs that appears down only one side of the stem and on leaf stalks. "These carry out a special function," he said. "They are readily wetted by rain and dew and retain a considerable amount of water. This is conducted down to the leaf-stalks, where some of it is absorbed by the lower cells of the hairs, and any surplus is passed further down to the next pair of leaves, and so on; the same process being repeated in each case." Chickweed does so well in fairly dry situations because it is able to make the best use of the water available.

In fact, common chickweed favors what botanists call "disturbed places." Here, they have little competition and can quickly spread across the surface. Disturbed places include cultivated fields and construction sites where turning of the soil will expose the seeds, some of which may have been dormant for years. Sunlight triggers germination, in effect telling the seed that it's in a suitable position to begin growing.

Common chickweed blooms from as early as March to as late as December—even in New England. It thus has one of the longest blooming seasons of any wildflower of northern climes. In milder temperate climates such as England's, it may bloom in every month of the year. This long season enables the plants to produce plenty of seeds but also exposes them to some harsh weather. To help handle this, the upper chickweed leaves can close over the buds of emerging flowers and new shoots at night, protecting them from possible damaging cold.

Also common, especially in lawns, is the closely related mouse-ear chickweed (*Cerastium vulgatum*), whose white, cleft-petal flowers are smaller than the three-quarter-inch flowers of *S. media*. A creeping plant whose fuzzy opposing leaves are shaped like the ears of a mouse, it grows throughout most of North America, including Alaska.

About 30 species of *Stellaria* and 25 of *Cerastium* can be found on this continent, though—as is often the case—the imports seem to be the most common and widespread. They are in turn members of the Pink family, which includes such common and oft-recognized flowers as the ragged-robin, campions, catchflies, bouncing bet, and—of course—the pretty pinks themselves.

Black-Eyed Susan

A PRETTY FACE

Black-eyed Susan recalls a lonely girl and a botanist's mentor.

Black-eyed Susan, an elegant native, gets its name from an old English song. The lower blossom is a "double" form.

Black-eyed Susan is a wildflower virtually everyone recognizes. "Many consider it . . . the prettiest of all the wildflowers," one writer said. However, it's also a plant whose common and scientific names are among the most unusual and sentimental. And while the plant is a North American native, both names find their origins thousands of miles away in Europe.

The popular name comes from a once-popular English ballad, written around 1720 by John Gay, a lyricist who wrote not only songs but also operas and poetry. The ballad tells of a young woman who comes aboard a ship looking for her sweetheart who's a crewmember. The song begins:

All in the dawn the fleet was moor'd,
The streamers waving to the wind,
When Black-eyed Susan came on board,
Oh where shall I my true love find?
Tell me, ye jovial sailors, tell me true,
If my sweet William, if my sweet William
Sails among your crew?

And ends:

The boatswain gave the dreadful word,
Her sails their swelling bosom spread:
No longer can she stay on board—
They kissed, she sighed, he hung his head:
Her lessening boat unwilling rows to land,
"Adieu," she cries, "Adieu," she cries
And waved her lily hand.

While the scientific name is scientific in origin, it is not without sentiment. *Rudbeckia hirta* is named for two 18th-century Swedish botanists. Olaus Rudbeck Sr. and Jr. were noted professors of botany at the University of Upsala in Sweden where a country minister's son named Carl von Linne came to study medicine in the 1720s. Olaus Jr. took a shine to the young man and his interest in botany; von Linne moved into Rudbeck Jr.'s house and earned money by tutoring four of the prolific professor's 24 children.

The student, who later called himself Linnaeus, went on to develop the binomial system still used today to name all life forms by genus and species. For reasons known only to him, Linnaeus decided that coneflowers of North America should recall the mentor of his youth and the mentor's father.

Hirta is Latin for "hairy," descriptive of the leaves and stalk. *R. hirta* is the type species for a clan of about 25 or 30 plants, usually called coneflowers and found throughout North America but mostly in the southern and western sections, including Mexico. Many coneflowers have bigger and more elongated center "buttons"—hence the name—than do black-eyed Susans.

If you look closely at the cone or flower head, you'll see that it is made up of hundreds of tiny seed-producing florets, which "bloom"—showing the yellow pollen—in a ring around the cone, starting at the bottom and working up to the tip. The yellow "petals" are not petals at all, but sterile florets that have given up their reproductive function to become flags, waving in the passing insects. Thus, each blossom is actually a composite of small, tightly clustered flowers and rays, an arrangement that yielded the plant's family name: Composite. The Composite family—also known as the Aster family—is the largest family of flowering plants, with more than 900 genera and 10,000 species throughout the world. The Composites are also probably the most recent family to appear on the earth, and among the most complex and highly developed of wild plants (see also the chapter on asters, beginning on page 271).

Black-eyed Susan's success at the business of survival is aided by its bright color, which attracts insects, its wealth of nectar that feeds them, and its abundance of yellow pollen. The pollen attracts short-tongued insects that can't get at the nectar, while the floret tubes hold nectar for insects—especially bees, butterflies, and moths—with tongues long enough to reach deep into the tubes.

Eastward Bound

Black-eyed Susan is a native of the western plains and prairies that humans have helped, both accidentally and deliberately, to spread across the continent. Before the 19th century, black-eyed Susan had been unknown in eastern North America, which had been forested territory until the Europeans arrived. When settlers felled trees for fields and pastures, they opened the land to the sun that the black-eyed Susan needed. The plant moved East in the 1830s, accidentally mixed with red clover seeds. By the 20th century, however, government officials were helping it to spread by encouraging its use, along with grasses and other native plants, to control erosion, especially on hillsides. It is now found in just about every state and most provinces, favoring dry meadows, roadsides, and waste places, and often appears in great numbers.

Waste places notwithstanding, the black-eyed Susan is one of our most beautiful common wildflowers, ranking 11th showiest in a 1940s poll of American and Canadian naturalists and botanists. But not everyone has been a fan. Nineteenth-century farmers in the East didn't like the newcomer befouling their fields. They spread reports that eating the plant could poison livestock such as sheep and hogs, though later experiments on the tall, or cutleaf, coneflower (*Rudbeckia laciniata*), long suspected by farmers of poisoning swine, found it caused little or no harm. In fact,

Gay's Beggar

John Gay (1685–1732), the English poet and songwriter who penned the lyrics to *"Black-eyed Susan,"* was also a playwright. His musical, *The Beggar's Opera* (1728), was such a success that it broke theatrical attendance records in England, where it was performed more than any other play during the 18th century.

Tiny Seeds

The black-eyed Susan produces abundant but tiny seeds. There are more than 1,700,000 of them to a pound.

Country Maids

Merry, laughing black-eyed Susans
grow along the dusty way,
Homely, wholesome, happy-hearted
little country maids are they.
Fairer sisters shrink and wither,
'neath the hot midsummer sun,
But these sturdy ones will revel till the
long, bright days are done.
Though they lack the rose's sweetness
and the lily's tender grace,
We are thankful for the brightness of
each honest, glowing face;
For in dry and barren places, where
no daintier blooms would stay,
Merry, laughing black-eyed Susans
cheer us on our weary way.
—Minnie Curtis Wait (1901)

the U.S. Department of Agriculture's *Range Plant Handbook* reported in 1937 that "in parts of Colorado and Wyoming, black-eyed Susan is accounted fair feed for cattle and fairly good for sheep, a condition which is probably directly associated with a paucity of better feed and may indicate locally impoverished soil conditions."

Chiefly because it's so widespread and pretty, black-eyed Susan has acquired many names. Among them are yellow daisy, golden Jerusalem, English bull's eye, brown betty, brown-eyed Susan, poorland daisy, and brown daisy.

Although *Rudbeckia hirta* has little history of use in herb medicine, American Indians such as the Chippewas employed tall coneflower (*R. laciniata*) to treat indigestion and burns. They called it *gizuswebigwais*, which means "it is scattering," perhaps a reference to its seeds or its tendency to multiply quickly in a field. Recent scientific research indicates that the black-eyed Susan has some antibiotic properties, and may be useful in treating staphylococcus infections and for increasing the body's ability to ward off other kinds of infections.

Easily Acquired

Black-eyed Susans are among our longest-lasting flowers, with the bright yellow rays remaining healthy for more than a month if the environment is right. The plants begin blooming in May or June, depending on how far north they are, and can still be flowering in October, if the weather remains mild enough.

They are easy to transplant. Despite their liking for dry sandy soils, their roots do not go too deep. Instead, they have many tiny rootlets that form a clump and that, by their sheer numbers, are able to collect enough moisture for the plant. Black-eyed Susans are biennials and self-sow readily. They favor sun all or most of the day.

In their first year, the plants usually display only a rosette of fuzzy leaves close to the ground. These leaves make and store enough food to send up the full-size, mature, flowering plants the next year. If you transplant, make certain you get some of the immature basal-leaf-only plants, too, so you won't have alternating flowerless years.

Though many people would consider the black-eyed Susan a weed, wildflower gardeners sometimes have trouble getting the plant to establish itself in their yards. Gardeners are either unaware that it is a biennial or they transplant it into rich soil. As the name "poorland daisy" suggests, black-eyed Susans thrive in poor soil.

Working with *Rudbeckia hirta*, American botanist Dr. A. F. Blakeslee (1874–1954) developed the Gloriosa daisy (*Rudbeckia tetra*), an annual hybrid that has become popular with gardeners. Perennial Rubeckias include the cultivars of *R. fulgida*, such as Goldsturm, Goldquelle, and Herbstsonne. Many are much larger than our wild *R. hirta* and wear such colors as mahogany, orange, red, and gold.

While many North Americans have waited till the development of hybrids to become interested in this genus, Europeans long ago imported the wild black-eyed Susans for their gardens, and still grow them. Who could fault their good taste?

Bindweeds

THE PRETTY STRANGLERS

Glory's cousins may be weeds, but they're still beautiful.

People see it and say it looks like a morning glory, but few know it by its common name. Yet from July into September, bindweed flowers can be found on vines climbing almost anything that's a few feet high—shrubs, fences, brush, fellow herbs, even garbage heaps. One of the most-viewed vines of any species in my hometown is a hedge bindweed that appears each year in a small evergreen hedge, surrounded by concrete and pavement, in front of the village post office. Everyone who goes to the post office sees and probably enjoys its flowers each summer, and no one has suggested that the weed be yanked.

Hedge bindweed, one of the most often-seen of the clan, bears large, bell-shaped flowers that may be pink streaked with white, or entirely white. The pink forms are particularly attractive. The "delicate pink flush is unequaled by the tint of many a highly cultivated flower," wrote F. Schuyler Mathews. In England, where flowers of hedge bindweeds are among the largest native blossoms, country girls used to weave wreaths of the blossoms for their hair. They often called the plant bearbind or bearbine and would sing:

> Thy brow we'll twine
> With white Bearbine
> And 'mid thy glossy tresses
> In sunny showers
> Its wand'ring flowers
> Shall wind their wild caresses.

However, British naturalist Marcus Woodward, noting that the flowers are short-lived like the morning glories, called them "the just emblem of fleeting joys."

The weedy hedge bindweed is closely related to the popular morning glory.

Glory's Cousin

It's no accident that hedge bindweed looks like a morning glory, for it's closely related to our common garden climbers, such as *Ipomoea purpurea* or *I. tricolor*, both natives of tropical America. Indeed, bindweed is often called wild morning glory, and it is a member of the small Morning Glory family

(Convolvulaceae), which has about a dozen North American genera. Some 28 species of bindweeds live in North America, and it is often difficult to tell them apart.

Hedge bindweed is found not only in North America but also in Europe, Asia, and Australia. It was long known as *Convolvulus sepium*, a scientific name literally meaning "entwining the hedge." Recently, the plant was reassigned to *Calystegia*, a genus of about 25 species worldwide called false bindweeds. They were found to differ enough from "true" bindweeds to warrant a genus of their own. However, most books continue to call them bindweeds rather than false bindweeds. "Hedge false bindweed," the official name, is now *Calystegia sepium*—*Calystegia* coming from the Greek, *kalyx*, a cup, and *stege*, a "covering"—descriptive of how the sepals clasp the base of the flowers.

The vines often climb the stems of plants, and while they don't feed on them they can choke some of the weaker hosts by "binding" the stem and strangling the plant. Moreover, the bindweed's roots form a deep, dense mass that tends to drain the food supply from the soil, starving out both host and neighboring plants.

In general, therefore, bindweed is not a wildflower that one would wish to introduce near a garden or important sensitive shrubs. It can, however, be an attractive vine on an otherwise dull fence or mixed into tall, weedy, and hardy plants like goldenrods.

Like other vines, hedge bindweed inches its way upward by "feeling" what's ahead. The tip of the plant turns round and round until it strikes an object. Then, by a method not fully understood by scientists but believed to involve hydraulic pressure changes, the vine stem winds around the discovered object and proceeds onward and usually upward, reaching 10 or more feet in length. In this way it rises above the masses to catch those all-important rays of the sun and to position its flowers high for passing insects to see.

Hedge bindweed turns its tip counterclockwise and away from the direction of the sun as it searches for a foothold, and winds that way once something is found. A botanist once discovered that if the plant is turned in another direction, it will die unless it can disengage itself and rewind in its natural, counterclockwise direction. Hedge bindweed is a rapid climber when compared with other vines, and the stem can describe a complete circle in less than two hours.

Insect Friends

"Every floral clock is regulated by the hours of flights of its insect friends," observed turn-of-the-20th century naturalist Neltje Blanchan. "When they have retired, the flowers close to protect nectar and pollen from useless pilferers," such as ants. Early in the summer, hedge bindweed blooms during the daylight hours when bees are active. However, an exception is nights with bright moonlight, when the flowers remain open and are visited by some species of Sphinx moths, Ms. Blanchan said. "In Europe," she wrote, "the plant's range is supposed to be limited to that of the crepuscular moth [named *Sphinx convolvuli* for its favored flower] and where that benefactor is rare, as in England, the bindweed sets few seeds; where it does not occur, in Scotland, this *Convolvulus* is

Underground Man

Ipomoea pandurata, a close North American relative of bindweeds, is called man-under-ground because its root system is said to be as large as a man. Weed expert Edwin Rollin Spencer reports that the plant can produce storage roots as long and as thick as a man's leg, and weighing up to 30 pounds! This huge root may reach down eight feet below the surface.

seldom found wild." Members of a related genus of southern Florida flowers, *Calonyction*, are called moon flowers or moon vines because they open in the evening to attract night-flying moths. (*Calonyction*, by the way, is Greek for "Good night!") Later in the season, when the plant has already produced a good deal of seed and nectar-thieves are not so great a concern, bindweed flowers stay open well into the night, even when the moon is not full.

In North America, hedge bindweed apparently relies more on bees than on moths for pollination. The flowers, especially pink ones, are attractive to bees that are guided into the narrow tubular nectary by the white stripes. The throat of the blossom is divided into five parts, and a cut-away of this area looks like the end of the barrel of a revolver.

Bindweeds, as well as other members of the Morning Glory family, play host to an unusual insect, the golden tortoise beetle (*Metriona bicolor*), which feeds on the leaves. According to Dr. Ralph B. Swain, an entomologist and author of *The Insect Guide*, the beetle can change the color of its shell from a dull reddish brown to a "glorious, glittering gold" in only moments. The glitter goes when the beetle dies, however, and the shell returns to a dull shade, much to the disappointment of beetle collectors.

William Hamilton Gibson, a 19th-century lecturer on natural history, said this beetle, which is quick and hard to catch, has several colors. "Nor is [the] golden sheen all the resource of the little insect; for in the space of a few seconds, as you hold him in your hand, he has become a milky iridescent opal, and now mother-of-pearl and finally crawls before you in a coat of dull orange." Ms. Blanchan said the insect looks like "a drop of molten gold climbing beneath bindweed's leaves."

In southern states another insect, the caterpillar of the yellow-banded wasp moth, is often found on bindweeds. In fact, it's so common on plants of the Morning Glory family that it has been named *Syntomeida ipomoeae*.

While hedge bindweed has made something of a pest of itself, the field bindweed (*Convolvulus arvensis*—"entwining the field"), has been even more hated. Found coast to coast, it creeps across farmers' fields, sinking roots that are even deeper and more difficult to eradicate than those of hedge bindweed. Roots of this plant have been found six or more feet deep. Field bindweed bears flowers that are smaller than hedge bindweed's, but they are equally pretty.

Many-Named and Useful

Being so common and widespread across three continents, hedge bindweed has picked up many folk names, among them lady's or old man's nightcap, hooded bindweed, bearbind (from the strength of its grip), great or greater bindweed (there's a "small bindweed"), bellbind, woodbind, pear vine, devil's vine, hedge lily, harvest lily, woodbine, creepers, and German scammony. Scammony, a name based on the Latin word for the herb, is a southern European member of the genus, used to produce a purgative widely sold in old apothecary shops. When *Convolvulus scammonia* wasn't available, *Calystegia sepium* was used instead.

Aunt Edith's Edict

"Hateful stuff—bindweed! Worst weed there is! Choking, entangling—and you can't get at it properly, runs along underground."
—Aunt Edith de Haviland, in *Crooked House* (1948) by Agatha Christie

While both scammony and hedge bindweed were used as purgatives in the Old World, jalap bindweed (*Ipomoea purga*), a native of Central and South America, was the chief ingredient in a New World purgative drug called jalap. Another tropical American species (*Merremia dissecta*, formerly *Convolvulus dissectus*) was used in the preparation of a Caribbean liquor, noyau. Still another, *C. rhodorhiza*, produced oil of rhodium, "which is so attractive to rats as to cause them to swarm to it without fear, even if held in the hand of a rat-catcher," Maude Grieve maintained. Oil of rhodium is also used by anglers as a fish attractant.

Of all the members of the genus, however, none is at once as useful and as popular as *Ipomoea batatas*, the tuberous-rooted bindweed. Though it is another tropical species, it often appears on dinner tables in North America, where it is well known as the sweet potato.

Deep Down

The bindweed roots pierce down
Deeper than men do lie
Laid in their dark-shut graves
Their slumbering kinsmen by.
—Walter de la Mare (1873–1956)

Deptford Pink

TINY BUT DIVINE

Deptford pink has popular relatives.

True pink is an uncommon color among autumn wildflowers in the northern United States and southern Canada. But one little grasslike plant, which begins its blooming season in late spring, is still popping pink blossoms well into October all across North America.

Deptford pink sounds English and, indeed, *is* British in origin. Named after the English town, now part of London, where it was once common, the plant was imported years ago, probably with grain or garden seeds. It has spread throughout the East as far west as the Mississippi, and out into Montana and the Pacific Northwest. Oddly enough, however, it is considered "rare" in its native England, according to *The Oxford Book of Wild Flowers,* and many British wildflower books don't even mention it. Here is yet another European immigrant that thrives in the freedom and wide-open spaces of North America.

Its scientific name is *Dianthus ameria.* Ameria is an ancient town in the Umbria region of Italy, where the plant must also be native. *Dianthus* is Greek for "divine flower," from *dios,* "god," and *anthos,* "flower." The name has caused some to wonder about the source; so heavenly a name, said one unappreciative writer, "hardly applies to these inconspicuous blossoms." However, the generic name was first used for one of Deptford pink's slightly larger siblings, *Dianthus caryophyllus,* which is found on limestone cliffs from southern Europe to China. Through centuries of complex cultivation, this small, five-petaled pink has been converted into the colorful, many-petaled carnations that fill bouquets and buttonholes, and that are among the most popular florist flowers ever created.

There are 200 species of *Dianthus,* some of them spectacular and all but one of them native to the Old World. A couple of European species, including *D. caryophyllus,* produce an oil used to enhance the scent of expensive perfumes. *Dianthus* is probably the biggest genus within the Pink family (Caryophyllaceae), of which there are around 30 genera and 600 species worldwide.

Deptford pink proves that pretty flowers don't need to be giants. This blossom is the size of a pinky fingernail.

Humble Surroundings

Those who would call Deptford pink "inconspicuous" probably have not really bothered to notice the flowers. To many, dandelions are inconspicuous—they are so common, they go unnoticed. But many writers tend to equate inconspicuous with small. While Deptford pink is certainly small, it's hardly inconspicuous.

Look at a blossom and you'll see five finely shaped petals, toothed at the ends, with delicate white dots near the center of the flower. The pink is pure and rich, and though the flower is small, the color always stands out like so many beacons in the humble surroundings this plant of waste places tends to frequent. No doubt, the flower's design helps to attract passing insects, whose eyes look for both color and patterns when hunting nectar. *Dianthus* species are supposed to be especially attractive and adapted to butterflies, though flies and beetles are said to visit them for their pollen.

Deptford pink makes up for its modest size with not only its bright color but also other attractive attributes. Its blooming season is among the longest of our wildflowers. Where I live, they are out from as early as June 20 until well into October. Several plants of Deptford pink, clustered together, can produce a dozen or more flowers at a time, making up in numbers and brightness what they lack in size.

In addition, Deptford pink decorates the so-called waste places of field guides, perhaps making them less of a waste. The plant takes to soil that most plants won't succeed in—dry, sandy earth in full hot sun, home also to the daisies, black-eyed Susans, and chicory in season. Interspersed with the white, yellow, and blue of these blossoms, the Deptford pink provides a lively contrast in color, and the company amplifies its pink.

Also called grass-pink because of its grasslike aspect, Deptford pink is easily transplanted in summer, but if you're willing to wait for next season, gathering seeds is easier. Since the plant is an annual, the seeds—little black dots like poppy seeds—are numerous throughout most of the season and have a good germination rate. They can be obtained by turning the dried, upright flower tubes into your palm and shaking out the contents.

Little packages can bring large joys. The appearance of these pink stars next year will reward the small effort of gathering a few seeds this year.

Without a Peer

And I will put the pink,
The emblem o' my dear,
For she's the pink o' womankind,
And blooms without a peer.
—Robert Burns (1759–1796)

The Great Field

"There is a little wilde creeping Pinke, which groweth in our pastures neere about London, and in other places, but especially in the great field next to Deptford, by the path side as you go from Redriffe to Greenwich."
—John Gerard (1633)

Milkweed

A SWEET GRABBER

Milkweed protects butterflies and entertains children.

Milkweeds are among the great toys of nature, known to almost any kid who grows up in the country. "The common milkweed needs no introduction," wrote naturalist F. Schuyler Mathews in 1894. "Its pretty pods are familiar to every child, who treasures them until the time comes when the place in which they are stowed away is one mass of bewildering, unmanageable fluff. Then there are vague talks about stuffing pillows and all that sort of thing; but the first attempt to manipulate the lawless airy down usually results in disastrous confusion, and whole masses go floating away on the slightest zephyr." He adds: "Of course, there is more fun in chasing milkweed down than in patiently stuffing a pillow; so the milkweed has its own way and goes sailing off to scatter its seeds hither and thither."

Alice Morse Earle had fond memories of milkweed in her 19th-century childhood. "That exquisite thing, the seed of milkweed, furnished abundant playthings," she wrote in *Old-Time Gardens.* "The plant was sternly exterminated in our garden, but sallies into a neighboring field provided supplies for fairy cradles with tiny pillows of silvery silk."

Wild Cotton

Bees visiting milkweed often become miniature Pony Express riders, complete with saddlebags.

The references to stuffing pillows were no joke. Both pillows and mattresses were filled with milkweed down from the Europeans' earliest settlement of North America. "The poor collect it and with it fill their beds, especially their children's, instead of feathers," wrote Peter Kalm in 1772. The silky hairs, or "pappus," gathered before the seam of the pod splits and spreads the seeds, were mixed with flax or wool, and woven to create a softer thread than either fiber yielded alone. Take a microscope, said Mr. Mathews, and "place some bits of white sewing silk beside [this] sheeny silk of Nature, and the former will look like a coarse white rope."

A 19th-century magazine article reported that milkweed's "chief uses were for beds, cloth, hats, and paper. It was found that from eight to nine pounds of the coma [seed hair] . . . occupied a space of from five to six cubic feet, and were sufficient for a bed. . . . A plantation containing 30,000 plants yielded from six to eight hundred pounds of coma." That seems an awful lot of plants and trouble to go through for about 100 mattresses, which may explain why milkweed mattresses are a thing of the past. However, during World War II, when all sorts of imported raw materials were in short supply, milkweed down was used extensively as a substitute for Asian kapoc in life preservers and for the linings of airmen's outfits. All these uses of the silky fluff have earned the plant such names as cottonweed, cottontree, silkweed, and wild cotton.

For a weed, this was a pretty handy plant in other ways. The French in Canada as well as some New Englanders in the 18th and 19th Centuries ate the tender shoots like asparagus. French Canadians also made a "very good, brown palatable sugar," according to one 18th-century author, by gathering and processing the flower heads in the early morning when they were covered with dew. Paper and even cloth could be made from the fiber in the stalks of the common milkweed (*Asclepias syriaca*). The fiber of swamp milkweed was so strong, it was made into twine and cord (see the chapter on butterflyweed, page 142). American Indians made dyes from the juice, and one modern expert on herbal dyes says milkweed can produce a wide range of colors. Rubber has been produced from the juice of various milkweed species, though commercial production has not been feasible.

American Indians made other good uses of milkweeds. Chippewas cut up and stewed the flowers of common milkweed, eating them like jam. They believed that consuming the flower-jam before a big meal would allow a person to eat more food than usual. The Sioux, or Dakotas, used to boil the tender young seed pods and eat them with buffalo meat. (Esclepain, a constituent of milkweeds, is supposed to be a good meat tenderizer.) Some Indians used the buds as food. Hopi mothers who were nursing ate milkweed to increase the flow of milk.

Incidentally, unless properly prepared, any part of the milkweed is bitter, and it may be poisonous. Cooking requires several changes of boiling water, and the water must be boiling when it comes in contact with the plant. Putting the plant parts in cold water and then turning on the heat will only serve to make them permanently unpalatable.

The root of *A. syriaca* has been used to treat typhoid fever, scrofula, and, in general, to help relieve inflammation of the lungs caused by a variety of ailments, especially asthma. Milkweed was imported to Europe by the early 17th century. Nicholas Culpeper, who called it swallow-wort, wrote, "the root, which is the only part used, is a counter-poison, both against the bad effects of poisonous herbs and the bites and stings of venomous creatures." As late as the 1930s, the tuberous roots of common milkweed could be sold to commercial concerns for six to eight cents a pound, about the same price paid at the time for butterflyweed, which was long listed as an official drug in the *U.S. Pharmacopoeia*.

It's no accident that the generic name, *Asclepias*, comes from Asclepius, the Greek hero of the medical arts. On the other hand, *syriaca*, meaning "of Syria," is probably an accident. This species is a native of America. Perhaps Linnaeus mistook the country of origin while classifying and naming the plant in 1753. Or perhaps the plant had already been imported to Syria for a crop experiment, and Linnaeus examined a specimen that had come from there. The rules of taxonomy require that the first name applied to a plant, even if based on mistaken assumptions, is the proper name. Some authorities haven't accepted this, preferring to use *Asclepias cornuti*, which was concocted in 1844. *Cornuti* means "horned," probably referring to the shape of the flower crowns.

Instant Bandage

The latex in milkweeds has led to an unusual medicinal use as an instant bandage. "The juice when applied to the skin forms a tough, adhesive pellicle [a thin film]," wrote Charles F. Millspaugh. "This has led to its use by the laity as a covering for ulcers and recent wounds. . . ."

North America can lay claim to 75 or more native species of milkweeds, some of them very difficult to tell apart. They represent more than half the known species in the world. *A. syriaca*, perhaps the most famous, is the type species for the genus and is found from Oregon and Saskatchewan and Kansas eastward, and down into the highlands of Georgia. The milkweed genus is in turn a member of the Milkweed family (Asclepiadaceae) of some 220 genera and more than 2,000 species, mostly tropical. In fact, only a half-dozen genera are found in North America. Several go by the name of milkweeds, though they are not of the *Asclepias* genus.

Milk Trap and Saddlebags

As the name suggests, milkweeds are known for their milk. In common milkweed, this white juice, which oozes out of the stems and leaves when broken, contains sugar, gum, fat, and other compounds. It is both acid and somewhat poisonous to animals. And it clots, like blood, soon after exposure to air.

Few creatures, including livestock and insects, will eat the plants because of the acrid fluid. What is more, since milkweed depends on flying insects for pollination, it doesn't want ants and other crawlers robbing its nectar supplies. When larger ants start creeping up the plant, tiny spikes in their feet pierce the green flesh, the flesh exudes the sticky fluid, and the fluid tangles up the ant's feet. As an ant struggles to clean off the goo, it gets even more glued and either becomes permanently stuck to the plant or falls off. No system, however, is perfect. I have seen small ants, probably light-footed enough to avoid breaking the skin, make it to the top and dine on the sweets.

To attract the kinds of insects they need, many milkweeds offer both color and extraordinarily sweet scent. The visitors are then given a little task to perform before obtaining their rewards. Although milkweeds come in various colors, common milkweed tends toward a hue that is difficult to describe—Mathews insists it's "lavender-brown"; Mrs. William Starr Dana says it's "dull purplish-pink"; Neltje Blanchan calls it "dull pale greenish purple-pink or brownish-pink"; Lawrence Newcomb describes it as "brownish pink or greenish purple"; and Roger Tory Peterson said it varies "in subtle shades of dusty rose, lavender, and dull brownish purple." Whatever the color, it and the strong sweet fragrance, attract a wide variety of bees, butterflies, and moths. Often a half-dozen insects will roam the umbels at one time. Once the insects have landed, the plant plays a reproductive trick.

Each flower has a slippery surface. When an insect lands, its feet slide around—often down between one of the five nectar-filled points in a flower's crown. If a foot gets briefly caught in a little slit, tiny pollen-coated devices, called pollinia, attach themselves. Ms. Blanchan said that these pollinia look like saddlebags, but they might also be likened to minuscule gnats with long amber wings. The pollinia drop off pollen as the insect visits other plants; eventually they fall away. If you watch closely as an insect crawls and often struggles around a freshly opened milkweed flower head, you may see one or several pollinia dangling from its legs.

Milkweed Thieves

Not all milkweeds are weedy. Efforts to reestablish the rare and threatened Mead's milkweed (*Asclepias meadii*) in prairie land east of the Mississippi were set back in June 1991 when the entire population of the plant was stolen from the Shawnee National Forest in Illinois. "This is a major setback for our cooperative efforts to reestablish the species east of the Mississippi River," said Forest Service chief F. Dale Robertson. The government offered a $5,000 reward for the arrest and conviction of the thieves.

Milkweed Pods

Little weavers of the summer,
With sunbeam shuttle bright,
And loom unseen by mortals,
You are busy day and night,
Weaving fairy threads as filmy
And soft as cloud swans, seen
In broad blue sky-land rivers,
Above earth's fields of green.
Your treasures you are hiding
In emerald velvet pouch,
You like no curious mortals
To gaze on them, I vouch;
But your woven fairy fabric
And magic spell concealed
In every tiny fibre
To nature's touch will yield.
The clasp of pouch unfastened,
Each tiny strand takes flight,
For they're surely downy feathers,
Of cloud swans soft and white,
That caught on sunbeams' shuttle,
Tho' you deftly wove with care,
Dame Nature has betrayed you, —
See, they're scattered on the air!
—Ray Laurance

It's hard to imagine a cleverer device for plant reproduction, and you must inspect a flower with a needle and magnifying glass to really appreciate it. Ms. Blanchan, a great admirer of the milkweed, said that "After the orchids, no flowers show greater executive ability, none [has] adopted more ingenious methods of compelling insects to work for them than milkweeds."

This system, like the sticky juice, is not perfect. Occasionally, bees, butterflies, and other insects can be found hanging dead from the flowers. Trapped in the pollinia-holding slit, they were attacked by spiders, ants, or beetles, or they were killed by heavy showers while struggling to get free.

The Butterflies

A few insects make use of the milkweeds in a different fashion. The caterpillars of the milkweed butterflies (*Danaidae*)—the most common of which is the orange-and-black monarch—feed on the leaves, usually in small enough quantity so as not to harm the host. The ingested acrid juice of the plant makes both the milkweed caterpillar and the subsequent butterfly distasteful to hungry birds. Some species of butterflies that are not milkweed eaters—such as the viceroy—mimic milkweed butterflies in color and design to take advantage of this strategy for survival.

Recent research has found that many common milkweeds contain potent, often poisonous, substances known as cardiac glycosides. Digitalis, a cardiac glycoside obtained from the foxglove, has been widely used to make heart muscles perform more efficiently after a heart failure. Various plants containing these substances have been used since ancient times to poison the tips of arrows. The glycosides in milkweed are strong enough to induce a heart attack in some grazing animals dumb enough to eat the bitter leaves.

It is probably these powerful cardiac glycosides that make monarchs unpalatable. Birds almost immediately become nauseous and vomit for up to a half hour after eating a monarch. After such an experience, most birds will simply bypass the monarch (and the look-alike viceroy). Some crafty birds, however, will catch a butterfly and sample a bit of a wing to see if it tastes bad, letting it go if it's a monarch. In Mexico and Central America, where our monarchs spend the winter, there are birds such as grosbeaks and orioles that have learned which parts of the monarch contain the smallest doses of poison and eat only those parts.

The monarch is the best known of the milkweed butterflies, recognized by almost every schoolchild and frequently seen fluttering around patches of milkweed. The monarch caterpillar lives most or all of its life on the plant and then constructs its bright green chrysalis under a leaf. Once the butterfly emerges, it feeds on the flower's nectar—a good reason for the caterpillar to refrain from overeating the host.

Survival

Milkweed uses the most convenient and available method of dispersing its seeds: wind. The seeds are topped with fuzz, or pappus, and breezes can carry these packages for miles. When the seeds land, they have a high rate of germination. Survival is also aided by the roots, which sink themselves deep in the earth and are hard to destroy. "Our milkweed is tenacious of life," wrote John Burroughs. "Its roots lie deep as if to get away from the plow." Moreover, common milkweed has a "mother plant," with the deepest roots, which sends out underground runners that sprout other plants nearby.

In some states milkweeds are considered field pests, hard to eradicate and a threat to stock. Farmers find it particularly annoying because few herbicides can harm it without repeated applications.

Many people would just as soon have a patch of milkweed. They are handsome plants, the flowers have a sweet scent (Mathews said too sweet), and the blossoms attract beautiful butterflies and sometimes hummingbirds. The French, in fact, imported them to their gardens in the 19th century. Many people have found the open dried pods attractive additions to dried flower arrangements or wreaths. The pods are sometimes gilded, and often the insides are painted in a bright color.

Because of the deep roots, successful transplantation of mature plants is difficult. Attempt it only with small offspring of the mother plant in the spring. Better yet, grab a few pods in late August or September and plant seeds in fairly dry soil that gets plenty of sunlight. Seeds may be planted in the fall or spring.

There are many varieties of milkweed, and some others should be mentioned. The swamp milkweed (*A. incarnata*), which is widespread from the Rockies eastward, was once commonly used as a source of fiber for twine and cord. While smaller and less fragrant than those of common milkweed, its flowers are more beautiful. The specific name means "flushed with pink," but the color is often deeper—purplish red or magenta. It can be planted in gardens with moist soils. Also rich in color is purple milkweed (*A. purpurascens*), common from the Plains eastward. Four-leaved milkweed (*A. quadrifolia*), unusual in that it favors shady forests instead of sunny fields, swamps, or roadsides, has pretty pink to lavender flowers. It, too, is found eastward of the Plains. A variety so red that it's called bloodflower (*A. curassavica*—"of Curacao") is common in the Gulf coastal states and in southern California. White-stemmed milkweed (*A. albicans*) favors the dry rocky deserts of the Southwest, while the showy milkweed (*A. speciosa*), with big, starlike, pinkish flowers, is found in a wide range of terrains from the central United States and Canada to British Columbia and California.

There is also the bright orange butterflyweed, a variety so handsome and interesting that it gets a chapter of its own (see the next chapter).

Teamwork

Two milkweed butterflies—the monarch and the queen—as well as the viceroy butterfly are all unpalatable and examples of "Müllerian mimicry." Named for German zoologist Fritz Müller, who proposed the theory, Müllerian mimicry might be considered a form of natural teamwork. Although unrelated, the three butterflies have developed similar appearances that warn other animals not to eat them. Thus, if a bird should sample any one of the species, it will avoid all three in the future.

Butterflyweed

A NEGLECTED BEAUTY

A source of both medicine and textiles, butterflyweed brightens gardens, too.

Orange is a fairly uncommon color among wildflowers, and butterflyweed makes use of it in spectacular fashion.

It's not shaped like a butterfly, nor does it act like a weed. Nonetheless, "butterflyweed" is certainly an improvement over "pleurisy root" as a name for this handsome wildflower.

Asclepias tuberosa, in fact, has many names, a couple of them just as unattractive as pleurisy root: fluxroot (in medicine, a "flux" is a fluid discharge from the body) and chigger flower (the little biting mites are a similar color). It's also called white root, wind root, Canada root, orange root, Indian posy, swallowwort, and yellow milkweed. Of course, a plant with a striking flower and many purported medicinal uses is bound to collect many names.

And yet, despite such recognition, butterflyweed has strangely been ignored by many fancy-flower fans, whose gardens would be much enlivened by its long-lasting, summertime color. At the 1876 United States Centennial Exhibition in Philadelphia, a bed of these flowers stirred considerable interest. Oddly enough, though the plant is a native of North America, the exhibited specimens had been grown in Holland and shipped over for the show. "Truly," wrote Mrs. William Starr Dana 20 years later, "flowers, like prophets, are without honor in their own country."

In *The Floral Kingdom*, published in 1877, Cordelia Harris Turner bemoaned the fact that butterflyweed was a "neglected beauty" and predicted that it "will no doubt one day be extensively cultivated in and out of doors, as its perennial roots, besides its native attractiveness, will specially recommend it."

Mrs. Turner was a good judge of beauty, but a poor prophet. Today butterflyweed is found in few gardens and fewer homes, though it's hard to find a more beautiful and decorative flower. The bright, rich orange is as striking a color as can be found in a wildflower, and a yellow variant that sometimes appears is just as brilliantly hued. The color and design earned butterflyweed enough votes in a 1940s poll of naturalists and scientists to rank it as the fourth most showy wildflower in North America.

Significant Medicine

Enough praise for the plant's appearance; butterflyweed has a long history of practical uses. An American Indian mound in Ohio, with remains dating from 700 B.C. to A.D. 1000, as well as excavations in the Pueblo region of the Southwest, contained textiles of butterflyweed fiber, which was used for cloth, rope, and string. In fact, even today, some Indians of the Rio Grande region make rope and string from the plant. According to the U.S. Department of Agriculture, it takes about five stalks to produce enough fiber to create one foot of cord.

However, among most Indian nations throughout much of North America, butterflyweed was best known as a source of medicine. Its thick root was used to treat various illnesses, such as pleurisy and rheumatism. The Delawares gave it to mothers after childbirth to help them produce milk, and Appalachian tribes employed it to induce vomiting. Penobscots treated colds with it, and the Menominees and many others used it for all sorts of skin injuries, pressing the pulverized fresh root or blowing the powdered dry root into the wound.

Butterflyweed became a significant medicine among American physicians in the late 19th century, when it was widely used as an expectorant and to treat smallpox. The rootstock was considered a major ingredient in at least a half-dozen medicines listed in the *U.S. Pharmacopoeia*, the official catalogue of acceptable drugs, from 1820 until 1905. In 1892, Charles F. Millspaugh said it had received more attention as a medicine than any of the milkweeds, and listed at least 14 uses, including treatment of dyspepsia, indigestion, dysentery, and eczema. According to John B. Lust, a modern naturopathy expert, the root has been recommended for colds, flu, and bronchial and pulmonary problems.

The monarch butterfly caterpillar loves milkweeds, such as butterflyweed. The larva eats the leaves and makes its chrysalis on the plant. The resulting butterfly drinks the nectar and lays its eggs on the leaves.

The Physician Asclepius

Milkweeds in general are so noted for their medicinal properties that their generic name recalls Asclepius, a mythical son of Apollo who was called the first great physician. Asclepius was so well loved by his patients that they eventually worshipped him as a god and erected temples to honor him. Asclepius, however, put beds in the temples and converted them into the first hospitals. As he visited patients, he carried a staff on which sacred serpents were wrapped. The serpents knew all the secrets of the earth and told him cures for diseases. Today this staff, called the caduceus, is the symbol of the medical profession.

According to Greek mythology, Asclepius became so good at his art that he could bring the dead back to life. He thereby incurred the jealousy and wrath of the gods, and Zeus eventually incinerated him with a thunderbolt. So much for pleasing the boss with good deeds.

Beloved

"The butterflyweed . . . is so named from the fact that it is beloved by butterflies. When the fritillaries are on the wing, one may often take a dozen specimens with one sweep of his net over a blooming plant of this species."
—Willard N. Clute, 1942

Fiber Feats

"A Sierra Miwok feather skirt or cape contained about 100 feet of cordage made from approximately 500 plant stalks, while a deer net 40 feet in length . . . contained some 7,000 feet of cordage, which would have required the harvesting of a staggering 35,000 plant stalks."
—*Michelle Stevens, Butterfly Milkweed (U.S. Department of Agriculture)*

Most parts of the butterflyweed are poisonous to some degree. Nonetheless, Indians of the West boiled the roots, possibly thereby removing the poisonous quality, and served the tubers as food. The Sioux made a sort of sugar from the flowers, and young seedpods were boiled with buffalo meat. Certain Canadian tribes were said to boil and eat the young shoots like asparagus.

Its common name comes from its ability to attract butterflies—indeed, the Delawares called the plant by a name that meant "where butterflies light." The bright, nectar-rich flowers attract many colorful species, including milkweed-loving monarchs, swallowtails, sulphurs, coppers, hairstreaks, and fritillaries, in addition to a wide selection of bees and other insects. (The relationship of monarchs and milkweeds is discussed in the chapter on milkweeds; see page 137.)

Found from New England to Florida and west to Colorado, Arizona, and southern California, butterflyweed blooms from mid- to late June in warmer parts of the country and in July in northern areas. The blossoms, which can last well into August and are among the longest-living of the wildflowers, are almost identical in form to their milkweed siblings. However, the brilliance of the orange makes the clusters or umbels glow like torches in a field on a summer's day, unlike the less bright purple, red, or white flowers of most milkweeds.

Finding Plants

The plants are from two to three feet tall with fuzzy, many-leaved stems. They thrive in full sun, with well-drained soils—preferably sandy and not too fertile. Thanks to their deep taproot, which burrows far under the ground for water, they can withstand long dry spells.

I have planted and spread hundreds of seeds over the years but have had no success in getting any to sprout in my yard, where they are probably eaten by birds and small rodents, and where my soil may be too rich for them. However, friends who start the seeds indoors have had better luck, and the U.S. Department of Agriculture says the plants are easily grown from seeds, which are "very viable." Sow them in the fall.

Acquiring butterflyweed plants from the wild—they often grow in waste places—is tricky because of that deep taproot. Take care to dig deeply to obtain as much of the thick white tuber as possible. Better yet, try to collect smaller, younger plants; they are more apt to survive because the roots are less deep and less likely to be broken in digging. Water the transplants well and you'll wind up with years of summertime orange—and plenty of butterflies.

Clovers

UBIQUITOUS AND USEFUL

Clovers help feed—and beautify—the world.

In summer, it seems that hardly a square yard of open ground lacks at least one member of the clover family. Although most of these plants weren't even here a few centuries ago, clovers have become so common and widespread that most flower fans don't even notice them, much less consider them worth noticing. Yet, observed close up or in large masses, many clovers are attractive flowers—some are even spectacular. Moreover, many have been of immeasurable value to farmers through the ages, and without the clovers, there would be many unhappy bees and a far poorer quality of honey than we now enjoy.

New Zealanders soon found out that without bumblebees to provide pollination, red clover won't set seed.

The word *clover* comes from *clava*, the three-pronged club used by Hercules in some of his Twelve Labors. All forms of clover are, of course, noted for their three-lobed leaves, a trait possessed by most members of the Pea family (and reflected in the "clubs" suit of cards). The weapon of the greatest hero of the Greeks and the strongest man of their mythology is somewhat symbolic of the fame and strength of these plants. Most were imported from Europe by farming settlers who knew the plants' value not only as a food for horses, cattle, and other domestic animals, but also as a soil regenerator.

The roots of the clover and many other members of the Pea family have nodules that play host to *Rhizobium* bacteria, which help to increase usable nitrogen in the soil and in the plant. Although 78 percent of our atmosphere is pure nitrogen, plants can't take this essential nutrient directly from the air. However, the bacteria convert the atmospheric nitrogen, found in tiny pockets of air in the soil, into ammonium, a nitrous substance the plant can absorb and use. This is a two-way, symbiotic relationship; in return, the bacteria obtain sugars created by the plant. Farmers frequently plant clover in poor soil to enrich its nitrogen content and growing capacity. Once the plant has finished its season—or its life if it's an annual—the farmer can simply churn it into the soil, providing further enrichment as a green manure. Because of their popularity for such uses, imported species have spread to almost every corner of temperate North America—and many other parts of the world.

Rare Future Food?

One of the rarest native clovers, running buffalo clover (*Trifolium stoloniferum*) was once thought to be extinct, but by 1984 tiny populations were rediscovered in West Virginia and later in Ohio and Indiana. In 1987, it was declared federally endangered. Today, more populations have been found, and some scientists are actually looking into its cultivation as a forage crop. The reason? Running buffalo clover has more leaves and thus more protein than do similar species, plus it's a perennial and doesn't need to be reseeded annually as most of the imports do.

Under Attack

If you think your life is tough, consider the red clover, susceptible to at least 45 different diseases, with names like bacterial leaf spot, Sclerotinia crown and root rot, leaf gall, dagger nematodes, red clover cryptovirus, and witches' broom virus. The last is so called because it produces a brushlike growth on the plant.

The Pea Family

The Pea family consists of nearly 500 genera and 15,000 species worldwide, including indigos, trefoils, alfalfas, medics, vetches, wild beans, soy beans, peanuts, and, of course, peas themselves. True clovers, called *Trifolium* because of their three leaflets, include at least 275 species worldwide.

Nearly 100 trifoliums are known in North America, but most occur in the western half of the continent. Only 20 or so clovers can be found in the East, and most of them are aliens. Though they may not be as common or widespread as the imports, the natives have many varieties. Among the most beautiful is the orange buffalo clover, which occurs throughout the central United States from Canada to the Gulf of Mexico. Some of the prettiest natives, both common and rare, live along the West Coast. And some natives are very limited in range. One variety, the threatened Kate's Mountain Clover (*Trifolium virginicum*) is found only in sparsely vegetated shale barrens in few mountainous locations in West Virginia, Virginia, Pennsylvania, and in one place in Maryland.

Most clovers have bushy, globe-like clusters of white, yellow, purple, or red tubular flowers and the namesake three-lobed leaves. Some species have the occasional tendency to produce four or more lobes, whence the four-leaf clovers that some people treasure. The leaves in many species, incidentally, close up at night, a habit more commonly found in flowers than in their greenery, and one apparently designed to help keep morning dew off the "stomata" (the openings on the underside of the leaf through which "transpiration"—the plant's form of breathing—takes place).

Buxom Rural Things

Clover is a kind of flower most appreciated in quantity. John Burroughs expressed it this way:

> Summer always comes in the person of June, with a bunch of daisies on her breast and clover blossoms in her hand. A new chapter in the season is opened when these flowers appear. One says to himself: "Well, I have lived to see the daisies again, and to smell the red clover." One plucks the first blossoms tenderly and caressingly. What memories are stirred in the mind by the fragrance of the one and the youthful face of the other! There is nothing else like that smell of clover. It is the maidenly breath of summer; it suggests all fresh, buxom, rural things, a field of ruddy blooming clover, dashed or sprinkled here and there with the snow-white of the daisies; its breath drifts into the road when you are passing; you hear the booming bees, the voice of bobolinks, the twitter of swallows, the whistle of woodchucks; you smell wild strawberries; you see the cattle upon the hills; you see your youth, the youth of a happy farm-boy, rise before you.

Burroughs was probably unaware that he was recording history when he wrote those words. The pastoral settings he describes are becoming rarer almost daily, as parts of the United States and Canada become less agrarian, and once-farmed fields turn to lawns or shopping centers, or revert to woodlands. Even where farming is still strong, there is more reliance today on chemicals to do the jobs that nature—including plants like clover—once did.

Yet old-fashioned fields can still be found, and the air over the flowers in them is full of bumblebees, honeybees, and butterflies, dipping and rising as they visit clover blossoms amid daisies, milkweeds, fleabanes, St. Johnsworts, wild carrots, and other summertime field flowers.

The nectar-filled tubes of red clover (*Trifolium pratense*) are designed for the larger bumblebees, which can easily open their the tubes and reach down for a drink, picking up pollen along the way. Except for the long-tongued butterflies—robbers who don't pollinate—virtually no other insect except the bumblebee can reach the nectar of the red clover.

Clovers rely very heavily on bees for survival. Experiments have been conducted in which netting was stretched across a patch of white clover (*T. repens*) to keep away bees, with the result that the plants produced only one-tenth the normal quantity of seeds. More dramatic was the experience of the New Zealanders who imported red clover seeds for fodder and had a bumper crop of it the first season. But there were no bumblebees in New Zealand, and the entire crop failed to set seed for the next year. Realizing the problem, the New Zealanders imported fewer than 100 bumblebees and within a decade were producing $1 million worth of red clover seeds annually, an example of the power of a symbiotic relationship.

Relying so heavily on bees for pollen transfer in the face of competition from so many other kinds of summer flowers, clovers—particularly white clover—have evolved an especially attractive nectar. Said to have a sugar content of over 40 percent, the liquid is so sweet that children used to pick and suck the blossoms. Burroughs describes the white clover as "the staple source of supply of the finest quality of honey," adding that celebrated European honeys "can hardly surpass our best products." Shakespeare called clovers "honey-stalks" and wrote:

> I will enchant old Andronicus
> With words more sweet, and yet more dangerous,
> Than baits to fish, or Honey-stalks to sheep.

Red clover, while also full of sweets, attracts its visitors with the help of its scent and its color, shades of red being especially attractive to bumblebees.

Wildlife, too, has taken kindly to imported crop clovers. At least 50 species of birds and mammals feed on their foliage and seeds. Clovers constitute as much as 25 percent of the diet of such fowl as the ruffed grouse, prairie chicken, and mountain quail, and such mammals as marmots and woodchucks.

Coming with the May

Crimson clover I discover
By the garden gate,
And the bees about her hover,
But the robins wait.
Sing, robins, sing,
Sing a roundelay,
'Tis the latest flower of spring
Coming with the May.
—Elaine Goodale Eastman
    (1863–1953)

Eat Me!

Farmers used to say that an acre of clover would produce as much food for horses and cattle as four acres of grass. Red clover was once a leading hay crop and is still valued for its high protein and mineral content as well as its ability to revitalize fields. A few years ago, two million bushels of seed were being grown annually, mostly in Illinois.

Mooo!

Red clover is the official state flower of Vermont. The state insect is the honeybee, the red clover's biggest fan and pollinator. And the state seal depicts a cow, whose favorite food is clover.

The Real Thing

One of North America's more unusual businesses is the Clover Specialty Company of St. Petersburg, Florida. The company, founded in 1939, raises four-leaf clovers for a variety of products, including clocks, jewelry, key chain tags, and cards. Clover Specialty grows white clover (*Trifolium repens*) plants, which, through selective propagation over 60 years, yield a higher than normal rate of four-leaf clovers—about one-tenth of 1 percent of the leaves are quadrifoil. The company prides itself in producing natural four-leaf clovers, noting that some "genetically altered" varieties are being sold.

While many plants have defenses to prevent them from being eaten, red and other clovers have evolved greens that are flavorful to grazing animals, apparently so they *will* be eaten. Being annuals, clovers must make certain their seeds are spread. They offer themselves—the entire plant, including seeds—as food for deer, cows, rabbits, and other herbivores that will later deposit the seeds in a mass of fertilizer. The seeds are especially thick-shelled, able to go through a mammal's or a bird's digestive system without being destroyed.

Not all feeders are welcome, however. Some clovers, such as white clover, have cells in their leaves containing two chemical compounds that, when combined, produce small amounts of cyanide. A slug eating a leaf will break open the cells, causing the chemicals to mix and create the distasteful chemical. Cyanide is also poisonous to plants, so white clover must store the ingredients separately.

Perhaps the cyanide "flavoring" has kept clovers from being very popular with human palates. Few authorities on edible wild plants promote clover. One suggested it may cause bloating while another reports it's hard to digest. However, the greens have been used in salads, and the dried flowers and seeds can be ground into flour. In times of famine, clovers have been eaten raw and boiled, and the flour has been used to make bread. Since the flowers are so high in nectar content, it's not surprising that they have been used to make wine.

Clover Types

Among the most prominent of our clovers, red clover is also called purple, meadow, honeysuckle, or broadleaf clover, as well as marlgrass, cowgrass, sugar plums, and knap. It stands up to two feet tall and produces deep red or purplish blossoms an inch or more around. It is interesting to watch bees move around a field of these flowers. The insects need to come no closer than a half an inch or so from a blossom before their sense of smell tells them whether previous visitors have cleaned out its nectar. Usually, the most attractive blossoms in full bloom are bypassed by bees, which seek out the freshly opened tubes of newer, less showy, but more food-filled heads.

Trifolium pratense (literally, "three leaves of the meadow") is the type species for the genus, and blooms coast to coast from May until November along roadsides and wood edges, as well as in fields. Since it is a crop plant, it is also widely sold commercially under such varietal names as Arlington, Flare, Cherokee, Kenland, Kenstar, Reddy, Redland, and Redman.

Alsike, or Alsatian, clover (*T. hybridum*) may reach three feet, making it one of our taller clovers. It bears flowers that mix cream and deep pink florets such that the heads, often flat-topped, are striking in their brilliance, especially if you happen across a little colony of them on a sunny summer day. Sometimes called Swedish clover, this variety was imported as a popular fodder crop and blooms throughout much of the growing season in much of North America.

White clover (*T. repens*, meaning "creeping") is the common clover found in lawns that haven't been poisoned with herbicides. Also called Dutch clover because it is native to northwestern Europe, white clover is particularly favored by bees and has long been used as a feed for livestock, even though the leaves can release some cyanide. White clover is also the kind on which you're most apt to find those coveted four-leaf clovers. But you may also find five or six leaflets—even nine. The fascination with four-leaf clovers is said to hark back to the times when anything in nature that bore the shape of Christ's cross was considered sacred or magical. Even the three-leaf form had its own religious significance, having been used, perhaps first by St. Patrick, as a symbol of the Holy Trinity ("three persons in one God").

The least hop, or suckling, clover, often called shamrock, bears the scientific name *T. dubium*. *Dubium* means "doubtful," indicating that it was uncertain at the time of its naming (1794) whether it was really a separate species. The name is still official, so the namer was probably correct. A European native now found throughout the United States and southern Canada, the least hop clover bears small yellow blossoms with from 3 to 20 florets per head as opposed to the 40 or more found on the other species. Some say it is the true shamrock used by St. Patrick for his religious instruction.

Rabbit's foot clover (*T. arvense*, "of cultivated fields") is an unusual but common variety. Also called dogs and cats, pussies, hare's foot, or pussy clover, it has cylindrical gray and pink heads that are fuzzy like a rabbit's foot, making it a favorite of children. It inhabits waste places in most parts of North America except the Southwest, blooming in midsummer.

Varieties of the genus *Melilotus* ("honey lotus") are called sweet clovers, although they are not true *Trifolium* clovers. Both white sweet clover (white melilot) and yellow sweet clover (yellow melilot) are tall—to 10 feet—bushlike plants with the typical pea-like flowers and elongated three-part leaves. Both have been used, dried and hanging, to sweeten rooms with their scent. One of their chemical constituents, cumarin, is purported to be the same substance that flavors vanilla, a member of the Orchid family. This sweetness has led to the use of the flowers in their native Europe to flavor snuff, pipe tobacco, and even Gruyère cheese. The flowers have also been an ingredient in a popular salve for skin sores. Both sweet clovers, which flower in June and July, are common throughout North America.

Clover flowers can take unusual forms, such as this hop clover, so called because they look like the cones of a hops plant.

True clovers have little history of medicinal uses. A tea from red clover was once used to treat whooping cough and other bronchial ailments, and some people enjoy the tea simply as a beverage, though they may add mint or other flavorings to liven it up. The plants have been credited with mystical powers in ages past. For example, witches were supposed to shun clover leaves, and all sorts of good luck—or even bad luck—was said to befall those who found clovers bearing more than the usual number of leaflets. Dreaming of clover is supposed to bring good fortune.

Sweet dreams!

Jewelweed

NATURE'S SALVE AND TOY

Soothing jewelweed feeds the hummingbirds and, unfortunately, the deer.

The dangling flowers of the jewelweed are popular with hummingbirds.

"Hey, Dad, wanna look for poppers?"

When he was three or four years old, my son asked that question several times during the summer. Since he had been barely able to walk, Ben had hunted "poppers" in our backyard, and later his younger brother, Mike, joined in the quest for these entertaining toys of nature.

Poppers, a word coined by Ben, are the energetic little pods of the jewelweed. The seeds are wrapped in an ingenious case that, when mature and disturbed, suddenly "pops" as the covering lets go like an uncoiling spring. The action sends the seeds flying as far as four or five feet. No wonder the plant is also known as touch-me-not, and no wonder it is so widespread.

Some people say jewelweed is so called because the colorful orange flowers dangle like earrings or pendants from the plant. Others say it refers to those coil-fired seeds. Still others say it's because the edges of the leaves, when wet with dew or rain, hold tiny drops of water that look like "scintillating gems, dancing, sparkling in the sunshine" to Neltje Blanchan.

"It is, indeed, a jewel," said William Hamilton Gibson. "Upon the approach of twilight each leaf droops as if wilted, and from the notches along its edge the crystal beads begin to grow, until its border is hung full with its gems. It is Aladdin's lantern that you set among a bed of these succulent green plants, for the spectacle is like a dream land."

Poison Ivy

Jewelweed is most famous as a balm to relieve the itching caused by poison ivy. I've found that it both relieves the itch and helps to clear up the rash, and many others have had equally good results. It is also supposed to prevent the rash from breaking out if you've touched the plant, apparently by attacking and dissolving poison ivy's oil before it can adhere long enough to cause blistering.

If you have a good supply of jewelweed in the yard, simply rub freshly picked leaves or, better, crushed stalks on the irritation. Ironically, jewelweed is often found growing with or near poison ivy, since both plants like similar situations—semishade and rich, moist soil.

Various American Indian tribes put the plant to extensive use as a skin salve, treating such things as athlete's foot and other fungi, and all sorts of itches in general. For the Nanticokes of Delaware, the leaves also served as a poultice for wounds. Colonial Americans used the juice of the jewelweed to dye wool yellow, and ate the leaves as a pot herb.

Hummingbird Heaven

Though people with the itch have long been fans of jewelweed, its biggest admirer is the ruby-throated hummingbird, which thrives on these flowers in midsummer. In fact, nature—more precisely, evolution—has designed the flowers to be pollinated by the bill of the hummingbird, which picks up the grains of white pollen from just inside the top front of one flower and deposits them on the inside top of the next.

Bumblebees, which also frequent these flowers, rarely pollinate them and cannot reach all the way back to collect all of the nectar. Some bees and wasps of sneaky bent will chew through the back of the flower to rob the nectar without even coming near the pollen. Consequently, it's not unusual to see little holes in the flowers.

In many places hummingbirds are not common. In such cases jewelweed can rely on its cleistogamous flowers to produce viable seeds without pollination. In fact, Charles Darwin discovered that in England, where this native American was introduced, only about 1 in 20 plants even bothers to put out showy flowers; there are no hummingbirds there, and bees are unlikely to pollinate the flowers there. This two-flower characteristic of the jewelweed led to its former specific name, *Impatiens biflora.*

Impatiens is a genus of succulent herbs that has about 10 other native members in North America, and more than 200 species worldwide, mostly in the mountains of Africa and Asia. The spotted jewelweed may be found in most states east of the Rockies, and in the Pacific Northwest to Alaska. Among the more common of the other species is the pale touch-me-not (*Impatiens pallida*), which favors northern climes and is common in southern Canada. The genus, in turn, belongs to the tiny Touch-Me-Not family (Balsaminaceae), which includes only one or two other genera.

Pick a Name

Jewelweed's most commonly used scientific name is misleading, and several other names have been employed right up to modern times. For more than 150 years, spotted jewelweed was known in most botanical circles as *Impatiens biflora.* The generic name is an allusion to the easily triggered seedpods, as if they were impatient to do their job. Several authors refer to the plant as *I. fulva*, a name that dates from 1818 and describes the tawny color, while some have used *I. nolitangere* ("don't touch!"). The current official name, however, is *Impatiens capensis.* The specific name here has the meaning, "of the Cape of Good Hope."

Magic Jewels

She brooks no condescension
From mortal hand, you know,
For, touch her e'er so gently,
Impatiently she'll throw
Her tiny little jewels,
Concealed in pockets small
Of her dainty, graceful garment,
And o'er the ground they fall.
Her tiny magic jewels
May be a fairy's gift,
For scattered by the brookside
They soon small leaflets lift.
What mortal knows the secrets
Of Flora's children shy,
Concealed in field and meadow,
That with the flowers die?
—Ray Laurance

Jewelweed Lotion

To make a jewelweed solution for poison ivy, pick leaves, stems, stalks, flowers—any part of the plant—and put them in a large pot with enough water to cover the vegetation. Stuff in as much as you can fit. Boil the plants until the color of the water becomes deep orange. This may take a half hour to an hour, depending on how much vegetation you have in the pot. Bottle and refrigerate the liquid. Freezing will preserve the decoction for long periods. When you have a case of poison ivy, just spread the fluid on the irritated area.

Why would botanists, who had a perfectly good name in *Impatiens biflora*, use one recalling the southern tip of Africa more than 8,000 miles from the plant's homeland? The Brooklyn Botanic Garden provided the answer: "The name *I. capensis* was published by Meerburgh in 1775, 13 years earlier than Walter's *I. biflora*. It has priority of publication and is therefore the correct name. Meerburgh described it from material cultivated in European gardens. He mistakenly thought it had been introduced from the Cape of Good Hope. The International Code of Botanical Nomenclature, in the interests of stability, does not permit changes in the specific epithet merely on the grounds that it is 'inappropriate.' Thus, *Impatiens capensis* remains the correct name."

Plants of the *Impatiens* genus have picked up folk names like silver-leaf, speckled jewels, silverweed, silver cap, slipperweed, ladies'-slipper (from the slipper-like shape of the flower), snapweed, quick-in-the-hand, ear-jewel, pocketdrop (as in a watch fob), ladies' ear-drop, wild or brook celandine, solentine, snapdragon, shining-grass, cowslip, weather-cock (pods burst in the wind and leaves wilt in the hot sun), kicking-colt, and wild balsam (the old-fashioned balsam of 19th-century gardens is in the same genus, though the flowers are completely different in shape). According to 18th-century botanist Peter Kalm, American Indians called it "the crowing cock" because of its shape.

Names like silverweed and shining-grass come from an interesting characteristic of the plant. If you turn a leaf upside down and dip it in water, it will take on a silvery or shiny appearance, probably because some coating on the surface holds a thin film of air.

It "Evaporates"

Jewelweed's blooming season in the Northeast is generally from mid-July through mid-September, although in years with mild winters, flowers—both showy and cleistogamous—will be out in middle to late June. The plants quickly wilt and die at the first appearance of cold weather; in fact, anything below 40 degrees Fahrenheit seems to do them in. Because such a high percentage of this succulent plant is water, once jewelweeds die, they quickly dry up and there is virtually no sign of them a few weeks later, almost as if they had evaporated.

It's no surprise then that jewelweed likes moist ground and is especially common around streams and woodland ponds, although it will sometimes spread into fairly dry shaded areas where its growth will be stunted. In ideal conditions, plants will grow almost five feet tall, even though the roots are short, relatively thin, and would seem to be unable to support such height in a plant. The trick is its hollow stem, a design at once lightweight and strong.

Although its root systems are not extensive, it is somewhat difficult to transplant jewelweed. If you want to try it, use small, young plants and put them in a wet, loose mulch. The best way to introduce jewelweed is by seeds, which you literally catch. Cup your hand around the quarter-inch pod and touch it. This will cause the pod to explode and shoot the seeds into your hand. Only the mature pods will pop, but it won't take you long to recognize which ones are apt to be ready to fly. Place the seeds into moist ground. If you do it early enough, the plant could mature and produce more seeds in the same season.

A Warning

Be forewarned, however. Once, after I had written a newspaper column about jewelweed, I quickly heard from an irate wildflower gardener who cursed the existence of the plant, which had overrun some of her nicest flowers. Indeed, jewelweed is a mover and a rabbit-like reproducer, so keep it in areas where it won't spread into your finer flowers.

The plant can be fairly easily eradicated if it becomes a pest. Just pull it out of the ground before it goes to seed; the small and shallow root system is easy to extract.

Ironically, two changes in ecology, particularly in the Northeast, are making jewelweed harder to find. The widespread invasion of garlic mustard, a spring plant that favors the same territory as jewelweed (see page 37), tends to push out young jewelweed plants. Yet jewelweed plants that live in places free of garlic mustard face becoming food for the vast herd of white-tailed deer. Twenty-five years ago, my backyard was literally bordered with jewelweed plants in late summer. Today, only a handful of plants appears in pockets near the house, where the deer fear to tread. Since jewelweed is so popular with hummingbirds, I wonder what the effect of the declining plant population will be on these birds, which use jewelweed to fatten up in late summer for their flight south.

If you are deer-free, jewelweed makes a nice annual hedge and mixes well with such wetland flowers as blue flags, nightshades, asters, and certain woodland sunflowers, which are not intimidated by jewelweed's numbers. They may attract wildfowl to your yard, for ruffed grouse, ring-necked pheasant, prairie chickens, and bobwhite quail all enjoy the seeds. And, of course, it's always handy to have around for first aid in case you run into some of that all-too-common but often unnoticed poison ivy.

Black Cohosh

CANDLES OF THE FAIRIES

Black cohosh is the bane of some bugs, but not others.

This photo shows why fairy candles may be a more appropriate name than black cohosh.

Summer is the time of glory for the showy wildflowers of open fields. The woodlands, where flowers show their splendor in the spring, are almost void of blossoms by midsummer. So it's often surprising, even to someone familiar with wildflowers, to run across the black cohosh brightly blooming in the shade of a deciduous wood in July and August. Although few American Indian names for plants are still in common use, *cohosh* is believed to come from a New England Algonquin word meaning "pointed." *Co-os* meant "pine tree," and *cohosh* probably refers to the spikes of flowers. Anyone who has ever seen its tall, furry, white racemes of flowers will know instantly why they have been called fairy candles. This less used, but more beautiful, name suits the plant perfectly.

American Indians held *Cimicifuga racemosa* in high esteem, using it to treat rheumatism, pneumonia, croup, and asthma, as well as "female complaints"—the plant is sometimes called squawroot. Many tribes also brewed a tonic from the root. Perhaps because the flower heads eventually form pods with loose seeds inside, rattling like a rattlesnake, some Indians used the plant to treat snakebite, giving rise to such names as black snakeroot and rattletop.

With the arrival of Europeans, black cohosh's importance and reputation for curative powers spread. The plant was used as a sedative, diuretic, astringent, and expectorant. It was also a treatment for whooping cough, consumption, bronchitis, diarrhea, and St. Vitus' dance (chorea). Physicians of the 19th century used it to speed up a woman's labor. The plant would "stimulate the uterus and cause rapid painless expansion of the parts," wrote Charles F. Millspaugh, who listed many uses for the plant in his 1892 work, *American Medicinal Plants*. In general, he said quaintly, "it will be found in most cases to act with far more constant success in females than in males, as its action upon the female economy is marked and distinctive."

So important were medicines made from its blackish, gnarled roots that herbalists listed black cohosh in pharmacopoeias of the United States and Britain well into the 20th century. While no longer so listed, the plant still appears in almost any modern herbal and is often recommended for dealing with two modern-day conditions: menopause (it's said to contain estrogen and to have a calming effect) and high blood pressure.

Bane of Bugs

Black cohosh was used not only for curing diseases but also for relieving another scourge—insect attacks. The fetid-smelling flowers, rubbed on the skin, served as a repellent to those little biting bugs of summer woods. From this comes another common name, bugbane. Even the plant's generic name, *Cimicifuga*, reflects this function, *cimex* is Latin for "bug," and *fugare* is Latin for "to drive away."

The plant's unattractive odor can, however, have just the opposite effect. While its flowers bloom virtually alone in and at the edge of woods, the brighter, more plentiful species of fields and other open spots attract the most plentiful pollinators: bees. What bee would bother to wander off into the dark woods in search of an occasional blossom when such a wealth of nectar and pollen can be easily found in the open sunlight?

So the cohosh has turned to deception to attract the kind of insects that would be available to carry its pollen from blossom to blossom. The flower, which smells like carrion, lures carrion and meat flies that feed on the carcasses of forest creatures. (Trilliums and skunk cabbages of spring use this same technique.) You should use it as an insect repellent, then, only if you don't mind a fly or two stopping by to see if you're dead meat.

Summer Ghosts

The fuzzy appearance of fairy candles comes from the numerous stamens on the many flowers along each spike. There are also small petals, but these fall off shortly after the blossoms open. The resulting fleecy wands, usually appearing in threes, sit atop plants that sometimes reach the striking height of nine feet. The fleecy flowers have inspired florid words from nature writers. "The tall white wands of the black cohosh shoot up in the shadowy woods of midsummer like so many ghosts," wrote Mrs. William Starr Dana. Neltje Blanchan called them tall white rockets, and Frances Theodora Parsons observed, "If we chance to be lingering when the last sunlight has died away, and happen suddenly upon one of these ghostly groups, the effect is almost startling." Recommending them in her book *Old-Time Gardens*, Alice Morse Earle wrote, "The succession of pure white spires, standing up several feet high at the edge of a swampy field or in a garden, partake of that compelling charm which comes from tall trees of slender growth, from repetition and association, such as pine trees, rows of bayonets, the gathered masts of a harbor, from stalks of corn in a field, from rows of foxglove—from all 'serried ranks.' "

The unusual flower form is not surprising, since black cohosh belongs to the Crowfoot family, a clan that includes flowers of such varied shape as the common buttercups, the larkspurs (delphiniums), mousetails, clematis, and columbines. The genus is small, consisting of only a dozen or so species. Six of those species are North American and include the unscented but similar-looking mountain bugbane (*C. americana*) of east-central woods. Two Pacific Northwest species are both rare: Mt. Hood bugbane (*C. laciniata*) and tall bugbane (*C. elata*). Another species, Arizona bugbane (*C. arizonica*) is found only in its namesake state.

Black cohosh is by far the most widespread species, ranging from New England to the

Deception

For the wandering woodland bug,
The fairy candles burn.
Yet, most come near and go "Ugh!"
And to other flowers turn.
But for a hungry, passing fly
The candles seem a treat.
The seamy scent is the reason why:
Flies think it's from dead meat.
—J. S.

A Nip of Cohosh?

The first large, successful
American business run by a
woman was said to be the Lydia
E. Pinkham Medical Company,
founded in 1875 by Lydia Estes
Pinkham. Her main product was
Lydia E. Pinkham's Vegetable
Compound, a patent medicine
to treat "all those painful complaints and weaknesses so common to our best female population"—in other words, menstrual pain. A main ingredient was
black cohosh, but the concoction's popularity might have
been due to its nearly 20 percent
alcohol content. In the late
1800s, when polite women did-
n't drink liquor, they could consume Pinkham's instead. It was
an especially big seller during
Prohibition. Today, Lydia
Pinkham Herbal Compound,
with black cohosh but minus the
alcohol, is manufactured by
Numark Laboratories Inc.

central plains and south to Georgia. Its other names include richweed (it favors rich soils), papoose root, rattleweed, rattleroot, rattlebox, tall bugbane, and bugwort. I myself like "fairy candles" and the image the name conjures up of sylvan fairies holding sparkling candles.

Black cohosh is an ideal flower to plant along the edges of the woods. It is attractive and long lasting, and spreads fairly quickly under conditions it likes—shade; rocky, rich, moderately acid soil; and hillside locations. Its main drawback in my part of the country is that deer often eat the flower stalks before they get a chance to bloom. Try starting cohosh from seeds, sowing them in August and September when they mature. The seeds must be exposed to a season of cold weather in order to germinate. These plants can also be obtained from many native-plant nurseries.

With a little luck, you'll keep the neighborhood fairies well lit and bug-free.

Chicory

THE ROADSIDE PEASANT

Chicory has a long history as food and drink for man and beast.

Chicory is a common "weed" that often provides the only splashes of blue in summer countrysides filled with yellow, orange, pink, and white flowers. So common is it along roadsides in Germany that it is called *Wegwart,* or "road plant."

In its European homelands, chicory is better known as a food than as a decoration. Egyptians ate its basal leaves thousands of years ago and still do. The Latin author Horace mentions its leaves as part of his own limited menu. By the 1600s, the plant was being cultivated as a green. In fact, chicory is a Composite, a family of wild plants—including the common dandelion, wild lettuces, and endive—often used for salad greens.

Popular Parts

As food, the leaves are good only when the plants are young. Some people place paper bags or other covers over the young plants to bleach the fresh leaves, preventing the bitterness that develops as the chicory matures. The French dig up the roots and place them in dark cellars, forcing them during the winter. The resulting white shoots are picked for a salad called *barbe de capucin,* or "beard of the monk." In Belgium, chicory is a big crop, and Belgians consider the leaves one of their major exports.

The English and especially the French prize its root, which is roasted, ground, and flavored with burnt sugar to make a coffee-like drink, or to add to coffee as a flavor enhancer. During the two world wars, when real coffee was in short supply, many people used chicory instead. Even today, when coffee prices periodically go out of sight because of crop problems in South America or Africa, widely advertised national brands of coffee are openly padded with chicory, both to keep prices down and—said the labels—to enhance the product's flavor. In the southeastern United States, many people prefer coffee to which chicory has been added, favoring the touch of bitterness it adds. The demand for the roasted roots in Europe has sometimes been so great that the chicory itself was adulterated with wheat or even acorns.

Some French authorities call chicory a contrastimulant, serving to "correct the excitation

Chicory flowers bloom for less than a day but are beautiful while they last.

caused by the principles of coffee," said Maude Grieve. "It suits bilious subjects who suffer from habitual constipation, but is ill-adapted for persons whose vital energy soon flags."

Chicory has also been used as a root vegetable. The young roots are boiled and eaten like carrots, to which the rootstock bears a resemblance.

During the 17th century, chicory and violet flowers were concocted into a confection called violet plates (see the chapter on violets, page 48). The flowers were also once used to make a yellow dye, while the leaves produced a blue dye—the opposite of what one might expect.

Ancient Medicine

Chicory roots have medicinal properties as well, though the plant has never been very popular with herbalists. The roots have been used for jaundice, spleen problems, and constipation. The milky juice of the leaves and a tea made from the flowering plant are said to promote the production of bile and the release of gallstones. The leaves are also useful for gastritis, lack of appetite, and digestive difficulties, according to herbalists. They were also applied as a poultice to injuries.

Nicholas Culpeper, the 17th-century herbalist, seemed to find a use for just about everything that grew from the ground. He maintained that chicory, which he knew as succory, was "effectual for sore eyes that are inflamed, or for nurses' breasts that are pained by the abundance of milk." He added that it was good for those who "have an evil disposition in their bodies." On this continent, some tribes of American Indians quickly took to the newcomer, chewing its fresh, spongy root like a gum.

For most people, however, chicory is just a wildflower, to be enjoyed for its color. Its three- to four-foot-high stalks are sparsely leaved and not much to look at, compared to the blossoms. The silver-dollar-size flowers, similar to hawkweeds and other Composites that lack the big center "eyes," or disks, are often described as sky blue—Emerson wrote of "succory to match the sky." As their brief life continues, some turn pinkish and then white in death. In fact, chicory plants bearing pink, white, or mauve flowers occasionally appear.

The flowers bloom in the morning, turn their heads toward and follow the sun, and fold up by noon on a bright day. On cloudy days or on days when the sun comes out early and is then covered by clouds, the flowers may not bloom at all, they may bloom and close early, or they may bloom all day.

Linnaeus, the Swedish botanist who established the botanical naming and categorizing system, used chicory as one of several flowers in a "floral clock." He determined that the flowers opened regularly at 5 A.M. and closed at 10 A.M. The period varies with the month and with the country; in England and the United States, the range is more like 6:30 A.M. to noon.

Its blooming characteristics gave rise to a legend in which the plant was once a beautiful maiden who refused the advances of the sun. In true male chauvinist fashion, the sun turned her into a flower, forcing her to stare at him each day and making her fade before his might.

Various authorities have described chicory as a biennial, a short-lived perennial, or a

Chicory Coffee

Those who would experiment with chicory brew should dig up the deep roots, thoroughly clean them, and roast them in the oven until the roots break with a snap and the insides are dark. Grind the roasted root as you would coffee. In brewing, use a bit less of the grind than you would for coffee; chicory is stronger.

long-lived perennial—one wag called it a birennial. Its life span may depend on its environment. With care, chicory can be transplanted to sunny gardens—or even better, to an open edge of the yard or to a field. It is especially attractive if there is a good-size colony of the plants. Like other common summer flowers, such as the black-eyed Susan, chicory favors poor soils where competition is not too great and where its deep root can tap into water that most plants can't find. Thus, unless you dig carefully, you will not get the entire root; and unless you transplant carefully, you will put it in a situation in which it will not grow well. Chicory may also favor soils with some limestone content.

Many wild plants will wilt for two or three days after transplanting. Water them daily and they will soon straighten up. With some kinds of plants it may take a week or two, but if you've gotten enough root, chicory should survive.

Happy Immigrant

Though not native to North America, the chicory has made itself at home as few natives have. It can be found wild from New Brunswick to British Columbia, and south from Florida to California. The plant was probably imported as a hay crop in the 1700s—by 1795, Thomas Jefferson was growing it at Monticello. In Europe, it is still grown and valued as hay, and farmers who use it maintain that chicory is better than alfalfa because it produces more hay in a season.

While modern farmers might use reapers to cut their chicory, there was a time long ago when only a golden sickle or a knife made from the horn of a stag could be used to cut the plant, which was harvested on certain special days, not as food for livestock but as an aphrodisiac for man. According to superstition, the plant was so powerful and sacred that if you talked while cutting it, you would die.

A plant as popular and as widely known as the chicory is bound to accumulate a variety of names. They include wild succory (especially in England), French or Belgian endive, bunk, cornflower, coffeeweed, witloof, blue or ragged sailors, blue daisy, blue dandelion, and bachelor's buttons. *Succory* is from the Latin *succurre*, "to run under," referring to the deep roots. *Witloof* is based on a Dutch word, meaning literally "white leaf," a reference to the practice of blanching the leaves to make them less bitter. "Blue sailor" may come from a sailor's blue uniform, and "ragged sailor" may come from the flower's typical aspect.

Its scientific name is *Cichorium intybus*. *Cichorium*, say some authorities, is a Latin term based on an Egyptian or Arabic word, *chikouryeh*, meaning simply "chicory." Other sources say it's from a Greek word, meaning a root or salad vegetable. *Intybus* simply means "relating to chicory," and is also derived from an Arabic word for the plant. Some say the words *intybus* and *endivia*, as in *endive*, both stem from the same Arabic word for the plant, *hendibeh*.

In Britton and Brown's *Illustrated Flora of the Northern United States and Canada*, chicory was the type species for a genus that included eight species, all natives of the Old World. Britton and Brown also set up a Chicory family (Cichoriaceae) that included 70 genera and 1,500 species

CHICORY

Presidentially Prized

In 1795, Thomas Jefferson wrote George Washington that chicory is "one of the greatest acquisitions a farmer can have" to feed his cattle. He also found it made a "tolerable salad."

worldwide. Most are herbs, but two are trees native to the Pacific Islands. Family members included the dandelion, sow-thistles, blue lettuces, and hawkweeds. However, Gray and other authorities consider chicory merely another genus within the huge Composite family, though they do now often recognize a Chicory tribe of the Composite family.

Color for Cracks

Like its cousin the dandelion, chicory has an amazing ability to show up almost anywhere that is sunny. I've seen it appear between the cracks of sidewalks and parking lots, where no more than a sliver of earth is open to rainfall. A field full of these flowers is striking, especially in a season when large blue flowers are generally lacking. They remind us that fall, with its many blue asters, is not too far off. Though each blossom has a short life, the chicory makes up for it with a long blooming season, from late June until early October.

And if its blue isn't enough color for you, consider the birds the chicory attracts. Goldfinches love chicory seeds. One of the prettiest views I saw on a trip over the Skyline Drive in the Blue Ridge Mountains of Virginia was a flock of those bright yellow birds fluttering amid chicory's sky blue flowers on a sunny summer's morn.

Not in Ladies' Gardens

Oh, not in Ladies' gardens
My peasant posy!
Smile thy dear blue eyes,
Nor only—near to the skies—
In upland pastures dim and sweet—
But by the dusty road
Where tired feet
Toil to and fro,
Where flaunting Sin
May see thy heavenly hue
Or weary Sorrow look from thee
Toward a more tender hue.
—Margaret Deland (1857–1945)

Bergamots

THE MONSTER MINTS

These flashy natives attract hummingbirds and taste good, too.

Most members of the Mint family bear flowers that only a bee would notice. Members of the genus *Monarda*, however, including bergamot, are showy enough to attract humans—and hummingbirds.

Wild bergamot is one of the most common and flashy of our early-summer flowers. This aromatic plant, a perennial that grows three to five feet tall, has large, globe-like blossoms from one to two inches wide. It is a denizen of dry, sunny localities, where it thrives as long as people or machines don't disturb its tall, delicate stems. Fewer and fewer of these places remain, which is why the once plentiful plant is seen less frequently, at least in parts of the Northeast.

Wild bergamot is a native of North America. John Tradescant Jr. (1608–1662) first noted the plant in the 17th century and sent samples back to England. (John was the son of John Sr., a gardener to King Charles I, who lent his name to the popular genus of spiderworts called *Tradescantia*.) The sharp citrus-and-mint smell of the crushed leaves was apparently similar to that of bergamot oranges, grown around Bergamo, Italy, and gave rise to the plant's name.

To botanists wild bergamot is *Monarda fistulosa*. The generic name recalls another early plant scientist, Nicolas Monardes (1493–1588) of Seville, Spain, a physician who from 1565 to 1571 published a massive text on the medicinal values of New World plants. *Fistulosa* means "full of pipes," descriptive of the long florets.

Most wild mints have tiny flowers. Wild bergamot is a giant.

Each flower head bears 20 to 30 of these florets, long tubular affairs holding enough nectar to satisfy the sweet tooth of many a flying creature. Dozens of varieties of butterflies and bees are drawn to the blossoms, whose pink, lilac, or purplish tints are particularly attractive to such insects, most of which serve to pollinate the flowers. As a careful observer might suspect, hummingbirds can also pollinate bergamot. Its vials of nectar perfectly fit the long beaks of the ruby-throated hummingbird, and a large colony of bergamots is almost sure to be frequented by these tiny birds.

The shape of the flower head, the hairs on its surface, and the construction of the florets all but prevent walking insects and those with short mouth parts from sampling the nectar. Despite these and other measures to stop pilfering by nonpollinating insects, however, there are always

Sweet Rhyme

Sweet will be the Flower
"Speak not, whisper not;
Here bloweth thyme and bergamot."
—Samuel Taylor Coleridge
(1772–1834)

Gooseberry-Bergamot Jelly

4 quarts of fresh gooseberries
3 big handfuls of chopped wild
bergamot leaves
White sugar (at least 12 ounces)

Wash the gooseberries, put
them in a large enameled pot,
and crush them. Mix in chopped
bergamot leaves. Add enough
water to cover and simmer.
When berries are soft, pour into
a clean jelly bag and allow mixture to drip overnight.

Add the sugar at rate of 12
ounces per pint of juice. Stir
over a low heat to dissolve the
sugar, then bring to a boil.
Continue boiling until the jelly
sheets on a spoon. Skim off any
skin that may form on the surface. Pour into hot sterilized jars
and seal.
—based on *"Just Recipes,"*
www.melborponsti.com

thieves about. In this case certain species of wasps chew holes in the base of each floret to suck out the nectar, without bothering to pick up any pollen.

A perennial, wild bergamot is easy to establish if you have a sunny, dry spot. It can be transplanted at almost any time of the growing season and can sometimes be acquired from places where the plant is clearly threatened with destruction, particularly from roadsides that are likely to be mowed by highway crews. If you come across a colony that is not endangered, a few plants may be divided off so that you can leave most of the group intact. The few you take, if planted in the right spot, can spread fairly rapidly over the years. Since the stems are susceptible to breaking, place the plants where people or animals are not apt to brush against them or knock them over.

Flashy Bee Balm

Though perhaps the most common member of the clan, wild bergamot is not the flashiest. Gardeners may be familiar with another *Monarda*, called bee balm, which is similar in form but bears bright red flowers. Despite its name it is probably less of a bee flower because its longer floral tubes allow only the largest of bees to access its nectar. Bee balm is more suited to hummingbirds, whose favorite color is bright red.

Although many American wildflowers are garden escapes, bee balm is a native that has found its way into many gardens. Explorer-botanists admired the plant and took it back to Europe. Bee balm and a half-dozen cultivated varieties developed from it are still popular there, decorating the landscape with their white, purple, pink, or crimson flowers.

My yard at one time had both bergamot and bee balm, growing about 40 feet apart. One year the bergamot didn't show up, a casualty apparently of a high water table brought on by sever-al unusually wet summers. A year or two later, my small but growing colony of bee balm, whose rare rich red I had enjoyed each August, also failed to appear, even though it had been lush the year before. I was surprised. I decided I must have miscalculated a spring run with the lawn mower and chopped off the young shoots. Two years later, however, in the very spot where the bee balm had been, a couple of plants bearing flowers almost the color of wild bergamot appeared and con-tinued to reappear for several years. The flowers were more reddish than my bergamots had been, but not nearly the deep red of bee balm. Had there been some sort of cross-pollination before the demise of the bee balm, and my bergamot-looking plant was really an off-colored offspring of bee balm and a neighborhood bergamot? Or did the union between my two colonies take place years before and some happenstance of nature delayed the offspring's appearance? Perhaps seeds of the hybrid had been buried years before, and some activity in the garden caused them to germinate.

Monarda didyma (*didyma* means "in pairs," referring apparently to its pairs of opposing leaves) is also called Oswego tea, a name of pre-Revolutionary origin. In 1743, a botanist named John Bartram (see the chapter on violets, page 48) was a member of a team of negotiators who traveled from Pennsylvania to upper New York State to make a treaty with the Indians. In the vicinity of Fort Oswego, Bartram came across the plant. He learned from the Indians that it was used in a tea to treat chills and fevers, and the name of the fort—the Indian word for the nearby river—became the name of the plant.

Actually, it is likely that by the 1740s, many back-woods colonists were already brewing teas from the aromatic leaves of both bee balm and bergamot as a substitute for imported teas not readily available far from coastal towns. After the famous Boston Tea Party, the plant became a widely used substitute for imported tea, at least until after the Revolution. If you want to try some, room-dry a bunch of leaves for a couple of weeks and then steep about three-quarters of a teaspoon per cup in boiling water. After drying, these and other kinds of wild tea leaves should be kept in sealed glass jars stored in a cool, dark place.

Like the various mints to which they are related, Monardas have been used to flavor food. Leaves and young plant tips have been added to salads, cold drinks, and jellies, particularly apple jelly. An oil from the plants, said to smell like ambergris, has been used in perfumes.

American Indians drank bergamot tea for headaches and sore throats, inhaled an oil extract to relieve bronchial congestion, used the leaves to treat acne, and applied fresh crushed leaves to soothe insect bites. Following the old Doctrine of Signatures, in which characteristics of plants are supposed to designate medicinal values, some herbalists believed that red bee balm is good for cleansing the red blood of impurities; some modern herbalists still vouch for this use.

The spotted bee balm, or American horsemint (M. punctata), which bears yellow and lavender flowers, was also popular with Indians from the East Coast to the Mississippi and into Texas and New Mexico. It was used chiefly to treat fevers and stomach ailments. Thymol, an antiseptic in mouthwashes such as Listerine and in many nose and throat sprays, has been obtained commercially from this plant as well as from bee balm.

About 15 Monarda species, often called horsemints or lemonmints, can be found in North America. Wild bergamot ranges coast to coast, though it's not found wild in California; bee balm is more limited in native territory, growing in and about rich woods from New York to Michigan and down into Tennessee and Georgia. However, as a garden escape—a term usually applied to alien species—bee balm is becoming more widespread and now is being found wild even on the West Coast.

In southern California, the closely related red monardella (Monardella macrantha) attracts several kinds of tropical hummingbirds with its bright red flowers. Its generic name suggests it's smaller than a Monarda, and indeed, these are generally low-lying plants.

The florets of Oswego tea attract hummingbirds.

Dr. Monardes

Nicolas Monardes, the physican from whom bergamots get their generic name, wrote the first herbal that covered plants of the Americas. Its English version was called *Joyful News Out of the New Found World*. Though he wrote extensively on American plants and had a garden full of them, Monardes never left Spain. Living in Seville, the center of commerce between Europe and the New World in the 16th century, he was able to get others to collect plants for him.

Nightshades

BEAUTIFUL, BUT DEADLY?

Our nightshades have an evil reputation, somewhat undeserved.

Climbing nightshade's beaked flowers . . .

Nightshade. The very word inspires images of villains, poisons, and death, of Gothic novels and Holmesian mysteries. But in the case of our common nightshades, the image is overplayed.

Climbing, or bittersweet, nightshade (*Solanum dulcamara*) is a common inhabitant of hedges, brush, and tall weeds from coast to coast in North America, as well as Europe and Asia. Easy to identify, this vine has purple blue flowers with pointed, reflexed petals and a conical yellow "beak" in the middle—a distinctive form shared by several more famous relatives, including the potato, tomato, and tobacco. Its greenery is distinctive, too: Each oval main leaf has two smaller wing leaves jutting out at the base.

Solanum, from the same Latin root as our word *solace,* means "quieting" or "healing," terms you'd hardly expect to be connected with a plant that can be toxic. And *dulcamara* is a corrupted form of the word for "bittersweet" (or literally, sweet-bitter), a characteristic of the plant. If you chew a leaf, the taste will at first be bitter, then sweet. This sensation is due to a substance called dulcamarine.

Another constituent, called solanine, is the more active ingredient. "It slows the heart and respiration, lessens sensibility, lowers the temperature, and causes vertigo and delirium, terminating in death with convulsions," one authority maintained many years ago. This substance, however, is found in tiny quantities and is not the same as the highly poisonous atropine contained in the related deadly nightshade (belladonna), the traditional weapon of mustachioed villains. In fact, modern authorities differ on whether eating berries or other parts of climbing nightshade will do any more than cause a mild stomachache—if that.

Several authorities agree that the berries have proved toxic to some degree in children, and it's safest to remove the plants from places frequented by youngsters inclined to eat such things. Actually, it's a good idea to warn youngsters against eating *anything* found outdoors. While most of our wild vegetation is harmless, a few plants can cause at least discomfort when eaten, and some might do more.

Some farmers, who've found that the berries of nightshades sicken their livestock, con-

sider the plant a pest. Agricultural inspectors have rejected whole truckloads of beans because a few nightshade berries were found mixed in, reports Richard Spellenberg, author of *The Audubon Society Field Guide to North American Wildflowers, Western Region.*

Climbing nightshade has been used for centuries as an internal and external medicine (whence *solanum*). The plant has been an ingredient in preparations for kidney ailments, skin diseases, rheumatism, jaundice, and respiratory problems such as catarrh, asthma, and whooping cough. John Gerard reported a rather specialized use: "The juice is good for those who have fallen from high places, and have been thereby bruised or beaten, for it is thought to dissolve blood congealed or cluttered anywhere in the intrals and to heale the hurt places."

Nicholas Culpeper, however, offered some of the most unusual uses: "It is good to remove witchcraft both in men and beast. . . . Being tied about the neck, it is a remedy for the vertigo or dizziness of the head, and that is the reason the Germans hang it about their cattle's neck, when they fear any such evil hath betided them."

Bright Berries

To many people and certainly to many birds, the berries are the outstanding product of the climbing nightshade. Coming from flowers that bloom in late spring and through the summer, the berries appear in midsummer and into September. Often there are both flowers and berries of various stages of ripeness, all on the same plant.

The fruits are at first green, then turn orange, and finally ripen to bright, translucent red that almost glows in the sunlight. "I do not know any clusters more graceful and beautiful than these," wrote Henry David Thoreau. "They hang more gracefully over the river's brim than any pendant in a lady's ear. Yet, they are considered poisonous; not to look at surely. . . . But why should they not be poisonous? Would it not be bad taste to eat these berries which are ready to feed another sense?"

. . . later become bright red fruits that many birds eat.

In his appreciative ecstasy, Thoreau may have overlooked the probable purpose of the bright color—to attract animals to eat the berries and thereby spread the species. Nightshade berries are popular with birds, which eagerly gobble them up. More than 30 species of birds dine on nightshade berries, including such songbirds as cardinals, catbirds, chats, magpies, meadowlarks, mockingbirds, orioles, various sparrows, thrushes, and thrashers, as well as such game birds as ruffed grouse, pheasants, wild turkeys, and bobwhites. Many mammals, especially skunks, also eat them.

Nightshades are among the relatively few wild herbs that offer showy, juicy fruits as an enticement for transporting their seeds. Perhaps that's because the plant blooms and fruits in the summer, the high season of flower and seed production, and has evolved something special to compete with the extravaganza of foods. The seeds are encased in a covering that prevents them from being damaged in passing through a bird's gut. As nature takes its course, the indigestible seeds may be deposited—complete with fertilizer—miles away.

Timing is important in the survival of the climbing nightshade, which can be found almost only where there are host plants to support it, and where the ground is not parched. For example, jewelweed and nightshade are often found together. In early spring, you're apt to see nightshade plants growing a foot higher than the masses of young jewelweed hosts; but a month later, the faster-growing jewelweed may outstrip the nightshades. They remain companions for the rest of the summer, the clinging nightshade sometimes becoming twice as long as its hosts are tall; it links from plant to plant horizontally over several feet so that it does not appear nearly its actual size.

As the nightshade matures, its hairy green stalks become smooth and woody, like a shrub, and turn grayish (in England, the plant is sometimes called woody nightshade). Though shrublike, nightshade is a perennial herb, which means that its aboveground parts die at the end of its season and new stalks come up in spring.

Other names for climbing nightshade include blue bindweed, felonwood, felonwort, poisonflower, snakeberry, scarletberry, dulcamara, and violet bloom. "Felons," blisters or boils especially around fingernails, were once treated with this plant. *Felon* is an interesting word; both this sense and that of an evildoer are believed to have come from the same origin—a word that meant someone or something that is full of bitterness. Bindweed, incidentally, is an inappropriate name, since climbing nightshade does not wrap itself around its host, as true bindweeds (*Convolvulus*) do. In other words, they don't bind, they just loosely loop around and lie across the hosts.

Nightshade flowers contain no nectar, but the pollen attracts some bees. The flowers do not require insect pollination, however, and apparently fertilize themselves most of the time. While few insects visit the flowers, the plant is not without its insect fans—various potato beetles enjoy its leaves as much as they do those of some 20 kinds of potatoes that are also members of the genus *Solanum*.

Other Nightshades

Solanum is one of the world's largest plant genera, containing more than 1,000 species, mostly in the tropical Americas; only about 40 species live wild in North America.

Black, or garden, nightshade (*Solanum nigrum*), a widespread European import, is occasionally called deadly nightshade because the leaves and the unripe berries are thought to be somewhat poisonous and, like belladonna's, the berries are black. However, black nightshade's toxicity is not nearly that of its European cousin and, in fact, Midwesterners used to add ripe black nightshade berries to pies. Children in South Africa are especially fond of them, as are African witch doctors, who use them in a rain-making concoction. Since cattle won't eat the greens, it's possible that the poisonous qualities, if any, lie only in those parts. Yet, the boiled leaves of black nightshade have been widely used for food, on our own continent and throughout Europe and even on the distant island of Mauritius in the Indian Ocean.

Black nightshade and the closely related American black nightshade (*S. americanum*, once called *S. nigrum americanum*) bear white flowers of the same shape as climbing nightshade's blooms and are found coast to coast. For centuries they were employed to treat dropsy, gastritis, and skin eruptions and injuries, and as a narcotic for nervous afflictions. American Indians, such as the Rappahannocks and the Houmas, used it to treat worms, sores, and insomnia. In Central Europe, mothers used to hang the plant over their babies' cradles as a hypnotic inducement to sleep. The narcotic or hypnotic effects of various nightshades may have inspired its name, the "shade" being a dark hallucination. True deadly nightshade has long been associated with the devil, and so has night. In general, it is a gloom-and-doom name, no matter how you look at it. (True deadly nightshade, (*Atropa belladonna*), the plant with which our subject is sometimes confused, is native to central and southern Europe and is very rare on this continent; only six states—California, Michigan, New Jersey, New York, Oregon, and Washington—reported sitings in the wild by 2002. Every part of the plant is extremely poisonous and dangerous.)

Speaking of the devilish side of nightshades, several are known for their thorns. For instance, silver-leaf nightshade, or horsenettle (*S. elaeagnifolium*), found coast to coast, is a prickly native with yellow berries and violet flowers; the name probably refers to the grayish leaves. Buffalo bur (*S. rostratum*) is another prickly native whose yellow flowers are found in almost every state and province. Its yellow prickers could be considered a blessing; they discourage animals, such as cattle, from eating its very toxic leaves. Several states, especially those where sheep are raised, classify it as a noxious weed. The burs that encase the seeds can get into the wool and, according to the Washington State Noxious Weed Control Board, "may cause damage and considerable loss in wool value in sheep."

Some *Solanum* species, such as *S. melongena*, a native of northern India that we call the eggplant, are quite familiar to us. The Incans first domesticated another sibling, *S. tuberosum*, on the slopes of the Andes Mountains centuries ago. Brought to Europe, the common potato became one of the most widely eaten vegetables in the Western world. True to its genus, however, the potato contains a bit of poison in its skin. Don't worry about eating your entire baked potato, though; cooking removes the toxicity.

The genus *Solanum* is in turn a member of the Nightshade, or Potato, family (Solanaceae) of some 90 genera and 2,600 species found worldwide, especially in South America. About 20 genera are found in North America. Among the most recognized members of the family is the tomato (*Lycopersicum esculentum*), believed also to be a native of the Andes or perhaps of Mexico. Few people would eat the tomato when the plants were first brought to Europe. The fruit, sometimes called love apple, was considered poisonous, and the plant was mostly used ornamentally. However, the Italians eventually started making spaghetti sauce from the fruit, and appreciation of its culinary value is said to have spread from there. Peppers, in the genus *Capsicum*, are also of the Nightshade family.

Another popular member of the family is the genus *Nicotiana*, or tobacco, with some 14 species on this continent. While experts may question whether our common nightshades are very poisonous, just read the little box on a package of cigarettes. There is no doubt expressed in its warning.

Bittersweet Flip

An anthologist included in her book Elizabeth Denison's poem, "Bittersweet," a stanza of which is reproduced with this chapter. She believed that the poet was describing *Solanum dulcamara*.. But was the anthologist confused? *S. dulcamara* is true "bittersweet," so called by the English before North America was settled. When the colonists discovered the unrelated woody vine *Celastrus scandens*, its berries reminded them of the bittersweet they had known in the Old Country and they called the New World plant American bittersweet. "Today bittersweet is now only a secondary name for the nightshade, and nightshade's namesake has become the 'true' bittersweet, without a verbal clue to its own respectable botany," says John Eastman in *The Book of Forest and Thicket*. "So much for descriptive accuracy."

Pokeweed

BOUNTY FOR MAN AND BIRD

Pokeweed feeds both man and bird,
but be careful what you eat.

Pokeweed's flowers are not much to look at . . .

Pokeweed. The word evokes images of a lumbering plant, slow to grow yet big when done. While our common poke is not particularly pokey, it is a giant among our summer herbs, a lummox long popular with both humans and birds.

While the name seems fitting for this large, coarse herb, it describes not its character but its aspect. *Poke* is from a Virginia Indian word, *pocan*, used for any plant that yielded a red or yellow dye. *Pocan's* roots are in the native word for blood. Thus, we also have puccoons, applied to various species of red or red-juiced flowers such as bloodroot (see page 22). In poke, the redness is found first in the stems, eventually in the leaves, and finally in the deep purple berries that were indeed used as a dye.

The flowers, however, generally escape whatever tints the plant sends upward. There is a hint of red in some of the petal-like sepals, but basically they are white or whitish. Usually five of them surround an ovary that looks much like a miniature green tomato. It is this ovary that later ripens into the plant's richly colored berry.

Summer is full of a thousand scents, but the most memorable are not always the most noticeable. Poke hardly qualifies as a sweet flower, yet the whole plant contributes summery smells to the passerby. In fact, poke is invariably described as strong smelling. That sounds almost like a euphemism for foul smelling, but it isn't. Poke offers a deep, earthy scent that's enjoyable, just as coffee or certain pipe tobaccos are both strong smelling and enjoyable.

Many writers dismiss the flowers as inconspicuous or unspectacular. I find them modestly elegant, however, and as I write this, a small bouquet of them sits on my desk. Some of the green-eyed blossoms are displaying their 10 stamens, tipped with anthers loaded with white pollen. This gives a certain lacy quality to the raceme. The pollen is much sought after by smaller bees and some flies, but one wonders how they ever manage to run across these modest, scentless flowers during a season when so many more visually spectacular and sweetly scented species are blooming. But insects look upon the world with different eyes, and see things we don't. If you inspect the blossoms closely with a magnifying glass, you'll see faint striations on the sepals, lines seemingly heading inward toward the "tomato." To an insect's ultraviolet vision, these may be much more visible and alluring than they are to our eyes, catching the insect's attention and guiding it to the pollen. One July day, I stood around a big poke plant in the backyard, watching to see what would visit so lowly a display. My poke was popular only with hover flies (probably *Toxomerus*), yellow-backed, bee-like little flies that, when they weren't hovering over the flowers, were gobbling up the pollen. Several European cabbage butterflies were flitting among the chickweed blossoms, but none would touch the poke. That was fine, though the larvae of hover flies feed on aphids and other pest insects while cabbage butterfly caterpillars are a major pest. I can remember them decimating the few heads of cabbage I used to grow each spring.

In stormy weather, the flowers can self-pollinate. The quality of the resulting seed may not be as good as the cross-pollinated kind, but self-pollination is better than no pollination.

The Pigeon-Berry

In southern New England pokeweed flowers appear in July, and by late August and September the berries are ripening—just in time for migratory birds that are fattening themselves up for flights south. This is the time of year when Thoreau, who used pokeweed stems as walking sticks, spoke of poke as being "all on fire with ripeness." The deep red-blue color draws many kinds of birds, especially mourning doves, but none was reportedly fonder of pokeweed than the late passenger pigeon, whence came the name "pigeon-berry."

Passenger pigeons once wandered North America in unimaginable numbers. In the early 1800s, one observer in Kentucky saw a single flock some 240 miles long and a mile wide, estimated to contain more than two *billion* birds. Such vast flocks, darkening the skies and taking many hours to pass by, were not unusual until the mid- to late 1800s when "pigeoners"—men who followed the flocks, using nets to capture the tasty birds by the tens of thousands—finally diminished their numbers enough to do them in. At one point 100 barrels a day of pigeons were being shipped to the New York grocery market alone. The last passenger pigeon died in 1914 in a Cincinnati zoo. "What a hideous mockery to continue to call this fruit the pigeon-berry when the exquisite bird whose favorite food it once was has been annihilated from this land of liberty by the fowler's net," wrote an irate Neltje Blanchan. The plant is also known as crowberry, but I don't think we have to worry about our corvid friends disappearing any time soon.

. . . but the resulting berries stand out, especially to hungry birds.

The range of the pokeweed and the range of the passenger pigeon just about coincide. Poke can be found from the Maritimes, Ontario, and Minnesota south to the Gulf states and out to eastern Kansas, Oklahoma, and Texas. Did the bird follow the plant or the plant the bird? I suspect the latter, since passenger pigeons ate many other foods besides pokeberries. The birds probably

Poke Sallet

A bunch of pokeweed leaves
    (young ones are best)
Water
3 slices of fried bacon
3 eggs
salt

Boil the pokeweed in at least
two changes of water—this gets
rid of the acrid element. Cook
bacon. When leaves are tender,
add to bacon drippings in the
skillet in which the bacon was
cooked. Add the eggs, one at a
time, scrambling them with the
pokeweed until well cooked.
Add bacon bits; salt to taste.

became the chief agents of dispersal, taking in the seeds in one place and leaving them in another, complete with fertilizer. The loss of billions of these wandering transports must have had some effect on the poke population, and I'll bet the plant is less numerous and widespread today than it was a century and a half ago.

That fact would disappoint "Poke Salad Annie" and many another old poke eater, for pokeweed has been widely used as a vegetable, and still is in parts of the South. I have had correspondents who eat the greens, or ate them in their youth, or whose parents ate them; several have told me that the plant is not as easily found as it once was. Of course, that may be because so many farms are turning into subdivisions or reverting to woodland. Pokeweed's favorite haunt is the edges of fields, where it gets plenty of sun but escapes the wrath of the farmer and his cultivator's blades. "It never invades cultivated fields," wrote John Burroughs, "but hovers about the borders and looks over the fences like a painted Indian sachem."

I once met a woman in her 80s who was living in a posh retirement community in Connecticut. She mystified her wealthy, city-raised neighbors by still eating poke all season. "Hereabouts people scoff at these delicacies," she said.

Yet pokeweed is still widely known as a food. Euell Gibbons called it a "wild potherb par excellence," and in the South, "sprouts," as the young shoots are called, have been sold in many markets, especially in spring. Plants were long ago brought to the vegetable gardens of southern Europe and northern Africa, where poke is now widely found in the wild. Among its biggest fans were the French, "always apt in testing and making use of every kind of food," observed Oliver Perry Medsger in *Edible Wild Plants*. They called it *raisin d'Amerique, herbe de la laque,* or *morelle a grappes.* The last name means "grape nightshade," reflecting the similarity of the berries to those of the nightshades, though they are not related. The plant has also been called American nightshade, mostly by Europeans.

The young shoots are cut, boiled in two changes of water, and served up like spinach or asparagus, with or without sauces. Folks in the midwestern United States used to fry the peeled leaves, and Southerners have made tasty pickles with them.

The plant was particularly valued because it could produce fresh greens year-round, thus helping to prevent ailments like scurvy. Farmers would dig up at least a portion of the huge rootstock (sometimes as thick as a man's thigh) and place it in a box of dirt in the cellar. All through the winter, the root would send up fresh shoots, which could be harvested at least once a week.

For some, pokeweed is even a cause to celebrate. Harlan, Kentucky, has an annual Poke Sallet Festival in late spring when, according to Marilyn Kluger in *The Wild Flavor*, everyone feasts on poke greens and you can even buy poke pizza. "The governor of Kentucky, who serves as the Chief Poke Warden, is charged with the duty of protecting the bounty of poke from greedy harvesters who would break the unwritten code of the hills concerning when and how to gather it," she says. A favorite dish at this festival is Poke Sallet, in which fresh leaves are sautéed in bacon fat, mixed with crisp, crumbled bacon, and served with the likes of black-eyed peas and cornbread. Bradford Angier's *Feasting Free on Wild Edibles* offers recipes for poke soup, pokeweed and eggs, and poke casserole.

The trick with pokeweed is to avoid the root when cutting the young greens. The roots and any older leaves or stems that have turned reddish are toxic and probably poisonous. So are the seeds inside the berries, though the berry meat and juice have been used as a coloring for confections such as icings and, sans seeds, as filling for pies. "I noted in my readings several years ago that the berries had been used for pies by frugal housewives, and often since have half determined to try pokeberry pastry, and the much-thought-of pie is still unmade and uneaten," wrote Charles Millspaugh in the 1890s. The berries were once used to color wines, much to the chagrin of drinkers. As a botanist named Charles Bryant wrote in 1783, "The Portugueze had formerly a trick of mixing the juice of the berries with their red wines, in order to give them a deeper colour; but as it was found to debase the flavour, the matter was represented to his Portugueze Majesty, who ordered all the stems to be cut down yearly before they produced flowers, thereby to prevent any further adulteration."

Nowadays birds are the chief consumers of the fruit. Many observers have reported birds that have eaten the berries behaving as if they were intoxicated. This is probably because of a narcotic effect of the seeds, but it could also be that the berries have gotten overripe and begun to ferment. The berries of autumn olive have been known to ferment and result in drunken birds staggering around the ground, sometimes even into traffic.

The seeds, incidentally, are long lasting. Some poke seeds buried on the grounds of an old agricultural experiment station in Arlington, Virginia, were still alive when uncovered nearly 40 years later as the site was excavated to house the Pentagon.

Pokeweed has also been widely used as a medicine, and it was once listed in the *U.S. Pharmacopoeia*. Many groups of American Indians used it as a slow-acting emetic and for treating rheumatism—a use still listed in herbals. They treated pimples and blackheads with it, and colonists used it to remove corns. "The root's close resemblance to the human shape caused it to be used by Indian doctors as an alternative in organic disorders where other simples [herbs] had failed and were not suitable," wrote herbalist Ben Charles Harris. In the 18th century, it was highly recommended for treating syphilis by one Dr. Clapp, of all names.

American Indians used a berry mash to treat sore breasts, and later farmers employed a tincture of poke to reduce swelling and caking of cows' udders. The plant was widely known as "garget," which is the name of an inflammation of the udders of livestock (the word's root is an old French word for "throat"; the word *gargle* has the same root). Mixed with lard, it was used to treat eczema, psoriasis, and ringworm. The juice of the plant can cause dermatitis, and its reaction with the skin has led to considerable experimentation with its use in treating skin cancers. Correspondents of Benjamin Franklin recommended poke as a cancer cure, and even today, reputable research scientists are exploring treatments for leukemia that use extracts from poke. Among some herbalists it was known as "cancer-root."

When it comes to using the plant as a medicine, however, we should probably leave poke alone. "Poisoning from the plant itself is rare, but overdoses of medicines made from it at one time caused many cases of poisoning," wrote Professor John M. Kingsbury in *Deadly Harvest*. There's evidence, too, that it can damage chromosomes.

Polk's Poke

Often, country folk called pokeweed polk. In fact, in the presidential election campaign of 1844, supporters of James K. Polk wore pokeweed leaves as their emblem. Either of the Bush campaigns could have saved tens of thousands of dollars on buttons by having followers pin sprigs of greenery to their lapels.

This poisonous property of the plant may be a defense against predators. I have watched long-legged flies (*Dolichopodidae*), their metallic backs glistening in the sun, scouring the leaves of poke for aphids and other leaf-eaters, but they always seemed to come up empty mouthed. On the other hand, Marilyn Berry, a poke-loving correspondent in Oklahoma, wrote, "Several years ago, my husband and I bought a house in Tulsa and were surprised to find poke growing wild in the yard. I went out one day to cut some and found bites had been taken out of the leaves. The next day, more bites were gone. And the third day, only tiny stubs of stems remained. We speculated that terrapins might have done it; we had spotted some in the yard around that time. The poke never grew back." Obviously, one creature's poison is another's nectar.

While the plant has been called inkberry, its use as an ink has not extended much beyond children's playing with it. The reason is that the color is not long lasting and eventually fades. Nonetheless, Indians made a blue stain from the plant for splint baskets.

Plant names could be the subject of a whole library of books, and poke would contribute more than its fair share to the volumes. To the scientist it's usually *Phytolacca americana*, though some texts maintain it should be *Phytolacca decandra*. *Phytolacca* is from a Greek word for "plant" and a French word for "lake"—*lake* as in the color, not a body of water. One would think that lake, as the name of a color, would be appropriate for shades of blue, but lake is actually a dark red. In the last half of the 19th century, the U.S. Post Office frequently issued the same stamp design over and over but varied the color with the years. Among serious philatelists, it's important to know the difference between "lake," "carmine lake," and "crimson lake"—the exact color changes the value of a stamp by hundreds of dollars.

Most authorities today go with the name *P. Americana*, though some still use *P. decandra*, which is preferred by noted American botanist Asa Gray. *Decandra* is a Greek word that refers to the 10 stamens. Literally, it means having 10 male organs, for *andros* is the Greek word for "man" or "male."

The plant's many folk names have included skoke, scoke, pocan, cokan, chongras, and cocum, probably variants of poke or American Indian words for the plant; jalap or cancer-jalap, referring to a member of the Morning Glory family that was employed as a purgative—a use to which poke has been put; bear's grape and *raisin d'Amerique*, references to the berries; and red-ink plant and redweed.

Pokeweed sprigs could be used as a decoration. "The purple-red foliage and fruit of pokeberry provides a lovely touch of color for fall arrangements in the home," wrote Nelson Coon, "especially when the bouquet can be put in front of a window where the sun can shine through the beautiful translucent leaves." Yes, even lummoxy leaves can be beautiful.

Sundews

THE CARNIVORES

Most wildflowers use insects. Sundews eat them.

Many plants, especially orchids, are known for their highly evolved ability to manage insects for pollination. Some plants, however, use insects in a different, more basic way: They kill and eat them.

I say "highly evolved" because it takes considerable cunning for a plant, just about the slowest-moving form of life, to catch a fast-moving insect. Yet sundews, and 17 other genera of carnivorous plants, have developed techniques to lure, capture, and consume both flying and crawling insects.

Although the round-leaf sundew (*Drosera rotundifolia*) is among the most widespread carnivores in North America, it may not be easy to find, both because of its size and its out-of-the-way habitat. The tiny, low plant lives in bogs, often in colonies along with sphagnum mosses. Acidic, boggy soils lack much nitrogen, so the sundew has turned to insects, which are abundant in bogs, as a supplemental source of this nutrient.

For most insects, plants provide food. Sundews turn the table. The glistening tentacles of round-leaf sundew are ready to grab a meal. PHOTO © ED KANZE

The upper side of sundew's flat, round leaves has many long reddish hairs or tentacles whose tips bear a clear drop of mucilage. This goo is sweet and lightly scented—one authority calls it a "delicate fungus-like odor"—which helps the plant to attract insects. A still more effective lure may be the way in which the droplets catch the light—like the namesake dew. To a passing insect on the wing, these droplets glistening in the sunlight must be tempting beacons. By laying its leaves almost flat on the ground, however, the sundew also makes itself easily accessible to ants and other crawlers who rely more on scent.

Once it is on the leaf, the insect immediately gets stuck in the drops of mucilage. Its struggles trigger the plant to ooze more fluid. Within about 20 seconds, the leaf hairs begin bending inward, wrapping around the victim. If the insect is too close to the edge of the leaf, the outer hairs can transport the captive inward toward the center where the maximum number of hairs can hold and process the prey.

This ability to ensnare victims by using relatively quickly moving tentacles has fascinated botanists, including Charles Darwin, and the mechanism is only partially understood. It involves rapid growth of cells on one side of the hair, forcing it to curl toward and around its catch.

Carnivorous Plants

What's this I hear
My Molly dear,
About the new carnivora?
Can little plants
Eat bugs and ants
And gnats and flies?—
Why, bless my eyes!
Who is this great diskiverer?

Not Darwin, love,
For that would prove
Unmeet for his parading;
Surely the fare
Of flowers is air,
Or sunshine sweet;—
They shouldn't eat
Or do aught so degrading.

If it alas!
Should come to pass
That Fido here should die,—oh, let
It not be said;
"The dog is dead,
Because one day
In thoughtless play
He went too near a violet."
—M. M. Dodge (1904)

Meanwhile, the victim dies, smothered by the fluid. The goo contains not only attractants and adhesives but also enzymes and an antibacterial agent. The enzymes, similar to those found in the human stomach, begin dissolving the insect's internal organs. The antibacterial chemical prevents the "meat" from spoiling during the process of digestion, which may take more than a week to complete. The tentacles transport the digested fluid to the leaves, which use its nitrogen and possibly other constituents as nutrition. After a couple of weeks, only the inedible exoskeleton of the insect remains, and after it blows away in the breeze, the plant may be ready for another meal.

Healthier Plants

While sundews can survive without ever capturing an insect, studies have shown that plants that have eaten insects produce more flowers and that the resulting seeds are larger and more numerous than in plants that have lacked such a meal. Charles Darwin and his son Francis were both fascinated by the sundew. "At the moment I care more about *Drosera* than the origin of all the species in the world," Charles wrote in the 1860s, after his book *The Origin of Species* had shaken the scientific world. In 1875, Darwin published the results of his studies in another book, *Insectivorous Plants*. His investigations found many interesting facts about the capture system. He determined, for instance, that an object simply striking the tentacles was not enough to trigger the capture mechanism; the tentacles needed to be touched a couple of times before the curling function would begin. This, he surmised, is the plant's way of ensuring that it doesn't waste its time and energy on a falling leaf or other useless debris. A real, wiggling insect was required. Darwin also determined that a sundew leaf could make up to three captures before the tentacles wore out and were no longer able to function.

While some carnivorous plants have spectacular flowers, the glistening red and green leaves pretty much steal the show in the case of *D. rotundifolia*. The small, white, five-petaled blossoms appear from June through August on leafless stalks that raise them five or six inches above the deadly leaves. Perhaps that relatively lofty flower position is designed to keep the pollinating insects far from the hazard below.

Lust Plant

The plant's ability to produce enzymes that dissolve flesh was not lost on herbalists, who have long prescribed the fresh leaves as a treatment for warts and corns. Less obvious is its long-standing use as a cough medicine and as an aphrodisiac. The Dutch, believing that cattle that ate the leaves would become romantically inclined, called the sundew by a name that translates as "lust plant." It's also been called youthwort, possibly because it evoked youthful lusting, but more likely because some thought it to be an herbal fountain of youth. "In America it has been advocated as a cure for old age," Maude Grieve wrote early in the early 20th century. "A vegetable extract is used together with colloidal silicates in cases of arteriosclerosis." It was also used as a freckle remover.

The round-leaf sundew, also called dew plant, red rot, dew grass, and moonwort, is one of our few "circumboreal" species—that is, it's native to North America, Europe, and Asia. On this continent, it lives from New Brunswick to British Columbia and south to Georgia and Mississippi, and throughout the northern prairie states to the Pacific Coast, where it can be found south into California. Round-leaf sundew is one of eight native *Drosera* species, the others being dwarf sundew (*D. brevifolia*) and pink sundew (*D. capillaris*), both found in the southeastern states and Texas; thread-leaf sundew (*D. filiformis*) of the Northeast; spoon-leaf sundew (*D. intermedia*) of eastern North America; slender-leaf sundew (*D. linearis*) of Canada and some of the very northern states; Tracy's sundew (*D. tracyi*) of the extreme southeast; and *D. anglica*, found in the Pacific Northwest.

The word *Drosera* is based on the Greek for "dewy," descriptive of the deadly drops atop the tentacles. Most of the species names describe the leaves—*rotundifolia* means "round-leaved."

More than 150 *Drosera* species exist worldwide, most of them in western Australia. Some 600 species of carnivorous plants, grouped into 18 genera, are found around the world. Virtually all live in wetlands, seasonal wetlands, or water. Many use sticky substances to trap their prey; others, like pitcher plants, drown them in a "cup" of water or, like the Venus flytrap, snare them in a trap.

Sundews, including the round-leaf, are uncommon plants. In many parts of the world, laws protect them from pickers and diggers. However, most sundews live in out-of-the-way places where humans are unlikely to be—in fact, where you shouldn't be. Walking in sphagnum bogs can kill the sensitive mosses and other plants, and is discouraged by conservation groups.

Because they are so unusual and often beautiful, carnivorous plants have a dedicated following, just as orchids and roses do. The International Carnivorous Plant Society, an organization of horticulturists, conservationists, scientists, and educators, is based in California and publishes a well-respected quarterly, *Carnivorous Plant Newsletter*. Sundews are obviously not candidates for the average wildflower garden; however, many people find them fascinating and challenging, and raise them as house or greenhouse plants in carefully regulated environments. Reputable nurseries that propagate and sell carnivorous plants and their seeds may carry such colorful names as California Carnivores, Dangerous Plants, The Carnivorous Plant Jungle, and even Triffid Park. The last recalls the science fiction movie *Day of the Triffids*, about man-eating plants that didn't just sit back and wait for a meal—they chased it down. Gulp!

It Counts and Remembers

Venus flytraps, perhaps the most famous of our carnivorous plants, can both count and remember. The "traps" close when certain hairs have been touched. But because the plant doesn't want to waste effort on a falling leaf or other debris, the triggers must be activated at least twice—as would happen if a fly were walking about on the trap. Thus, the plant can count—to two. What's more, the Venus flytrap can "remember" for up to 40 seconds that the trigger hair was touched once. After that interval, it's unlikely that an insect would remain motionless. The plant resets its memory, awaiting another chance for a double trigger.

Bloodthirsty Miscreant

"Here is a bloodthirsty little miscreant that lives by reversing the natural order of higher forms of life preying upon lower ones, an anomaly in that the vegetable actually eats the animal!"
—*Neltje Blanchan* (1900)

Purple Loosestrife

SUMMER'S DEADLY GLOW

Purple loosestrife almost drove Darwin "mad."

Its spectacular color makes purple loosestrife hard to hate, but the alien is pushing out many natives.

Bicycling north of Boston on the Minuteman Bikeway one August day, I came upon one of the most immense stands of wildflowers I had ever seen. Acres and acres literally glowed purple in the early-morning sun. I stopped and stared. It was an incredibly beautiful sight. It was also a vivid and deadly example of the hazards that some imported plants pose to our environment.

The flowers were purple loosestrife, an alien species that has been taking over vast wetlands, crowding out many native plants and robbing others of food and shelter. An unusual battle is underway to curb the spread of a plant that has been called one of the most beautiful summer wildflowers. The weapons are not chemicals or even mowers or shovels; they are *Galerucella calmariensis* and *G. pusilla*, two little beetles from Europe. Some say the battle will succeed, but others feel it's unnecessary and some even oppose attempts to eradicate the plant.

A native of Eurasia, where it is not nearly so common, purple, or spiked, loosestrife had arrived in North America by 1850, probably imported for gardens. The plants begin blooming around the Fourth of July, peak in August, and remain flowering as late as mid-September in the Northeast.

Lythrum salicaria is a member of the Loosestrife family (Lythraceae), consisting of about 21 genera and more than 400 species worldwide. Most are tropical, and only seven genera and about 25 species are found in North America. About a dozen of these species are of the *Lythrum* genus, and probably the most common is our purple loosestrife, found coast to coast, and missing only in Arizona and New Mexico and the extreme southeastern states. While purple loosestrife is an alien, many of our loosestrifes are natives, such as California loosestrife (*L. californicum*), a shrub of the Southwest; Florida loosestrife (*L. flagellare*), found only in Florida; and winged lythrum (*L. alatum*), which grows in all states and provinces east of the Rockies.

Gore and Peace

Purple loosestrife is a true loosestrife, as opposed to the genus of primroses, also called loosestrife (such as yellow loosestrife, whorled loosestrife, and moneywort—each discussed elsewhere). As if to confuse us more, those plants bear the Latin name *Lysimachia,* which literally means "loose-strife." However, our purple loosestrife has a less-than-peaceful Greek name. *Lythrum* means "gore," of the blood-and-guts kind that would be seen in a battle. It seems incongruous for a plant to be called loosestrife in English and gore in Greek, but the Latin name probably stems from the color of the flowers. What's more, there is some history of the plant's being used as a styptic poultice for wounds, and the connection with the primrose loosestrifes was probably drawn from that association.

Purple loosestrife's more popular medicinal uses were internal. It was once widely used to treat dysentery and diarrhea, and was also a respected treatment for fevers, liver diseases, constipation, and cholera. It has also been employed as an eye freshener and a gargle for sore throats.

Salicaria, incidentally, means "willow," because the leaves are similar in shape to willow leaves. In France, the common name for the purple loosestrife is *salicaire,* a word that has given rise to such English folk names as red sally and flowering sally. In Europe, where it is widely distributed, purple loosestrife has acquired many other folk names, such as spiked soldiers, purple grass, killweed, willowweed, purple willowherb, grass polly, foxtail, and salicare.

Purple loosestrife is a big, hardy herb. Plants run from three to five feet tall—sometimes to 10 feet—and bear as many as 30 to 50 flowering branches. They like wet feet, and grow in meadows, along stream banks and ponds, and near swamps. They also prefer full sunlight. This species is, incidentally, one of the relatively few plants whose seeds require light for germination; seeds of most plants seem indifferent to light and in fact most germinate in the dark. This need for light probably helps assure that loosestrife's seeds will sprout in an area that is sufficiently sunny. Indications are that the seeds do not attract birds or other granivorous creatures, perhaps because of some distasteful constituent. This is a reasonable defense strategy in a plant whose seeds germinate only when exposed to light—and therefore also to many seed eaters.

Pushy Perennial

Purple loosestrife is a downright pushy perennial, spreading rapidly by a variety of means. Plants produce vast numbers of seeds, which are often transported by both wind and water to new locations. When they arrive, their settling in is prodigious. According to Professor Bernd Blossey of Cornell University, an expert in purple loosestrife and its biological control, the seeds have a germination rate of more than 90 percent and between 10,000 and 20,000 seedlings can sprout in one square meter of land.

Survival techniques don't end there. The root system produces what botanists call "adventitious shoots," thus spreading in territory in which it has already gained a foothold. If that's

Poetic License?

In old England, loosestrife was called long purples, which has led some authors to wonder about a line from *Hamlet.* Shakespeare, considered almost as expert in floral culture as in playwrighting, wrote in Ophelia's death scene:

> *There with fantastic garlands did she come*
> *Of crow-flowers, nettles, daisies, and long purples.*

All but the long purples are spring flowers in England, leading at least one author to suggest that Shakespeare "for once made a mistake." However, it could also be that the bard simply had some other flower in mind or employed poetic license.

90/90

"In Europe, there are several insects which act together to control purple loosestrife. As a result, only small, scattered stands of the plant exist. The current program includes the introduction of these *Galerucella* spp., the weevil *Hylobius transversovittatus* and the planned release of two flower-eating species which are also specific to purple loosestrife. It is predicted that upon establishment of these species, North American purple loosestrife will be reduced by 90 percent over approximately 90 percent of its present range."

Biological Control: A Guide to Natural Enemies in North America, edited by C. R. Weeden, A. M. Shelton, M. P. Hoffmann (Cornell University; www.nysaes.cornell.edu/ent/biocontrol)

13 Hours

Before a purple loosestrife will begin flowering, there must be 13 hours of daylight.

not enough, pieces of the stem readily throw out roots to form new plants. Even if you mow them down, the "corpses" can sprout new plants.

With so many methods of assuring survival, and with no native enemies, it's easy so see why purple loosestrife can quickly blanket a sizable piece of land. That's what has so many botanists and environmentalists worried. In making itself at home, this energetic alien dispossesses many native plants that are unable to compete. In the process, many mammals, birds, insects, and other creatures that use native plants for food or shelter are also dispossessed. Meanwhile, purple loosestrife itself offers little in the way of food, cover, and nesting materials for native wildlife. No wonder this plant has been called the purple plague and has been included on The Nature Conservancy's list of America's Least Wanted—The Dirty Dozen.

Scientists shun using herbicides on purple loosestrife because the chemicals could cause environmental damage. Cutting down the plants is useless because the stems root so easily. Pulling them up is backbreaking work and requires immense numbers of laborers.

So instead, plant scientists like Dr. Blossey have turned to natural enemies. In Europe, purple loosestrife is kept in check mostly by insects that feed on its leaves and flowers. After extensive testing, scientists determined that the two European beetles mentioned earlier, *Galerucella calmariensis* and *G. pusilla,* could help control purple loosestrife populations by eating its leaves. When this happens year after year, plants die. State, provincial, and national governments are reluctant to import insects for fear they will attack native plants, and it took years of investigation to determine that the beetles would eat only purple loosestrife and would be safe to introduce. By 1992, the beetles had been released in New York, Pennsylvania, Maryland, Virginia, Minnesota, Oregon, and Washington state in the United States, as well as in locations in Canada. Other states have followed suit. A weevil, *Nanophyes marmoratus,* which eats loosestrife flowers, has also been introduced, and Dr. Blossey expects that, eventually, there will be a 90 percent reduction in the purple loosestrife population in North America.

Not all scientists are alarmed over the invasion. Wildlife biologist John Eastman, author of *The Book of Swamp and Bog,* argues that nature eventually reins in species that invade and dominate a region. Diseases and parasites attack the newcomer. Over the years, such checks and balances reduce populations, and the invaders meld with their new environment and with native species.

The most spectacular example I've seen of natural checks of an invasive species occurred in connection with the periodic infestations of gypsy moth caterpillars, a species introduced to New England at the turn of the 20th century. These eruptions occurred every eight or so years when millions of the fuzzy caterpillars would hatch in the spring and defoliate countless trees. The cyclical outbreaks kept getting bigger until finally, in the late 1980s, both a virus and a fungus appeared that together decimated the gypsy moth larvae. Today, gypsy moth caterpillars are no more numerous in my neighborhood than is any other species.

Purple loosestrife has not been without its outright fans. "One who has seen an inland marsh in August aglow with this beautiful plant is almost ready to forgive the Old Country some of the many pests she has shipped to our shores in view of this radiant acquisition," wrote Mrs. William Starr Dana at the turn of the 20th century. Even as late as 1970, the U.S. Department of Agriculture's 450-page *Selected Weeds of the United States* did not so much as mention purple loosestrife. What's more, even though most states have declared it a noxious weed, nurseries continue to sell *L. salicaria* as a garden plant.

Beekeepers love purple loosestrife blossoms, not only for the dark honey they produce but also for the flowers' availability. "Loosestrife is one of the few plants that blooms in midsummer, when everything else is dying back from the heat," a commercial beekeeper from Connecticut once told the *Hartford Courant.*

Trimorphic

Purple loosestrife fascinated Charles Darwin. Although at casual inspection the flowers seem ordinary enough, they are constructed in an unusual fashion, designed to ensure cross-fertilization. The flowers are "trimorphic"; that is, they come in three forms: long-styled, in which the pollen-catching stigma is on a long style, and the stamens, bearing pollen-producing anthers, are medium and short length; medium-styled, in which the style is medium in length, and the stamens are both long and short; and short-styled, in which the style is short and the stamens medium and long.

Each plant has flowers all of one kind. The pollen produced by the long-stamened anthers is large; the medium-length anthers have smaller pollen, and the short ones, smaller still. Pollen from anthers on long stamens will fertilize only the stigma on long styles. Medium-length stamens fertilize medium-length stigma. And so for the short ones.

Thus, when a bee enters a flower, it picks up one size of pollen on one part of its body. The bee must move on to other flowers with different configurations in order to unload the pollen. This trimorphism, which guarantees that inbreeding will not take place, amazed Mr. Darwin, who studied it at great length. He once wrote to noted American botanist Asa Gray: "I am almost stark, staring mad over *Lythrum* . . . For the love of Heaven, have a look at some of your species, and if you can get me some seeds, do!"

Whoops

"Horticultural cultivars of purple loosestrife were developed in the mid-1900s for use as ornamentals. Initially, these were thought to be sterile, and therefore safe for horticultural use. Recently, under greenhouse conditions, experimental crosses between several cultivars and wild purple loosestrife and the native *L. alatum* produced hybrids that were highly fertile. Comparable, subsequent experiments performed under field conditions produced similar results, suggesting that cultivars of purple loosestrife can contribute viable seeds and pollen that can contribute to the spread of purple loosestrife."
—*Lowell Urbatsch, Department of Plant Biology, Louisiana State University, writing in* USDA Plant Guide (2000)

Yarrow

THE FIRST-AID KIT

Yarrow has treated many maladies for many centuries.

Yarrow, imported as a medicine, can be found along many inhospitable roadsides.

As soon as March rolls around, when the sun is higher in the sky and the air is a tad warmer, wildflower fanatics hit the trail in search of some sign of life. Among the earliest greens are strange little combs that sprout from the earth almost as soon as the snow has melted. These early leaves of common yarrow are tantalizing, but it will be several months before the plant spreads open its clusters of white flowers.

Chippewas called yarrow *adjidamowano*, which meant "squirrel tail." The feathery "tails," so small in March, are the finely segmented leaves that also earned *Achillea millefolium* its name, *millefolium*, as well as its common English name, milfoil. The name may be an exercise of poetic license, however. Though I've never taken the time to confirm it by counting, there probably aren't a thousand leaves on the plant, just as there aren't a thousand feet on a millipede or a hundred on a centipede. Nevertheless, the name well suits the appearance, as does a popular Spanish name in the Southwest, *plumajillo*, which means "little feather."

Botanists, no poets when it comes to description, call these leaves bipinnate, which means leaflets branch off the stem, and from them, smaller subleaflets branch off, giving an overall lacy effect. Ferns with this appearance would be called twice-cut, and indeed casual observers of plant life sometimes mistake the flowerless yarrow for a fern. Some leaves are even tripinnate.

Fit for Survival

Far from being a primitive fern, the yarrow is a member of the Composite family and thus is among the highest forms of plant life. Each flower is composed of disk and ray florets, but yarrow is unusual in having only five or six rays per blossom, much like a simple, five-petaled flower. The sparsity of rays is balanced by a plenitude of flowers. While other Composites such as daisies and sunflowers have a few large blossoms composed of many disk and ray florets, yarrow has many small blossoms, each of which is composed of a few tiny disk and ray florets.

These clusters, or "umbels," of flowers are one of yarrow's ways of surviving. The plant flashes a sizable and bright display to passing insects, which find the wealth of closely packed blossoms easy pickings. The plant offers those flowers from May or June through summer and some-times into November. I have even seen them blooming at the end of December, despite many nights of below-freezing temperatures. This long flowering season virtually guarantees pollination despite the floral competition. A feeding insect will easily fertilize many flowers with pollen since all are so close together.

Other survival techniques include the perennial's ability to spread not only from the many seeds it produces but also from underground runners that are difficult to eradicate—much to the annoyance of farmers. While grazing animals shun the bitter leaves, hunger may force cows to eat yarrow, with the result that their milk has an off-flavor, which also irks farmers. The poor flavor and camphor-like scent are additional means of protecting the plant from predators. Not just mammalian grazers but many kinds of insects, such as the Japanese beetle, shun yarrow. In fact, the effect of the plant's scent is so powerful that yarrow is said to protect nearby plants of other species from insect attack.

Because it favors poor soils, yarrow can be useful in preventing erosion and in decorating an otherwise bleak landscape. One of its favorite haunts is the roadside, where doses of sand, salt, and petroleum pollution fail to daunt its annual appearance.

Many Milfoils

While there's no doubt that European settlers brought common yarrow to this continent, many botanists believe that yarrow was here long before the Europeans arrived. The U.S. Department of Agriculture's plant database, which calls *Achillea millefolium* both "native and introduced," lists 11 subspecies of yarrow that it considers native. Among these are western yarrow (*A. millefolium occidentalis*) and California yarrow (*A. millefolium californica*). Many of these subspecies were once considered species of their own. Thus, common yarrow may have been a circumboreal species, and over the millennia pockets of slightly different plants evolved—not different enough to make them species, but enough to make them notable.

Yarrow's Old World connections might be guessed from its generic name, which recalls the Greek hero. However, among the nine species of *Achillea* occurring in North America, only one other is considered truly native: Siberian yarrow (*A. sibirica*), found from Alaska through central Canada and into Montana, North Dakota, and Minnesota. The rest have been introduced. The only other import that has made any name for itself in North America is the sneezewort, or white tansy (*A. ptarmica*), so called because it was once dried and used as snuff to encourage sneezing as a headache remedy.

Most of the genus's 85 or so species live in Europe and Asia. Probably none is as widespread as *A. millefolium*, which is found throughout Europe, Asia, northern Africa, North America, and Australia.

The Absinthe Connection

Yarrow has long been used as a mild sedative, and the reason may lie in one of its constituents, thujone. This chemical is also found in absinthe, the illegal liqueur made from the related wormwood plant. The toxicity of thujone may be what led absinthe to be banned in most of the world and what contributed to the insanity and death of absinthe addict Vincent van Gogh.

Symbolic Yarrow

Emblem of our equal land,
Where men and women helpful stand,
And love and labor, high and low,
Type of the low! Thou lovely plant!
Teach the proud-hearted how to know
The sacred worth of nature's grant
The strength of bitterness, and the
  sweet
Humility of nature's feet.
—Annie Adams Fields
  (1834–1915)

Rust of Achilles

With a name like Achillea, you can bet a few tales have been told about yarrow. In one, Chiron, the centaur, is supposed to have taught Achilles about the healing virtues of yarrow, and he used it extensively to keep his armies healthy—so much so that the plant took on his name almost immediately.

Another story involved misinterpretation of the name. When Achilles and the Greeks were on their way to attack Troy, Telephus, a son-in-law of King Priam, tried to stop them. Clumsy Telephus tripped over a vine; Achilles caught and seriously wounded him with his spear. Later, an oracle told the ailing Telephus that only "Achilles," meaning yarrow, could cure his worsening wound. Telephus misunderstood and went straight to Achilles, promising to conduct his army to Troy if he would heal the wound. Agreeing, Achilles scraped some rust off his spear and from the filings arose a yarrow plant, with which he treated Telephus's wound. (Ancient tribes that settled what is now Hungary and Finland also believed that the scrapings from a weapon that caused a wound could cure the wound—more of the old "hair of the dog that bit you" theory.)

Its early use by armies earned yarrow such names as soldier's woundwort and *Herba militaris*.

The Woundwort

Throughout the centuries, healing wounds has been yarrow's chief use, probably because constituents in the plant help clot the blood. From the Greeks before Christ to the American Indians of the West and soldiers in the American Civil War, yarrow has been a medicine for the wounded. The Medieval English called it woundwort ("wound plant"), the same name used by the Utes in their own tongue. In fact, the word *yarrow* is said to have come from the Anglo-Saxon *gearwe*, a name used as early as A. D. 725 that may have meant "to repair," reflecting the plant's healing applications.

Herbals and herb histories go on at length about the medicinal uses to which the leaves and dried flower tops of yarrow have been put. Ancient herbalists claimed that its thousand-parted leaves were a sign from above of its thousand uses, and that it has been eaten, drunk, smoked, snorted, rubbed on, and bathed in by many peoples. All sorts of skin problems—from ulcers and burns to the eruptions of measles and chickenpox—have been treated with yarrow ointments, although some sensitive people can wind up with skin irritations from its use. It has even been studied as a possible cancer-preventing agent.

"An ointment of the leaves cures wounds, and is good for inflammations, ulcers, fistulas, and all such runnings as abound with moisture," wrote Nicholas Culpeper in 1649. "The leaves of yarrow doe close up wounds, and keep them from inflammation, or fiery swellings," noted John Gerard in 1633. He added that "the leaves being put into the nose, do cause it to bleed, and ease the paine of megrim"—a rather messy way of dealing with a headache. Oddly enough, in 1640 herbalist John Parkinson recommended putting the leaves in the nose to stop bleeds.

Milfoil tea was well known as a treatment for stomach problems and possibly as a sedative. The plant's content of iron, calcium, potassium, and other minerals led to its use as a tonic. It has treated hypochondria, cramps, dysentery, hemorrhoids, diabetes, and disorders of the lungs, kidneys, and the liver. The leaves were chewed to relieve toothaches. American Indians employed it for many problems, including balding, earaches, and sprains, and as a contraceptive, sweat herb, cold medicine, and appetizer. Its wide use among the natives may vouch for its status as a native plant. Iroquois, Micmacs, Chippewas, Chickasaws, Delawares, Menominees, Objibwas, Mohawks, Utes, Meskwakis, Piutes, Zunis, Miamis, Illinois, Winnebagos, and other tribes all used yarrow. Despite all this, the *British Pharmacopoeia* dropped yarrow as an official medicine in 1781 and the *U.S. Pharmacopoeia* did so in 1882.

Yarrow is not without other uses. The leaves are pungent—it was called old man's pepper—and it was once used to pep up salads and as a snuff. The Swiss made a vinegar from an Alpine variety. An extract obtained from the flower heads is used as a flavoring for soft drinks, and liqueurs have been made from several European species. The Swedish, who call it "field hop," once used it in making beer; Linnaeus, the father of plant and animal classification, maintained that yarrow-brewed beer was more intoxicating than hop-brewed.

Good and Evil

The forces of both good and evil have put yarrow to use. Witches employed it for spells, prompting such names as devil's nettle and bad man's plaything. On the other hand, the plant was woven into garlands that were hung in homes and churches to ward off evil spirits. Hanging some yarrow in the crib could also discourage baby-stealing witches. The Chinese cast yarrow stems like lots to divine the future, a technique described in the *I Ching*.

Love, too, was closely connected with yarrow. English country maids who wanted to find out who their future husband would be would wrap an ounce of dried yarrow in flannel, place it under their pillow at night, and chant:

> *Thou pretty herb of Venus' tree,*
> *Thy true name is Yarrow;*
> *Now who my bosom friend must be,*
> *Pray tell thou me to-morrow.*

Another version of this prayer, recorded in the Devon region of England, went:

> *Yarra, yarra, I seeks thee yarra,*
> *And now I have thee found,*
> *I prays to the gude Lord Jesus*
> *As I plucked ye from the ground.*
> *Gude night, purty yarra,*
> *I pray thee sweet yarra,*
> *Tell me by the marra*
> *Who shall my true love be.*

Yarrow Parasite

While many creatures shun yarrow, at least one plant seeks it out to survive. The purple broomrape's seeds germinate only when in contact with the roots of *Achillea millefolium* or a few other related plants. The broomrape's roots tap into the yarrow's roots to obtain all the nutrition they require—but not so much that they kill the host. Thus, broomrapes don't need chlorophyll and lack any green parts.

Some maidens believed that if they cut the stem crossways, the initials of their future husband would appear. And when the fellow was found, having him eat yarrow at the wedding ensured that he wouldn't take off—for seven years, at least.

A messier system of prognostication was also practiced. In a rather odd custom, country folk in England would tickle the inside of the nose with a yarrow leaf while singing:

Yarroway, Yarroway, bear a white blow,
If my love love me, my nose will bleed now.

Yarrow's many uses and its unusual leaves have earned it many other names, among them knight's milfoil, thousand weed, thousand seal, nose bleed, bloodwort, staunchweed, sanguinary, noble yarrow, and dog daisy. Since carpenters were apt to cut themselves in their work, it was also called carpenter's weed, especially in France, where it's known as *herbe aux chapentiers*.

While sometimes disparaged for its weedy ways, yarrow makes a bright addition to a wildflower garden as company for such fellow "weeds" as the daisy, black-eyed Susan, St. Johnswort, and later the goldenrods and asters. Its fragrance is fresh, and the flowers are long lasting in summery bouquets. It's easily transplanted to well-drained, well-sunned spots.

A. millefolium will often produce pinkish flowers, especially at higher altitudes. However, there are cultivated bright pink and red varieties (*rosea* and *rubra*), popular with gardeners. Yarrow is even used as a ground cover that can be walked upon, though not heavily. As such, the bright green leaves, not the flowers, are wanted, and the plants must be mown regularly. Imagine, though, how soft and luxurious "yarrow grass" would feel to the barefoot stroller!

Queen Anne's Lace

THE ROYAL CARROT

Both loved and hated, Queen Anne's lace is a wildflower whose family history has been much debated.

Queen Anne's lace is another of those hardy, weedy, but attractive summer wildflowers that will inhabit places most plants disdain. Though it is one of our most handsome wildflowers, it is also among the most hated.

Daucus carota, also commonly called wild carrot, is a native of the Old World that, like the daisy, dandelion, and other sun-loving imports, spread across the continent with ease and abundance. It is found in all of the lower 48 states and most Canadian provinces. Queen Anne's lace favors dry, unmown fields and the edges of sunny roads, blooming from late June into October. However, they are in their glory at midsummer.

The lace-like delicacy of the plant's flat-topped, circular clusters of tiny, white flowers inspired its common name. Queen Anne, who ruled England from 1702 to 1714, was said to have been fond of wearing lace on her dresses. One story has it that the Queen challenged her ladies in waiting to create a lace as finely designed as the *Daucus carota* in her garden. She joined in the competition, and guess who won? A close look at the umbels shows they are actually composed of many smaller clusters of flowers, or "umbellets," all lacily laid out and probably quite as exquisite as anything the Queen created or wore.

This huge mass of tiny flowers is a flashy display to passing insects. More than 60 kinds have been found visiting the blossoms. These include flies, bees, butterflies, wasps, and beetles, some perhaps drawn by the somewhat strong smell of the plant.

Daucus, the generic name, is from the Greek, *dais*, "to burn," and is descriptive of the acrid taste of the root and leaves. *Carota* comes from a Greek word for "carrot" that may in turn have been based on the word for "head," a reference perhaps to the showy display of flowers. Maude Grieve says the word is Celtic for "red of color." Calling a redhead a "carrot top" may have ancient roots.

The flower heads of Queen Anne's lace are variable; the plant may have only a few dozen florets or, like this one, a few hundred.

One of a Kind?

Is Queen Anne's lace the cultivated carrot run wild or the wild parent of the cultivated carrot? Or is it neither? Various authorities say the carrot we grow in the garden or buy in the market is really

Recipes

Spicy like the seeds of celery, Queen Anne's lace seed can be used to season soups and poultry, herb bread, or "campfire stew." To collect them, simply shake the brown "nests" into a small paper bag or a can. (Make sure, of course, that you're not shaking the nest of a poisonous hemlock.) To clean the seeds of the chaff, rustle them in a light breeze.

Country Trick

Country folk used to have fun by coloring Queen Anne's lace flowers. To try it yourself, cut some flowers and stick the stems in cans of water to which vegetable dyes of various colors have been added. After six or eight hours, the white flower heads will turn to pretty shades, suitable for offbeat bouquets.

the same species as this wild carrot. Cultivated carrots carry the scientific name *Daucus carota sativa*, indicating they are a subspecies of wild carrot. The cultivated carrot, said to have originated from the area of Afghanistan, has spread around the world to every continent and was in North America by 1609. Known to ancient Greeks and Romans before Christ, it was prized as a medicine—it is rich in vitamin A, among other things. Though it has long been eaten, the root was not very popular as a food until fairly modern times, and was not widely consumed raw until this century. (However, E. Lewis Sturtevant reported that in the 19th century, "So fond of carrots are the Flathead Indians of Oregon that the children cannot forbear stealing them from the fields, although honest as regards other articles.")

Some authorities believe that the eating variety was cultivated from the wild while others believe just the opposite—that Queen Anne's lace is merely some bastard offspring of cultivated carrots gone wild. Others disagree with both contentions. "Still another fiction," wrote Neltje Blanchan in 1900, "is that the cultivated carrot, introduced to England by the Dutch in Queen Elizabeth's reign, was derived from this wild species. Miller, the celebrated English botanist and gardener, among others, has disproved this statement by utterly failing again and again to produce an edible vegetable from the wild root. When the cultivation of the garden lapses for a few generations, it reverts to the ancestral type—a species quite distinct from *Daucus carota*." Nonetheless, Dr. Sturtevant said, "Vilmorin-Andrieux obtained in the space of three years roots as fleshy and as large as those of the garden carrot from the thin, wiry roots of the wild species."

While the garden and wild carrots have very similar fernlike leaves, underground parts are noticeably different. Wild carrot has a white root that burrows deep into the rather dry ground in search of water. The roots of cultivated carrot are red orange outside (the bark) and yellowish inside (the wood). By the intention of the cultivators, the roots don't go nearly so deep and favor richer soils. Mrs. Grieve, a turn-of-the-20th-century herbalist, said the wild carrot has a "strong aromatic smell and an acrid, disagreeable taste" while the garden carrot has a "pleasant odor and peculiar, sweet, mucilaginous flavor."

Poisonous Relatives

Queen Anne's lace is one of only two members of the *Daucus* genus in North America. Rattlesnakeweed (*D. pussilus*) has smaller flower heads and is found in the southern and western states. They are in turn members of the Carrot, or Parsnip, family (Apiaceae) of about 50 genera in North America, including cicelies, parsleys, parsnips, pimpernels, and fennel. While many of these have been used as foods, two genera include the highly poisonous water hemlock (*Cicuta maculata*), summer bloomer of wetlands, and the poison hemlock (*Conium maculatum*), found throughout the United States and southern Canada, and said to be one of the most poisonous plants in the world.

In many cases, identification of different species in this family is difficult and can be done only by studying the seeds. Queen Anne's lace is quite like some other less common members of the clan but can usually be identified with certainty by the one or several tiny deep purple flowers that often appear in the center of the white-flowered umbel. No one knows for certain why these purple flowers appear, but children used to be told that Queen Anne pricked her finger, causing a drop of her blood to stain the lace. Poison hemlock has no purple flower but does have purple-spotted stems, which are lacking in Queen Anne's lace.

Bird's Nest

After the flowers die, the umbel curls up so that each head forms what looks almost like a bird's nest, which is one of the folk names for the plant. The shape of this "nest" has led some to believe certain insects are specially adapted to make their homes in their heads. Certainly, spiders find it handy, but one well-circulated story—and probably only a story—was that a species of bee would dwell only in the dried umbels of wild carrots.

These nests often fall off and roll away in the breeze, like tumbleweeds. If they roll across or come to rest in the right environment, the seeds that fall out will eventually germinate. Thus the nests may actually be a clever evolution of nature that provides vehicles to carry loads of seeds for establishing new colonies.

Over the centuries, wild carrot has been used to treat a wide selection of ailments, everything from kidney problems and gout to hiccoughs and flatulence. "Though Galen [a second-century Greek physician] commended garden carrots highly to break wind," wrote Nicholas Culpeper in 1649, "yet experience teacheth they breed it first, and we may thank nature for expelling it. . . . The seeds of them expel wind indeed, and so mend what the root marreth." In many cases only the plant's seeds, which are plentiful, were used to obtain the medicinal essences and oils and were a food flavoring.

Wild and cultivated carrots also had an odd use during the reign of King James I, when it was the fashion for ladies to decorate their hats with leaves, in the manner of feathers. "One can picture the dejected appearance of a ballroom belle at the close of an entertainment," observed Mrs. William Starr Dana. One could also picture the dejected look on the belle who used a once-popular concoction of questionable efficacy. Boiled in wine, the flowers were supposed to be a love potion that was also a contraceptive.

Transplanting flowering Queen Anne's lace is tricky because by maturity, the plant's root has sunk itself deep into the ground. These deep roots were one reason the plant was among the most hated of weeds; farmers found it almost impossible to eradicate from fields and often called it devil's plague. Dairy farmers especially dislike Queen Anne's lace because it gives an unpleasant taste to the milk of cows that eat it.

Queen Anne's lace is a biennial that produces only lacy, almost fernlike leaves in its first year. In the second year, the flower head appears. While most plants grow from one to three feet tall, I have seen specimens reach seven feet. Several forms of *D. carota* are known, including ones with all pinkish or purplish flowers.

Other names for Queen Anne's lace include crow's nest, lace-flower, parsnip, and rantipole. The last—an old word for a wild, roving, reckless, or ill-behaved person—was undoubtedly first applied by a farmer, not a flower fan.

Fair Ladies

In the fields and blooming meadows
Among the grasses green
And the dainty pink-faced clover,
Fair ladies can be seen.
Decked out in snowy laces,
Heirlooms of nature old,
"They've long been in the family,"
Flower gossips have been told.
Gauzy gowned in fairy network
And caps of finest lace,
Dames colonial of the roadside
In the summer find a place
In nature's glad procession,
That pay all homage due
To their wise and bounteous mother,
They're proud and loyal too!
—Ray Laurance

Gardening Guides

To establish Queen Anne's lace in your wildflower garden or field, dig the young, first-year plants, easily identified by the distinctive, feathery leaves. Dig deep to get the full root. Do this two years in a row since the plants are biennials that bloom only in the second year. The plants will self-sow. You can also gather the seed in late summer and plant them in the fall.

Dayflowers

AN EMBARRASSING MEMORIAL

Looking like blue Mickey Mouse ears, dayflowers are one of our few common "weeds" from Asia.

The Asiatic dayflower appears to be a two-petaled flower, but look for the lowly third.

Stacey Wahl, who wrote a children's book that uses flower petals to teach number groups, told me that one of the most troublesome numbers to represent was "two" because there are so few two-petaled flowers.

"How about the dayflower?" I asked her.

"That would be cheating," she replied. "I would never cheat a child."

Indeed, while at first glance it seemed to be one of few two-petaled flowers, the Asiatic, or common, dayflower (*Commelina communis*) has a third petal, barely visible below the main part of the blossom. Unlike the pair of larger sky blue petals, the lower one is whitish and wan, looking as if it were a useless mistake of nature.

This petal arrangement, a characteristic of the whole dayflower clan of some 95 species worldwide, inspired an 18th-century botanist to employ some humor in naming the genus *Commelina*. According to Neltje Blanchan, "delightful Linnaeus, who dearly loved his little joke, himself confesses to have named the dayflower after three brothers, Commelyn, Dutch botanists, because two of them—commemorated in the two showy blue petals of the blossom—published their works. The third, lacking application and ambition, amounted to nothing, like the inconspicuous whitish third petal!" Linnaeus himself was less blunt in his own explanation, saying only that the Commelina are "flowers with three petals, two of which are showy while the third is not conspicuous, from the two brothers Commelin, for the third died before accomplishing anything in botany."

Odd Flowers

Our dayflowers are interesting not only for their name, but also in their odd form and habits. No plentiful flowers in the United States and Canada look anything like the dayflowers, which seem as if they would be more at home in a jungle. Each flower rises from boatlike bracts, with two large petals looking like blue Mickey Mouse ears. The flowers open with the sun, remain open long enough to be fertilized by passing bees, then close, usually by midday, never to open again—

hence, dayflower. (If the sky becomes cloudy after a flower opens, the blossom may last longer, sometimes all day.)

The bright petals, almost the color of many of our gentians, are probably what prompted the importation of the Asiatic dayflower in the 19th century. However, they are attractive not only in their hue but also in their large numbers, their long blooming season (June through October), and their peculiar tendency to sparkle in the sunlight. Examine a blossom closely and you'll see hundreds of tiny shiny spots, like so many miniature diamonds or dewdrops set off nicely by the blue. Under a microscope these appear to be clear cells scattered throughout the more plentiful blue-tinted ones. The sparkle occurs when sunlight hits the juice in the colorless cells. The petals are very succulent; crush one in your fingers and you'll find much moisture and little substance— and a blue tint to your skin. It is possible that these sparkles act as beacons to distant bees, luring them in so that they will notice and be attracted to the blue color of the flowers.

A Second Chance

The flowers, incidentally, give the bees two chances to dine. When the petals wither in late morning or early afternoon, they collapse into a gelatinous mass that remains blue but mixes with the remaining nectar. Bees love this sweet mixture and while dining on it, may leave a bit of pollen on the pistil, still erect and able to be fertilized.

Almost as odd as the flowers are the leaves, which clasp or wrap around about a half inch of the plant stem before spreading out in normal leaf fashion. If they were not so common outdoors, the exotic Asiatic dayflowers would probably be a popular and prized houseplant.

And they are common, almost ubiquitous, in parts of the continent and particularly around older established properties. Dayflowers can be found growing out of cracks in sidewalks, around the bottoms of utility poles, and almost anywhere there's a bit of fairly moist soil. These annuals can spread quickly, forming an 8- to 12-inch-high ground cover in sunny or even somewhat shady locations, such as the edges of lawns, where they make a nice transition between the grass and shrubs. They spread rapidly and easily because the stems flop over and creep along the ground, sinking new bunches of roots from their joints. (If you should use dayflower as a ground cover, keep them away from territory inhabited by delicate plants.)

Members of the small Spiderwort family (Commelinaceae) of 25 genera and 350 species, all with three-petaled flowers, dayflowers are among the few temperate-zone members of their genus and family. Mostly natives of the tropics, spiderworts are represented by only three genera in North America. One genus, called spiderwort (*Tradescantia*), has the unusual ability to register the level of nuclear radiation. Under exposure, the stamen hairs turn from blue to pink, the degree of change reflecting the strength of the radiation.

Commelina species include two common natives. Despite its name, the perennial Virginia dayflower (*C. virginica*) has a huge range—from Pennsylvania south to Florida and Texas through Central America into South America as far down as Paraguay. Its "mini-petal" is blue. The perennial

Dayflower Dishes

"The young leaves and shoots may be added to salads. We get so many of these plants in our garden that I pull handfuls of the shoots, wash the roots and add them to Chinese stir fry. Entire flower is edible sheathed in a connate sepal, as are seeds (also tucked in that sepal sheath). This is free food that comes up every year; get it started and it will become one of your favorite weeds. I eat the plant (flowers in summer and shoots in spring) in salads; leaves, flowers, shoots are delicious. In late summer, flowers keep coming and you can eat seed pods for a healthful dose of essential oils and phytosterols."
—Jim Meuninck,
"Herbal Odyssey,"
www.herbvideos.com

slender dayflower (*C. erecta*) has a white mini-petal, but stands upright and doesn't flop over like its Asiatic sibling. It's found from the East Coast to Arizona. Eight *Commelina* species live in North America, mostly in the southern states. The Asiatic dayflower, found in all states and provinces east of the Rockies, also ranges into Central America, where it is among several plants known as *hierba de pollo*, or "herb of cooked chicken," a possible reference to its use as a flavoring. The western, or birdbill, dayflower (*C. dianthifolia*) occurs in the Southwest and has a third petal that's larger and bluer than the others.

Uses of the dayflowers have been somewhat limited. One source reports, however, that the Asiatic dayflower increases sexual potency of senior citizens. The Chinese dry the leaves and use them for tea.

Nature's Makeshift

Of course, this alien can be considered a weed in that it has become so common and widespread. That doesn't mean that it is necessarily a pest or worthless. Weeds can be admirable plants and certainly were to John Burroughs, the American naturalist who wrote the following in 1881:

> Weeds are nature's makeshift. She rejoices in the grass and the grain, but when these fail to cover her nakedness, she resorts to weeds. It is in her plan or a part of her economy to keep the ground constantly covered with vegetation of some sort (which, incidentally, protects the soil erosion and the terrain from flooding), and she has layer upon layer of seeds in the soil for this purpose and the wonder is that each kind lies dormant until it is wanted. . . . .
>
> Ours is a weedy country because it is a roomy country. Weeds love a wide margin, and they find it here. You shall see more weeds in one day's travel in this country than in a week's journey in Europe. Our culture of the soil is not so close and thorough, our occupancy not so entire and exclusive. . . . . The European weeds are sophisticated, domesticated, civilized; they have been to school to man for many hundred years, and they have learned to thrive upon him: their struggle for existence has been sharp and protracted; it has made them hardy and prolific; they will thrive in a lean soil, or they will wax strong in a rich one; in all cases they follow man and profit by him. Our native weeds, on the other hand, are furtive and retiring; they flee before the plow and the scythe, and hide in corners and remote waste places. Will they, too, in time, change their habits in this respect?

Certainly the Asiatic dayflower, from a faraway continent, has found its niche in North America and is doing its best to clothe nature when and where she needs it.

No Spiders

Spiderworts don't look like spiders, nor do they attract them. They were named in error for another plant that was supposed to cure the bite of a poisonous spider.

Late Summer & Fall

Knotweeds

KNOTS UNDERFOOT

Most knotweeds are lowly plants, but at least one is towering.

Lady's thumb, a typical tiny knotweed, has buds, flowers, and seeds all in one pink cluster.

Some are called knotweeds, some smartweeds, water-peppers, and persicaries. One is even called smartass. But doorweed and doorgrass are the names I like best, the names that recall the friendly old farmhouses that the most common of these weeds once surrounded.

John Burroughs explained it. "Knotgrass . . . carpets every dooryard and fringes every walk, and softens every path that knows the feet of children, or that leads to the spring, or to the garden, or to the barn. How kindly one comes to look upon it! . . . It loves the human foot, and when the path or place is long disused, other plants usurp the ground."

Burroughs was describing the prostrate knotweed, *Polygonum aviculare*, one of the many polygonums that inhabit North America and much of the world. The Germans called it *wegtritt*, literally "path step," for these plants are so often underfoot. Like flies, mice, and roaches, they seem to follow humans wherever they go. Unlike vermin, however, they are not necessarily pests; they serve a useful purpose, and they can even be beautiful.

Polygonum is a widespread and botanically elementary genus of more than 100 species worldwide and some 70 on this continent. Everyone has seen them. However, few people bother to notice most of them, much less learn their names, because the flowers are so small. However, as Burroughs urged, "examine it with a pocket glass and see how wonderfully beautiful and exquisite are its tiny blossoms."

Tiny Flowers

In many *Polygonum* species, the flowers are pink (though some are whitish or greenish). Although they are only an eighth of an inch or less long, the flowers of Pennsylvania smartweed (*P. pensylvanicum*) are clustered in groups of from a few to 50 or more. Their often bright and rich pink color can stand out nicely against the green foliage of leaves and nearby grass. Their color is especially appreciated because, in many parts of North America, pink wildflowers are uncommon in late summer and autumn. And since they thrive in hard, well-packed soils, such as paths, they are often the only vegetation that colors the more downtrodden parts of our planet.

If you take Mr. Burroughs's advice and inspect the smartweed flower cluster, you'll find that the vast majority of blossoms are closed, as if they were all just buds. Among the dozens on a smartweed spike, only one or two flowers will open up at one time, usually at random and without order. When they finish blooming, the five-part, petal-like calyx closes back up, still pink and bud-like in appearance. Inside, however, seeds are now growing. Thus, a cluster of knotweed flowers can be a collection of buds, blossoms, and seed-hiding calyxes, all looking alike from a distance and retaining their color for weeks. In many flowers, once the blooming has ended, the distinctive color disappears. In Pennsylvania smartweed and related species, the flower head, still pink after blooming, may be the plant's attempt to flash as much color as possible to attract insects to the few flowers that are actually blooming in the cluster.

These flower clusters—appearing to be so many little knots—may be the source of the name knotweed. Sports fans, however, may view the buds not as knots but as miniature pigskins, for in many species they are elliptical, just like footballs.

Polygonum is a member of the Buckwheat family (*Polygonaceae*) of some 50 genera and nearly 1,200 species around the world, including rhubarbs and docks. Buckwheat itself (*Fagopyrum esculentum*) is found throughout the northern United States and in much of southern Canada as an escape and as a descendant of cultivated plants brought over from Europe. *Fagopyrum* is from the Greek, meaning literally "to eat wheat," and Americans have long been fond of buckwheat pancakes, a traditional winter meal. The English grew it only as food for pheasants. Native to Central Asia, buckwheat has long been cultivated by the Chinese, Hindus, and Japanese. Russians are fond of honey made by bees that have gathered the nectar of buckwheat flowers. Many *Polygonum* species also offer nectar that attracts bees, and the genus is considered an important honey source by beekeepers.

Japanese knotweed, the largest of our Polygonum species, is a tasty pest from Asia that can grow 10 feet tall.

To wildlife, members of the *Polygonum* genus are valuable food sources. Many kinds of birds, especially game birds and waterfowl, eat the seeds or the whole plant. *Aviculare* means "of the birds," and the plant has been known as birdgrass, birdweed, and goosegrass for centuries. Probably from seeing how birds sought out the knotweeds, American Indians collected the seeds to add to others to grind into flour.

Self-Defense

Because most of these plants are a foot or less tall, their nectar stores are likely targets for pilfering by ants and other pedestrian insects that are not apt to pollinate the flowers. Consequently, many species have evolved defenses. For example, the long-bristled smartweed (*P. cespitosum*, meaning "of

Knotweed Pie

Euell Gibbons, who wrote *Stalking the Wild Asparagus*, loved Japanese knotweed pie. Here's how he made it:

Pick large young knotweed stalks with long "knots" at leaf junctures.

Peel off the purple rind.

Slice green inner walls into short pieces.

Mix 1½ cups of sugar, ¼ cup of flour and ¾ teaspoon of nutmeg.

In another bowl beat 3 eggs.

Gradually beat flour mixture into eggs.

Beat 4 cups of the chopped knotweed into the mixture.

Pour into an ordinary piecrust.

Bake for 50 minutes at 400 degrees Fahrenheit.

Cool and eat.

the ground") has long white hairs situated just below the spike of flowers or intermixed with the bottom few blossoms. These discourage crawlers from passing to the sweets above.

Long-bristled smartweed and many other *Polygonum* species also have distinctive sheaths that wrap around junctions of stems and stalks, almost like tape that is holding the pieces together. In the long-bristled smartweed, and in some other species, hairs project from the top edge of the sheath, again discouraging crawlers.

Several members of the genus are called tearthumbs, such as the arrow-leaved tearthumb (*P. sagittatum*, meaning "arrow-like"), because they have rows of tiny prickers on their leaves and stems. These devices probably evolved as obstacles to thieving ants and other crawling insects. If rubbed across the skin, they might make a weak scratch, but hardly a tear.

P. aviculare does not possess these hairs, since its few, dull-looking flowers produce no nectar. That's because prostrate knotweed relies on breezes, not bees, to carry its pollen to fertilize distant flowers.

Though it has unremarkable flowers, this knotweed has many names. Aside from the three avian names already mentioned, it has been called bird's tongue or sparrow tongue because of the shape of its little leaves; allseed, because it was, like its cousin buckwheat, used as a grain; armstrong, because it's hard to pull up from invaded gardens; pigweed, pigrush, swine's grass, hogweed, and cowgrass, because livestock eat it; centinode, ninety-knot, and nine-joints, because of its characteristic stem joints; red robin, probably because of its reddish seeds; beggar grass, because it usually inhabits poor soils; wild buckwheat, because of that cousin; and wire weed, because it's wiry.

In nature, especially nature inhabited by humans, prostrate knotweed performs a useful function in covering what is called stressed ground—soil that has been compacted in one way or another, but especially by feet. Few plants grow in such soil. In covering trails and other trampled ground, prostrate knotweed helps to prevent erosion. At the same time, the plant benefits from the mammalian feet that traverse these trails. Be they paws or shoes, they pick up seeds and transport them down the line to sprout new knotweeds. What's more, these seeds are especially long-lived, and may be viable for 50 or more years, thus greatly increasing the odds that they will find a suitable home for germination.

A peculiar *Polygonum* that needs neither bees nor breeze to propagate is the swamp, or shoestring, smartweed (*P. muhlenbergii*), which relies so much on its shoestring-like roots to spread its numbers that it rarely puts forth many flowers. In fact, acres of these wetland plants may be seen in season without producing a single flower. The species is named, incidentally, for the Rev. Heinrich Muhlenberg, a minister who was also a noted naturalist. His name is more commonly seen in connection with an endangered turtle called Muhlenberg's, or the bog, turtle.

Despite its name Pennsylvania smartweed is found from the Atlantic to the Pacific. Also called pinkweed, the plant bears its pink clusters atop one- to two-foot stems and is found around house foundations, paths, and roadsides. "Its erect pink spikes direct attention to some neglected corner in the garden or brighten the field or roadside," wrote Mrs. William Starr Dana.

Throughout spring and early summer, long-bristled and Pennsylvania smartweeds are but low, barely noticeable weeds. However, in mid-August, they stand up and show off their colors—in the process, burying remnants of the past. I have had long-bristled smartweed in a spot reserved in the spring and early summer for daisies, black-eyed Susans, yarrow, and hawkweeds, and the smartweed stands up just in time to surround and cover over the unattractive dying or dead remains of its predecessors.

Smarting Weeds

Russians have experimented with and used various smartweeds for tanning leather and as feed grains, going so far as to irradiate the seeds to increase the percentage of protein in them. Because of the plant's high nitrogen content, agricultural experts have recommended Pennsylvania smartweed as an excellent fertilizer for poor soils; it's grown and then plowed under.

The name smartweed comes from the bitter taste of the leaves of some species. One such smarting smartweed, found around pond edges, is often called mild water-pepper (*P. hydropiperoides,* meaning "water-pepper-like") and is one of our more common native species. More common and more attractive is the amphibious swamp smartweed (*P. amphibium*), also called longroot smartweed, which can live on dry land, on land sometimes submerged, and in water with its leaves floating. The terrestrial form, often seen around summer-dry drainage ditches, has striking stems striped with crimson (it was once called *Polygonum coccineum,* meaning "scarlet"). This native plant possesses a characteristic of many polygonums—swollen joints where the leaves join the stem; hence, the generic name, *Polygonum,* which means "many knees." Many people believe that these joints are also the source of the "knots" of knotweed.

P. persicaria, another common weed and an import from Europe that's found coast to coast, is edible as a salad green and was once used to produce a yellow dye. It is called lady's thumb because the leaves bear a design that some have imagined to look like a thumbprint of the Virgin Mary. Its specific name, *persicaria* means peach-like, and many polygonums were formerly classified under the genus *Persicaria,* because their leaves resemble those of the peach tree. Though it was not native, lady's thumb quickly spread across the continent with the European settlers and was so established by the late 19th century that American Indians in the Midwest were using it to treat stomach ailments.

A Medicine Chest

Among the most interesting and widely known of the *Polygonum* clan is *P. hydropiper,* another European immigrant, which has a myriad of names and medicinal uses. Its folk names include water-pepper (the translation of *hydropiper*), biting persicaria, bity tongue, ciderage, red knees (the color of the joints), bloodwort, snakeweed, redshanks, sickleweed, and pepperplant.

Packaged for each of its traditional herbal uses, this water-pepper could probably fill an old-time pharmacist's whole shelf. In various solutions, it was supposed to have cured epilepsy and treated gravel, dysentery, gout, mouth sores, dropsy, jaundice, colds, coughs, and bowel com-

Viviparity

Some plants, especially those that grow in alpine climates with short seasons, bypass the flower-and-seed process and produce new plants from "bulbils," small bulbs that fall off the mother and start new plants. This process is called viviparity, a word whose roots mean "to bring forth live." The Alpine Bistort (*Polygonum viviparum*) produces a few flowers but usually many more bulbils. It grows in the Rockies and in other cold regions of northern North America, Europe, and Asia.

plaints. It was used as an antiseptic and a stimulant. Extracts of the plant were applied to ulcers and hemorrhoids (hence, two of its more earthy folk names, arsesmart and smartass).

Because of the old Doctrine of Signatures, which asserted that plants bear outward signs of their value to humans, water-pepper was often employed to treat sore and swollen joints. "It is very good for sciatica, gout, or pains in the joints, or any other inveterate disease," said Nicholas Culpeper, "if the leaves are bruised and mixed with hog's grease and applied to the place, and kept on four hours in men and two hours in women, the place being afterwards bathed with wine and oil mixed together, and then wrapped up with wool or skins, after which they sweat a little." Another signature found on many *Polygonum* species is spotted leaves, which gave rise to the plant's use in treating pimples and acne.

Americans treated cholera with it by wrapping the patient in a sheet soaked in water-pepper tea. Mexicans used the plant as a diuretic and for rheumatism. People who once believed that a certain kind of worm caused earaches used to apply a few drops of the juice to the ear as a cure. Some herbals recommended the plant for getting rid of fleas in a room, and maintained that chewing the leaves would eliminate toothaches—perhaps because the mouth pain would divert attention from the tooth.

There are even more ailments for which it was used, but suffice it to say that among past practitioners of folk medicine, water-pepper was a must.

Pest from Asia

Though most polygonums are low-lying plants, one import is a giant, reaching 10 feet in height. In fact, the Japanese knotweed (*P. cuspidatum*) is so big and spreading, it's often mistaken for a shrub. The first time I came across a specimen, I didn't know its identity. There it stood, nearly five feet tall, bushy, and loaded with sweet-smelling tiny white flowers. The kids and I had watched it grow from the day in the spring when we first saw its asparagus-like shoots at the edge of the pavement. By late August, it was big and spreading and unlike anything I had seen before.

There were clues to its identity, including hollow stems. When it consisted of little more than several shoots, two or so feet high, the boys had broken one and, noticing the empty middle, stuffed a stick into it. They wanted to see how long it would remain, stick in shoot. It was still there three months later, but hidden by the luxurious growth of large oval leaves and all the drooping branches of small white flowers.

We had also noticed that the stalks were wrapped here and there by paper-like bands, similar to the joints on the lowly knotweeds nearby. By comparison, however, this mystery plant was as an elephant would be to a mouse. Several wildflower field guides didn't have the answer, but George W. D. Symonds's *The Shrub Identification Book* (1963) did. Oddly enough, Japanese knotweed shouldn't have even been in the book. Mr. Symonds explained that although the plant is not a woody shrub, it looks more like a shrub than the herb it is. Shrubs last year-round, but herbs die back to the ground at season's end. And since Japanese knotweed dies back, bears flowers, and grows wild, it's a wildflower.

Equine Cruelty?

Equestrians of old found water-pepper useful. The ancient Scythians believed that if **Polygonum hydropiper** was placed under the saddle, a horse would be able to travel faster than usual without stopping for food or water. Pity the horse.

This native of Japan arrived in England in the 1800s when a Belgian botanist introduced it. From England it soon made its way to America. Keepers of gardens, perhaps Oriental gardens, probably introduced the plant because of its sweet scent or simply because of its abundance of flowers and handsome leaves. During the 20th century, Japanese knotweed spread to such a degree that Nelson Coon, in *The Dictionary of Useful Plants*, called it the worst of the *Polygonum* weeds and almost impossible to eradicate. The plant is spreading steadily and can be found on both coasts; in the Northeast there are miles-long stretches of railroad track with Japanese knotweed growing along it.

The plant is also called Japanese, or Mexican, bamboo because of its similarity to that Oriental plant; it's also weedy, like bamboo. However, knotweeds are not even closely related to bamboo, which is a grass. *Cuspidatum*, from the Latin, means "having a cusp or point," probably referring, in this case, to the point of the leaf. The word is from the same root that gives us cuspid and bicuspid, our one- and two-pointed teeth.

Although Japanese knotweed may be a pain in the green thumb to gardeners who suddenly find it spreading rapidly through their prized hybrids, Euell Gibbons saw in it a source of a considerable variety of foods. In his best-selling *Stalking the Wild Asparagus* (1962), Mr. Gibbons devoted a full chapter to Japanese knotweed, treating it as a combination fruit and vegetable. Boiled like asparagus and served with butter and maybe a little sugar to counteract the tartness, the young shoots make a pleasant vegetable, he maintained. He also gave recipes for aspic salad, a sweet-and-sour sauce, Japanese knotweed jam, and *Polygonum cuspidatum* pie.

Whether you want this "food" on your own property is questionable. It can spread annoyingly and become difficult to get rid of. Some people consider Japanese knotweed the most serious plant pest around today, a threat to many native wild species that is spreading too rapidly and too extensively. Many states list it as a noxious weed because, as the Washington State Department of Ecology puts it: "The species forms dense stands that crowd out all other vegetation, degrading native plant and animal habitat. This perennial plant is difficult to control because it has extremely vigorous rhizomes that form a deep, dense mat. In addition, the plant can resprout from fragments; along streams, plant parts may fall into the water to create new infestations downstream."

What's more, their sweet though not overpowering scent seems to attract many stinging insects—not so much bees as yellow jackets and sundry species of wasps and hornets. A bush-full of those could unnerve someone who is sensitive to insect venom.

Better to try to eliminate the plant than introduce it. Most chemicals are ineffective because the rootstock—up to five feet deep—is difficult to kill. One technique is to cover the invaded area in the spring with sheets of black plastic. Do that for a year or two and you'll starve the root. Of course, you'll also kill everything else under the plastic, but in war, desperate measures are sometimes necessary. Another technique that requires more vigilance is to continually cut down the shoots as they try to rise up and spread leaves. This, too, may take a couple of years because the roots are so strong and long lasting.

And if you have a hankering for *Polygonum cuspidatum* pie, you can always visit the local railroad tracks.

Indian Pipes

GHOSTS OF SUMMER'S WOODS

"Palpably ghastly" to some, Indian pipe mystifies others.

Indian pipe is an epiparasite and thus needs no green chlorophyll to survive.

Coming across a cluster of Indian pipes is an eerie, almost shocking experience. Ghostly and pale in the dark of the midsummer woods, the plant's freakish white flesh makes it look more like an oddly formed fungus than the wildflower it is. These albinos of the flowering plant world are somewhat closely related to the dogwoods, heaths, and even the evergreen laurels and rhododendrons. Like some of these cousins, Indian pipe has learned ways to take advantage of other life forms in order to live in places where few plants could survive.

The white or bluish white, almost leafless, plants bear a single five-petaled flower that, when young, faces downward. The shape of the plant resembles a clay pipe whose stem has been stuck in the earth, and the flower is not unlike the bowl. Scientists call it *Monotropa uniflora*, meaning "once-turned" and "single-flowered." "Once-turned" refers to the fact that the flowers face the ground early in their life and then turn straight upward once they begin to produce seeds.

The Indian pipe is a member of a tiny clan of two to four species—scientists disagree on the number. Of these, only Indian pipe and pinesap (*M. hypopithys*) live in North America. Indian pipe is found from Maine to Florida, and from Washington to northern California. The plant also ranges across southern Canada and into Alaska.

Monotropa is in turn a member of the Indian Pipe family (*Monotropaceae*), a small clan of 10 genera and 12 species, mostly found in the temperate Northern Hemisphere. They include the equally unusual pine drops, pigmy pipes, snow plants, and cone plants, none of which are common.

An Epiparasite

The Indian pipe is strange not only in appearance but also in lifestyle. Botanists at first thought it was a parasite, feeding directly off the roots of other plants. But Indian pipe's own thick, brittle cluster of roots never touches those of other plants. Then scientists decided it was a saprophyte (from the Greek for "rotten plant"), living chiefly on the decaying parts of other plants, particularly trees. However, botanists now believe the plant is an "epiparasite"—a parasite that forms a relationship with another parasite to obtain its nutrients. Its roots employ certain mycorrhizal fungi in the soil to obtain food from the live roots of green plants such as trees. The fungi connect the Indian pipe with the host's roots by means of filaments. Scientists have not yet figured out whether the fungus gains anything from its attachment to the Indian pipe—it seems to serve only as a conduit between the tree root and the herb. However, botanist A. Randall Olson, a longtime fan and student of *Monotropaceae*, has come across an "obscure report from a botanist who died before he had a chance to publish his findings that phosphorus in some form may be transferred to the fungal partner."

Though it may not look much like a typical blossom, the Indian pipe flower has most or all of the equipment found in typical flowers. It offers both nectar and pollen, and while little research has been done on the range of insects that will visit it, small bumblebees have been seen on the flowers. "I suspect that certain flies would not be out of the question either," said Dr. Olson, who is head of the Department of Environmental Sciences at Nova Scotia Agricultural College. Dr. Olson said that while the flower has no scent that is discernable to humans, "the floral organs may be releasing other substances detectable to the insects alone." What's more, he said, while Indian pipe's whitish color is bright to human eyes, insects may perceive colors that make the plant even more attractive, helping it to stand out like a beacon on the shaded forest floor.

Since it obtains all needed nutrients from other plants, Indian pipe doesn't require leaves, the food-making factories that most plants possess. Thus, in the long process of evolution, only vestiges of leaves remain in the form of scale-like appendages on the stems. Nor does the plant need chlorophyll, the green chemical employed by most plants in using sunlight to create carbohydrates for food. Thus, the entire Indian pipe lacks any trace of green.

Indian pipes favor beech woods, but they will live in other areas, and it is said that the best time to find them is after a heavy, soaking midsummer rain. They always live in shade, never in open sun. The roots send up shoots only when the plants are ready to bloom. Since they don't need the sun to manufacture food, they don't require a long season of aboveground parts. As soon as blooming and seed making is completed, the aboveground parts turn black and wither away.

The plant can't be picked for display—not that anyone would want it for a bouquet—because its flesh soon turns black and oozes a clear, gelatinous substance when cut or even bruised. Its natural color and tendency to "melt" on picking earned it the name ice plant. Other names include ghost flower, corpse plant, and wax plant. "This curious herb well deserves its name of corpse plant, so like is it to the general bluish waxy appearance of the dead," wrote Dr. Charles F. Millspaugh. "Then, too, it is cool and clammy to the touch, and rapidly decomposes and turns black even when carefully handled."

"It is the weirdest flower that grows, so palpably ghastly that we feel almost a cheerful satisfaction in the perfection of its performance and our own responsive thrill, just as we do in a good ghost story," said Alice Morse Earle. Its common name comes, of course, from the shape of the plant and probably from the fact that it was first known as an Indian herb.

Pinesap, North America's only other *Monotropa*, is a circumboreal species found throughout the Northern Hemisphere north of the tropics. In England, it's known as the yellow bird's nest, reflecting its tangled cluster of thick roots. Indian pipe's roots are similar, and it has been called nest root and nest plant.

Sad and Cold

Pale mournful flower, that hidest in shade
'Mid dewy damps, and murky glade,
With moss and mould,
Why dost thou hang thy ghastly head
So sad and cold?
—Catherine Beecher
(1800–1878)

Whose Pipe?

"Why should it have been named Indian pipe?" naturalist F. Schuyler Mathews wondered early in the 20th century. "It occurred to me once, when I was climbing the slopes of South Mountain in the Catskills and came across a pretty group of the ghostly Indian pipes, that they were wrongly named; they should have been called the Pipes of Hudson's Crew. Those of us who have seen the ghostly crew in Rip Van Winkle can easily imagine the gnomelike creatures smoking pale pipes like these." Perhaps Mathews didn't know that the plant has also been called Dutchman's pipe.

Woodland Puffs

Most folk names for Indian pipe aren't very attractive. One, however, surely is: fairy-smoke.

For Bright Eyes

Its use as a medicine has earned Indian pipes even more names. American Indians employed the plant as an eye lotion—whence the name eyebright—as well as for colds and fevers. Americans of the 19th century treated spasms, fainting spells, and nervous conditions with the plant and called it convulsion root, fitroot, and convulsion weed. Mixed with fennel, it was once also used as a douche.

Dr. R. E. Kunze, writing more than a century ago in The Botanical Gazette, told this story: Fourteen years ago—it was in the early part of July—I went woodcock-shooting with two friends, near Hackensack, N.J., and while taking some luncheon in a beech grove along the course of Saddle River, I found a large patch of ground literally covered with Monotropa uniflora in full bloom; it covered a space some five feet wide by nine feet long, a beautiful sight of snow-white stems and nodding flowers. Being in need of some just then, I proceeded to fill my game-bag; and to the question, what it was used for, answered: "Good for sore eyes"; little thinking that the party addressed was suffering from a chronic inflammation of the eye-lids, the edges of which had a very fiery-red appearance. No sooner said than he proceeded to take in his game-bag a supply also, and he made very good use of it, as I ascertained afterwards. His inflamed lids were entirely cured in four weeks' time, and he has had no further trouble since, by applying the fresh juice of the stems he obtained while it lasted.

Today, few herbals even mention Indian pipe, possibly because the plant contains toxic substances.

Unforgettable

Indian pipes, once seen, are never forgotten. I can remember finding them as a child on Nantucket Island and being told their name. That, the daisy, black-eyed Susan, and violet were probably the only wildflowers I could name till well into adulthood.

They are not the stuff of wildflower gardens. While Indian pipe produces seeds, gardeners shouldn't be optimistic about having them germinate into flowering plants. Conditions must be just right, including the presence of the correct fungi. You can always try, but remember that the plants need total shade in summer. Clarence and Eleanor Birdseye, the frozen-food folks who wrote a book, *Growing Woodland Plants*, pointed out that it's virtually impossible to transplant Indian pipe. That makes sense since digging up the plant would break its vital fungal connections with its host neighbors.

Nature writers who prefer showier plants have given Indian pipe some bad reviews. Explaining its colorless and parasitic qualities, Neltje Blanchan penned a lengthy attack, including:

"No wonder this degenerate hangs its head; no wonder it grows black with shame on being picked, as if its wickedness were only just then discovered. . . . . To one who can read the faces of flowers, as it were, it stands a branded sinner." Arthur Craig Quick suggested that its ancestor was "an honest plant" that "must have been imbued by some evil genius with the idea that the world owed it a living. . . . . Forthwith it began its search for a way to get its living through the work of others."

Poet Mary Potter Thacher Higginson (1844–1941) offered a more pleasant description of these unusual plants:

> In shining groups, each stem a pearly ray
> Weird flecks of light within the shadowed wood,
> They dwell aloof, a spotless sisterhood.
> No Angelus, except the wild bird's lay,
> Awakes these forest nuns; yet night and day,
> Their heads are bent, as if in prayerful mood.
> A touch will mar their snow, and tempests rude
> Defile; but in the mist fresh blossoms stray
> From spirit-gardens, just beyond our ken.
> Each year we seek their virgin haunts, to look
> Upon new loveliness, and watch again
> Their shy devotions near the singing brook;
> Then, mingling in the dizzy stir of men,
> Forget the vows made in that clustered nook.

From a wicked degenerate to saintly nun; such are the extremes of the human imagination.

Mulleins

THE BEARDED WEEDS

Mulleins offer beauty, a beverage, and even a light,
and they hang out with hags.

Common mullein can grow to a height of six feet. Its leaves once served as dollhouse blankets.

Weeds they are—common around the world, often found where little else will grow. Nonetheless, mulleins are wonderful weeds, both in form and utility. They are represented in North America chiefly by two plants: common mullein, known for its leaves, and moth mullein, known for its flowers.

Common, or great mullein (*Verbascum thapsus*), the more easily seen of the two, has been known by more than 40 folk names and has a long list of uses—everything from a torch to a restorer of hair color. Practically everyone has seen the plant, although few people today know its formal name or its reputation as anything but a weed. Growing from five to eight feet in height, common mullein bears thick, velvety, grayish leaves that have earned it such names as ice leaf, Our Lady's flannel, Adam's flannel, beggars flannel, velvet dock, blanket herb, velvet plant, woolen, feltwort, fluffweed, and hare's beard. Because of its uprightness, it has been called shepherd's club, Aaron's rod, Peter's rod, Jacob's staff, or Jupiter's staff—depending, no doubt, on the caller's religious persuasion.

Hag's Torch

Mulleins have been appreciated since ancient times. In fact, it was said that Ulysses used common mullein, long believed to ward off evil spirits, to protect himself against the wily Circe. Romans and subsequent civilizations dipped the dried plant in fat and lit it. These torches, called *candelaria*, were often used in funeral processions and other ceremonies. Later civilizations that burned mullein for light called the plant high taper, hig-taper, hedge taper, torches, and candlewick plant. The colorful name hag's taper may have come from the belief that witches used mullein to illuminate sinister ceremonies or that people used the tapers to repel witches. However, most authorities think that *hag* is just a corruption of the Old English words *haege*, *haga*, or *big*, meaning "hedge," and was applied because the plants are common along English hedgerows.

Common mullein has for centuries been used to treat diseases of the lungs, earning it the names lungwort and ag-leaf. Europeans, colonial settlers, and many groups of American Indians smoked the dried leaves to obtain relief from coughs due to consumption and asthma, though one wonders how smoke could ameliorate breathing problems.

"The seeds, bruised and boiled in wine and laid on any member that has been out of joint, and newly set again, takes away all swelling and pain," wrote 17th-century herbalist Nicholas Culpeper. *The Ladies' Indispensable Assistant* in 1852 said steeped mullein "is good for a lame side, and internal bruises." The leaves were also used in a different way to relieve soreness; as a substitute for flannel, they were rubbed on rheumatic joints, the gentle friction creating a soothing warmth. Among other ailments the plant was used to treat were diarrhea, colic, piles, gout, mumps, toothaches, ringworm, burns, migraines, earaches, and warts. It was even used for removing slivers.

Of all the medicinal and cosmetic forms of mullein, none is more noted than mullein tea, used for coughs, colds, or simply as a tonic. The English mix a cup of boiling water with a tea-spoon of leaves that have been dried and powdered. Euell Gibbons recommended cough syrup made from red clover, white pine, mullein, and wild cherry bark. Before you run out and brew some tea or syrup, though, be aware that cows and other grazing animals shun the common mullein because its hairs are irritating to the mucous membranes. To be safe, the tea should be filtered through fine muslin or a similar material.

Common mullein can be purchased commercially from herbal medicine suppliers and goes by such names as Mullein Leaf, Mullein Leaves Tincture, Mullein Flower Oil, and as an ingredient in mixtures like Ayurvedic Bronchial Formula.

Exotic Uses

Common mullein had some rather exotic uses, too. The seeds, considered somewhat narcotic, were thrown into water to intoxicate fish and make them easier to snare. Figs and other fruits were wrapped in its leaves to prevent rotting. This has led to some modern speculation that the mullein may contain an antibiotic that inhibits the growth of various bacteria. The velvety leaves were placed inside socks or shoes to warm the feet and increase circulation—and perhaps to act as a sort of natural Odor Eater.

From the yellow flowers, Roman women obtained a dye to give them blond hair. The plant's ashes were made into a soap that was said to restore gray hair to its original color (possibly true, if the original color was black). "Pale country beauties rub their cheeks with the velvety leaves to make them rosy," noted Neltje Blanchan in 1900.

Professional flower arrangers today use the spring rosettes of leaves at the base of displays. In *Using Wild and Wayside Plants*, Nelson Coon says the leaves make fine blankets for children's dollhouses.

The down on the leaves and stems was once gathered as tinder; when dry, it would ignite at a spark. Hummingbirds have been seen gathering the down to line their tiny nests, and many other bird species, especially goldfinches and woodpeckers, can be found picking the seeds off the stalks.

Nature's Blanket

Several species of beetles make their summertime home on milkweed and only milkweed. But one variety, *Labidomera clivicollis*, often moves elsewhere for the winter. It seeks out the thick, fuzzy, curled-up leaves of the common mullein as a place to hibernate.

One would think that with all those uses, mullein would be a popular plant. It was, once. Years ago, many gardeners grew common mullein to provide not only medicine but also beauty. The statuesque plant was admired both for its plentiful yellow flowers and for its handsome foliage. In fact, it was widely grown in the British Isles and especially in Ireland around the turn of the 20th century. "I have come 3,000 miles to see the mullein cultivated in a garden and christened the 'velvet plant,'" wrote a surprised John Burroughs, the American naturalist, on a trip to Great Britain.

Hirsute Family

Common mullein's ability to live in inhospitable places—full bright midsummer sunlight and dry, poor soil—is due in part to its ingenious design. The long leaves wind around the stem in whorls that point upward, an arrangement that captures every drop of rain possible and directs it down the stem to the thirsty roots. These roots are found both near the surface, to catch the sprinklings of showers, and deep in the earth, to collect the more consistently available moisture far below the evaporating heat of the sun.

The hair that covers both leaves and stem is more complex than that found on most plants. Seen under a microscope, these hairs contain branches and collectively look like a forest after the leaves have fallen. The hairs probably serve several purposes. One, apparently, is to discourage animals and insects from eating the plant—although slugs, usually hair haters, are able to chew up mullein. The hairs also discourage crawling insects, especially ants, from making the long climb up to the flowers, where they could rob the nectar without pollinating the stigmas.

The hairs are also believed to form a barrier against the harsh sunlight that might otherwise damage the delicate cells in the leaves or simply sear the plant's flesh. The hairs may also serve as a barrier to dust particles that are plentiful in the dry soils in which mullein is often found; dust can become layered enough on a leaf to prevent the cells from receiving the sunlight and carbon dioxide needed to function properly.

The flowers have hairs of their own. Common mullein has five stamens, three of which are shorter than the others and bear small purple hairs that exude a sweet "sap." Both the color and sweetness of these hairs lure bees and other insects, which visit primarily for the flowers' pollen. These hairs are probably the source of mullein's generic name, *Verbascum*, a word that is probably a corruption of *barbascum*, from the Latin, *barba*, a "beard" (whence *barber*).

Hack Plant

Common mullein was sometimes called *herbe de St. Fiacre*, after an Irish-born priest who lived and gardened in France in the 17th century and became the patron saint of gardeners. In France, a *fiacre* is an old-fashioned cab, named after the Hotel de Saint Fiacre in Paris. If you enter the name *herbe de St. Fiacre* into some language-translating computers, you'll get back "grass of St. Hackney carriage."

If you'd like to try adding them to your garden, collect the seeds and plant them in the fall. While some states list common mullein as an invasive plant, most herb gardeners don't find it to be pushy or a prolific producer of offspring. They consider it an attractive and useful plant. In fact, Audrey Wynne Hatfield, in *How to Enjoy Your Weeds*, says common mullein actually benefits gardens by sinking both deep and shallow roots that drain and ventilate the soil. "This is but one more example of how weeds can work to the advantage of the cultivated plants in one's garden," she says.

Moth Mullein

Moth mullein (*Verbascum blattaria*) is a rather different sibling whose leaves are not unusual, but whose flowers can possess a strikingly delicate beauty. Field guides usually list moth mullein under yellow flowers, but this is one of a handful of wildflowers that will play tricks on you. As often as not, moth mullein's flowers are white or even light pink. In all color forms, however, the blossom is purple toward its center, where it bears what appears to be a little ball of purple wool. This purple-on-white or purple-on-yellow combination, probably aimed at guiding insects to the nectar and pollen, is unusual in flowers of midsummer, and a roadside stand of moth mullein will easily catch and hold the eye.

Like the dayflower or chicory, moth mullein opens in the early morning but usually wilts by midday. Each blossom lasts one day, sometimes two, then drops off to leave a rounded seedpod with a long tail on it. (I've seen some blossoms open for a second day, but only after having fallen away from their connection with the plant; they were merely dangling from the seedpod tail on which they had been snagged. Unlike the proverbial chicken without its head, it was a head without its chicken!)

Some believe that moth mullein is so called because it attracts moths. Other observers point out that the flower is not designed for moths and that the blossoms are closed at night when most moths are about. I have seen bees and particularly pollen- and nectar-gathering flies on the flowers (which can, in a pinch, fertilize themselves), but never a moth. It is more likely that the name came from a fancied resemblance of the white or pinkish flowers to the insect. The purple hairs, which appear in tufts on the stamens, could be likened to the furry body of a moth.

If the plants bloomed in large numbers and if the flowers lasted longer, moth mullein would no doubt be popular with gardeners. However, what pleases the gardener is not necessarily best for the plant. Like its common sibling, moth mullein is a biennial that sends up a low, non-flowering rosette of leaves the first year and a tall flowering stem the second. Living only two years, the mullein must rely on seeds to keep the species alive and therefore produces prodigious numbers of them. To do this most efficiently, the plant puts out a few fresh flowers a day rather than many at once. It thus spreads over several weeks the effort needed to provide an attractive display for potential pollinators and to get many flowers fertilized. The pods in turn ripen successively over a period of weeks, increasing the chances for nature—via showers, wind, birds, or other means—to disperse the seeds.

Burly Weed

Burly weed, with your mittens and
    cloak,
Standing tall in the sun, tell me
    whether
You're a straying of Eskimo weather,
Or a phoenix of tropical smoke?
Was it summer, or winter, that
    wound you
In your waterproof duffle and felt?
Are you dreaming of snowdrifts
    around you,
Or a climate where buttercups melt?
—Theron Brown (1832–?)

Such untamed flowers are always a challenge to cultivators, who've managed to develop mullein hybrids that are available in a variety of colors and are long blooming. Most are offspring of purple mullein (*Verbascum phoeniceum*), a Mediterranean species, and bear such varietal names as Jolly Eyes, Pink Domino, Copper Rose, and Gainsborough. "Verbascums are the talk of the gardening world and the essential complement to any garden," said one British flower catalogue in 2001.

The Names

Some sources say common mullein, *V. thapsus,* was named for the Greek island of Thapsos, where the plant is supposed to come from; others maintain that the name refers to a town in Sicily or the city of Thapsus in the North African nation of Tunisia. (It was there that Julius Caesar defeated the partisans of Pompey in 46 B.C., reportedly killing 50,000 people.) Whatever the geographical origin of the name, the plant was hardly concentrated in one town, and was widely spread around the Mediterranean, Europe, and western Asia by the time Linnaeus named it. Common mullein came to this continent with 18th-century settlers, who appreciated its medicines and beauty. Today common mullein is found in all of the lower 48 states and most provinces. Its journey across North America was apparently rapid; one explorer reported in 1802 that he couldn't find it west of the Alleghenies, and another 17 years later he saw it growing along the Missouri River on trails frequented by westward-traveling settlers and trappers. It "follows closely on the footsteps of the whites," wrote Edwin James in 1819.

The scientific name for moth mullein (*V. blattaria*) comes from the Latin, *blatta,* meaning "cockroach," an insect that this plant was once believed to repel. Though less common, moth mullein is equally widespread in North America.

The origin of the word *mullein* itself has been a subject of considerable speculation. Some say it is from the French, *melandre,* meaning "leprosy" or, generally, "diseases of cattle or the lungs." The plant is sometimes called cow's, or bullock's, lungwort because it was used to treat ailments of those animals. However, other authorities say the name is from the Old French, *moll,* meaning "soft," and refers to the plant's flannelly leaves. Or, it's a corruption of the Old English, *wolleyn,* meaning "woolen." The venerable *Oxford English Dictionary* suggests that it might come from *molegn,* an Old English word for "curds." But it doesn't say whey—oops, why.

The genus *Verbascum,* with nearly 300 species worldwide, is a member of the Figwort family, which consists of about 165 genera and 2,700 species, including the familiar but oddly shaped butter-and-eggs, snapdragons, turtleheads, beard-tongues, speedwells, monkey flowers, betony, and louseworts—among the latter, the rare and now famous Furbish's lousewort, whose discovery along a stream in Maine once halted a multimillion-dollar dam project. Such respect the mulleins will doubtless never get.

St. Johnsworts

CHASING THE BLUES WITH YELLOW

Many believe St. Johnswort can chase away depression.

Good press can do wonders for a weed. In 1996 St. Johnswort, a relatively obscure plant, quickly became one of the hottest herbal treatments when an article in the prestigious *British Medical Journal* praised its ability to treat depression. "Move over, Prozac," proclaimed *Newsweek* a few days later, and scores of other publications around the world carried word of this "new" wonder drug.

Is this the same plant that ancient Greeks waved to ward off evil spirits? The same that is supposed to sport bloody spots on August 29, the day its namesake was beheaded? The same noxious weed hated by farmers coast to coast?

Few people beyond serious herbalists and wildflower enthusiasts had ever heard of St. Johnswort until the British announcement. The medical authorities weren't conservative in their praise for *Hypericum perforatum*, either. "Hypericum extracts were significantly superior to placebo and similarly effective as standard antidepressants," said the *British Medical Journal.* "The herb may offer an advantage, however, in terms of relative safety and tolerability, which might improve patient compliance."

St. Johnswort is also inexpensive. Assuming you don't grow and grind your own for free, you can buy a daily dose of St. Johnswort pills at a cost of between 27 and 50 cents, depending on the brand and the store you buy it from. That's a far cry from the cost of Prozac and similar prescription drugs.

Europe has been the center of interest in St. Johnswort as a treatment for both depression and anxiety. In fact, in Germany at the turn of the 21st century, St. Johnswort was the most-used antidepressant, outselling Prozac eight to one. The growing interest in the herb prompted the U.S. government's National Institutes of Health to announce in 2001 that it was conducting a three-year study of the efficacy of the herb. In 2002, a study published in the *Journal of the American Medical Association* indicated that St. Johnswort was of little value in treating depression of "moderate severity."

Common St. Johnswort has been called the new Prozac, but studies have yet to prove its ability to treat depression.

Golden Flames

How cheery, warm, and bright,
With golden yellow light,
The hillside pasture this midsummer
    day,
As through the fragrant fern
The starry flowers burn
With all the brilliancy of noontide
    ray!
Was it for this of old—
This blazing gleam of gold
From petals shining as from altar
    flame—
For token of their praise
That men in olden days
Should give St. Johnswort for this
    flower's name?
Because its flame was seen
Kindled in pastures green
At times when he, the Baptist, came
    on earth,
Of whom it was foretold
By sainted prophets old,
That many should have gladness at
    his birth?
—Isaac Bassett Choate
    (1833–1917)

Ancient Medicine

While some old-time herbalists suspected what modern scientists are finding, the plant was more famous in the past for other uses. Greeks and Romans considered St. Johnswort as a treatment for wounds, for reducing fevers, and as a diuretic. The herb continued to be used throughout the Middle Ages and the Renaissance, but by the 19th century it had pretty much fallen out of official use and was even dropped from pharmacopoeias, the official listings of medical drugs. "In scientific medicine, it has become obsolete long ago," wrote one noted physician in 1884.

It was long ago suggested, however, that St. Johnswort might be useful in the treatment of mental problems. In 1799, William Lewis, an English expert on medical herbs, reported that "*Hypericum* has long been celebrated . . . in maniacal disorders; it has been reckoned of such efficacy in the latter as to have thence received the name *fuga daemonum*." Back then, many kinds of mental disorders were lumped together as demonic possession—*fuga daemonum* means "scare the devil." "Taken internally, the plant cures melancholy, 'if it is gathered on a Friday in the hour of Jupiter, and worn away about the neck,' " wrote Charles M. Skinner in 1911, reporting what an ancient herbal had to say.

A few years before the British announcement about the depression studies, there was another flurry of excitement—this one over another possible problem St. Johnswort might treat: AIDS. In 1988, *The Proceedings of the National Academy of Sciences* suggested that hypericin, an active constituent in St. Johnswort, had been shown to inhibit retroviral infections in laboratory animals. Retroviruses are a group of tumor-producing viruses, including the type that causes AIDS. However, later research found possible serious interactions between hypericin and other drugs used to treat AIDS. Normal doses of St. Johnswort extract actually deactivated the therapeutic function of one anti-AIDS drug, and in February 2000, the U.S. Food and Drug Administration issued a public health advisory warning of St. Johnswort's dangerous interaction with indinavir, a drug used by AIDS patients.

Another study of patients given synthetic hypericin suggested that the substance was not only useless in fighting the retrovirus, but also that about half the participants developed skin rashes. St. Johnswort has long been known to cause photosensitivity in the skin of livestock and some humans. Needless to say, people thinking of treating themselves with any herb should first consult a physician and be aware of any of the possible drug interactions and warnings—in this case, the possibility of getting a rash.

Mystical Past

St. Johnswort's names, both common and scientific, reflect a mystical past. For hundreds of years Europeans believed that bloody spots appeared on the leaves on August 29, the anniversary of the beheading of St. John the Baptist, for whom the plant is named. But they also believed that on June 24, St. John's birthday, the plant should be hung from windows to keep away the likes of ghosts, devils, imps, and even thunderbolts. In fact, some people believed that the clear spots on the leaves were places where the angry devil stabbed them with a pin—*perforatum*, as in "perforat-ed," is how scientists describe these clear spots.

Hypericum is the ancient Greek word for St. Johnswort. Some authorities say the the word is a combination of the Greek, *hyper* and *eikon*, meaning "over an apparition," because some people believed that the plant had power over evil spirits and could frighten them away. What would probably have scared them most was the scent, for common St. Johnswort isn't a pleasant-smelling plant, unless you like the smell of turpentine or rosin.

The yellow flower petals turn red when crushed, which some herbalists took to mean that the plant could treat bleeding problems. John Gerard wrote that St. Johnswort could make "an oyle of the coulour of bloud, which is a most precious remedy for deep wounds, and those that are thorow the body, for sinewes that are prickt, or any wound made with a venomed weapon."

Over the ages it was also used to treat bedwetting, cancers, hemorrhoids, stomach ulcers, and insomnia.

Watch Your Step

One of the most colorful superstitions associated with the plant comes from the Isle of Wight, off the south coast of England. There, if you accidentally stepped on a St. Johnswort plant, a fairy horse might rise from its roots right under your legs and you'd be instantly and helplessly astride the ani-mal. All through the night the horse would ride until dawn, when it would disappear into the ground, leaving you stranded miles from your home.

The plant has picked up many names over the centuries. Herb gatherers shortened *Hypericum* into "percum-leaves." Another folk name was tutsan, probably an abbreviated form of *toute saine*, "heal-all." Its many other names include amber, devil's scourge, goatweed, grace of God, hard-hay, Klamath weed, St. John's grass, tipton weed, *mellepertuis* ("thousand perforations"), rosin rose, and witches' herb.

Shrubby St. Johnswort is popular with bees, which like its abundance of pollen.

The name Klamath weed may stem from some association with a nation of American Indians of that name, who live in the Pacific Northwest. The plant has long been hated on the West Coast. In California, St. Johnswort has been considered a noxious weed since the 1920s. In 1946, two species of beetles that prey on this plant were imported from Europe as a biological con-trol and have apparently been successful.

Mangosteens

Common St. Johnswort is a member of the Mangosteen family (*Clusiaceae*) of six North American genera, of which *Hypericum* is the most common, numerous, and widespread. True mangosteens are evergreen trees of the genus *Garcinia,* found in Malaysia and represented on this continent by four tropical species, including the saptree.

There are about 60 species of *Hypericum* in North America, of which common St. Johnswort is perhaps the most widespread and best known. However, other well-known members of the clan include shrubby St. Johnswort (*H. spathulatum*) and spotted St. Johnswort (*H. punctatum*). Though it's a herbaceous plant, shrubby St. Johnswort is so big and full of branches by midsummer that it looks like a bush. Its flowers produce a rich bounty of pollen that bees delight in harvesting.

Common St. Johnswort blooms from June through September in sunny, dry locations, such as fields and waste places. The one- to two-foot-high plants are easy to identify: their flowers have five bright yellow petals that turn dark red if you rub them. Hold up the leaves to the light and you'll see the transparent spots, which are actually oil glands.

St. Johnswort can be established from seed or by transplanting wild specimens. Seeds are readily available through herb houses or can be acquired from wild plants in the fall. If you choose to transplant, dig way down and get a good clump of soil; because the plant favors dry locales, St. Johnswort has a deep taproot for seeking out underground water. It also has shallow roots that wander outward and establish new plants. Thus, once planted, St. Johnswort may be hard to get rid of. Put it where it won't be a problem or where you can keep it under control.

Baptist's Beheading

Common St. Johnswort bears dark red spots on the flowers and clear spots on the leaves. Tradition says that the red spots represent the blood of St. John, spilled at his beheading, while the clear spots are the tears shed by his followers.

Avens

BOTH BLESSED AND CURSED

The wandering avens are lowly plants with lofty backgrounds.

Avens are plants that few people recognize when they're blooming but many people curse when they're fruiting. They are among the late-season grabbers that rely on mammals—from woodland wildlife to humans—to spread their population.

The fruits appear in late summer and early fall, usually as little green clusters of seeds. At the end of each seed is a tiny hook, similar to that on a Velcro fastener, that quickly grabs onto fur or clothing, seeking a free ride to a new home. "Whoever spends an hour patiently picking off the various seed tramps from his clothes after a walk through the woods and fields, realizes that the by-hook-or-by-crook method of scattering offspring is one of Nature's favorites," wrote Neltje Blanchan.

These hooking devices are actually transformed styles. The "style" connects the pollen-catching stigma to the seed-producing ovaries in the pistil. In most plants the style withers away after fertilization, but in the avens, it does double duty, becoming stronger and developing the hook. I once heard the inventor of the Velcro fastener report that he got his inspiration for the device after a walk in the woods, where he observed how some hooked seedpods—quite possibly a species of avens—had attached themselves to his clothing and his dog's fur.

The seed head of the avens may have inspired the inventor of Velcro fasteners.

Natural History

The genus *Geum* comes in several common and often different-looking varieties in North America, including white avens, or redroot (*Geum canadense*); rough avens (*G. virginianum*), which has cream-colored flowers; yellow avens (*G. aleppicum*), probably the most common; purple, or water, avens (*G. rivale*), perhaps the best known; large-leaved avens (*G. macrophyllum*), a yellow-flowered variety widely found in the Pacific states; prairie smoke (*G. triflorum*), an odd-looking species with bell-shaped pink flowers found in the sagebrush plains of North America; and herb bennet (*G. urbanum*), a native of England that is now found on this continent.

Most of our avens varieties have small flowers, about the size of a nickel, and bear five rounded petals and a bushy green center that later becomes the traveling seed cluster. Sixteen species live across North America, most favoring cool climates. Showier species, whose hybrids have become garden flowers, are found in Europe and South America.

The flower has the aspect of a wild rose, which is not surprising since it is a member of the Rose (Rosaceae) family. Other closely related members of the Rose family with similar-looking flowers are wild strawberries, blackberries, and cinquefoils. Most of those plants are low or shrubby; avenses often run two to three feet tall and are quite herblike or, as some would say, weedy looking.

The small flowers and weedy habits of this perennial have left the avens clan ignored by many modern wildflower writers. Yet the genus is rich in history, both botanical and ecclesiastical.

Satan Flies Away

Known to the ancients as a medicinal herb, avens was called by the Romans *avencia*, a word whose origin is obscure and which meant simply "avens." *Geum*, the generic name, is from the Greek, *geno*, which means "to yield an agreeable fragrance" or possibly from the Greek, *geuein*, which means "to give a taste of." Either origin probably stems from the clove-like scent that the roots of some species give off when pulled from the ground, especially in the spring.

Perhaps because of the fragrance, the plant was worn as an amulet. *Ortus Sanitatis*, a medieval guide to good health published in 1491, maintained, "Where the root is in the house, Satan can do nothing and flies from it, wherefore it is blessed before all other herbs, and if a man carries the root about him, no venomous beast can harm him."

In America and in England (where the common species is *G. urbanum*, which is also found as an escape here), the plant is also called bennet, way bennet, or herb-bennet. This is a corruption of either *Herba benedicta* ("blessed herb") or "St. Benedict's herb." The latter was a term applied to several plants used as antidotes. According to legend, the name comes from St. Benedict, the man who founded the Benedictine order of monks. A fellow monk once gave a cup of poisoned wine to St. Benedict, but as the saint blessed the wine, the poison—likened to a devil—flew out of it with such power that the cup disintegrated, thus disclosing the murder plot.

Most avens plants bear leaves of three. In medieval times, these leaves and the five golden petals of the blossoms symbolized the Holy Trinity and the five wounds of Christ. By the 14th century, the plant was often used as an architectural decoration for church columns and walls.

Avenses, particularly *G. urbanum*, have been used to treat diarrhea, sore throats, skin afflictions, agues, bronchial catarrh, and fevers. "The root in the spring-time, steeped in wine, doth give it a delicate flavor and taste, and being drunk fasting every morning, comforteth the heart, and is a good preservative against the plague or any other poison," said Nicholas Culpeper. It has been employed even as a freckle remover and as a treatment for bad breath.

With constituents similar to those of *G. urbanum*, *G. rivale* was once well known across America as Indian chocolate; its roots were used to concoct a drink that looked somewhat like hot chocolate, though it tasted more like cloves. Mixed with sugar and milk, it treated dysentery, colic, stomach problems, and other ailments. Called throatwort it was also used as a gargle.

One of the most popular uses for the European avens was as a flavoring for beers, including the famous Augsburg Ale. It is also supposed to preserve such drinks.

From architecture to ale: not a bad background for such a lowly tramp.

Hello! Hello!

In an article in *The American Botanist* in 1918, Lucinda Haynes Lombard reported that some people believed that friends who held avens leaves in their hands were able to converse telepathically over many miles.

Herbal Hat?

"As a corruption of the monkish title, [herb-bennet] is sometimes called herb-bonnet, a name quite meaningless in itself, but a fair illustration of the way in which, when a name ceases to be understood, it becomes perverted into something else that is at least English in sound, though devoid of sense."
—*Professor F. Edward Hulme*
(1881)

Mints

OLD AND LIVELY SCENTS

Only Mickey wouldn't like the mints.

The first time I ran across a spearmint plant, all I could think of was gum. In fact, for much of my life, I had thought of spearmint as nothing more than a confectionary flavoring. I was amazed when I picked a weed at the edge of a road that smelled exactly like the Wrigley gum I'd chewed as a kid.

Truth is, if it weren't for its aroma, spearmint—and the several other North American mints—might hardly be noticed at all. For *Mentha spicata* bears tiny flowers, appreciated by few but the several dozen species of flies and bees that visit them. Yet their aromatic leaves have earned the mints fame that has endured since long before Christ.

Mints are a large family of 3,200 species in 160 genera worldwide, including the genus *Mentha*, with 30 species. About a half-dozen mints are found in North America, but only one of them is native. *Mentha*, the Latin, and *Minthe*, the Greek, are words based in mythology. Minthe was a sweetheart of Pluto, but like many mythological relationships, this one led to trouble. A properly jealous Proserpine—Pluto's wife—turned Minthe into the plant that bears her name. Wrote Ovid:

> Could Pluto's queen, with jealous fury storm
> And Minthe to a fragrant herb transform?

Wild mint (Mentha arvensis) *is a native that makes a tasty tea.*

She could. What's more, "Proserpine certainly contrived to keep her rival's memory fragrant," wrote Neltje Blanchan. "But how she must delight in seeing her under the chopping knife and served up as a sauce!"

Indeed, mint sauce or jelly is almost as much a part of a lamb dinner as cranberry sauce is of a turkey dinner. Spearmint is usually the variety of mint used in concocting the sauce, but other species can be used. So long have such sauces been paired with lamb that one of the plant's common folk names is lamb mint. Its use for flavoring seafood dishes earned it two other names, mackerel mint and fish mint.

Paying Tithes

Before Christ, the Pharisees paid tithes with mint, anise, and cumin. "In Athens, where every part of the body was perfumed with a different scent, mint was specially designated to the arms," reported Maude Grieve.

Virgil maintained that deer injured by hunters sought out spearmint to heal their wounds, but John Gerard warned that injured men shouldn't consume it because "whoever eat mint when wounded will never be cured." Romans, who introduced spearmint into Britain, cultivated it for food preparation, for preventing coagulation of milk, for love potions, and as an old-time Alka-Seltzer—a use to which many of the mints have been put. Ovid recommended scouring serving platters with the green leaves.

Arabs and Persians were the first to use spearmint to flavor drinks. In fact, the word *julep* is from the Arabic, *gulab,* which means "rose water," another plant-flavored drink. A fine and flavorful tea can be brewed by steeping the dried leaves in hot water. Wild food forager Euell Gibbons liked to add a little spearmint to a tea made from the dried flowers of red clover (*Trifolium pratense*).

Amatus Lusitanus wrote in 1554 that the plant was "always" found in gardens, and Dr. E. Lewis Sturtevant reports that later botanists confirmed this statement from Europe.

"The smelle rejoiceth the heart of man, for which cause they used to strew it in chamber and places of recreation, pleasure and repose, where feasts and banquets are made," wrote Gerard. Spearmint was for centuries added to bath water "as a help to comfort and strengthen the nerves and sinews," wrote John Parkinson in 1629. "It is much used either outwardly applied or inwardly drunk to strengthen and comfort weak stomackes." Nicholas Culpeper, another herbalist of the period, cited 40 different ailments treated with spearmint, including something that would please Mr. Wrigley—sore gums. Even today children enjoy picking and chewing the leaves for the flavor. But be warned: Culpeper also claimed that the plant "stirs up venery, or bodily lust."

Spearmint probably first arrived with the Pilgrims. It's mentioned in a list of plants brought over to Plymouth, demonstrating the esteem in which it was held. Although a native of southern Europe and Asia, the plant was widespread in America by 1739, when a botanist found it growing wild in various parts of Virginia. This suggests that it had been popular in early colonial gardens. Its popularity prompted one of its most common titles, garden mint.

Mint Sauce

A popular recipe for mint sauce calls for mixing two tablespoons of chopped fresh spearmint, one-half tablespoon of sugar, one tablespoon of warm water, and the juice of two lemons.

Mouse Be Gone

Mint has been used to whiten teeth, perfume soaps, flavor toothpaste, cure chapped hands, and relieve stings. "Mice are so averse to the smell of mint, either fresh or dried, that they will leave untouched any food where it is scattered," Mrs. Grieve maintained. Pennsylvanians used to pack bundles of spearmint with their grain to keep out rodents.

Spearmint is picked just before it blooms in August or September. The herbs are hung in bunches till dry, and the leaves are then removed and ground into a powder. The powder can be stored and used as needed, or it can be mixed with corn sugar syrup to form a basis for various mint sauces.

So popular was spearmint as a flavoring that by 1930 some 50,000 pounds of it was being grown annually, primarily in Michigan and Indiana. Ten to 20 pounds of spearmint oil could be obtained from an acre of plants. Though its flavor is as popular as ever, the plant itself is not consumed commercially quite as much as it used to be because carvone, the oil in spearmint that cre-ates the attractive flavor, is now being produced synthetically and more cheaply from waste orange and grapefruit peels. However, chewing gum fans will be glad to know that Wrigley still uses natu-ral flavorings from both spearmint and peppermint (*M. piperita*) plants.

In North America spearmint is a weed, a garden escape that will grow almost anywhere that is moist enough and not too sunny. Our native wild mint (*M. arvensis*) also favors moderately shady situations but will survive in full sun if the ground is not dry. It normally grows to about two feet in height.

Mints are difficult to start from seed and propagate chiefly by sending out underground runners that produce new plants. The resulting colonies can be incredibly hardy. Twenty-five years ago, I found some wild mint plants growing in a narrow strip of soil between road pavement and a stone wall. The location is often inundated with snow, plus sand and salt from snowplows. The colony is still alive and well today.

Acquiring wild mint or spearmint is as easy as digging up several plants and moving them to your yard. A warning, however: Both wild mint and spearmint can become a nuisance, spreading like a weed into parts of the garden where they are not wanted. If you introduce these plants, either select a spot where they can spread without causing problems, or set up borders around the plants. The borders can consist of one-by-six-inch boards buried upright, bricks placed end-up, or fairly deep stone. Spearmint also does well in boxes.

Another possible problem with mint is a form of rust, peculiar to the genus and for which there is no cure. Afflicted plants should be destroyed to prevent the disease from spreading.

Many Names

Among the many names applied to spearmint over the centuries are common mint, sage of Bethlehem, brown mint, Our Lady's mint, green mint, spire mint (*spear* and *spire* refer to the plant's tall, narrow shape), and St. Mary's herb. Some authors list it as *Mentha viridis*, a name applied by noted American botanist Asa Gray. However, most modern authorities call it *M. spicata*. The specif-ic name means "spike," again referring to the shape.

Wild mint's *arvensis* means "of the field." Its dried leaves make a tasty tea, as do spearmint's. The plant is circumboreal, found native in Europe and Asia as well as North America.

Wild mint's purplish tube-like flowers grow in tight clusters around the leaf axials. This technique of clustering elongated flowers is a plant's way of protecting the nectar against thieving insects that don't provide pollination services. For instance, various wasps whose tongues aren't long enough to reach the nectar-rich bottom of the flower will cut a hole through the base of a tube to reach the sweets. By clustering the blossoms, the plant prevents robbers from gaining access to the base of at least most of the flowers.

53 Square Miles of Gum Flavoring

Wrigley, the gum maker, uses both spearmint and peppermint in flavoring its products. According to the company, "a vast area of farmland is required to raise all the mint the Wrigley Company needs. If added together, this farmland would equal 53 square miles, or approx-imately 30,550 football fields.

Mints have confused and confounded botanists for years, and it can be difficult to identify them positively. They often hybridize. For instance, peppermint, *M. piperita*, is now actually considered a hybrid of spearmint (*M. spicata*) and water mint (*M. aquatica*), and that hybrid has a number of variations. Euell Gibbons observed, "If the first sprig of wild mint you taste doesn't exactly delight you, don't thereby conclude that you don't like wild mint. Keep searching, and eventually you will find a mint that is exactly tailored to your tongue."

If you grow spearmint, plan to grow it, or have access to it, you might wish to try this old-fashioned mint punch: Pick a quart of fresh spearmint leaves, wash and dry them, then mash them till soft and cover with freshly boiled water. Set aside for 10 minutes. Strain, cool, and chill. Add two cups of cold grape juice plus lemon juice to taste. Mix in sugar till sweet enough and add a quart of ginger ale. Spike it with what you wish, if you wish.

But watch out for venery . . .

Tasty

Mint is but a lowly weed
But a useful weed, indeed;
For unlike a fancy tulip,
You can add it to your julep.
—J. S.

Cardinal Flower

AMERICA'S FAVORITE

Cardinal flower is a showy member of a potent clan.

"America's favorite." That is how Roger Tory Peterson described the brilliant red cardinal flower, the most stunning of our midsummer wildflowers. Mr. Peterson's terse evaluation, contained in a field guide almost void of comment, has a sound basis. In the 1940s, Dr. Harold N. Moldenke, curator and administrator of the herbarium at the New York Botanical Garden, surveyed more than 1,000 botanists and naturalists throughout North America, asking them to list the dozen most showy, conspicuous, and interesting wildflowers in their regions. More than 500 responded, and the tally left little question as to which was the favorite. Cardinal flower amassed 213 votes; the next closest was the showy lady's slipper with only 155 votes.

Cardinal flower, another favorite of hummingbirds, was once voted the most beautiful wildflower in North America.

"There is no other wild flower which approaches it in color," wrote F. Schuyler Mathews, who studied floral colors in the late 19th century. "It is not so much something colored as color itself," said naturalist John Burroughs.

Red is particularly attractive to hummingbirds (a friend had a hummingbird fly up to inspect a red flower print on her dress as she was sitting near her garden one day), and cardinal flower's shape—a long tube at the bottom of which is a pool of nectar—is well suited to this long-beaked, hovering bird. What's more, the flower's reproductive organs, the pistil and stamen, project from the mouth of the flower tube in such a way that they will touch the head of the visitor. This is a "protandrous" flower: the male, pollen-bearing stamens develop first, then the female, pollen-receiving pistils. This "sex change" occurs from the bottom up on a wand of flowers, and visiting hummingbirds will go to the male flowers first, because they are the most nectar rich.

Cardinal flower (*Lobelia cardinalis*), also called red lobelia, red betty, slinkweed, and hog's physic, is found from New Brunswick to Florida and west into Texas, Colorado, the Southwest, and parts of California.

It has been said that the relative rarity of hummingbirds in north temperate climates is due to the relative rarity of red flowers. Both hummingbirds and red flowers are much more common in tropical America. In northern parts of North America, the range of the ruby-throated hummingbird and the cardinal flower is almost identical, probably demonstrating the closeness of their relationship. The decline in the number of cardinal flowers has no doubt aided the decline in the number of ruby-throated hummingbirds, the only species that regularly visits the eastern half of North America. But the opposite can also be true: Since cardinal flowers rely on hummingbirds for survival, any decline in the hummingbird population hurts the plants. It's a catch-22 affair.

A plant endowed with so much beauty has, to no one's surprise, won the praises of almost every writer of natural history, not the least of whom was Mr. Burroughs. "The cardinal [flower] burns with [an] intense fire, and fairly lights up the little dark nooks where it glasses itself in the still water," he wrote. "One must pause and look at it. Its intensity, its pure scarlet, the dark background upon which it is projected, its image in the still darker water, and its general air of retirement and seclusion, all arrest and delight the eye. It is a heart-throb of color on the bosom of the dark solitude."

Some people believe that the native red bird inspired the flower's name, but even our handsome cardinal does not match the flower in the brilliance and magnificence of its fire-engine red. The name comes from the color of the vestments of the princes of the Roman Catholic Church. Ironically, it is said that one of the first European gardens to have a blooming specimen of this plant belonged to Cardinal Francesco Barberini, a well-known 17th-century Roman prelate. The North American native had arrived in Europe in 1626, collected by John Tradescant, who was sending back plants for the botanical gardens of England. Once it had been discovered, cardinal flower quickly became a popular addition to the gardens of wealthy Europeans who coveted and collected exotic flowers of the new lands being opened up by explorers and traders.

Cardinal flower is one of those plants whose beauty is so captivating that unknowing or thoughtless admirers are tempted to pick it, and too often do. Overpicking can spell disaster for the cardinal flower because the plant tends to be a short-lived perennial and relies a good deal on its seeds for survival. A worse problem, however, has been the loss of habitat. Cardinal flower likes wetlands, and over the last three centuries, many of these have been drained for agriculture and development.

Cardinal flower does, however, have another method of spreading. The mother plant sends out little shoots that, in their first year, appear only as basal rosettes of leaves. The next year, those shoots mature to flowering plants three to four feet high. Left alone, a fairly good-size colony can establish itself by shoots and seeds.

Naturally, they should never be picked or transplanted. The best way to obtain them is by collecting seeds from the wild or by acquiring the seeds, rootstock, or plants from a reputable nursery. Cardinal flowers are not particularly fussy about such things as soil pH or richness, but it is essential that the ground be moist and the location fairly sunny. Cardinal flower's usual haunts are streamsides and wet meadows. Some authorities have found the plant sensitive to winter kill, perhaps in the northern reaches of its range, and it is said to do best in ground that doesn't freeze hard, such as near water. I have seen a 10-year-old plant growing alongside a subdivision house— right next to the downspout of a roof gutter that apparently provided just the kind of dampness it wanted.

Scarlet Rain

At least a half-dozen other writers have noticed the beauty of the flower reflected in nearby water. Justice Oliver Wendell Holmes put it into poetry:

The cardinal, and the blood red spots
Its double in the stream:
As if some wounded eagle's breast
Slow throbbing o'er the plain,
Had left its airy path impressed
In drops of scarlet rain.

A Blue Sibling

The genus *Lobelia* has around 43 North American species, some of which sport brilliant blue flowers and some of which are tiny-flowered weeds. Perhaps the most striking sibling is great blue lobelia (*L. siphilitica*), which in late August and September bears handsome flowers with the air of a rare gentian.

The great lobelia has rather tube-like flowers about an inch long, each with an upper and a lower lip. The upper lip is divided into two petals while the bottom has three petals marked with white. This shape has prompted some botanists to suggest that lobelia may be an important evolutionary link between the simpler tube-like flowers and the more complex and advanced Composites—like daisies and asters—which usually have a center disk of tubular florets surrounded by florets that have turned into rays. Lobelia petals, experts say, are on their way to becoming rays. In fact, botanists have classified lobelias in the Bellflower family, just below the Composite family, reflecting a high degree of evolutionary development.

Some botanists believe that blue is the high end of the evolutionary progression of floral coloring, which started with green, then went through phases of white and yellow, then developed reds, and finished at bright blue. Blue attracts bees best, and it is probably no coincidence that bees are among the most highly evolved of the insects. Great blue lobelia is also visited by hummingbirds.

The beauty, size, and hardiness of the great lobelia have made it popular with some gardeners here, and with more in Europe. They are easy to plant from seed or to transplant, and though they look rare, are not. Great lobelia has about the same range as cardinal flower, though it is not found as far west.

Lobelia siphilitica is a rather unattractive name that reflects its former use as a treatment for syphilis. It was also a medicine for dropsy, diarrhea, and dysentery. Cherokees treated nosebleeds with it, and Iroquois considered it a cough medicine.

Indian Tobacco

Indian tobacco (*L. inflata*) is a small-flowered species common east of the Rockies. The plant has long been known as a medicinal herb. Even though grazing animals will not touch it because of its acrid taste, and the plant sometimes proves poisonous, quacks of the 19th century concocted many a medicine from it because it was believed that anything that set the insides afire was beneficial to health. However, even serious physicians used Indian tobacco for all sorts of ailments, and more modern experts suspect that the plant's narcotic effect may have been the actual cure.

American Indians were perhaps more skilled at its use, and employed it to treat sore eyes, breast cancer, and coughs. Creeks used it to ward off ghosts, and Meskwakis considered both red and blue lobelias as magical, especially when used as love potions. As its name suggests, Indians chewed the leaves, and it is said that the effect was to induce drowsiness. About its only real value was as an emetic, whence it picked up such unappetizing names as vomitroot, puke weed, and

Thomsonians

In the early 19th century, a "root doctor" named Samuel Thomson promoted the powers of Indian tobacco to treat almost any ailment. Thomson, who has been called the father of the patent medicine, founded the Friendly Botanical Societies, which he claimed numbered more than three million members by 1839. Thomsonians believed that herbs could cure most ailments and improve life. Thomson's success came despite his having been arrested in 1809, charged with killing a man by administering lobelia. His accuser was a physician, and Thomson was acquitted after claiming he hadn't used lobelia on the victim and demonstrating that the doctor couldn't even identify what a lobelia plant looks like.

gagroot. "If yer ever wants to get rid of what's inside yer," a Canadian farmer told an interviewer in 1879, "jist make a tea of lobelia leaves and I'll bet my team of hosses out there it'll accommodate you."

Oddly enough, while Indians had many uses for the plant, smoking was apparently not one of them. Professor John Uri Lloyd, a pharmacist writing in the 1880s, noted the plant had been called wild tobacco, but added: "From Wild tobacco it is quite natural that it should acquire the name Indian Tobacco, as it would be presumed a tobacco that was wild would be used by the Indians. As a matter of fact, however, we have no record that the Indians ever made use of the plant in the manner of a tobacco."

Because it has an effect similar to nicotine, several modern-day patent medicines, such as Bantron, have employed Indian tobacco's "lobeline" extract as a stop-smoking medication. However, the U.S. Food and Drug Administration reported in 1993 that Bantron and similar over-the-counter products did not work, and banned their sale. The FDA said at the time that it "believes that allowing ineffective products to stay on the market discourages research to find effective ones."

Lobelia cardinalis is reported to have many of the same chemical properties as *L. siphilitica* and *L. inflata* but has seen limited use as a medicine, perhaps because people would rather look at it than eat, drink, or smoke it. It was once employed as a nervine, and some American Indians rid themselves of worms by eating it. Cherokees, however, used it instead of great blue lobelia in a concoction to treat syphilis.

Lobelia is a name that recalls Matthias L'Obel (1538–1616), a Flemish botanist and herbalist who became physician to James I of England and was known as Lobelius. Most of the plant's 43 North American species are found east of the Rockies. More than 250 species exist worldwide. The genus is a member of the small Bellflower, or Bluebell, family (Campanulaceae), which is said to have nearly 90 genera and some 2,000 species worldwide, including exotic tropical and alpine plants. Among the many lobelias that appear in summer is one that provides a rare example of humor—or at least punning—in a plant name. The native pale-spike lobelia (*L. spicata*), which is among the tallest of the genus, has been called the highbelia.

Marriage Counselor

Among the Meskwaki Indians, the root of the great blue lobelia was used to prevent divorce. Seeing discord between a couple, a tribe member would mash the root, secretly add it to the food of both husband and wife, and love would return.

Bouncing Bet

SOAP WITH BOUNCE

Bouncing bet made cloth nicer and hands cleaner,
but cows had to stay away.

Many of our most abundant summer wildflowers are natives of Europe that were brought over to fill colonial gardens or that snuck over with crop seeds. Bouncing bet falls in the first category, and it was probably used for both practical and decorative reasons. Today, however, few gardens display its pinkish blossoms. Like so many other imports, bouncing bet has run wild and become a weed, growing along railroad tracks, beside highways, around parking lots, and in other waste places. Just as the human immigrants did, it found much freedom in America.

The one- to three-foot-tall perennial bears clusters of five-petaled phlox-like flowers, whose color was described by F. Schuyler Mathews as "the most delicate crimson pink imaginable—a tint so light that we might call it pinkish white." Unfortunately, because the plants are often found in dusty waste places, the flowers frequently turn out to be dirty pink.

Purpose of Color

The natural color has a purpose. The petals are attached to a long tube, at the bottom of which is a pool of nectar. Only a creature with a long tongue can easily reach the pool. While the light pink is not particularly attractive to butterflies, which have long tongues but which are usually drawn to brighter colors, the shade is perfect for attracting the large sphinx and other night-flying moths. It is no accident that the flower's scent is strongest just after sunset.

Saponaria officinalis is a member of the Pink family, which includes such common summer plants as evening lychnis, ragged-robin, catchflies, and campions. Within the genus *Saponaria* are about three dozen species, all natives of Europe, Asia, and northern Africa. Bouncing bet is the type species, the only one found in North America, and certainly the most widespread variety of the genus. On this continent it can be found in each of the lower 48 states and most Canadian provinces.

Bouncing bet cleaned the hands of farmers in the field and boatmen on canals.

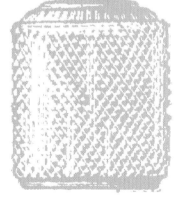

London Pride

Before there were sewers, people in England called bouncing bet London pride because its sweet, nighttime perfume helped hide the city's stench.

In Monkish Fashion

"By the brothers in European monasteries, centuries ago, its virtue as a capital cleansing agent was well understood, and they employed it for scouring cloth and removing stains. They gave it, in monkish fashion, a Latin name, *herba fullonum* . . . ."
—Charles Francis Saunders, *Edible and Useful Wild Plants* (1920)

Cleaning Up

Saponaria is based on the Latin word *sapo*, "soap." The plant is usually called soapwort in England. It contains a juice called saponin, a glucoside that appears when the leaves are bruised. Saponin not only produces suds but also dissolves oils, fats, and grease. Farmers—and it was around farms that the plant was most often found wild—would use the leaves as soap, whence names latherwort, bruisewort, scourwort, crowsoap, soaproot, and soapwort gentian. The root has been used in homemade toothpastes and shampoos.

Medieval monks, who used it to clean cloth, called the plant *herba fullonum*, which means "fuller's herb." A fuller was someone who increased the weight and bulk of cloth by such techniques as shrinking, beating, and pressing. Well into the 19th century, North American fullers were using bouncing bet as a cleaning agent, and they often planted fields of it near their mills for a handy supply. Today, long after the fulling mills have disappeared, the plant is still found around old mill sites. It is also common today along old canals because the immigrants who worked their boats in the 19th century often planted it along the banks for a ready soap supply, wherever they were.

Centuries ago, brewers would slip some of the plant's juice into their beer to improve head frothiness. Brewers still do that kind of thing today but use more modern head-builders.

Like so many other plants of old-time gardens, bouncing bet served as a medicine as well as a decoration. As might be expected, it was used as a skin wash for the likes of dermatitis, itching, poison ivy rashes, and tumors. John Gerard said it would "beautifie and cleanse the skin." It has also been used as an expectorant for respiratory congestion, as a cure for venereal diseases such as syphilis and gonorrhea, and for treating jaundice. However, most modern authors warn of the somewhat poisonous or at least very irritating effect of saponin on the stomach. Cows and other livestock avoid it as well as its sibling, cow cockle (*S. vaccaria*), which has been known to make animals ill.

Bouncing bet is a widespread July and August bloomer—"a stout, buxom, exuberantly healthy lassie among flowers," according to Neltje Blanchan. Naturalist John Burroughs also appreciated its name and admired its "feminine comeliness and bounce." Actually, *bet* is a version of *betty*, an old term for a laundress, and is supposed to reflect a fancied resemblance of the flowers to a washerwoman, seen from the rear as her flounces bounced while she scrubbed the clothes up and down the washboard—presumably in a solution of soapwort!

Among this plant's many North American and European names are sweet betty, hedge pink, old maid's pink, Boston pink, chimney pink, sheepweed (from its pastoral settings), wild sweet William, lady-by-the-gate, wood's phlox, mock-gilliflower, and dog's cloves.

Bouncing bet likes full sun and moist soil. It multiplies by producing many seeds and by forming colonies via thick underground runners. If your wildflower garden or yard needs some bounce, you can easily transplant bouncing bet—few would complain about digging up a plant or two since it's on the "invasive weed" list in several states. However, if you like your "bet" tamed, cultivated double-flowered varieties of *Saponaria officinalis* are available in either pink or white. It "makes a great rock garden plant and also should be considered for areas that are difficult for growing other types of plants," says Plantstop.com, an Internet nursery in Plantersville, Texas.

Evening-Primrose

AN OWL-LIKE SWEET

Evening-primroses offer beauty in the night.

Some of the most parched patches of earth are home to the evening-primrose, an often overlooked but useful and unusual plant with flowers that like the dark better than the day.

As its name suggests, the evening-primrose blooms as the sun sets. Each four-petaled yellow flower opens handsomely to form a cross, a form echoed by a cross-shaped stigma. By late the next morning, when the sun's rays have beaten down on the delicate blossoms, the flowers fold up their petals and leave a rather ratty-looking collection of wilted corpses.

Mrs. William Starr Dana, a turn-of-the-20th-century writer on wildflowers, waxed almost poetic when she described the flowers' nocturnal habits. "Along the roadsides in mid-summer, we notice a tall rank-growing plant which seems chiefly to bear buds and faded blossoms. And unless we are already familiar with the owl-like tendencies of the evening-primrose, we are surprised some dim twilight to find this same plant resplendent with a mass of fragile yellow flowers, which are exhaling their faint delicious fragrance in the evening air."

Though chiefly a night bloomer, the flower stays open a bit longer in late summer and early fall. Mrs. Dana suspected the flower's tendency to remain open for part of the following day might be due to the diminished strength of the sun as the winter solstice approaches.

The plant's internal clock opens flowers by night to seek the services of moths, such as the pink night-moth and the many miller and sphinx moths. The lemonish scent and the color—a yellow that is striking to the eyes of night-flying insects—draw them to the plant. Some botanists have postulated that the flowers are unusually visible at night because the petals are slightly phosphorescent, able to produce light if stimulated by some source. Writing in 1894, Charles Millspaugh said that technically speaking, they did not generate light but merely "stored" sunlight absorbed during the day. He compared it to the calcium sulfide, obtained from crushed oysters, that was used at the time for luminous clock faces.

For naturalist John Burroughs, who didn't mind pulling himself out of bed for a sunrise stroll, the evening-primrose was a "coarse, rankly growing plant; but, in late summer, how many an

Evening-primroses are flowers of the night, aimed at attracting moths instead of bees.

Secret Guides

Many flowers have "honey guides," designs that direct an insect's eye toward the nectary. Humans can see many of them, but not those of the common evening-primrose. While the flowers look all yellow to our eyes, they bear a pattern of lines that insects can see and follow night and day, but that are visible to us only under ultra-violet light.

Ach Du Lieber!

You can't always trust names. Common evening-primrose, a North American native, was imported to Europe by 1614 and became especially popular in Germany as a salad herb. Generations later, enterprising nurserymen tried to sell the same plant to American gardeners under the name of German rampion.

untrimmed bank is painted over by it with the most fresh and delicate canary yellow!" And Neltje Blanchan added: "Like a ballroom beauty, the evening-primrose has a faded, bedraggled appearance by day. . . . . But at sunset a bud begins to expand its delicate petals slowly, timidly—not suddenly and with a pop, as the evening primrose of the garden does."

Occasionally, a moth will even be found sleeping in daytime within the tent formed by the wilted evening-primrose petals.

Variability

Its fragrant breath is apparently produced inconsistently. John Burroughs observed that "our evening-primrose is thought to be uniformly sweet-scented, but the past season, I examined many specimens, and failed to find one that was so. Some seasons, the sugar maple yields much sweeter sap than in others; and even individual trees, owing to the soil, moisture, and other conditions where they stand, show a difference in this respect."

This variability interested a Dutchman named Hugo de Vries, who lived from 1848 to 1935, and to whom the evening-primrose was a laboratory of sorts. de Vries was suspicious of Darwin's theory that all changes in species occurred exceedingly slowly, requiring thousands of years. Studying some 50,000 evening-primrose plants and the hundreds of thousands of flowers they produced, de Vries very occasionally discovered odd blossoms—such as ones that were much bigger or smaller than usual, or that bore more or fewer petals. He found that in breeding these errant forms together, the unusual characteristics survived. He called the variant forms mutants, and their different characteristics mutations. Thus, he theorized, these occasional accidents of nature could cause major changes in evolution very quickly.

Contradictions

Evening-primrose's name seems full of contradictions. It is neither a rose nor a primrose, but an evening-primrose, a botanical family all of its own that is not even closely related to either of the other two clans.

What's more, the *prim* of its name has nothing to do with its aspect. *Prim* is from *primus* or *primula*, Latin for "first," because some true primroses bloom early in the season—usually in April—and are among the first garden-type flowers to appear. The *rose* of primrose is probably not a reference to the flower. The Old English version of primrose was *primrole* or *pryme rolles*, a corruption of the French, *primevere*, which meant "first of spring." While evening-primrose may look similar to an Old World primrose, it doesn't blossom very early. Flowers begin to appear in July, reach their peak in August, and can bloom as late as early October.

The Evening-Primrose family (Onagraceae) consists of about 25 genera and 600 species distributed worldwide, but mostly in the Americas. Some, like fuchsias, are popular with gardeners. Although only about a dozen genera are known on this continent, the evening-primrose genus, *Oenothera*, alone has at least 100 species living in North America, mostly in the central and western states and Mexico. Our common evening-primrose, *Oenothera biennis,* is not only common but also widespread, found coast to coast, from southern Canada south. Most evening-primroses are yellow- or white-blossomed, though one beautiful species—rose sundrops (*O. rosea*) of the Southwest—is rosy purple. In the West the better-known varieties often inhabit sandy locations, such as deserts and beaches, and many are called primroses instead of the more accurate evening-primrose.

Like the common name, the plant's scientific name has ancient roots. One authority says that *Oenothera* is Greek for "wine-scenting" because the roots of the plant were once used for that purpose. Another says it means "wine-hunting" or "wine-drinking" and referred to another, apparently similar, plant eaten to create a desire for wine (just as peanuts or olives are eaten by some people for that end). There's also a story that the plant "dispels the effects of wine." *Biennis* means "biennial," which the plant is.

Other English names include night willowherb, four-o-clock, king's cure-all, fever-plant, scurvish, wild beet, and scabish. I especially like evening star. Some names reflect its use in folk medicine, especially as a cough treatment and for skin irritations. The French in Quebec as well as some American Indians such as the Ojibwas considered it excellent for healing wounds.

Modern scientists are delving into the possible values of the evening-primrose. Since the 1960s, European researchers have been experimenting with the oil from the seed, finding it rich in vitamin F and using it as a treatment for burns and other skin wounds. Scientists in England in the 1970s were looking into using a seed extract to prevent heart attacks by reducing the blood's ability to clot. Researchers in Europe and Canada were also finding this extract of some help to multiple sclerosis patients.

By the late 1980s, evening-primrose oil, commercially manufactured from the seeds, was growing in popularity and is now readily available in pharmacies and from herbal suppliers. The oil is rich in an essential fatty acid called gamma linolenic acid (GLA), and is used as an anti-inflammatory for treatment of eczema, allergies, breast pain, arthritis, and even hangovers. In Europe and Australia, it is one of the most widely prescribed pharmaceuticals used for skin ailments. Evening-primrose species, including *O. biennis,* are grown commercially in at least 15 countries.

Sweet and Nutritious

Among animals, mule deer and pronghorns are especially fond of it, and many varieties of birds seek out its seeds, which are rich in fats and often available well into the winter. Their "bare stalks are cafeterias for hungry birds who seem delighted to find these little cups of seeds held high above the snow line especially for them," wrote Arthur Craig Quick in 1939. "I have counted as many as ten birds at a time on a single stalk." The dried seedpods, incidentally, have long been popular for decorations in flower arrangements and herb wreaths.

Humans have also appreciated the plant as food, enough so that the native was transplanted first to Italy and then, by 1614, to England, where it is still cultivated as a garden plant and is now found growing wild. First-year roots were boiled to create a dish described as both nutri-

Night Crew

Most flowers blossom in the day,
Which is the very common way,
But some plants like to bloom at night
When there's hardly any light.
While this seems to make no sense,
It might be a matter of self-offense:
For the after-dark offers its own crew
Of pollinators who've got night-
    view.
So these nocturnal flowers offer drinks
To thirsty moths like the sphinx.
—J. S.

tious and sweet, with a taste similar to that of parsnips, though it's said that if the roots are not pulled at the right time, the flavor can be peppery. Both the French and the Germans used the young shoots in salads, and the Germans treated it like scorzonera, a European vegetable.

Though it's called wild beet, that name probably reflects the shape of the biennial's first-year root more than the taste. It's fat and round, full of food stored to give it strength to send up the flowering plant in the second year.

Probably because of its use as a food, the common evening-primrose, a North American native, has been spread around the world. It is found in the wild in Europe as well as in temperate regions of Africa and South America. It is particularly well established in England.

Even Fries

If you want to taste evening-primrose, find some first-year roots, peel them, boil them in two changes of salted water, and serve with butter. Several authors even recommend evening-primrose French fries: peel, boil twice, dip in batter, and pan fry.

Hardy Fellow

The common evening-primrose is a hardy fellow, able to survive in unpleasant places and preferring dry, sandy soils—perhaps this is why so many others of the genus are widespread across the dry plains and deserts of the West. I once found a sizable plant growing in about two inches of sand atop a large roadside culvert; the thick root crept inside that thin coating around the pipe for about two feet until it could wind its way down into more substantial soil, still sandy and only sometimes wet during the summer. Almost all members of the genus require sandy soil, whether it's in the desert, the suburbs, or along an ocean beach.

Even in the common evening-primrose, which usually lives in sandy soils far from deserts, the root appears to have the ability to store water for quite a spell. In this connection, it is interesting to note that evening-primroses are only a couple of families removed from the Cactus family.

The evening-primrose sows so easily that the simplest way of obtaining some for your "desert" is to gather the seeds in September and October and plant them. The seeds are tiny—it takes more than 1.3 million of them to weigh a pound. New plants should self-sow for years afterward. Since evening-primrose is a biennial, it takes two years to get a mature plant from seed. The first-year plant consists only of what Ms. Blanchan called "exquisitely symmetrical complex stars"—the basal rosette of leaves. The plants may require a bit of special care: Evening-primrose leaves are one of the favorite foods of the Japanese beetle, which will quickly devour them.

Toadflax

OLD TOAD FACE

Toadflax is a plant of many names, most of them colorful.

Yellow toadflax, also called butter-and-eggs, is one of our common and pretty imports, found in sunny, dry, waste places from June until early fall. Botanists call it *Linaria vulgaris*. *Linaria* is from the Latin, *linum*, meaning "flax." From the same root word comes *linen*, a cloth made from flax. Before it blooms, toadflax's slender, stringy leaves look much like flax, although the flowers bear no resemblance. *Vulgaris* simply means "common."

And common it is, as long as it can find the sandy, sunny spots that it favors so much. The plants produce thousands of seeds to start future generations, and its creeping rhizome can establish sizable colonies—much to the chagrin of farmers, who have given the attractive flower some unattractive names.

The Bees

The flower itself is quite handsome, shaped much like the garden snapdragons (*Antirrhinum*) to which it is closely related. While most of the blossom is yellow, the area around the closed lips is bright orange—a color and placement with a purpose. Orange attracts bees, particularly bumblebees, and various researchers have reported that bumblebees and large honeybees are about the only insects strong enough to open the lips and large enough at the same time to reach down inside the lower spur-like tube to obtain the nectar. In the process, they rub against the stamens, which dust the bees' backs with pollen.

This closed-door policy is a marvelous example of having your cake and eating it, too. Unlike so many flowers, toadflax doesn't have to waste energy opening and closing each day or night, or when it rains. It's always closed to pilferers, and yet always open to the right insects.

No system is perfect, however. Certain butterflies and moths, also drawn to orange, are sometimes able to dip their long tongues inside the flower to steal the sweets without pollinating the flower. Yet such thefts don't really do any harm, for toadflax is able to fertilize itself—one more reason for its success at survival.

The flower's lips, incidentally, probably led to its peculiar and ancient name. As far back as 16th-century England, the plant was called toadflax because the orange mouth is shaped some-

Toadflax, also called butter-and-eggs, is a tight-lipped flower that manages to entice bees into opening its mouth.

what like that of a toad. Children sometimes take the flowers, squeeze them just behind the lips, and make the toads "talk."

There is also an old story that the name originated from an observation that "toads will sometimes shelter themselves amongst the branches of it." The plant's slender, grasslike leaves couldn't provide much shelter from either sun or rain, however, and the first explanation seems more believable. (Some people say that the name comes from the whole flower's form, which resembles a tadpole, but that explanation seems stretched too far.)

Still another explanation for the name—perhaps the most reasonable—comes from Willard N. Clute, author of *The Common Names of Plants and Their Meanings*. "The useful and phlegmatic toad has several plants named for it . . . because they are not of much account . . . . The toadflax . . . is a flax-like plant of no value for spinning."

Mary Durant, in *Who Named the Daisy? Who Named the Rose?* reports that toadflax is also called ranstead (ramstead or ramsted) because a Welshman named Ranstead was said to have introduced it to America. He settled near Philadelphia and planted toadflax in his garden. From there—and probably other sources—it headed for the wide, open spaces.

Many Names

Today, the plant has spread across not only this continent but also across the temperate zones of the world. Such a widespread flower is bound to generate many folk names, and there are no fewer than 30 recorded for *Linaria vulgaris*, the most common being butter-and-eggs, named for its color combination. Others include fluellin, patten and clogs, flaxweed, snapdragon, churnstaff, dragonbushes, brideweed, toad, yellow rod, larkspur, lion's mouth, devil's ribbon, eggs-and-collops, eggs-and-bacon, bread-and-butter, devil's head, pedlar's basket, gallwort, rabbits, doggies, calve's snout, impudent lawyer, Jacob's ladder, rancid, wild flax, wild tobacco, devil's flax, devil's flower, deadman's bones, continental flower, and rabbit's weed. Several names refer to the shape of the flower, which some liken to a dragon's face, or to shoes, or things familiar around a farm. Gall was a disease of chickens, treated with the plant. The colors yellow and orange recall sulfur, and sulfur years ago recalled hell, giving rise to so many devilish names. Those evil names may also relate to the fact that farmers considered the plant a pest. The origin of "fluellin" is discussed in the chapter on speedwell (see page 58). As for "impudent lawyer," one of our more unusual and colorful plant names, its source is probably the expression on the face of the flower. But why a *lawyer*?

Like so many other imports, toadflax may have been brought here as a source of medicine as well as beauty. Through the ages it has been used to treat several ailments, including jaundice, liver diseases, dropsy, hemorrhoids, and eye difficulties. The plant was added to bathwater to relieve skin rashes and diseases and it is said to be a diuretic. "This is frequently used to spend the abundance of those watery humours by urine, which cause the dropsy," said Nicholas Culpeper. However, herbalist John Lust suggests that toadflax is rather powerful and warns against internal use without medical supervision. Since its juice, mixed with milk, was widely used as a fly poison

Toadflax in 1842

"Wherever it prevails, it is very destructive in wheat fields, and where it has long been known, as in some parts of Massachusetts, it is pronounced one of the most obstinate and difficult weeds to destroy."
—Luther Tucker, editor, the *Cultivator* (June 1842)

Eggs-and-Collops

One of the many names of toadflax is eggs-and-collops. A collop was a slice of bacon or ham on which a fried egg was served. In England, Collop Monday was the day before Shrove Tuesday, and eggs-and-collops was the appropriate dish.

centuries ago and cattle won't eat the plant, there's reason to heed the warning. Germans, incidentally, obtained a yellow dye from the flowers.

Toadflax may bloom rather variably, apparently depending on climatic conditions. One year I found them in bloom in an elevated part of my hometown on July 4 while the next year, on July 17 in the same place, the buds weren't even out. Yet, that year in a warmer valley, hundreds flowered on July 15. Some authors describe them as flowers of the late summer, although they clearly can bloom earlier in my part of the Northeast.

Transplanting them is easy—just dig up a bunch and place it in an arid, sunny spot. Unless they get strong sunlight, however, the plants will fail to produce blossoms each year. They should also be intermixed with other plants, such as grasses. Toadflax needs neighbors because it's one of our few common parasitic herbs. Its roots tap into the roots of other plants to steal both water and salts. Its thieving, however, is done in moderation—it does not want to kill its hosts and lose the assistance they supply.

Toadflax is a member of the Figwort family (Scrophulariaceae), which in North America includes about 60 herbaceous genera as well as some shrubs and trees. Among the figworts are foxgloves, mulleins, turtleheads, monkeyflowers, and speedwells. More than 150 species of *Linaria* grow around the world; some 14 are found on this continent. Several European and North African species, mostly purple-flowered, have been popular with gardeners and rock gardeners.

Goldenrods

THE ALL-AMERICANS

The goldenrods could be a national flower.

The goldenrods, wrote Mabel Osgood Wright, "are a byword among plant students, who say that if a botanist is ever condemned to the severest punishment that the underworld can mete, the penalty will be to write a monograph, accurately describing and identifying all the known goldenrods."

To describe goldenrods in terms of torture seems a shame, but the point is well taken. Throughout the world, 125 species of goldenrod are known; of these, around 90 are found in North America. The Northeast, and particularly New England, is home to up to 50 kinds. They vary from widespread species found from Newfoundland to California, to species of very restricted ranges, such as one found only on the shaded cliffs of the Wisconsin River in Sauk County, Wisconsin. "To name all these species, or the aster, the sparrows, and the warblers at sight is a feat probably no one living can perform," observed Neltje Blanchan.

There is a certain challenge to being able to identify goldenrods—with the help of a good guidebook, of course. While many are distinctive, many others are similar to each other, and quite a few kinds may be found in one location. F. Schuyler Mathews tells of coming across "no less than 15 varieties" in a quarter-mile length of road in Campton, New Hampshire.

The plumes of goldenrods, which come in several forms and many species, are made up of many small aster-like flowers. This is tall, or Canada, goldenrod, S. canadensis scabra.

Visual Delight

Goldenrods, however, are better as visual delights than objects for cataloguing. In late summer and autumn, their tall wands and plumes wave over fields and roadsides in such profusion that they are perhaps the dominant ground coloring of the season. In eastern North America, they are so common and adaptable that there is almost no spot—outside an inner city—where one can stand outdoors in September and not see their bright color.

"Goldenrod, collectively, is a delight to the eye, for its color and indispensable factor in the landscape," said Mrs. Wright in 1901. "For decorative purposes it is eminently satisfactory, sought out and beloved by all men, as is amply proved by 'goldenrod weddings,' and by the numerous jars, pitchers, water cans, and bean pots filled with it that decorate suburban stoops." In

Europe, where only a couple of not very showy species are found as natives, some of the more lux-uriant North American varieties have been carefully cultivated in gardens and have been popular as border plants.

Certain goldenrods, as well as steeplebush, are unusual among plants with spikes of flow-ers in that the blossoms at the top open first and the blooming creeps downward. In most other plants, the bottom-most flowers open and the blooming moves upward. (However, John Burroughs found that in teasel, "The wave of bloom begins in the middle of the head and spreads both ways, up and down.") The top-to-bottom flowering of the spike-shaped goldenrods may be connected with their competition for insect attention. When the plant first blooms, many of the late-summer flowers are competing to attract bees, and thus the highest, most visible flowers come out first. Later, as the competition fades in the cooling breezes of fall, goldenrod is one of the few flowers left, and it has no trouble flagging down hungry bees with its lower-blooming blossoms.

Another creature attracted to goldenrods is the praying mantis, the large green insect famed for eating so many garden pests. The former fire chief in our town, who had been a trained entomologist, told me one fall day that the best place to find mantis egg cases is on the dead stalks of goldenrod. To prove his point, a few hours later the chief showed up in my office with a dry stalk of goldenrod, mantis eggs attached. (I kept the stalk outdoors over the winter and when spring arrived, the mantises hatched and headed out, presumably to devour local pests.) Why do these Mantids favor goldenrods? Possibly because the mother mantises spend a lot of time perched on goldenrods late in the season. They prey on the many flying insects drawn by the color and scent to the wealth of nectar in the goldenrod flowers. When they are done hunting and ready to lay eggs, they pick the nearest handy place.

One creature that shuns goldenrod—thank heaven—is the white-tailed deer. While these herbivores are overpopulated in some parts of the country and are decimating many species of native wildflowers, they avoid goldenrod. That's probably no accident, for goldenrod seems to be among the plants that have evolved chemical "flavorings" that make them distasteful to grazing mammals.

Sun Medicine

European herbalists and physicians have long recognized goldenrods as important plants, though they are not nearly as plentiful in the Old World as here. Even their generic name, *Solidago*, means "to make whole," referring to their supposed medicinal benefits. Chippewas had an even better name for the Goldenrod family in general, calling it *gizisomukiki*, which translates as "sun medicine." The plant has been used to calm stomachs, allay nausea, pass stones, cure wounds, and to treat diphtheria, bronchitis, and tuberculosis. Old-time Californians employed the appropriately named *Solidago californica* to treat sores and cuts. They called the plant *oreja de liebre*, which means "jackrab-bit's ear," reflecting the shape of the leaf. Zunis chewed the flowers to extract the juice, which they swallowed to treat sore throats. Among the Alabama Indians, a poultice of goldenrod roots was used to relieve toothaches.

Golden Rubber?

Thomas Edison experimented with using goldenrod's milky juice as a source of rubber. In the 1930s, a scientist named L. G. Polhamus continued the research and found at least two species with appreciable amounts of rubber that could be used commercially. He even rec-ommended developing latex-rich varieties from these plants. His ideas were not pursued.

Yellow Flowers

"How the eye loves to linger upon yellow flowers! Of the three primary colors, yellow always seems to me the most harmonious under all conditions, from the first marsh marigold to the last brave wand of goldenrod. . . . . Roughly speaking, without attempting a census, it seems to me that taking the year through, the majority of landscape flowers are yellow."

—*Mabel Osgood Wright* (1901)

Goldenrod "is a sovereign wound-herb, inferior to none, both for inward and outward use," wrote herbalist Nicholas Culpeper centuries ago, referring to the European species, *S. virgaurea*, meaning "rod of gold." It has been used to treat so many maladies that it's as much a panacea as any plant could be, says Donald Law, a modern English herbalist.

The Great Saladin (1137–1193), the poor boy who rose to be caliph of Egypt and fought King Richard in the Third Crusade, was said to have greatly treasured goldenrod as a medicine and pioneered its cultivation into the Middle East, where it was an important crop for centuries. When it was first introduced into Elizabethan England as a medicinal herb, Mediterranean-grown *S. virgaurea* was much sought after and commanded high prices—as much as a half crown an ounce. When people discovered that the very same plant could be found growing wild in parts of the English countryside, however, its monetary value plummeted, and so did its popularity among herb users. That prompted John Gerard to observe: "This verifieth our English proverb: 'Far fecht and deare bought is best for ladies.'"

Ancient Brews

Brews of goldenrod were popular on many fronts. Witches were said to have used goldenrod in potions. In Europe, the leaves were sometimes concocted into what was called Blue Mountain wine. Teas made from several species, especially the more aromatic ones, have been brewed in both Europe and in North America, particularly by the Indians. "No preparation is better than a tea of the herb made from the young leaves, fresh or dried," Nicholas Culpeper said. Medicinal extracts and tea leaves made from such aromatic American species as fragrant or anise-scented goldenrod (*S. odora*) were exported in the 19th century to China, where they were much admired and commanded high prices.

Bees harvest the nectar in great quantities in the flower-starved autumn. In fact, goldenrods are considered one of the most important "bee plants." And if you should annoy one of those drinking bees, you could try the sting lotion that the Meskwakis once concocted from the flowers of the stiff goldenrod (now called *Oligoneuron rigidum*, but long known as *S. rigida*).

The flowers of various species of goldenrods have been used to make yellow dyes for cloth. While their excellence as dyes has been recognized for several centuries, goldenrod colorings for some reason were little used professionally and were popular mostly in the home. Ancient diviners believed that the plant could be used to point the way to underground sources of water, hidden springs, and even to troves of silver and gold.

With so much beauty and so many uses to its credit, it's not surprising that two states—Kentucky and Nebraska—have proclaimed it their official state flower.

While it has long been known as a curative, goldenrod has often been blamed as a chief cause of hay fever, probably because it blooms in such great numbers at the height of the hay fever season. It's a bum rap, as we explain in the chapter on ragweeds (see page 236).

Common Species

Among the many widespread goldenrods are:

◆ Blue-stemmed goldenrod (*Solidago caesia*), also called the wreath goldenrod, has tufts of blossoms on bluish or purplish stems, and is found east of the Mississippi, as well as into Texas. "None is prettier, more dainty, than this common species," says Ms. Blanchan.

◆ Canada goldenrod (*S. canadensis*), with spreading plumes, may grow five feet tall or higher and is unusually widespread; it can be found from Labrador to the Pacific states, where it is more commonly called meadow goldenrod. Its roots are among the deepest of common American herbs, growing as many as 11 feet down into the prairies of Nebraska—enabling it to find deep subterranean water in very dry seasons. Meskwakis, who believed that some children were born without the ability to laugh, would boil this goldenrod in water with the bone of an animal that died when the child was born. Washing the baby in this brew supposedly guaranteed that the child would be cheerful and blessed with a good sense of humor.

◆ Tall goldenrod (*S. canadensis scabra*, formerly *S. altissima*) is a variety of the above species that may reach eight feet in height and can be found from the Atlantic to Wyoming and Arizona. Chippewas, who called this plant squirrel tail, used it to relieve cramps.

◆ Early goldenrod (*S. juncea*), a small and common variety with comparatively few blossoms, is true to its name by blooming as early as late July, an occurrence that some New Englanders take—without cause—to presage an early winter. Nonetheless, its appearance does put a psychological chill into the viewer, warning that despite all this midsummer warmth, the cold is not so far off. Years ago this plant was dried as a winter decoration, and Chippewas used it to treat convulsions and "women's ailments."

◆ Gray goldenrod (*S. nemoralis*), a two-foot-high species found mostly in sterile fields east of the Rockies, was considered by F. Schuyler Mathews as "the most brilliantly colored of all goldenrods." Probably following the doctrine of signatures, which says that a plant's value can be told by its outward signs, the Houma Indians made a tea from its roots to treat yellow jaundice.

◆ Lance-leafed, or flat-topped, goldenrod (*Euthamia graminifolia*, formerly *S. graminifolia*), a very common variety in the East, has a flat top of flower clusters, is sometimes confused with tansy, and is quite fragrant. (*Euthamia* is from a Greek word describing the clustered flowers.)

◆ Rough-stemmed goldenrod (*S. rugosa*) is another tall variety, whose specific Latin name means "with wrinkled leaves." The word *rugged* is based on the same root; apparently something that's rough and wrinkled was considered rugged or tough. Since this species survives in dry soils and on dusty roadsides, the name is doubly appropriate. It's found from Texas to Wisconsin and eastward.

◆ Sharp-leaved, or Atlantic, goldenrod (*S. arguta*) is sometimes reported as the earliest goldenrod, with full bloom in mid-July. Flowers appear greenish yellow.

Afire

Willow trees are turning,
Maple leaves are burning,
Goldenrod's afire!
Fairy torches glimmer,
Woods are in a shimmer
And the flames leap higher!
November rain is all in vain
Down, down, it dashes.
O goldenrod! Goldenrod!
You've burned the woods to ashes.
—Angelina W. Wray

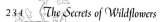

◆ Narrow goldenrod (*S. simplex*, formerly *S. spathulata*), another wide-ranging species found on both the East and West Coasts and across Canada, is interesting in that it thrives in such variant locations as coastal sand dunes and mountain slopes. It's so called because its flower heads are composed of narrow clusters. The species has many variants.

◆ Sweet goldenrod (*S. odora*), also called Blue Mountain tea, is noted for its strong anise scent. During the American Revolution it was frequently used as a replacement for British teas. Charles Francis Saunders, in *Edible and Useful Wild Plants of the United States and Canada*, calls it "a pleasant and wholesome drink," and Euell Gibbons recommended its sweet-aromatic flavor and aroma. This was the only goldenrod ever to make the *U.S. Pharmacopoeia*, the official list of recognized medicinal substances, but it was dropped by 1882.

◆ White goldenrod (*S. bicolor*) is more colorfully called silverrod. Its flowers are white or creamy and so unlike typical goldenrods that few people recognize them as such. Silverrod is also called belly-ache-weed from its use as a carminative—an herbal Gas-X.

All goldenrods are perennials. Most are showy and long lasting enough to make fine border flowers, and are easily established by transplanting or gathering and spreading the seeds. Their decorative blossoms remain fresh in bouquets for several days, and I can't imagine an autumn flower arrangement without goldenrods.

Nor can I imagine a late-fall walk without seeing the dried, gray, fuzzy-topped wands that John Greenleaf Whittier recalled in "The Last Walk in Autumn":

> Along the rivers summer walk,
> The withered tufts of asters nod;
> And trembles on its arid stalk
> The hoar plume of the golden-rod.

National Flower?

"The goldenrod is certainly our representative American wildflower," wrote Mathews in 1895. A few years before, when the subject of a national flower was widely discussed, a Boston man published an essay suggesting that either the arbutus or the goldenrod be chosen, and asking the people to make known their preference. "The response was decisive," F. Schuyler Mathews reported. "And the vote was cast by an overwhelming majority for the goldenrod."

In the 19th century, goldenrod was touted as a symbol of the United States. "It symbolizes a country where the people rule, for many tiny flowerets are needed to make a perfect head, just as in our composite nationality many races combine to form the true flower of American manhood and womanhood," wrote one author.

No Rival

The goldenrod, the goldenrod
That glows in sun or rain,
Waving its plumes on every bank
From the mountain slope to the
*   main,—*
Not dandelions, nor cowslips fine,
Nor buttercups, gems of summer,
Nor leagues of daisies yellow and
*   white*
Can rival this latest comer!
—Edna Dean Proctor
(1829–1923)

Ella Gilbert Ives put the idea to song. Here's an excerpt:

Sing a song of goldenrod!
The truest bit of gold
That ever gleams by woodland streams
Or on the wayside wold,
Till o'er and o'er, from shore to shore,
The echoes sweet are rolled.
O goldenrod! Dear goldenrod!
We'll sing your praises ever.
Though but a weed
Your voice we'll heed,—
"Our Union none can sever."

Were it not for its misrepresentation as a hay fever flower, goldenrod might well be in the running today as our national flower.

Ragweeds

THE SEASON FOR SNEEZIN'

If ragweed is so annoying, why is it ambrosia?

Common ragweed's cone-like green flowers, hardly noticed amid its handsome foliage, give off countless grains of sneeze-provoking pollen.

The end of summer is the season for sneezin', when breezes bear pollens that bring tears to eyes and tickles to noses of millions of hay fever sufferers. Ragweed pollen is the chief source of the irritants that cause late-summer hay fever. Although there are many species in the ragweed genus, the main culprits are common ragweed (*Ambrosia artemisiifolia*) and great ragweed (*A. trifida*).

Many people have found it strange that such devilish plants should be called ambrosia, which was the food of the Greek gods. (If they consumed both ambrosia and nectar, the drink of the gods, humans could become immortal, too.) However, *ambrosia*, which can also mean simply something that tastes or smells good, was the plant's ancient classical name, first applied no doubt to a finer-flowered or better-tasting member of the clan, whose identity today is unclear. John Gerard wrote 400 years ago that the mystery plant's scent "hath moved the poets to suppose that this herbe was meate and food for the gods."

Artemisiifolia, sometimes spelled *artemisiaefolia*, means its leaves are like those of the wormwood plants, members of the genus *Artemisia*.

Common ragweed, originally from eastern North America, is now found coast to coast, and from Canada to Brazil. It forms colonies along roadsides and on the margins of woodlands. The plants also invade fields where cows will eat them if they're desperate enough. The resulting milk is tainted by the bitterness of the plant (whence another name, bitterweed). Experiments in the Midwest in the 1940s found that cattle favored—even over alfalfa—hay made by harvesting ragweed before it bloomed and curing it with a little salt. Sheep and pigs like the plant fresh (whence another name, hogweed). For them, at least, it *is* ambrosia.

Common ragweed's fernlike leaves are quite attractive, and a grove of the plants looks almost like a stand of ferns. Above the leaves, wands of dangling green male flowers rain down the pollen on the less numerous females, hidden in clusters of bracts below. Because ragweed does not use the services of insects, it has not had to evolve showy, scented blossoms. Its flowers are green, the same as the rest of the plant, and have no markings or scent to woo passing bees.

The pollen can also fertilize more distant flowers. Tiny and light, designed to be borne by air and not by insects, the pollen is manufactured in massive quantities so that at least a few grains will pollinate a female flower somewhere. If you're a hay fever sufferer, you know how successful such a system can be. Just consider your nose to be a flower. When you start sneezing away, you've been well pollinated.

Pestiferous Pollen

Ragweed pollen itself is no worse than the airborne pollen of some other weeds, but ragweeds are the most common and prolific producers in many areas from August through September. Nationwide, ragweeds spew a quarter of a *billion* tons of pollen into the air each season. A single plant can produce several million grains of pollen and, spread by the wind, these can easily travel a mile or two from the parent plant.

Between 5 and 10 percent of the population is allergic to pollen. That's up to 30 million people in just the United States. Some 75 percent of them are allergic to ragweed pollen, which the Connecticut Lung Association calls the "single, most important pollen" in causing hay fever, and is responsible for more of the hay fever–causing pollen than all other plants combined. The allergic reaction can include repeated and prolonged sneezing, a stuffy and watery nose, redness, swelling and itching of the eyes, and various breathing difficulties. Over some years of exposure to the irritations, some people can develop chronic sinusitis and even asthma.

Annihilating the weed would be almost impossible, according to an official of the Connecticut Lung Association. While setting up pollen-counting stations around Connecticut some years ago, the official said he was "just dumbfounded" at the number of ragweed plants he saw. "It was everywhere—in fields, cracks in driveways, along sidewalks, in flower gardens."

In fact, the number and perhaps the size of ragweeds has probably been increasing in the past century. Recent studies by Dr. Lewis Ziska, a plant ecologist with the U.S. Department of Agriculture, and Dr. Peter Wayne and a team at Harvard University, suggest that the increasing levels of carbon dioxide in the atmosphere are probably helping ragweeds thrive—and causing more people to suffer. Dr. Ziska estimated that the quantity of ragweed pollen in North America may have doubled in the last century because of global warming and the interrelated increase in CO_2, the gas that plants breathe. "When you give plants more CO_2, you find some plants respond strongly and some respond weakly," Dr. Ziska told *USA Today* in 2000. "We're finding some weeds survive better than (desirable) plants." Dr. Wayne's team found that ragweeds grown in atmosphere with double the normal carbon dioxide levels were taller, fuller, and produced more seeds—and 61 percent more pollen.

The lung association official said that while the pollen can be airborne over long distances, the highest concentrations are within a few hundred yards of a plant, so destroying them could bring some relief to nearby sufferers. In some places, it is illegal to allow ragweed to grow, and you can be fined for not destroying plants that appear on your property. Law or no law, pulling up any ragweed you see is doing a service for the many hay fever sufferers. Often when my children were small and we went for a walk, we'd all yank up any plants we ran across. They are

The Wonder of Artemisia

Artemisia was a person as well as a part of the scientific name for common ragweed. She was the wife—and sister—of Mausolus, a Persian satrap and ruler of Caria and Rhodes, who died in 353 B.C. Artemisia erected a huge and elaborate tomb in her husband's memory. The edifice became one of the seven wonders of the ancient world, and the satrap's name became our word for an aboveground burial place, *mausoleum.*

Achoo!

"Achoo," says you,
As you view
This bright September morn.
"Oh my," says I,
And I cry:
"A sneeze of pollen born!"
Ragweed, indeed,
—Please take heed—
Is making you wheeze and sneeze.
It's here, it's there,
It's everywhere,
Until the fall's first freeze.
Those grains are banes,
Respiratory pains,
On such a beautiful day.
So yank this crank
From field and bank,
And throw nasal strain away.
—J. S.

annuals that establish themselves very easily and quickly, so ripping up one may prevent a colony of dozens from forming over a couple of years.

Other plant pollens or spores can be equally annoying to sensitive people. In the spring, certain trees and grass pollens can cause symptoms; into the summer and early fall, there are mold spores and airborne pollens from cockleburs, plantains, sheep sorrel, and some other plants.

Goldenrods, which bloom extensively at the same time that ragweed flowers bloom, are often blamed for hay fever, a sort of guilt by association. In fact, the heavier goldenrod pollen is designed to be bee-borne, not air-borne, and hence is not considered among the culprits affecting hay fever sufferers.

Common ragweed's other names, many as unattractive as the problems it causes, include stickweed, stammerwort, blackweed, carrotweed, Roman wormwood, tasselweed, and hay fever weed. Hay fever, incidentally, is a misnomer, since neither traditional "hay" nor a fever is involved. The ailment's technical names are allergic rhinitis or pollinosis.

Value in a Villain

Even villains have their value. The Delaware Indians used the plant as a poultice to prevent blood poisoning, and in the 19th century the leaves were rubbed on poison ivy inflammations to provide relief. Cheyennes treated bowel cramps with ragweed tea, and Nanticokes considered it a laxative. Mexicans recognized it early in this century as an official drug for reducing fevers. Its leaves have been used to produce a long-lasting green dye. And its use as a hay may become more extensive when farmers realize that some weeds can be their friends as well as foes.

Old herbals recommended ragweed as an antidote for hay fever—a little hair of the dog that bit you. While few modern herbals even mention ragweed, those herbalists of the past had the right idea. Today scientists have developed hay fever treatments that use ragweed pollen. In allergen immunotherapy, a patient is given a series of shots—like vaccinations—with increasingly larger doses of ragweed pollen extract to enable the sufferer to build up immunity to the pollen.

Perhaps the greatest value of ragweed is as a soil preserver and conditioner. It is quick to arrive and patch up the earth's wounds, such as swathes cut by floods, fires, or even bulldozers, thus helping to prevent erosion. The nutrients and especially the fibers contained in the above- and below-ground parts of the plant enrich and condition the soil, paving the way for other plants.

The Great One

Two dozen species of ambrosia live in North America, including some with very limited ranges such as the San Diego burr ragweed (*Ambrosia chenopodiifolia*), found only in San Diego County, California.

Almost as common as *A. artemisiifolia* is the great ragweed (*A. trifida*), whose name aptly describes its size, not its popularity. While the green flowers are similar to those of common ragweed, the leaves are "trifid"—three-lobed—and quite different. A fan of rich soils, great ragweed often grows from 10 to 15 feet tall—an immense size for an annual. F. Schuyler Mathews said it's the tallest member of the huge Composite family, though some of the related sunflowers and wild lettuces can give it a run for its money. Great ragweed ranges from the entire East Coast to Manitoba and New Mexico.

Although it, too, is a prolific producer of sneezy pollen, the great ragweed plant has also had its friends. Smart wheat farmers used to appreciate its arrival after their spring crop was harvested. Rich in nitrogen and other nutrients, great ragweed would be allowed to grow until just before blooming time and then plowed under as a green manure.

The plant has also been called horseweed and horse-cane because those animals supposedly like it (or perhaps because it's as tall as a horse). Either explanation may also apply to buffalo weed, a name more common in the Midwest. Unless you're an equestrian, buffalo herder, or a wheat farmer, however, it's best pulled from the ground early in its career—before it gives you or a neighbor the wheezes and sneezes.

Giant Great

In the 1800s, naturalist William Hamilton Gibson claimed to have measured an 18-foot, 4-inch specimen of giant ragweed.

Tiny Grains

Ragweed pollen is so small that, laid side by side, 100 pollen grains would be needed to reach across the head of a pin.

Joe-Pye Weed

A NOBLE LUMMOX

Joe Pye is long gone, but his weed still graces many meadows.

Joe-Pye weed was named for a New England "yarb man."

The American Indian has given us many words, mostly place-names like Connecticut, Mississippi, and Chicago. However, in the East at least, it's unusual to find a plant with a common name of Indian origin, and especially one with the name of an individual Indian.

Folklorists tell us that Joe Pye, sometimes written Jopi, was a traveling medicine man or, as early New Englanders would have called him, a "yarb man." One tale says he came from a Maine tribe and used to sell his herb wares around the Northeast at about the time of the American Revolution. Another had it that Joe Pye owned a lot of land near Salem, Massachusetts, in early colonial times. Though he befriended European settlers and helped them with his herbal medicines, Joe Pye was eventually chased off his land and forced to live in an Indian village in western Massachusetts. He is said to have used his "weed" as a treatment for typhoid fever, possibly because the plant could make people sweat profusely. He must have had some success—or at least a lucky batting average—for the plant has borne his name for more than three centuries.

Actually, Joe-Pye weed refers to several different "weeds," all members of the genus *Eupatorium*, although there has been confusion over whether some plants are distinct species or just variations of others. At least three Joe-Pye weeds—spotted (*E. maculatum*), sweet (*E. purpureum*), and hollow (*E. fistulosum*)—are widespread, found in most states east of the Rockies. *E. maculatum* has crossed the Great Divide and is found on the West Coast, both in the United States and Canada.

Some botanists suspect that spotted Joe-Pye weed, identified by its spotted or "dashed" stem markings, may be a race of sweet Joe-Pye weed. The ovate hairy leaves grow in whorls of four or five, and the many flower heads are in several bunches of six or seven, all so jammed together that the plant often seems to have one flat-topped cluster. Sweet Joe-Pye weed, considered rare and treasured in some of its range, is easily identified by the vanilla-like odor of its crushed leaves. While all species attract butterflies, sweet Joe-Pye weed's scent and color probably make it the most attractive of the lot. Hollow Joe-Pye weed has a hollow stem, absent in the other two varieties.

Huge Genus

Eupatorium is a huge genus, with some 500 species worldwide. In North America, there are 50 species, including the several kinds of Joe-Pye weeds, a few bonesets (see the next chapter), sundry snakeroots, and a thoroughwort or two.

Joe-Pye weeds are members of the Composite family. Unlike such common Composites as daisies, asters, and sunflowers, Joe-Pye weeds have no rays and are all composed of tubular "disc" flowers, favored by the long-tongued butterflies and bees. Although these insects pollinate flowers while dipping for goodies, Joe-Pye weed can pollinate itself. Because the flowers are so closely packed, pollen-bearing stamens of one flower head can come in contact with the long pollen-catching stigma of a neighboring head, accomplishing the job that insects usually have to do in Composites.

The plants are found in moist or wet lowlands, especially in meadows near ponds and streams, and can grow to 12 feet, making them among our tallest herbs. Their flowers range from pink to light purple, coloring that inspired F. Schuyler Mathews to write in the 1890s that "a good patch of Joe-Pye weed under a hazy August sky produces one of those delicious bits of cool pink, set in dull sage-green, such as an impressionist likes to paint."

Purple-shaded Joe-Pye weeds—one author likens their color to crushed raspberries—are a sort of transition from the white of midsummer's Queen Anne's lace and the purples of loosestrife and vervain to the tinted whites and deeper purples of fall's asters, and serve almost as a harbinger of the cooler weather to come. If you mark the passing of the seasons with the color of flowers, you might shiver just a little in the heat of August when you see Joe-Pye weed.

Actually, Joe-Pye weeds' season is fairly long, and I've seen the plants in bloom as early as July 15 in Connecticut, although the great groves of them aren't out in true color and height until mid-August. The flowers are usually gone by mid-September.

Many people enjoy the Joe-Pye weeds' beauty indoors and out. Country inns in New England often display bouquets of Joe-Pye weed in August or early September. The purple clusters liven up tables and counters, and one fancy Connecticut inn used to fill a whole corner of its dining room with the tall flowering stalks.

More Blood

Eupatorium means "of a noble father" and was reportedly named for Mithridates Eupator (or also called Mithridates the Great), the overly ambitious ruler of the Asia Minor kingdom of Pontus from 120 to 63 B.C. Why him? Some authorities say it's because he was the first to use one of the genus as a medicine. Others tell the story of how Mithridates had discovered that a species of *Eupatorium* was an antidote to poison, and he consumed it regularly to protect himself from poisoning by his enemies—including his mother. (This same technique is used today to treat asthma, and some have called Mithridates the world's first immunologist.) He was eventually captured by an enemy and, since he preferred death to being a prisoner, he tried to poison himself. He had so much antidote in his system, however, that nothing worked, and he finally had a comrade stab him to death.

Mithridatism

"Mithridatism" is a term meaning an immunity to poison, acquired by administering increasingly larger doses of a poison. It is named for Mithridates Eupator, Joe-Pye weed's scientific namesake.

The Killer

White snakeroot, once the most notorious member of the *Eupatorium* genus, may have killed thousands of Americans in the eastern half of the country, including Nancy Hanks Lincoln, Abraham Lincoln's mother. Eaten by cows when fodder was in short supply, the plant tainted the milk with a poison that caused an often fatal disease called milk sickness. For decades people did not know the source of the disease, and suspected everything from poison ivy to bacteria and vapors from under the earth. So devastating and feared was milk sickness, especially in the first half of the 19th century, that whole villages were permanently abandoned after it struck. Dairy cows may still occasionally eat white snakeroot and while their milk would be equally toxic today, it is diluted with other milk in such huge quantities that the poison has no effect. White snakeroot was long known as *Eupatorium urticaefolium* or *E. rugosum*; recently, it was assigned the name *Ageratina altissima*. Though it's poisonous, many nurseries offer white snakeroot as a native plant that will do well in partial shade.

If that tale seems far-fetched, there are those who believe that the name recalls Mithridates' penchant for bloodshed—shed blood being somewhat similar in color to European varieties of our Joe-Pye weed. Always warring with the Romans, Mithridates once ordered the massacre of all Roman and Italian cities in Asia, and it is said that 80,000 people were killed in one day in the winter of 88 B.C. Thus, like the purple loosestrife discussed earlier (see page 176), this plant's name may have a gory origin, making one wonder whether botanists—or at least taxonomists—are a bloodthirsty lot.

Sweet Joe-Pye weed has several folk names. It is called queen of the meadow (sometimes "king," more in keeping with the meaning of *Eupatorium*), trumpet flower (if you have a good imagination, the upward-pointing whorl of leaves could look like the end of a horn), kidney root, gravel root (it was used to treat kidney ailments), marsh milkweed (no relation to true milkweeds), quillwort, and motherwort.

Medicinal Uses

Indian Joe may have found a medicine for typhus in this plant, but 19th-century Americans used it chiefly to treat kidney and urinary illnesses. One American Indian tribe—maybe Joe's—even favored it as an aphrodisiac. Perhaps less interested in its libidinous virtues, Chippewas employed solutions of Joe-Pye weed to treat inflamed joints. Potawatomis made poultices for burns from its leaves and considered the flower heads to be good luck charms, especially when gambling. Ojibwas believed that washing a papoose up to the age of six in a solution made from the roots would strengthen the child. Children who were fretful and couldn't sleep were put in a bath to which a Joe-Pye weed decoction had been added, causing them to relax and nod right off.

Wildflower gardener and former U.S. senator George D. Aiken called Joe-Pye weed "a good natured lummox, willing to grow anywhere for anyone." It makes an excellent border flower or pond-edge plant, self-sowing readily. All that's needed is some wet soil and good sunlight, and they can be transplanted easily.

Mixed with goldenrod, sunflowers, and some of our earlier tall white asters, Joe-Pye weed creates a colorful late-summer hedge, especially in front of a wood. And you can always use it to fire your imagination, as did a *New York Times* writer some years ago: "Those eddying mists of this [August] morning could have been more than a swirl of vapor. If old Joe Pye's spirit was there, he must have been appraising the season's yield."

Boneset

A BITTER TEA FOR THE AILING

From mending fractures to charming deer,
boneset was both popular and feared.

Not too long ago the drying leaves of boneset dangled from the rafters of many a country attic. The plant was one of the most widely used—and widely hated—medicinal herbs of old America. Boneset tea, the scourge of children who dreaded its bitter taste, was extensively used as a "febrifuge," a fever reducer, from the times of the first settlement of North America well into the 20th century.

Boneset is a July and August flower of wet, sunny meadows and waste places. Although it has been likened to milkweed, with which it often grows, boneset is no relation, and is, in fact, a member of the huge Composite family of such plants as daisies, asters, and goldenrod. Its white (rarely blue) rayless blossoms are packed in rounded heads, with long white "threads" projecting far beyond each floret, giving a fuzzy appearance to the clusters.

However, the leaves, not the flowers, are the more distinctive feature of *Eupatorium perfoliatum*. *Perfoliatum* refers to the stem's "perforating" the leather-like, veiny leaves. Actually, the leaves clasp and entirely surround the stem, making it appear as if the stem has perforated one long leaf with pointed ends.

Eupatorium, the genus to which boneset belongs, literally means "of a noble father," but reportedly referred to Mithridates Eupator, bloodthirsty ruler of Pontus, whose warring exploits are described in the chapter on the closely related Joe-Pye weed.

Extracts of boneset made American Indian and colonial medications that were popular but vile tasting.

Widely Used

Like Joe-Pye weed, boneset was long ago employed as a medicine among American Indians, who called it a name equivalent to "ague weed." Our ancestors often referred to it as Indian sage. "It has always been a popular remedy in the United States," wrote British herbalist Maude Grieve. "Probably no plant in American domestic practice [has had] more extensive and frequent use." At one time it was listed in the *U.S. Pharmacopoeia* as an official medicine.

There are still some old-timers who can recall a grandfather's or grandmother's attic with

If He's Black or Purple...

"To cure rattle-snake bites . . . put thoroughwort leaves pounded on and keep wetting them with water. If person is very sick, black or purple, let him drink a little of the juice. Renew the application after 2 hours."
—*The Ladies' Indispensable Assistant* (1852)

dozens of boneset plants, hanging to dry. "To one whose childhood passed in the country some 50 years ago, the name or sight of this plant is fraught with unpleasant memories," wrote Mrs. William Starr Dana in 1893. "The attic or woodshed was hung with bunches of the dried herb, which served as many gruesome warnings against wet feet, or any overexposure which might result in cold or malaria." A friend who grew up in the 1930s remembered its being collected and dried by her grandmother. Much to her chagrin, the friend was also fed its tea for colds and fevers.

Mrs. Dana described the taste of boneset tea as "nauseous." Mixing boneset extract with a candy such as taffy made the medicine more palatable to an ailing child. Yet Alice Morse Earle, author of books on early-American life, recalled boneset tea as having "a clear, clean bitter taste, no stronger than any bitter beer or ale."

Whatever the taste, the tea was a common and inexpensive method of relieving fevers, and was especially popular among African Americans in the South. When medical supplies were short during the Civil War, boneset tea instead of quinine was given to Confederate troops. Many drugstores carried the leaves by the middle of the 19th century.

Bones of Contention

Boneset was used to treat dengue, a disease once common in the South. Transmitted by mosquitoes, the ailment was also called break-bone fever because the pains were so severe that bones seemed broken. Perhaps as a consequence, the plant that relieved the pain was called boneset.

Another theory has it that the name came from the doctrine of signatures, the belief that God gave plants outward signs as to what they were good for. Since the opposing leaves of boneset were joined at the stem, folks believed that a poultice of the plant would help broken bones to knit. Still another theory—perhaps the most reasonable—was that boneset tea was given as a pain reliever to people who had broken bones.

The herb was also used to treat constipation, rheumatism, catarrh, pneumonia, influenza, and ringworm, and for expelling tapeworms. Some authorities say that because it stimulates immune cell function, boneset can help fight off minor viral infections, such as colds and the flu, the same way echinacea does. As a remedy for snakebites, its decoction was drunk as a tea, and its crushed leaves were applied to the bite.

Because of its thoroughness in treating so many kinds of fevers and ailments, boneset was also popularly known as thoroughwort (from *wort*, meaning "plant"). Some authorities believe that its only real value was in causing fever victims to sweat, and consequently it was popularly known as sweating plant and feverwort.

Charles F. Millspaugh described one dramatic case of boneset's effectiveness in the 19th century:

When a young man, living in the central part of this state, he was attacked with intermittent fever, which lasted off and on for three years. Being of a bilious temperament, he grew at length sallow, emaciated, and hardly able to get about. As he sat one day, resting by the side of the road, an old lady of his acquaintance told him to go home and have some thoroughwort "fixed" and it would certainly cure him. (He had been given, during the years he suffered, quinine, cinchonine, bark and all its known derivatives, as well as cholagogues, and every other substance then known to the regular practitioner, without effect; the attacks coming on latterly twice a day.) On reaching home, with the aid of the fences and buildings along the way, he received a tablespoonful of a decoction of boneset evaporated until it was about the consistency of syrup and immediately went to bed. He had hardly lain down when insensibility and stupor came on, passing into deep sleep. On awaking in the morning, he felt decidedly better, and from that moment improved rapidly without further medication, gaining flesh and strength daily. No attack returned for 20 years, when a short one was brought on by lying down in a marsh while hunting.

Charming Deer

The Chippewa Indians rubbed the plant's root fibers on the whistles they made for calling deer. As such it was considered a "charm," a substance that had the power to affect something—in this case, deer—without coming in contact with it.

Other names for boneset include crosswort (the pairs of leaves whorl around the stem so that, as you look down on them, each pair crosses the next below), wild sage (the leaves bear some resemblance in shape), thoroughwax, thoroughgrow, and throughstem. In some cases *thorough* may be a variation of *through*, as in throughstem, because of the stem's projecting through the leaves.

About 50 species of *Eupatorium* are found in North America, mostly in the East, and several of them are called bonesets. However, no other boneset has the distinctive perforated leaves and none is as common and widespread as is this species, which ranges from the East Coast to the Dakotas and down into Florida and Louisiana. East Texas has a variety, *E. compositifolium*, whose white flower clusters are more pyramid-shaped than flat-topped and that carries the suspicious name, Yankee weed. The plant doesn't come from the land of the Yankees, so the Texans must hold the weed in such contempt that they named it after their favorite "enemy."

Although F. Schuyler Mathews found the flowers "dull and uninteresting," healthy plants are attractive, even "desirable," according to Edwin Steffek in *Wildflowers and How to Grow Them*. However, the handsomely shaped leaves often turn yellowish in the wild and are frequently attacked by leaf-eating insects that do not have children's tastes. To maintain healthy-looking plants, the ground should be continuously moist, and you may have to spray for insects. Transplant stock in late spring or early summer, as soon as the plants are recognizable. These short-lived perennials self-sow readily, and you'll soon wind up with enough plants to load up your rafters and fill many a cup of tea.

The Doctor's Story

Mrs. Rogers lay in her bed,
Bandaged and blistered from foot to
*   head.*
Blistered and bandaged from head to
*   toe,*
Mrs. Rogers was very low.
Bottle and saucer, spoon and cup,
On the table stood bravely up;
Physics of high and low degree;
Calomel, catnip, boneset tea;
Everything a body could bear,
Excepting light and water and air.
I opened the blinds; the day was
*   bright,*
And God gave Mrs. Rogers some
*   light.*
I opened the window; the day was
*   fair,*
And God gave Mrs. Rogers some air.
Bottles and blisters, powders and
*   pills,*
Catnip, boneset, sirups and squills;
Drugs and medicines, high and low,
I threw them as far as I could throw.
"What are you doing?" my patient
*   cried;*
"Frightening Death," I coolly replied.
—Will Carleton (1845–1912)

Sunflowers

BEAUTY AND BOUNTY

Sunflowers feed and entertain humans and birds, and inspire artists.

Sunflowers, like this tall specimen, Helianthus giganteus, *have a long history of helping humans in countless ways.*

If ever a clan of flowering plants was put on this earth to help humans, it would be the sunflowers, whose golden-rayed blossoms seem so symbolic of late summer. Some of them are downright amazing in their usefulness. Sunflowers have been used to feed people, birds, pigs, and bees; to clear swamps; to encourage egg laying, make paper, fill life preservers, and stuff cigars. In one species nearly every part of the plant is or has been of economic value—even its ashes.

Sunflowers are New World plants. *Helianthus*, the generic name, comes from the Greek *helios*, "sun," and *anthus*, "flower." Sunflowers, in turn, are members of the large Composite family. About 70 species are known in the Western Hemisphere, but 50 to 60 of them are North American. More species are found in the Midwest and West than in the East. Because so many sunflower seeds are purchased to feed wild birds, odd species and hybrids can pop up almost anywhere. Identification is often difficult for this reason and because, even among the wild native species, hybridizing is possible.

A Popular Style

Neltje Blanchan observed at the turn of the 20th century that one-ninth of all the then-known flowering plants in the world belonged to the Composites. More than 1,600 species were found in North America north of Mexico, and more than half of these are of the "daisy pattern," Ms. Blanchan wrote, calling it "the most successful arrangement known." And of these, the majority are wholly or partly yellow.

Of the yellow daisylike Composites, sunflowers are the most conspicuous. In many cases their flower heads are the largest and their stalks the tallest. Tall, or giant, sunflower (*H. giganteus*) and common sunflower (*H. annuus*) can reach 12 feet in height. These features help assure survival: bright yellow flags waving high above the masses easily attract pollinating bees. Later, though minus their color, the seedy heads still wave high, readily spotted by hungry birds that help disperse the seeds.

The king of the genus is the common sunflower, although in parts of the continent other varieties may be more common. It is royal both in its history and as the parent of most garden and agricultural sunflowers grown for their seeds. One scion—the mammoth, or Russian, sunflower—has a head up to a foot wide that bears 2,000 or more good-size seeds.

Early History

Because there is virtually no written record of pre-Columbian North and South America, fairly little is known about the early history of this popular plant. Natives in Mexico and Peru used the flowers, so similar in form and in color to the sun, in ceremonies honoring the sun god. Aztec priestesses wore the flowers in their hair, and the conquering Spanish found many representations of sunflowers, wrought in pure gold, embellishing Aztec and Incan temples. Today, the sunflower is the national flower of Peru.

Although the common sunflower is probably native to western North America, trade among the American Indian nations made the species well known and widespread across the continent by the time European explorers arrived. Champlain found the Hurons growing it in 1615, to use the stalks as a source of fiber for cloth, much as flax was used. They used the leaves as fodder, the flower rays as a yellow dye, and the seeds for both food and hair oil. Some tribes made black and purple basket dyes from the seeds. Senecas roasted the seeds and boiled them with water to make a coffee. Some tribes believed that to eat the seeds improved the eyesight. Ojibwas made a poultice for blisters from the leaves.

Lewis and Clark found that the Plains Indians, who often grew sunflowers intermixed with their corn crops, added the ground seeds to marrow of buffalo bones to form a sort of hard pudding. (Euell Gibbons mixed boiled beef marrow, sunflower seed meal, and salt to make a tasty spread for bread or crackers.) Peter Kalm reported that by 1749 Indians in Loretto, Canada, were cultivating sunflowers and mixing the seeds in maize soup. Indeed, in Russia and elsewhere, powdered sunflower seed is today often used as a thickening agent for soups.

Early settlers, especially in Canada, quickly saw the plant's value and fed it whole to livestock. They also sent it to Europe, where it became very popular. John Gerard, the 17th-century herbalist who exper-

Sunflower Cookies

1 cup sunflower margarine
1 cup granulated sugar
1 cup brown sugar, packed
2 eggs
1 teaspoon vanilla
2 cups all-purpose flour
1 teaspoon baking soda
½ teaspoon baking powder
¼ teaspoon salt
2 cups oats, rolled
1 cup coconut, flaked
1 cup raw or roasted sunflower kernels

In medium-size mixing bowl, combine margarine and sugars until well blended. Add eggs and vanilla. Stir together the flour, baking soda, baking powder, and salt; mix well. Add to margarine mixture. Stir in oats, coconut, and sunflower kernels. Drop by rounded tablespoons onto ungreased baking sheet. Bake at 350°F for 8 to 10 minutes, or until cookies are brown around the edges. May substitute chocolate chips or raisins for coconut. Makes 4 dozen cookies.

—*National Sunflower Association*

imented extensively with discoveries from the New World, wrote: "We have found by triall that the buds before they be flowered, boiled and eaten with butter, vinegar and pepper after the manner of artichokes, an exceeding pleasant meet, surpassing the artichoke far in procuring bodily lust." He also found broiled buds tasty.

Many Uses

In the years that followed the Europeans' discovery of the common sunflower, a multitude of uses for it and its hybrids and siblings were developed. The seed has been for centuries ground into meal and used to make a palatable and nutritious bread. Sunflower seeds have a high food value, containing vitamins A and B, calcium, phosphorus, and other minerals.

With 16 percent albumen and 21 percent fat, the seeds have been valued for feeding and fattening chickens, hogs, and milking cows. With hogs, all the farmer needs to do is plant the seeds of *H. tuberosus*; the animals will root out the tasty underground tubers themselves. Sunflowers are said to encourage the egg-laying ability of poultry. The leaves also make an excellent fodder. The stems and seedless heads, when dried, serve as litter in poultry houses. Dahlgren & Company, a Minnesota firm that processes sunflower seeds for food uses, sells the discarded shells for turkey bedding.

The pith of the sunflower stalk is one of the lightest natural substances known, having a specific gravity of 0.028, compared to 0.24 for cork. Consequently, it was used to stuff life preservers. The stalks were burned in heaps to obtain large quantities of potash from the pith to use as fertilizer. Well into the 20th century, perhaps still, the Chinese used the stalk fiber to blend with the silk cloths. This fiber has also been used to make paper in fairly modern times. The shells were once ground and made into blotting paper.

Seeds are pressed cold or under moderate heat to obtain a vegetable oil that is much like olive oil and is readily available in supermarkets today. It's used in food preparation, including the manufacture of margarine. The oil was also used as fine lamp fuel, as a lubricant, for soap and candle making, and as a drying oil in paints. Sunflowers are now Argentina's most important oil-producing seed; before its breakup, the Soviet Union was the biggest seed producer, but Argentina now leads all nations. Sunflowers are also said to be the only major crop plant to have originated in the United States, and are still widely grown on the Plains. About 2 million tons of seeds are produced annually for oil and confection markets—about 500,000 tons of that are sold for bird food. North Dakota is the biggest grower of commercial sunflowers, with some 1.7 million acres planted in the year 2000. That was second only to wheat as a crop.

People have eaten the seeds, raw or roasted, in many forms, and today sunflower seeds are still popular as a snack food. One manufacturer's product, roasted in soybean oil and seasoned with sea salt, contains more than 200 calories an ounce—not exactly the stuff of diets. In Russia, where the seeds are as popular as peanuts are here, large bowls of hybrid sunflower seeds are often found on tables in restaurants or the seeds are sold on street corners. Roasted seeds have also been used to brew a coffee-like drink, particularly in Russia and in Hungary, where sunflowers are also a popular crop.

Follow the Sun?

Many people have believed that sunflowers follow the sun. Sir Thomas Moore described this trait in a poem:

As the sunflower turns on her god
*   when he sets*
The same look which she turn'd when
*   he rose.*

In fact, although the buds tend to follow the sun, the flowers don't. According to the National Sunflower Association, once the flower opens, it faces eastward. No one knows why for certain, though the tendency may protect the plant from the desiccating rays of the sun on very hot days.

In herb medicine, various parts of the plant were employed to treat bronchial and pulmonary diseases, malaria, and fevers. Linoleic acid, extracted from the oil, has been used by herbalists to slow the progress of multiple sclerosis. Today, however, most practitioners of herbal medicine do not use sunflowers for anything other than food.

The carefully dried leaves have been used as a tobacco substitute and, according to one 19th century author, "the flavor . . . is said to greatly resemble that of mild Spanish tobacco." The leaves have been smoked both as a medicine and for enjoyment, especially in Germany.

The plant is said to have a remarkable ability to dry damp soils. "Swampy districts in Holland have been made habitable by extensive culture of the sunflower," reported Maude Grieve. Research has found that a sunflower's leaves transpire six gallons of water over its 18-week growing season. That's several times the plant's total weight.

In nature, bees find sunflowers useful for obtaining not only large quantities of nectar but also wax for their hives.

Our Artichoke

Among the many varieties of sunflowers found in America, *Helianthus tuberosus* is probably the least known as a sunflower, though it is well known as the Jerusalem artichoke. Various nations of Indians cultivated this plant, also called earth apple and Canada potato because of its starchy tuber. Chippewas, who simply dug it up and ate the root uncooked, called it by a name that translates as "raw thing." The Indians passed the plant on to the settlers, who sent it to Europe as early as 1617. By 1630, it was widely used as a vegetable.

Italians cultivated it and called it *girasole aricocco*—"sunflower artichoke"—and it is believed that a mispronunciation of *girasole* led to the popular but geographically incorrect name, Jerusalem. The plant was as well used as the potato, to which it is about equal in food value, until the latter was introduced into Europe in the 18th century and became more popular.

Stronger Than Cement

Obviously, sunflowers have many attributes. One of the strangest is their strength. Naturalist John Burroughs described an unusual seedling back in the early part of the 20th century:

> One of the most remarkable exhibitions of plant force I ever saw was in a Western city where I observed a species of wild sunflower forcing its way up through the asphalt pavement; the folded and compressed leaves of the plant, like a man's fist, had pushed against the hard but flexible concrete till it had bulged up and then split, and let the irrepressible plant through. The force exerted must have been many pounds. I think it doubtful if the strongest man could have pushed his fist through such a resisting medium. . . . It is doubtful if any cultivated plant could have overcome such odds. It required the force of the untamed hairy plant of the plains to accomplish this feat.

Kansas Man

The sunflower is the state flower of Kansas, a fact noted on at least three U.S. postage stamps bearing its likeness. Alf Landon, the Republican from Kansas who ran for president in 1936, used sunflower-shaped campaign buttons. In response, Democrats noted that sunflowers die in November. Landon, of course, lost.

Although large-flowered varieties—the bird food kind—are readily available, Frank C. Pellett, who set up a large wildflower sanctuary in Iowa back in the 1940s, shunned the mighty annuals and hybrids in favor of smaller wild varieties whose flowers he found more delicate and numerous. The plants can be relied upon to send up flowers in larger numbers each year. They require very little care, he said, and are not fussy about their situation, as long as it is sunny. My favorite wild variety is the tall, or giant, sunflower (*H. giganteus*), which likes semishaded moist territory and which each year produces many delicate and long-lasting flowers, about 2¼ inches in diameter.

In the 19th century, Alice Morse Earle reported, "the sunflower had a fleeting day of popularity, and flaunted in garden and parlor. Its place was false. It was never a garden flower in olden times, in the sense of being a flower of ornament or beauty; its place was in the kitchen garden, where it belongs." Nonetheless, more than two dozen garden hybrids of *H. annuus*, with petals bearing shades of red, pink, maroon, and red, were developed in the 20th century. In the 1990s, sunflowers became almost a fad, and not only in gardens. Apparel, food packages, cosmetics containers, greeting cards, and even wine bottle labels bore pictures of sunflowers.

Whether or not you choose to grow wild or cultivated varieties for their beauty or your kitchen, you are providing food naturally for many wild birds; more than 45 species have been observed eating them. If you feed birds, you probably can't help having a few of the cultivated sunflowers spring up from seeds dropped or cached by birds or buried by feeder-robbing squirrels. You can either let the birds pick away at the heads as they stand on the stalk (or after they inevitably fall over onto the ground), or you can cut the heads with mature seeds, dry them, and save them for winter when food is scarcer. The larger heads may be suspended from trees or the house, using thin fishing line so that squirrels have difficulty pilfering the seeds. For an added treat, the head can be coated with melted suet, wrapped with pieces of suet, or dabbed with peanut butter.

Thus, everyone—humans and beasts—can enjoy the beauty and the bounty of the amazing sunflowers.

Expensive Sunflowers

Vincent van Gogh liked to paint sunflowers, and people like what he painted. In 1987, one of his sunflower works sold at auction for $39.9 million.

Turtleheads

THE TALKING HEADS

How turtleheads can provide entertainment, natural and otherwise.

"We're going to look for some turtleheads," I told my three-year-old son as we got into the car. He looked at me, puzzled, and asked: "Just the heads?"

"They're flowers," I replied. "They look sort of like the head of a turtle."

He paused again and asked: "Do they have eyes?"

"No," I said, "but they have big mouths and you can make them talk."

He seemed to accept that explanation, and once we reached the edge of the swamp where I had seen the flowers in years past, he began asking where the turtleheads were. When we finally found some mixed among tall grasses and cattails, he stared for a moment at their peculiar shape.

"What do they say?" he asked.

I picked one blossom from a cluster, squeezed its sides, and played ventriloquist as its mouth opened and closed.

"That's pretty funny, Daddy," he said. And for the next 10 or 15 minutes, he insisted that the turtlehead "say something."

Turtleheads challenge bees but still manage to be pollinated.

Masticating Flowers

Unfortunately, he didn't get to see a more natural performance that is both funnier and stranger than his father's. Turtleheads rely almost exclusively on larger bees for pollination. When they squeeze between the closed lips and then wiggle and twist around to reach the nectar supplies deep inside the one- to two-inch-long flower tube, they cause the front lips to open and close as if the flower were chewing its own food instead of providing it. To come upon one of these flowers "masticating" is a most entertaining sight, which we missed that day for lack of bees.

Fluffy fur-like hairs on the lower lip keep out crawlers, and few flying insects are strong enough to push their way between the lips and then past an arm-like sterile stamen that must be moved aside to reach the nectar. In the process of all this maneuvering, the bees get well dusted with pollen.

Seed Case Attacks

The seedpods of the turtlehead can be a miniature world of life and death. Tiny caterpillars of certain moths and flies feed on the seeds. Ichneumon wasps land on and crawl about the seed cases, probing through them with their ovipositors until they find a victim and then stab the caterpillar to implant eggs that soon hatch larvae that eat their host, from the inside out.

Enigma

The turtlehead's a tightlipped plant—
It keeps its secrets sealed
And, unlike the banana, can't
Reward you as it's peeled.
Yet, what's so great inside that shell
That makes the bee elate?
And when it blooms each day, pray
*   tell,*
Does it "open"—or "inflate"?
—J. S.

Turtleheads are "protandric," which means that the male parts mature first, then the female parts. Since the flowers open from the bottom to the top of the stalk, the older, lower flowers are females, and the ones above, male. The male flowers have closed or nearly closed lips, while female flowers open wider—making it easier for bees to deposit pollen than to pick it up.

Figworts

Turtleheads are fairly common flowers of wetlands, swamp fringes, and stream banks, blooming in August, September, and sometimes into October. *Chelone*, the plant's generic name, is from the Greek for "tortoise," referring to the shape of the top of the flower, which is like a tortoise's head. *Glabra*, its specific name, means "smooth," and describes its smooth, hairless stems and leaves.

It is a member of the Figwort family (Scrophulariaceae), a family of around 225 genera and 4,500 species, whose members include the butter-and-eggs, or toadflax, covered in another chapter (see page 227), and the garden snapdragons. The similarity between these and the turtleheads can easily be seen in the flowers' mouthy construction.

While there are four North American species of *Chelone*, *C. glabra* is probably the most widespread, found from southern Canada to Alabama, and from the Atlantic to the Mississippi River watershed. In the South, there are attractive purple and pink species. *C. glabra* is generally known as a white flower, but pink-tinged specimens are not unusual.

Dining Spot

A nectar-loving butterfly makes use of the turtlehead, not for the flowers' sweets but for the plant's leaves. The Baltimore checkerspot (*Euyphydryas phaeton*), a black-and-white species with brick red or orange spots along its wing edges, is found over a wide area of the northeastern United States but is extremely local in its living habits. In fact, guidebooks tell butterfly collectors who hunt the Baltimore to look first for turtleheads and to expect the insect to be not more than 100 yards away.

The Baltimore lays its eggs on the leaves, on which the resulting spiny orange-and-black caterpillars feed exclusively. If you see a turtlehead with holes in its foliage, odds are that a Baltimore caterpillar was there for dinner. In the fall, groups of the caterpillars will spin thick webs over a plant and spend the winter together. The next spring the caterpillars feed on the leaves and then construct their blotched grayish chrysalises on the underside of the turtlehead or other leaves.

Though odd of shape and plain of color, the turtlehead is nonetheless a handsome flower, and its tight clusters produce many blossoms over many weeks. The perennials grow from one to six feet high. You might consider starting some if you have a moist sunny spot on your property, though the late Vermont senator George D. Aiken maintained that they also do well in fairly dry soils. While you can transplant them in the spring, they are not common enough to be removed from the wild and should be left alone, unless they are threatened with destruction. They can be started from cuttings taken in the summer, but the best method of establishing turtleheads is from their seeds, which have a good germination rate. Seeds should be easy to obtain in

September or October, if you know where to find the plants. Many native plant nurseries sell one or more species of *Chelone*.

Fish and Snakes, Too

Among *Chelone glabra*'s popular names, most of which are derived from the flower shape, are turtle-bloom, snakehead, codhead, fishmouth, bitterherb, salt-rheum weed, and shellflower (probably from the fancied resemblance of the top of the flower to the shell of a turtle or tortoise). It has been called hummingbird tree because those long-billed birds seek out its sweets early in the morning before the blossoms close. Some people call it white closed gentian because of a similarity to the blue closed gentians; there is no botanical relation.

The plant has also been called balmony among people who practice folk medicine and have used the leaves to make a salve for a variety of skin irritations, such as tumors and ulcers. It was popular among some tribes of American Indians as a tonic and a laxative, although the leaves from which the medicines were concocted have a markedly bitter taste. The Malecite Indians of Canada's Maritime Provinces used the plant as a contraceptive. Other medicinal uses included treatment of worms, jaundice, consumption, and dyspepsia.

Not one to mince words, herbalist Ben Charles Harris says that the turtlehead is good for "the removal of toxic sludge from the stomach and intestines."

Personally, I'll stick with using it for puppetry.

Tortoisehead?

The Latin name means "tortoise," but the English name is turtle. What's the difference between the two creatures? Tortoises are turtles that live on dry land rather than in the water. Since these are water-loving plants, turtlehead is probably the more appropriate name. If they lived in the desert, they'd be better called tortoiseheads.

Vervain

A FAVORITE OF PRIESTS AND WITCHES

Vervains are plants of magic and mystery.

Blue vervain's wands were used in sacred ceremonies.

As a kid, did you ever play with sparklers, those pyrotechnic wires that burned brightly but slowly down the wand, spitting out sparks along the way? Think of blue vervain as a floral sparkler, except its flame starts at the bottom of the wand and works its way up. The fire, of course, is the burst of bright blue flowers.

Blue vervain (*Verbena hastata*) is found in meadows, brook sides, and pond shores in the heat of mid- to late summer, and produces a candelabrum of floral stalks. As the blooming works its way from the bottom to the top of the spike, you'll typically find seeds below the flowers and buds above. If the spikes are short and tightly clustered, the display can be spectacular; if they are stringy and loose, they will be less showy but still interesting.

What the plants might lack in showy beauty, however, they make up for in legend and lore. For the common American vervain and its European sibling belong to a clan of plants that has had uncountable magical, mystical, and medicinal qualities attributed to it for thousands of years.

A Mystical Name

The word *vervain* is applied to both a genus and a family of plants. *Verbena*, the principal genus within the Vervain family, *Verbenaceae*, includes from 100 to 200 species found mostly in the tropics. While all but a few species are natives of North or South America, the type species is the European vervain, *Verbena officinalis*, which is now also found throughout the United States as a sneak-across weed or a garden escape.

Theories about the origin of vervain's name are many. Some say that *verbena* is a corruption of *Herba veneris*, "herb of Venus," a name used because the ancients thought vervain was an aphrodisiac able to rekindle the flames of dying love. Others say that the name was simply the Latin word for "altar plants," because vervain was so frequently used in connection with Roman religious ceremonies. *Webster's New International Dictionary* traces the word to the Latin *verber*, meaning a "rod" or "stick," which describes the shape of the plant. Country children have used them as toy swords and arrows.

Still others, especially Italians, believe *verbena* is a variation of the Latin *herbena* or *herbeus*, which means "green." Or it could be a corruption of *herba bona*, "good plant." Finally, there are those who feel that *vervain* and perhaps *verbena* are connected with the ancient Celtic word *ferfaon* or *ferfaen*, meaning "to drive away stone." This name reflects a former use of the plant in treating bladder disorders.

Colorful Past

Vervain also has many folk names, such as herb grace, holy herb, enchanter's plant, Juno's tears, frog's feet, pigeon grass, herb of the cross, and simpler's joy. Our native species is also called American vervain, wild hyssop, ironweed, and purvain. Many of the names recall vervain's colorful past.

The Druids were supposed to have put the plant in their lustral water, used in rites of purification. Their priests gathered it "when the dog-star arose from unsunned spots," and held it between their hands during ceremonies. When they picked it from the ground, Druid priests would have to leave fresh honey on the spot to make amends for having robbed the earth of so sacred a plant.

Priests of early Rome believed the flowers were formed from the tears of Juno. They called it *Herba sacra* and employed it in decorating sacrificial animals, altars, and headdresses. Roman ambassadors carried it as a symbol of peace and friendship when visiting other nations. Vervain also figured in ancient Jewish ceremonies, and Christians used it as well as hyssop as an "aspergillum," a device for sprinkling holy water on the faithful.

The forces of both good and evil used vervain. Considering it miraculous by association, Christians in the Middle Ages believed it to be a cure for many ailments because it was found growing on Mount Calvary. An old legend said it was used to dress Christ's wounds—hence such names as herb of grace or herb of the cross. When gathering vervain, people used to chant a song that began:

> Hallowed be thou, Vervain
> As thou growest in the ground
> For in the Mount of Calvary
> There thou wast first found.

On the other hand, vervain was purported to be among the most common ingredients in the brews of witches. Magicians and sorcerers used it in sundry rites and with incantations. For example, magicians taught that smearing the juice of vervain on the body would guarantee that a wish would come true, or would make the worst enemies friendly. John Gerard didn't think much of such goings-on: "Many odde wives fables are written of Vervaine tending to witchcraft and sorcery, which you may read elsewhere, for I am not willing to trouble your eares with reporting such trifles, as honest eares abhorre to heare." In fact, he believed the Devil himself deceived physicians into believing vervain was good as a medicine for the plague.

Valuable Vervain

Among the members of the family Verbenaceae is the famous and valuable Burmese teak tree, which has one of the hardest woods in the world.

Party Plant

Party people should love vervain. According to the Latin writer Pliny, "If the dining chamber be sprinkled in water in which the *herba verbena* has been steeped, the guests will be merrier."

Despite this, vervain was thought to repel evil spirits and bring good fortune. To keep the devil out of their homes, English peasants in the 17th century hung vervain and dill, along with a horseshoe, over doorways to keep the devil out. "Vervain and dill hinders witches from their will," it was said. The plant was worn around the neck as a charm against headaches, snakebites, insect stings, and "blasts" (sudden infections), and was also carried for good luck. When they went courting, French peasants presented vervain to young ladies, believing that it would help win their hearts. In Germany a hat made of vervain was given to a bride to protect her from evil. In 18th-century West Sussex, England, parents hung dried vervain leaves in black silk bags from the necks of their "weakly children," hoping to give them strength.

Nicholas Culpeper listed many uses for the plant in the 17th century. "Used with lard," he wrote, "it helps swellings and pains in the secret parts." But it also "causes a good colour in the face and body." So valuable was vervain a few centuries back that "simplers," people who gathered wild herbs would always find a purchaser for the plant; thus, the name simpler's joy.

Nerves to Worms

While medicinal and superstitious uses of the European vervain were legion, American blue vervain, also called swamp vervain, has been popular in folk medicine, too, and has been listed in several modern herbals. Vervain tea, made from our vervain, was famous not too many years ago as a tranquilizer and as a relief for symptoms of fevers and colds, and for chest congestion. The herb has been used to treat insomnia, as a poultice for external wounds and sores, and even to drive out intestinal worms. American Indians in California made a flour from the roasted, ground seeds of a western species; the seeds' bitterness was reduced by soaking them in a couple of changes of cold water. Chippewas "snuffed" the dried flowers to treat bloody noses.

Although their *Complete Guide to Herbal Medicines* (2000) lists more than 25 uses to which vervain has been put, pharmacists Charles Fetrow and Juan Avila point out that not a single scientific study has found evidence that either European or American vervains have any medicinal value at all.

A total of 31 species of *Verbena* live in North America. Only two natives besides *V. hastata* are found coast to coast, and big-bract vervain (*V. bracteata*) and hoary vervain (*V. stricta*) are both considered invasive weeds in some parts of their range.

Also fairly common in the eastern half of North America is the white vervain, *V. urticifolia*, much like blue vervain in the size and shape of the plant, except that the flower spikes are taller and the blossoms are, of course, white. Weed expert Edwin Rollin Spencer calls the species the homeliest of the genus, adding that it's also sometimes a pest to farmers.

If you have open wetland or a pond on your property, blue vervain makes an attractive plant that blends in well with other flowers of the season, such as Joe-Pye weed, boneset, early goldenrods, and ironweed, all of which favor moist ground. Vervain is easily transplanted and spreads readily from seed and from its rootstock. What's more, vervain is a source of winter food for some songbirds. The wands of seeds, four to five feet tall, offer their fruit long after the plant itself has died, and they attract cardinals, juncos, song sparrows, and other species.

Aspergillum

Vervain was once an aspergillum
—Now there's a word to rhyme!
Priests would take the wands and
*   fill 'em*
At a holy water time.
They'd dip the spindly stick and
*   shake it*
At a special sacred hour;
To spread good grace, they'd make it
A flower-power shower.
—J. S.

Groundnut

SWEET FROM TIP TO TOE

Barefoot boys were among groundnut's many fans.

Wildflower watchers often overlook vines, many of which are considered troublesome weeds. But at least one native vine, the groundnut, has been treasured for centuries for its sweetness, both above- and belowground. Those who have read John Greenleaf Whittier's idyllic celebration of youth may recall that "The Barefoot Boy" knew not only the ordinary wildflowers but also these vines with hidden treats:

Oh for boyhood's painless play,
Sleep that wakes in laughing day,
Health that mocks the doctor's rules,
Knowledge never learned of schools
Of the wild bee's morning chase,
Of the wild-flower's time and place,
Flight of fowl and habitude
Of the tenants of the wood;
How the tortoise bears his shell,
How the woodchuck digs his cell,
And the ground-mole sinks his well;
How the robin feeds her young,
How the oriole's nest is hung;
Where the whitest lilies blow,

Where the freshest berries grow,
Where the ground-nut trails its vine,
Where the wood-grape's clusters
* shine;*
Of the black wasp's cunning way,
Mason of his walls of clay,
And the architectural plans
Of gray hornet artisans!
For, eschewing books and tasks,
Nature answers all he asks;
Hand in hand with her he walks,
Face to face with her he talks,
Part and parcel of her joy,—
Blessings on the barefoot boy!

Groundnut flowers are sweet smelling and its corms sweet tasting.

The groundnut is a member of the Pea family and, as every barefoot boy once knew, frequents moist thickets. The vines bear distinctive fronds consisting usually of two or three pairs of opposite leaves and one end leaf at a right angle to the rest. However, the more distinctive feature of the plant is its flowers. Blooming in tight clusters of a dozen or two blossoms from July through September, they are of an unusual color. Some describe it as purplish brown or even chocolate. They look almost good enough to eat, especially after you smell them; the scent is among the strongest and the sweetest in our wildflower world. "Although too inconspicuous in itself to be

Sadie's Quest

Price's groundnut (*Apios priceana*) was discovered by and named after Sadie Price (1849–1903), a Kentucky schoolteacher who collected specimens of more than 2,000 species of mid-American plants and discovered two other new ones, Price's dogwood (*Cornus priceae*) and Price's sorrel (*Oxalis priceae*). She once described for *The American Botanist* how, outfitted in a full-length Victorian-era dress and hat, she went hunting for a fern: "To collect it a humbling of my pride was necessary, as I had to cast aside hat and botanical equipment, and crawl under the projecting rock, with scarcely room for head and shoulders to enter. It meant sore muscles and a fresh accumulation of mud on the dress that had already passed recognition, but it also meant a treasure to gloat over."
—As reported by Robert H. Mohlenbrock in *Where Have All the Wildflowers Gone?*

called a landscape flower," wrote Mabel Osgood Wright in 1901, the groundnut "pays its tithe in fragrance."

Since the flowers are often hidden behind the vine's own leaves or those of the host plant, you may have to rely on your nose to find them. Mrs. Wright added that the groundnut vines help to add fullness to greenery in that each vine "brings into uniformity much that would otherwise be unsightly, straggling growth."

Tasty Roots

The sweetness doesn't end with the flowers. The tuberous rootstock—from pea- to egg-size lumps linked like big beads on a chain—was cherished by the American Indians, explorers, and barefoot farmboys alike for its sweet, somewhat nutty, taste recalled in its common name. Groundnut offers more than good taste, however. The U.S. Department of Agriculture says "groundnut tubers are a good source of carbohydrates and contain between 13 percent and 17 percent protein by dry weight, or about three times more than potatoes or any other widely used vegetable root."

Groundnuts may be eaten raw, boiled, roasted, or fried, but several enthusiasts say they taste best if you peel and parboil the tubers with salt, and then roast them or chop and fry them. The meat should always be eaten while hot; a cold groundnut is said to be as tasty as a wet towel.

Many Indian tribes, including Sioux, Delawares, Omahas, Dakotas, Cheyennes, Osages, Pawnees, Hidatsas, and Wampanoags, considered the groundnut an important food, and many cultivated it. British explorer Bartholomew Gosnold found Indians of Martha's Vineyard eating groundnuts in 1602, and Massachusetts Bay Indians introduced the plant to the Pilgrims, who ate them to help get through that first difficult winter at Plymouth. Europeans knew of the plant by 1590, when Thomas Hariot, writing about Sir Walter Raleigh's early but unsuccessful attempt to establish a colony in Virginia, told of "openask," with its "very good meate." Early Swedish immigrants in the mid-Atlantic colonies were using groundnuts for bread in the 1700s. Once, when his potato crop failed, Henry David Thoreau turned to digging up groundnuts and found them quite tasty. (Nelson Coon says that for diabetics they make a good substitute for potatoes.)

Explorers and soldiers on long trips through the middle of North America sought out the groundnut, and one trick was to look for the burrows of field mice, which often collect and store the tubers as winter food. One expedition reported finding a peck of roots from the stores of mice.

Raleigh was reportedly impressed enough with the groundnut that he brought it back to England as a "potato." Dr. Asa Gray, the noted 19th-century botanist, was of the opinion that had civilization started in the New World instead of the Old, the groundnut would have centuries ago been cultivated and developed as a commercial crop and would now be an everyday vegetable. Some American farmers in the past made an attempt at cultivating the groundnut but were never successful at gaining a wide enough market to profit from growing them. Perhaps the European palate simply didn't like groundnuts as much as it did other discoveries from the Americas, such as the true potato and the tomato. However, groundnut is also a labor-intensive crop because the plants don't cooperate with the regimentation that farm equipment would impose on them. As the U.S. Department of Agriculture puts it, "groundnut is difficult to cultivate mechanically because each tuber can sprout and grow in the spring, filling in spaces between rows." Thus, weed control is very difficult.

Many Names

Groundnut is also called wild bean and is, in fact, a relative of our garden beans. It produces a small edible pod of seeds in the fall. (Several other related plants are also called wild bean.) Other folk names include hyacinth bean, Indian potato, pig potato, bog potato, potato bean, white apple, ground pea, trailing pea, and Dakota potato. French settlers called it *pomme de terre*, or "earth apple."

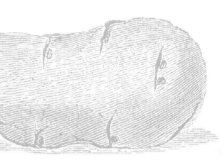

    Its scientific name, or names, are almost as plentiful as its common ones, and different authors have used different names depending on when they wrote. In 1753 Linnaeus named the plant *Glycine apios*; *glycine* means "sweet," and *apios* is Greek for "pear," referring to the shape of the tuber. By the 1800s it was being called *Apios tuberosa* by some, including Dr. Gray. By the 1890s, it was *Apios apios*. In 1913, Britton and Brown were calling it *Glycine apios* again, but today it is known as *Apios americana*, probably the most suitable of the lot since it is a widespread native, one of two members of the genus to live in North America. The other, often quaintly called traveler's delight (*Apios priceana*) is quite rare, and is found only in rocky woods of a few counties in Illinois, Tennessee, Kentucky, Mississippi, and Alabama. Also called Price's potato-bean or groundnut, the species is officially listed as "threatened" by the U.S. government. *A. americana*, on the other hand, is widespread and fairly common, at home from eastern Canada to Florida and west into Texas and Colorado, North Dakota, and Saskatchewan.

    Only a handful of *Apios* species are known in the world; two live in China and one in the Himalayas.

For Your Own

Perhaps because its flowers aren't huge, *Apios* species or cultivars have not been popular with gardeners, except in France during the 19th century. (The closely related wisteria has fared better.) Nonetheless, nurseries here and in Europe sell cultivated versions. For example, Plantsman Nursery in Devon, England, says in its catalogue: "We rave about this plant. . . . . The combination of luxuriant growth and reliable heavy flowering puts this vine in a class of its own."

    Groundnut is easy to grow from the tubers transplanted in the spring or from seeds collected in September or October. It needs moist, rich soil, a host plant or fence, and not too much sun. Although it does not spread rapidly and overrun an area, it is difficult to eradicate once established, so select planting places with care. One 19th-century gardener, writing in the *Canadian Horticulturist*, suggested planting them with tall summer roses: "It would do them no harm, but lend a beauty to them after they had done blooming."

Rejected in Ireland

In the late 1840s, as the potato famine was devastating Ireland, attempts were made to introduce the American groundnut as a replacement vegetable. The effort failed, not only because it took two to three years to get a "nut" of edible size, but also because groundnut tubers multiply in all directions from the mother plant, making it almost impossible to weed a field of them.

In your garden it may be picked freely to bring its fragrance into the home, but avoid picking it in the wild. While not an endangered species, groundnut is not as common as it once was and should be encouraged to self-sow seeds where it is not a pest. (The last patch of it in my neighborhood was pushed out by invasive Japanese knotweed.)

We should do all we can to give barefoot boys—and girls—of the future a chance to find its trailing vine.

Groundnut Chips

"Slice the 'nuts' and simmer with butter, pork or bacon in a saucepan until tender; then dry off rapidly, cooking in such salt and pepper as desired in the last few minutes."
—Fernald and Kinsey,
Edible Wild Plants of Eastern North America

Ladies'-Tresses

ORCHIDS OF AUTUMN

The little ladies'-tresses send bees up, down, and around.

To many of us, the word *orchid* conjures up images of large, showy flowers of fine color and exquisite form. Ladies'-tresses may not be large, finely colored, or particularly showy, but their form has made them a favorite of those who hunt for the seeming handful of early-autumn flowers that don't fall within the aster or goldenrod clans.

Ladies'-tresses are among the last of the Orchid family to bloom in northern North America, and some say that they are the most common variety of wild orchid in the eastern United States. In my territory, they are hardly common—none of the wild orchids is—and I once got a call from an orchid enthusiast visiting the area who wanted to know where he might view some ladies'-tresses, even if it took a good bit of hiking. It did take a bit of a walk, but the reward was twofold. He got to view the flowers, but also he got to see them in an environment where nature was repairing damage made by humans. The orchids were growing in the middle of an old sand and gravel excavation—now part of a preserve—that was ever so slowly returning to a natural state.

To the casual wildflower observer, such interest may seem odd, for none of the ladies'-tresses species gets to be more than 18 or so inches in height. Their spikes of small white flowers are slim and often difficult to pick out from their surroundings, which frequently includes small white asters and grasses. Yet, the delicate, cleverly designed flowers are well worth seeking out and inspecting, even if doing so requires a magnifying glass.

Among the last orchids of the season in many areas, nodding ladies'-tresses have cleverly designed flowers that manipulate bee visitations.

Nodding, Slender, and Fragrant

Some 25 species of ladies'-tresses are found throughout North America and 300 worldwide. In the eastern half of the continent, the genus is most apt to be represented by three species: nodding ladies'-tresses (*Spiranthes cernua*), northern slender ladies'-tresses (*S. lacera*), and fragrant ladies'-tresses (*S. odorata*). Nodding ladies'-tresses inhabit the typical haunt of the genus—swamps and wet fields—while northern slender ladies'-tresses favor dry, sandy places, particularly hillsides; I've seen them happily growing amid the ugliness of that old sandpit. They are widespread, found from Newfoundland to Florida, and westward to New Mexico. The South is home to the largest-flowered of the genus, fragrant ladies'-tresses, which has a scent that hints of vanilla. Representatives of the Pacific states include Western ladies-tresses (*S. porrifolia*) and hooded ladies'-tresses (*S. romanzof-fiana*). Both are summertime rather than autumnal bloomers. Hooded ladies'-tresses are found throughout northern North America as well as in Europe, especially Ireland, where they are known as Irish ladies'-tresses.

The genus got its name from the way in which the flowers are displayed. They seem woven into the stem, giving it the appearance of a woman's braid—which is an old meaning of *tress*. The plants have also been called ladies'-traces, *trace* being another form of *tress*. *Spiranthes* comes from *speira*, a "spiral," and *anthos*, "flower," Greek words descriptive of the manner in which the flowers wind their way around the stem like a spiral staircase. Thoreau called it a "dense spiral cone like the thread of a screw." Actually, the flowers appear on only one side of the stem, but the stem twists to make them seem to be attached spirally.

Britton and Brown called this genus *Ibidium*, from a fancied resemblance of the flowers to the head of an Ibis. The genus has also been called *Gyrostachys*, Greek for "twisted stalk." *Cernua* means "nodding," because the flowers are downward-turned; *lacera* means "torn," referring to the fringes on the labellum; *porrifolia* suggests its leaves are leek-like; *odorata* reflects the scented flowers; and *romanzoffiana* refers to the Russian count Nikolai Romanzoff, who in the early 1800s sponsored explorations of North America and the Pacific Islands.

The Climbing Bees

Despite their size and lack of vivid color, ladies'-tresses attract many bees, without which they and half the other flowers in the world would disappear. Thus, it is important that flowers have something—be it size, color, or scent—to attract the interest of these insects and then reward them for their effort. In this case, a sweet fragrance draws them.

The complex relation between bees and ladies'-tresses fascinated Charles Darwin, Asa Gray, William Hamilton Gibson, and other noted students of nature. If you observe a bee visiting a colony of the plants, you'll find that the insect always starts at the bottom of the spiral spike of flowers and works its way up to the top, then flies to the bottom of the next plant's spike, works upward, etc. Why the bee uses this bottom-to-top system is uncertain. Darwin suspected it's just easier for bees to climb up than back down. "I believe," he wrote, that "bumblebees generally act in this manner when visiting a dense spike of flowers, as it is the most convenient method—on the same principle that a woodpecker always climbs up a tree in search of insects."

More important, however, it is a system that enables the plants to survive and to which the ladies'-tresses probably adapted themselves during their long evolution. In a maturing spike, the lower flowers are older, and have grown to the point where they are designed to be receivers of pollen. The blossoms toward the top are newer, less developed, and can only give pollen. Thus, having picked up grains from the top flowers of one plant, the bee moves to the bottom of the next

Unbounded Passion

"Beautiful as is the orchid, there was nothing beautiful in its origin, for the first Orchis was the son of a nymph and a satyr, hence a fellow of unbounded passion. At a festival of Bacchus, being warm with drink, he attacked a priestess, whereupon the whole congregation fell upon him and rent him limb from limb. His father prayed [to] the gods to put him together again; but the gods refused, tempering their severity, however, by saying that whereas the deceased had been a nuisance in his life, he should be a satisfaction in his death, so they changed him to the flower that bears his name."
—*Charles M. Skinner* (1911)

to deliver the pollen and fertilize those flowers. Gradually, the ability to receive pollen moves up the spike so that most of the flowers—perhaps with the exception of the uppermost—are fertilized.

Goo for Pollen

Even the method of dispensing pollen is unusual. As the bee inserts its tongue into a new flower to sip the nectar, it splits a little disk inside, releasing a very sticky glue that dries almost instantly and that helps assure that a tiny "boat" carrying pollen adheres to the bee. Apparently, having little pods of pollen on their tongues does not annoy the bees too much, for they continue to visit other flowers. When a bee visits the lower, older flowers, it finds the channel for its tongue has widened a great deal as the flower has matured. This allows the pollen-catching stigma to be exposed to the bee's pollen-bearing tongue, effecting pollination.

The intricate relationship between bees and ladies'-tresses becomes even more intricate and involved in Ute ladies'-tresses (S. *diluvialis*), found in the upper Rockies and included on the U.S. threatened species list. Two researchers, plant biologist Sedonia Sipes and Dr. Vincent Tepedino, an entomologist, found that the bumblebees that visit Ute ladies'-tresses can obtain only nectar from the flowers; they must have other flowers to supply their pollen needs. Thus, unless appropriate pollen-rich flowers are in the vicinity, it's unlikely that bees will visit the Ute ladies'-tresses and assure their survival.

Aphrodisiac

Ladies'-tresses have seen limited use in the practical world. A European species was once thought to be an aphrodisiac, and has been used to treat eye, kidney, and skin ailments. A Chilean variety is considered a diuretic.

Other names for these plants include wild tube-rose and screw-auger for S. *cernua*, and green-lipped ladies'-tresses, twisted-stalk, and corkscrew-plant for S. *lacera*. Fragrant ladies'-tresses have also been called fragrant tresses as well as tidal tresses.

These plants grow from tuberous roots. They should be transplanted only if they are in certain danger of destruction. Like most orchids, they're fussy about their surroundings, and they probably require the presence in the soil of certain kinds of fungus that help the young plants to grow. If you're patient, you can try planting from seed. In the case of S. *lacera*, you'll have to wait three years before flowers will appear.

Some varieties are available commercially, and one of the easiest to find and maintain in a garden is called *Spiranthes cernua odorata*, Chadds Ford, the parent of which was found in the 1960s in a wet Delaware ditch on land about to be subdivided.

Hyacinthine Bells

. . . Ah, then in shady lane and
   grassy field,
What new delight thy slender spires
   to find,
With tress of hyacinthine bells
   entwined!
Fragrance like thine no rose of June
   can yield;
No lily can eclipse thy snow, dear
   prize,
Flung backward by sweet summer as
   she fields.
—Emily Shaw Forman

Dogbane

A FLY'S WORST FRIEND

Dogbane is not likely to knock off Fido.

Dogbane may punish a thieving fly with death. Photo © Ed Kanze.

September is when summer's flowers produce their bounty of flying, floating, popping, and dropping seeds seeking a foothold for next year's crop. Dogbane sports one of the more unusual of the season's seed containers. The long, slender seed cases dangle from the stems in pairs, looking like the pajama bottoms of long-legged elves. Each pod contains seeds attached to fluffy fibers, much like those of the milkweeds. In fact, the shape of the pods as well as other features of the plant hint of the Milkweed family and, indeed, dogbane was once classified as a milkweed. Today, it's in a genus (*Apocynum*) and family (Apocynaceae) of its own, one step away from the milkweeds.

Dogbane is a common shrubby herb whose handsome pink flowers bloom in July and early August, and whose green pods disperse their seeds at the beginning of fall. Spreading dogbane, *Apocynum androsaemifolium*, is both the type species and our most common example of this small genus. It is found throughout the United States and southern Canada, except in the extreme Southeast. *Apocynum* means "dogbane" while *androsaemifolium* refers to the similarity of the leaf form to those of the androsaemum, an Old World plant.

Only a dozen species of *Apocynum* exist worldwide, and only three are found in North America. However, the whole Dogbane family consists of around 130 genera and 1,100 species, mostly tropical. Only nine genera are found in North America, four of them in the Northeast.

Like Rubber

Spreading dogbane is peculiar in a couple of ways. One is its feel. Touch the leaves, stems, and especially the pods, and it feels like rubber. Perhaps it is not surprising that the milky white juice inside the plant dries like soft rubber when exposed to the air.

Spreading dogbane, which grows to four or five feet in height and is usually found in colonies, bears small pinkish flowers that resemble lilies of the valley. F. Schuyler Mathews, author of *Familiar Flowers of Field and Garden*, wrote:

The flowers are quite as beautiful as many small garden favorites and in my estimation, they are individually more attractive by reason of their delicious dainty pink flush than the lily of the valley.

This seems flat heresy, but in defense of the preferences for a common wild flower, I would venture to predict that if some horticulturist should succeed in producing a lily of the valley with the dainty pink coloring of dogbane, such a flower with its charming perfume would be wildly admired by every lover of flowers. Such is the disadvantage of the wild flower that its beauty is discounted if it has not reached an abnormal development, and its charms are unheeded if it does not throw out a perfume strong enough to entice the passerby.

Bane of Bugs

These flowers, so admired by Mathews, may be the bane of foolish dogs, but they are certainly the bane of flies and various smaller insects for whom they are a deathtrap. Dogbane flowers are designed to attract butterflies, whose tongues are dabbed with a cement-and-pollen mixture as they dip for the sweets. Bees may also feed and then transfer pollen. However, flies and other weaker flying insects that are not valued as pollen carriers are apparently unwelcome and often wind up dead for their trespassing.

Neltje Blanchan describes the process this way:

Suppose a fly falls upon this innocent-looking blossom. His short tongue, as well as the butterfly's, is guided into one of the V-shaped cavities after he has sipped; but getting wedged between the trap's horny teeth, the poor little victim is held prisoner there until he slowly dies of starvation in the sight of plenty. This is the penalty he must pay for trespassing on the butterfly's preserves! The dogbane, which is perfectly adapted to the butterfly and dependent upon it for help in producing fertile seed, ruthlessly destroys all poachers that are not big or strong enough to jerk away from its vise-like grasp. [Another author maintains that scales are actually triggered by touch and bend inward to clasp the victim.]

One often sees small flies and even moths dead and dangling by the tongue from the wicked little charmers. If the flower assimilated their dead bodies as the pitcher plant, for example, does those of its victims, the fly's fate would seem less cruel. To be killed by slow torture and dangled like a scarecrow simply for pilfering a drop of nectar is surely an execution of justice medieval in its severity.

Hands Off!

Are humans the bane of dogbane? Researchers at the University of Pennsylvania in the 1990s found that in two test groups of Indian hemp (*Apocynum cannabinum*) growing in the wild, most of the group whose plants had been gently touched by humans were eaten by insects and many died. The untouched group remained healthy. The findings puzzle scientists, who are uncertain why human contact may lead to the plants' demise. However, they suspect that *Apocynum* may react to touch by releasing a chemical that protects it from humans but winds up attracting insects. Some plants, such as sulfur cinquefoil (*Potentilla recta*) and butter-and-eggs (*Linaria vulgaris*), seem to have the opposite reaction, and thrive on human touch.

Whoops

While poisonous, dogbanes are not as potent as once thought. A 1939 text on poisonous American plants reported that only 15 to 30 grams of dogbane leaves could kill a horse or cow. Subsequent investigation has found that this statement was based on erroneous data published in 1922 by the New Mexico agricultural experiment station, which had confused dogbane with the related and very poisonous oleander.

In the Middle

Apocynum cannabinum and *A. androsaemifolium* often combine to create what scientists now tongue twistingly call *Apocynum x floribundum Greene* (pro sp.) [*androsaemifolium x cannabinum*], which is found in almost every state and province. The name used to be a lot simpler. For years it was called *Apocynum medium*, a name that suggests it's in the "middle" of two species.

Poisonous?

Dogbane is considered mildly poisonous, to humans as well as to dogs, and in that sense it could be considered a bane of any mammal. The name probably stems from a related or similar European species or genus. The only apparent connection between the American plant and dogs was its occasional use to treat people bitten by mad dogs. No dog would be foolish enough to eat the leaves, which have an intensely acrid taste: the plant was once called bitterroot.

For several insects, however, dogbane is not only harmless but also tasty. The caterpillar of the monarch butterfly and other milkweed butterfly larvae treat dogbane as a milkweed, feed on it, and build their chrysalises under the leaves. Once ingested by the caterpillar, the acrid juices of this and the milkweeds make the insect unattractive to birds and thus form a natural chemical defense against predators. The dogbane leaf beetle (*Chrysochus auratus*), a shiny green-backed beetle, spends most of its life on the leaves, which are both food and a place to lay its yellow eggs.

Powerful Drug

Humans have also found the plant useful; it was listed in the *U.S. Pharmacopoeia* as recently as 1952. Apocynum, one of the digitalis group of medicines, was once made from it and was considered a powerful drug for slowing the pulse. Dogbane has also been used to treat rheumatism, syphilis, and scrofula, and there has been recent research into its use to fight tumors. The folk name wild ipecac suggests it has been employed to induce vomiting.

American Indians, including Crees and more western tribes, used to peel the skin off the outside of the stems of a white-flowered dogbane called Indian hemp (*A. cannabinum*) and use its fibers in making string. They frequently manufactured fishing lines and nets from it, and sometimes wove cloth with the fibers. Swedes who settled in New Jersey and Pennsylvania two centuries ago favored dogbane over other materials for bridles and nets, and traded with local natives for their "Indian hemp" rope. "The Swedes usually got 30 feet of these ropes for one piece of bread," reported a contemporary author. Some traders!

Because dogbane flowers are so rich in nectar, American Indians and settlers used to obtain small quantities of sweetener from the blossoms when sugar was not available. Chippewas of Minnesota and Wisconsin, who used it as a medicine and a charm, called spreading dogbane *makwonagic odjibik*, which translates into the rather unattractive "bear entrails root."

Dogbane is also known by a host of other names, including flytrap, catchfly, honeybloom, rheumatismwood, western wallflower, and wandering milkweed.

Spreading dogbane is a fairly handsome plant with smooth dark green leaves and reddish stems. You may wish to consider it for portions of property that are sunny and fairly dry, with poor soil and lots of space. You can transplant, divide roots, or sow seeds collected in September and October. But be forewarned that this perennial, as its name suggests, can spread and choke out smaller, more delicate plants. In addition, if you have small children who might be tempted to taste its leaves or seedpods, it would be best to avoid having this somewhat poisonous plant around.

If you like butterflies and hate flies, however, dogbane may be right for you.

Thistles

WATCH YOUR STEP!

Although thistles have been cursed for ages, you don't have to be an ass to enjoy them.

Thistles are so well known for their prickly nature that many people call any plant with stickers a thistle. Yet, even though they were thought to be a curse from God, thistles are important, often attractive, plants that have many points—other than sharp ones—worth appreciating.

Many varieties of thistles are literally covered with thorns from head to foot, a defense against insects as well as four-footed—or two-footed—animals. The stickers that adorn the thistle heads are designed to discourage grazing animals from eating them and to keep crawling insects, such as ants, away from the unusually sweet nectar in the flowers.

The blooms of the flower heads, which range from the size of a marble to almost as big as a tennis ball, burst from the tops with thin, hairlike petals of bright purple or deep pink. Some species are yellow, and a few star-thistles (*centaurea*) are blue.

Poor PR

Though brilliantly colored, thistles suffered from some pretty poor PR over the millennia. "Cursed is the ground because of you," God told Adam in the Garden of Eden. "Thorns and thistles it shall bring forth to you." Shakespeare called them "rough thistles" in the same breath with "hateful docks." In his book, *All About Weeds*, biology professor and farmer Edwin Rollin Spencer labeled the Canada thistle (*Cirsium arvense*) "perhaps the worst weed of the entire United States. The plant does not have a single virtue so far as man is concerned."

So despised have thistles been that Australia passed an Act of Parliament around the turn of the 20th century, imposing stiff fines on persons who failed to destroy the plants, which were taking over thousands of square miles of fields Down Under. The government even appointed inspectors to search out scofflaws. England enacted a similar measure, and no fewer than 37 states have officially declared the Canada thistle *planta non grata*.

With such an unpleasant history, there would seem to be no redeeming value to this prickly family, whose very name is said to come from an ancient Saxon word for "to stab." However, both humans and beasts have appreciated thistles, in both fact and legend. For instance,

The bull thistle is among the largest and thorniest of the common thistles. Its handsome flower attracts many butterflies and bees, and nest-building goldfinches favor its down.

No, Canada

The Canada thistle isn't Canadian but a European species that was introduced into North America, probably with crop seeds. Perhaps because it arrived via Canada, it picked up the name; in Europe, the plant is usually called creeping thistle.

Kinds of Spines

Thistle spines are actually exaggerated serrations of leaves and bracts. While they exist solely to provide protection against grazing animals, other plant spines seem to have evolved to protect the plant from heat. On cacti, for instance, leaves probably developed into spines because the sun and dry air would have desiccated traditional leaves. In the case of a cactus, the green trunk assumes the food-production functions that leaves perform in most plants, so the spines wind up providing a degree of protection and perhaps even shading.

many varieties of birds love thistle seed, as do bird-feeding fans, who will pay several dollars a pound for it. And a pound of tiny thistle seed isn't much.

Butterflies love its nectar, and bees make fine honey from it. When crushed to destroy the thorns, thistles leaves have been found to be excellent food for livestock and were once widely used for that purpose in Scotland. Stripped of their spines, the young leaves of many *Cirsium* species make excellent salad greens and cooked vegetables. The peeled stems are said to be tasty either cooked or raw, and the roasted root is sweet. From the flower heads, the British have made golden thistle wine, which is supposed to taste like dry sherry. The seeds have been pressed to obtain oil; perhaps that was what Theophilus Thistlebottom of tongue-twisting fame was planning to do after successfully sifting thistles.

"Two or three of our native species are handsome enough to be worthy of a place in gardens," wrote British herbalist Maude Grieve. Indeed, some years ago, it was common in the British Isles to find Scotch, or Scots, thistle naturalized about the ruins of old castles in whose gardens it had been cultivated. It and members of its genus are still mentioned as border plants in a few gardening books.

Then, there is the scent. The despised Canada thistle is as fragrant and sweet as the most delicate and cultivated of garden flowers. One plant's perfume fills the air for yards around. The pasture thistle (*Cirsium pumilum*), a large pricker-studded fellow of the Northeast, is also called the fragrant thistle and once had the scientific name *C. odoratum* because of its fine scent.

Thistle Clans

About a dozen thistle genera occur in North America, all members of the large Composite family. Many species were unintentionally imported from Europe with crop seeds.

Cirsium is one of the larger thistle genera, with more than 90 species in North America. Its name comes from a Greek word that reflects the species' former use as medicine to treat swollen veins. Chippewas used native species for back pain during pregnancy. Mohegans of Connecticut employed the imported *C. arvense* as a mouthwash for infants.

Much of the farmers' hatred for thistles stems not so much their prickly aspect as from their prolific and persistent nature, able to take over fields and stay there. In fact, their taste for good quality soil is legend, and the British used to tell of the blind man who was choosing land to buy for his farm. "Take me to the thistle," he said. A 16th-century poet, writing on husbandry, advised:

> If thistles so growing proove lustie and long,
> It signifieth land to be hartie and strong.

The perennial Canada thistle has roots that not only go deep but also creep along just under the surface, sending up many new shoots. If left alone for a couple of years, a single plant can establish a sizable colony. And if it finds a mate, a true population explosion can occur. *C.*

arvense is a "dioecious" species, having both males and females, and unless plants of the opposite sex are close by, fertile seeds will not be produced. A male plant will produce only colonies of males via the underground runners, and females will make only females. But, to the dread of farmers, a colonizing male near a colonizing female can soon produce scads of seeds, which goldfinches and other birds scatter everywhere.

Incidentally, though thistle heads are equipped with a generous supply of down designed to lift away seeds in the wind, relatively few seeds find their way aloft. In many species, most seeds reach the ground when the flower head dies and falls off. While the down may do little for future generations of thistles, it kept past generations of Americans warm. Thistle-down quilts were great for snuggling under in winter, and the fluff was also popular with woodsmen, who used it as tinder for their campfires. The down is a major ingredient in the nests of American goldfinches, which also enjoy eating the seeds.

The tall, or roadside, thistle (*Cirsium altissimum*), is a closely related species that, as both the English and Latin names suggest, is one of our loftier herbs. A native that's widespread east of the Rockies, it can reach 10 feet in height.

Blessed among the Cursed

Among the other alien species that grow in North America is the blessed thistle (*Cnicus benedictus*), a seeming contradiction in terms. It may have been so called because of its extensive reputation and use as a cure for many maladies in the Middle Ages, when religion and medicine were closely connected. There is also a legend that the plant's veins were made white by the Virgin Mary's milk as she fed the infant Jesus. The plant was considered so powerful that it was used to treat the plague. *Cnicus* is the Latin word for "bastard saffron" or "mock saffron," perhaps reflecting some ancient use of the plant, which is found throughout the United States and southern Canada.

Scotch thistle, or cottonthistle (*Onopordum acanthium*), is found coast to coast, and in many states is considered a noxious weed. *Onopordum* means "asses' thistle," an ancient name possibly indicating that "stupid asses" would eat it, thorns and all. *Acanthium* means "thorny."

Scotch thistle may be the "true" thistle of Scotland, emblazoned on coins, flags, coats of arms, and the like. It was originally the emblem of the House of Stuart—so ordered by James IV on the occasion of his marriage to Margaret Tudor ("The Thistle and the Rose" of poet William Dunbar). In 1540, James V created the Order of the Thistle for knights of Scotland. Its motto, *Nemo me impune lacessit* ("No one attacks me with impunity") became the motto of Scotland and might well be the motto of the thistle itself. Even today in the United States, a long-running public radio show carrying Celtic music of Scotland and Ireland is called *The Thistle and Shamrock.*

Scotch thistle is a tall, erect, single-flowered, and very thorny plant of open fields. Legend has it that when the Danes or Norsemen invaded Scotland a thousand years ago, the soldiers stole up to a Scottish camp one quiet night by marching barefoot. However, one hapless

Thistledown

Set loose from summer's churlish
*   hand,*
All day they pass my door;
White voyagers to no man's land,
To ports without a shore.
—Lizette Woodworth Reese
    (1856–1935)

Good Food?

"The thistle is not cultivated assiduously; indeed, legislatures have fulminated against it, and it is usually treated as the enemy to be rooted out of the soil wherever found. Yet the ass thrives on it, and the question is put to doubters of its nutritive value, 'Did you ever see a dead donkey?' "
—*Charles M. Skinner* (1911)

Invasion!

"The increase of the Canada thistle for the last 10 years has been great; and if it continues to spread in the same ratio, for the 10 subsequent years, it will cover whole farms, and even townships. Borne on the 'wings of the wind,' in a clear day, we may see countless numbers of its seed, many hundreds of feet in the air; and whose fates can decree on whose soil they will lodge and vegetate?"
—Orson Cardin, Tompkins County, New York, writing in the *Cultivator* (November 1841)

Dane inadvertently stepped on a thistle and let go a loud yelp that aroused the sleeping Scots, who thereupon slaughtered the Danes and saved themselves and their country from being conquered. Hence, the respect paid in Scotland to the thistle.

In England and elsewhere, thistles were long valued as a medicine for convulsions and cricks of the neck, as a spring tonic, and to restore hair. "Though it may hurt your finger, it will help your body," advised Nicholas Culpeper. Country maidens believed they could use thistles to determine who would be the best candidate as a husband. They'd place thistle heads, one for each suitor, in the corners of their pillow at night, and the head that had grown a shoot by the next morning represented the most faithful admirer.

Perhaps the thistle was better used as a prognosticator of the weather. If the flower head closed during the day, it was a sign of impending rain. Later, the down was a forecaster: "If the down flyeth off coltsfoot, dandelyon, or thistles when there is no winde, it is a signe of raine," wrote a 17th-century Englishman.

Of all the thistles that have been used as medicines, the blessed milkthistle (*Silybum marianum*) is probably the best known. It has treated liver ailments for two millennia. It has also been widely used as an antidote for poisonous mushrooms. A native of Europe, this introduced species is found throughout much of North America. The plant is called blessed, supposedly because an angel instructed Charlemagne, as he prayed for a cure for a plague, to shoot an arrow into the air; the plant it landed on would provide the right medicine. It struck *S. marianum*.

One of our largest species is the bull thistle (*Cirsium vulgare*), which can grow to five feet and bears big reddish purple flowers atop an amazing display of bracts bearing long spines. A mature, flowering plant is handsome and often visited by butterflies and bees. Farmers dislike it in their fields and pastures, but because it's a biennial, bull thistle is not quite the pest that sibling Canada thistle can be.

Thistles have worked their way into history in many ways, both good and bad. Perhaps the most creative and nefarious use for the plants was discovered by some evil-doers in South America. When Charles Darwin was in Argentina sailing aboard the *Beagle*, he asked a native whether robbers were numerous in an outlying district he wished to explore.

"The thistles are not up yet," the fellow replied.

The answer quite rightly confused Darwin. But later on during his visit, he learned that the fields of the "great thistle . . . were as high as the horse's back" in some parts of the territory. "When the thistles are full-grown," he said, "the great beds are impenetrable, except by a few tracks as intricate as those of a labyrinth. These are only known to the robbers, who at this season [late summer] inhabit them, and sally forth at night to rob and cut throats with impunity."

Asters

THE STARS OF AUTUMN

But most of our asters aren't really asters anymore.

Asters, someone once said, "are stars fetched from the night skies and planted on the fields of day." Indeed, it often seems as if there are as many asters as stars when September and October roll around. And to those who have studied the subject a little, it seems almost as if there are as many aster species—and, lately, aster genera— as there are asters.

Aster, of course, means "star," as in *astronomy* and *astronaut*, descriptive of the star-like form of the flowers. This Latin generic name is one of the few that has caught on as a common English wildflower name as well. Asters were once more frequently called starworts (*wort* means "plant") and are still so called in England.

Until the 1990s, more than 150 North American plants were included under the genus *Aster*. However, close study, using DNA testing and other techniques, has determined that our "asters" are not quite the same as Old World asters. Almost all North American plants once classified under the genus *Aster* now bear such tongue-twisting generic names as *Symphyotrichum*, *Oclemena*, *Chlorolepis*, *Eurybia*, and *Doellingeria*. In fact, only one native *Aster* species is left in North America: the pretty Alpine aster (*Aster alpinus*), found only in Colorado and Alaska. Dr. Guy L. Nesom, a research botanist, did most of this taxonomical work, which was published in 1994.

Although some 250 species called asters in English grow around the world, the majority, at least 150, are natives of North America, and about 50 might be considered common and widespread. While so many of our common wildflowers have come from Europe, none of our asters is an immigrant. In fact, Europe has relatively few asters. *The Oxford Book of Wild Flowers* lists only one species of note in the British Isles, and most of the European varieties are rather unimpressive. Indeed, Donald Culross Peattie wrote in 1935, "Europe has no asters at which an American would look twice."

The calico aster is so called because its center disks are first greenish, then yellow, then purplish red, and flowers of many disk shades may be found mixed together on a single plant.

Bee Medicine

While European asters didn't do much to perk up ailing humans, they were recommended as a sort of medicine for bees by no less than Virgil, the great Latin poet. Book IV of his *Georgics* is devoted to the natural history and care of bees, and therein Virgil offers a suggestion for ailing colonies, using a European aster (probably *Aster amellus*):

The meadows know a flower, yclept by swains

"The Starwort": 'tis an easy one to find

For from one root it rears a mighty forest.

Its disc is gold; its many petaled fringe

Pale purple shadowed with dark violet.

Often the altars of the gods are decked

With chaplets wreathed of it; 'tis rough to taste;

In sheep-clipped dells and near the winding stream

Of Mella shepherds gather it. Take thou

And seethe the roots in fragrant wine, and serve

Full baskets in the doorway of the hive.

The Hunt

Of our native asters, some 75 are found east of the Rockies and 55 of them in the northeastern United States and southeastern Canada. The Pacific states seem to have fewer of them, but those few include the beautiful and widespread leafy aster (*Symphyotrichum foliaceum*), with beautiful purple- or lavender-rayed flowers. Since there are so many species, aster spotting is almost an autumnal sub-hobby of wildflower hunting. With so many varieties—some exceedingly rare—amateur flower sleuths could spend many hours not only in finding but then in identifying asters.

This is sometimes no simple task, for most wildflower guides do not pretend to list every species you might come across. Even armed with an extensive catalogue, identification can be tedious and technical, requiring close inspection of the leaves, seeds, or other parts. In addition, asters in the wild tend to form hybrids and to create tiny races that sometimes become distinct enough to be classified by some botanists as species. What's more, one species may have many varieties. For instance, the old leafy aster (*S. foliaceum*) comes in at least four varieties: Canby's aster, Parry's aster, and two called Alpine leafybract asters. And, of course, unless you have a very new guide, almost all of the scientific names will be out of date.

You don't need a botany degree, though, to identify most of the common asters. Actually, it's fun and challenging and, in the process of trying to separate similar species, you can learn a good deal about plant identification and structure.

The season for aster hunting starts in August when the white wood asters (*Eurybia divaricata*) and other early species appear. September is the best time, since virtually every variety is in bloom sometime during the month. The flowers are a prelude to autumn's bright colors. John Burroughs observed: "How rich in color before the big show of the tree foliage has commenced, our early roadsides are in places in early autumn—rich to the eye that goes hurriedly by and does not look too closely—with the profusion of goldenrod and blue and purple asters dashed upon here and there with the crimson leaves of the dwarf sumac."

Blues, purples, and variations thereof are common colors among asters. Many white varieties are also common, though often the white species will produce blossoms with subtle pastel tints of violet, pink, or blue. In many species the center disks start out yellow but turn to purple or brown later on.

Success Story

Members of the huge Composite, or "Aster" (Asteraceae), family of flowers, the various genera of asters are the most typical examples of Composite construction—a center disk of florets (almost always yellow) surrounded by rays that, while they look like petals, are actually sterile florets lengthened through evolution in a design to attract insects.

Neltje Blanchan wrote an interesting essay on the Asteraceae that is fitting to pass on here because, according to some botanists, asters are among the most successful Composites and hence among the most successful flowers:

Evolution teaches us that thistles, daisies, sunflowers, asters, and all the triumphant horde of Composites were once very different flowers from what we see today. Through ages of natural selection of the fittest among their ancestral types, having finally arrived at the most successful adaptation of their various parts to their surroundings in the whole floral kingdom, they are now overrunning the earth.

Doubtless, the aster's remote ancestors were simple green leaves around the vital organs, and depended upon the wind, as the grasses do. . . to transfer the pollen. Then some rudimentary flower changed its outer row of stamens into petals, which gradually took on color to attract insects and insure a more economical method of transfer. Gardeners today take advantage of a blossom's natural tendency to change stamens into petals when they wish to produce double flowers.

As flowers and insects developed side by side, and there came to be a better and better understanding between them of each other's requirements, mutual adaptation followed. The flower that offered the best advertisement, as the Composites do, by its showy rays; that secreted nectar in tubular flowers where no useless insect could pilfer it; that fastened its stamens to the inside wall of the tube where they must dust with pollen the underside of every insect, unwittingly cross-fertilizing the blossom as he crawled over it; that massed a great number of these tubular florets together where insects might readily discover them and feast with the least possible loss of time—this flower became the winner in life's race. Small wonder that our fields are white with daisies and the autumn landscape is glorified with goldenrod and asters!

The New England aster, much more widespread than its name suggests, is among the most beautiful of the group.

White wood aster, one of the earliest asters, has fewer rays than most but is nonetheless elegant in design.

The structure of the aster flower is a bit more complex than Blanchan describes it. The center disk has two kinds of florets: Those in the center have both stamens and pistils and can provide pollen to visiting insects. The more numerous outer-disk florets are female, having only pistils, and are therefore capable only of receiving pollen. This arrangement probably encourages cross-pollination. The insect lands on the flower head and begins working the florets from the outside toward the center. In so doing it gives the outer-floret pistils pollen from the previously visited blossom. As it reaches the center, the insect picks up new pollen to pass on at the next blossom.

The Celebrity

Asters are found in all kinds of situations: fields, dry sand, salty beaches, swamps, woods, leaf mold, thickets, limestone cliffs, and, of course, along roadsides. Some thrive in bright sun while others favor shade.

Autumn Stars

Thoreau was pleased at how late in the season he found the calico aster (*Symphyotrichum lateriflorum*) in bloom. "You thought Nature had about wound up her affairs," he wrote in his journal in September 1856. "You had seen what she could do this year, and had not noticed a few weeds by the roadside, or mistook them for the remains of summer flowers now hastening to their fall; you thought you knew every twig and leaf by the roadside and nothing more was to be looked for there; and now to your surprise, the ditches are crowded with millions of little stars."

Among the most beautiful of the genus is the New England aster, about which the "critics" seem to agree:

"Probably no (aster) is more striking. . ."—Mrs. William Starr Dana, 1893
"Surely this is the most admirable of all the asters."—Mabel Osgood Wright, 1901
"The flower-heads . . . shine out with royal splendor."—Neltje Blanchan, 1900
"Our most showy wild aster."—Roger Tory Peterson, 1968

Even the staid, scientific Britton and Brown called it "one of the most beautiful of the genus." And in that poll of hundreds of naturalists and botanists in the 1940s, New England ranked it as the third most popular flower in North America.

From late August through early October, New England aster colors moist roadsides and fields with varying shades, including violet, magenta purple, violet purple, pink rosy lilac, and reddish purple. Occasionally, a red or white bloom is found. The 40 to 100 rays on each flower are stunningly set off by the center disk of yellow, creating a blossom an inch to an inch and a half across. Were these only solitary flowers on single stems, they would probably be admired. As it is, up to 50 blossoms may appear in a single two- to five-foot-tall plant, creating a spectacular display.

For the scientist, the renaming of the asters has brought accuracy and order. For the rest of us, it's removed some colorful names and created some polysyllabic nightmares. New England aster used to be *Aster novae-angliae*, which could be translated as "star of New England." Now, as *Symphyotrichum novae-angliae*, it's literally "fused hairs of New England." However, for the botanist, the meaning of the words is not as important as having words that apply to one and only one species, and to do so in accordance with certain rules. The word *Symphyotrichum* was created in 1832 to describe the hairs on the seeds of a European plant. According to Dr. John C. Semple, a noted aster expert at the University of Waterloo in Ontario, the name actually described "an aberrant condition in a garden cultivar. Nonetheless, the name was validly published and is the oldest generic name applicable to the group of asters" to which it has now been applied.

Though New England aster is a geographical name, this aster is by no means limited to New England, and can be found across southern Canada to the Rockies and Pacific Northwest, and south in the United States to the Gulf Coast. Since many nurseries sell New England asters, the plant's range and numbers will probably expand.

This perennial likes plenty of sun and fairly rich, moist soils, and spreads slowly by roots and by seeds. Because it is such a common, hardy, and easy-to-grow flower, it is well worth trying to establish it in your yard or garden. The best way is to transplant in late spring or early summer. Since the plants are usually found in large colonies, removing a couple will do little harm, either to the scenery or to propagation. The experts say that the most successful time to transplant is June, but I have moved them in late July without trouble. Transplanting in fall is risky unless you get a complete clod of roots.

Planting seed is easier, but less likely to succeed because the germination rate in asters isn't great. If you give it a try, use many seeds, gathered and sown in October or November.

The lower leaves on the New England aster tend to die and dry up, making the plants somewhat ratty looking by blooming time. To prevent this, mulch the plants heavily over the winter, remove the mulch in the spring, and replace it once the new growth has hardened. Mulching also produces better-quality flowers.

New England aster is the parent of many garden asters, cultivated widely especially in Europe. Among the more common hybrids are Barr's Blue and Barr's Pink, Crimson Beauty, Snow Queen (a white variety), and Harrington's Pink. The similar and beautiful New York aster (*S. novi-belgii*) is parent of the famous and widely grown Michaelmas daisies.

While deer seem to shun many asters, our experience has been that these herbivores like New England asters, especially the flower heads. For that reason we have given up trying to keep New England asters, but have plenty of white wood asters, Lowry's asters, heath asters, and others that the deer don't touch.

Useful Stars

Among Europeans and the colonists, asters found fame as medicinal herbs, although the Shakers brewed solutions from them that supposedly cured skin rashes, and the ancient Latins were said to have used some species to treat snakebites and sciatica. Nicholas Culpeper recommended a couple of European varieties for such things as fevers, asthma, and "swellings in the groin."

Nonetheless, American Indians found plenty of uses for asters, treating many problems—from skin rashes and earaches to stomach pains and intestinal fevers—with various species. Nervines and cures for insanity were made from some asters. Others were eaten. For instance, Ojibwas of the Midwest and settlers in Maine and Quebec favored the flavor of the young leaves of the large-leaved aster (*Eurybia macrophylla*). Even the smoke was important. Meskwakis used aster smoke in their sweat baths. By feeding the smoke into a paper-like cone fitted into a nostril, they revived unconscious people. Both Chippewas and Ojibwas smoked the New England aster and other asters in pipes as a charm to attract game, especially deer.

Although they may have little practical value, asters have long been recognized as decorations. The flowers of most species last several days after being picked and put into vases, though many—like New England asters—close up at night. Almost all are perennials that don't suffer from picking. Mixed with plumes of goldenrod, what finer bouquet can adorn a table in an American home than these two handsome and colorful autumnal natives?

Gentians

THE ROYAL FAMILY

Gentians are flowers with Moxie—literally.

The bottle gentian never opens, but strong bees still manage to get inside.

If there were ever a royal family of wildflowers, it would be the gentians. Most are brilliant in color, extraordinary in dress, finicky in situation, and few in number. Even their name has a regal origin.

To discover a fringed or a closed gentian on an early-autumn hike is a treat not soon forgotten. Thoreau described the color of the fringed gentian as "surpassing that of a male bluebird's back," and William Cullen Bryant called it "heaven's own blue." The several closed, or bottle, gentians, less sung by poets, are almost as blue but tend toward purple and are not as showy.

Although their seasons coincide—late August through early October—and they share similar hues, little else about our two best-known gentians seems the same. The fringed variety likes sunny meadows while the closed favors the forest's shade. Fringed is biennial, appearing two years after the parent plant spreads its tiny seeds; closed is a perennial, long-lived and often forming large colonies. Fringed is showy, among our most beautifully shaped flowers; closed is more conservative, so much so that it never opens its petals—hence its name.

The Nun of Flowers

"A bud and yet a blossom!" wrote John Burroughs. "It is the nun among our wild flowers, a form closely veiled and cloaked." Burroughs and other naturalists have marveled at the closed gentian's ability to reproduce itself without opening its petals to pollen-transferring insects. Burroughs, in fact, long believed that bees could not pollinate the flower. "The buccaneer bumblebee sometimes tries to rifle it of its sweets," he once wrote. "I have seen the blossom with the bee entombed in it. He had forced his way into the virgin corolla as if determined to know its secret, but he had never returned with the knowledge he had gained."

Burroughs later learned that larger bees and bumblebees can indeed safely extract the flower's nectar, though it is with considerable effort that they force their way inside. Although their petals are ever closed, the flowers are actually designed to attract and serve the bee. Being closed protects the nectar from rain and pilfering insects of lesser strength, and the flower tips are specially coded to let the bees know which ones have already been drained of their sweets.

William Hamilton Gibson once watched a bee as it made the rounds of some asters, and then moved over to a closed gentian. Once there, it pushed its way into only one of the five blossoms on the plant, and then moved on to more asters. Curious as to why the bee stopped at only one, he examined the blossoms and found that the flower the bee visited was a young one, marked with white where the bee entered at the tip of its corolla. Older flowers—from which the nectar had already been extracted—had turned purple around the opening. They had lost their honey guides, as botanists call them; it was the plant's way of telling the bee not to bother with these blossoms.

In the 1920s a German botanist named Fritz Knoll experimented with similar honey guides. On a dark blue piece of flat paper, he drew white circles; in the middle of each was a hole through which sugar water was available. A hummingbird hawk-moth, which in the wild feeds at a European flower with a white ring on a dark blue background, quickly learned to go to the circle to find its treat. The shape of "flower" had nothing to do with the moth's interest—it was all color. The insect ignored other combinations, such as white rings on yellow or gray paper. Knoll later placed a sheet of glass over the blue paper. The moth still went to the rings, and little tongue-marks remained on the glass where it tried in vain to dip into the covered hole at the center.

It is not always easy to see bees entering closed gentians. Possibly the bees will not expend the energy needed to get at the nectar unless they are fairly desperate for food. Bees burn much fuel simply flying about on their nectar quests, and must be careful not to use up more than they collect. F. Schuyler Mathews spent many seasons watching closed gentians in a vain effort "to catch the robber in the act."

Mathews, however, may have lived with "lazy" bees. When I once wrote an article on gentians for the *New York Times* and mentioned the infrequent bee visitations, I received a letter from a clergyman in upper Wisconsin who not only often observed bees opening closed gentians, but also enclosed pictures as proof. "Maybe these bees are Scandinavians—industrious and all that sort of thing," the priest wrote.

So what drives a bee to go through all that trouble? John Eastman, in *The Book of Swamp and Bog*, reports that the closed gentian "is one of the richest of all flowers in nectar quantity (up to 45 milliliters) and sweetness (40 percent sugar)."

Uncommon but Plentiful

The closed gentian is not commonplace, but in its place, it can be common. I have seen the plant in the wild in only one spot in my hometown, and there it grows literally by the hundreds. When I first saw this colony in 1972, it consisted of several dozen plants. Ten years later, there were 1,000 or more of them.

The sight was all the more satisfying because this grove of uncommon flowers was thriving in the middle of dirt roads that had been cut through woods for a huge housing development. Before the subdivision ever got to be more than dirt roads, however, the wise town fathers decided

Microseeds

If you order bottle gentian seeds from a nursery, don't expect a heavy package. It would take nine million seeds to make one pound.

to purchase the 550-acre woodland as a refuge. So often developments destroy wildlife and their habitats. How nice to see the flowers, for once, having the last laugh!

The closed, or bottle, gentian (*Gentiana andrewsii*), also called the blind or barrel gentian, is named for Henry C. Andrews, a noted English painter of flowers at the turn of the 19th century. It is found from Canada to Georgia and out to the states along the Mississippi and into Colorado. Much like it in shape, color, and range is the slightly smaller *G. clausa*, also called the bottle, or closed, gentian.

These closed gentians are not difficult plants to grow. The tiny seeds can be gathered in October or purchased from a specialty nursery. They should be spread on damp soil and lightly tamped into the surface. Be careful not to plant on ground that is either too wet or that will dry out. *G. andrewsii* will grow from one to three feet high, but the taller ones often lie down along the ground, as if unable to bear the weight of the clusters of up to a half-dozen flowers at the top.

Edwin F. Steffek, author of *Wild Flowers and How to Grow Them*, said the bottle gentian is less finicky about soil than is its fringed cousin, and will grow in most damp, shaded places. Perhaps it is because we have lost so much of our old forests, whose fringes are the favored haunt of the bottle gentian, that the flower is not as common as it could be.

Fringed Gentian

Many consider the fringed gentian our most attractive wildflower. Indeed, in the 1940s continent-wide poll, it ranked eighth of the most beautiful wildflowers.

The four petals of the vase-shaped flowers each end in long, fine fringes. While these add to the flower's showy beauty and may help to attract passing bees, they probably evolved chiefly to keep crawling insects, especially ants, away from the plentiful supply of nectar. Some become tangled in the fringe and give up their expedition while others, surprised by the fringe's lack of support as they try to climb over it, simply slip off and fall to the ground. So characteristic are these fringes that the greater fringed gentian has been named *Gentianopsis crinita*, the specific name meaning "hairy" or "with long hair." (This species was long known as *Gentiana crinita*. The new *-opsis* suffix means that it is "like" a *Gentiana* gentian, but is not one.)

When the sun is not shining, the tops of the petals wrap themselves tightly around each other, forming a pointed cap and protecting the interior from rain that might dilute the nectar or from night-flying insects that might steal the bait without providing pollination. The flowers are plentiful and large, two inches tall on a healthy plant, which may itself reach three feet. A single plant may bear from 1 to an impressive 100 blossoms.

Fringed gentian is probably the fussiest and least predictable of our well-known flowers. These characteristics, combined with its biennial nature and the temptation among wildflower gatherers to pick it, have made it rather rare. The seeds need just the right moisture (not too wet and never dry), neutral to moderately acid soil, and, some authorities say, the presence in the soil of a certain kind of root bacteria. Thus, transplanting is almost always a waste of time and removes the plants—and the seeds—from a natural habitat, eliminating future generations from appearing on proven ground.

Spirited Soda

America's first mass-marketed soft drink, Moxie, contains gentian extract as an ingredient. The drink, which is still sold, was once so popular that its name has become a common word meaning skill, know-how, and spirited action.

From Seeds

The acquisition of some seeds, either from a plant (they must be fresh) or from a nursery, is the safest method of establishing plants. You can try just spreading them in a wet meadow, as nature does, or you can follow one of the several indoor planting methods outlined in books on wild-flower cultivation. The late U.S. senator George D. Aiken of Vermont, one of the best authorities on the horticulture of fringed gentian, devoted a full chapter to the subject in *Pioneering with Wildflowers*. The senator maintained that the flower is "easy" to grow.

In nature, the plant is not necessarily stable in situation. Being a biennial "with seeds that are easily washed away, it is apt to change its haunts from time to time," wrote Mrs. William Starr Dana. "So our search for this plant is always attended with the charm of uncertainty. Once having ferreted out its new abiding place, however, we can satiate ourselves with its loveliness, which it usually lavishes unstint-ingly upon the moist meadows which it has elected to honor."

There is a spot in my town where fringed gentians appear each year. Some years only three or four plants will show up—possibly because conditions, such as the amount of rainfall, were not good. Other years, more than two dozen plants will bloom. Since one pod can contain many hundreds of seeds, the future crop each year for this meadow depends on the success of the plants two years earlier. If a big rainstorm hits at seed-spreading season, the next generation may disappear literally down the drain—the site is only a few feet from a well-traveled highway.

Royal Medicine

Gentian, the name of several species of flowers and a small family of plants, recalls King Gentius of Illyria, the country where Shakespeare set *Twelfth Night* and which is now roughly where Albania and what was once called Yugoslavia are. The king supposedly discovered that some species cured a strange illness that had infected his troops. Nonetheless, it wasn't powerful enough to deal with a worse problem; the Romans conquered him and his men in 168 B.C.

A thousand years later in Hungary, people were dying of a plague. The story goes that King Ladislas (1040–1095) went into the fields and prayed for a cure. He said he would shoot an arrow into the air and asked God to direct the falling shaft to a plant that would cure the plague. It landed on a gentian, which later stemmed the disease. Perhaps for his faith, if not his aim, Ladislas was canonized a saint in 1192, and the local gentian was thereafter called *Sanctus Ladislas Regis Herba*. A similar story is told about Charlemagne, but the plant his arrow landed on was a thistle.

Old herbals describe the use of European gentians for myriad ailments such as colds, skin itches and ulcers, worms, kidney stones, ruptures, bruises, and even stitches in the side. "A more

The fringes of the fringed gentian are a beautiful defense mechanism.

Faithful

*I know not why but every sweet
     October
Down the fair road that opens to the
     sea
Dear in the wayside grasses tingeing
     sober
Blooms my blue gentian faithfully for
     me.*
—S. R. Barlett

Cerulean Flower

*Thou waitest late, and com'st alone
When woods are bare and birds have
     flown,
And frosts and shortening days por-
     tend
The aged year is near his end.
Then doth thy sweet and quiet eye
Look through its fringes to the sky,—
Blue—blue—as if that sky let fall
A flower from its cerulean wall.*
—William Cullen Bryant
     (1794–1878)

sure remedy cannot be found to prevent the pestilence than it is," wrote Nicholas Culpeper. "It strengthens the stomach exceedingly, helps digestion, comforts the heart, and preserves it against faintings and swoonings." It was also good for "the biting of mad dogs and venomous beasts." Gentian leaves are supposed to be a refrigerant, an agent that lowers abnormal body heat, and they have been placed on open wounds and inflammations to cool them.

In modern times yellow gentian (*Gentiana lutea*), a native of Eurasia, has been used to stimulate the appetite and to treat a variety of stomach problems and other ailments. In Switzerland and the Alpine regions of Austria and Germany, several liqueurs and cordials are made from a sugar obtained from its roots. A European concoction known as gentian bitters is sold today in better American food markets as an after-dinner drink to aid digestion. The popular Angostura Bitters, used to flavor cocktails, also contains gentian.

Fringed gentian apparently possesses chemicals similar to those of the yellow gentian, for American Indians, including the Delawares, used to brew a tea from its roots to purify the blood and strengthen the stomach. The mountain folk of the Appalachia made a similar tonic from the striped gentian (*Gentiana villosa*) and would even wear the root for strength.

The *Gentiana* and *Gentianopolis* genera are members of the Gentian family (Gentianacea), which includes the marsh pinks, sabbatias, centauries, columbos, felworts, pennyworts, and other obscure plants. Among the 60 or so North American members of the two genera, only the fringed and bottle gentians seem to be widespread east of the Mississippi. Many gentians favor colder climates, such as high mountains—particularly the Rockies—and some are very particular about where they settle. In 1900, one species had been found only on Nantucket Island and at Portsmouth, Virginia, while another, only rarely seen even in the 19th century, was occasionally sighted in the Grand Rapids section of Saskatchewan.

The Rocky Mountains are home to at least 20 kinds of gentians, and at least a half dozen live in the Pacific Northwest, especially in wet places. Most common varieties are blue or purple, though some yellow species exist. One of the most striking Rocky Mountain species is the western fringed gentian (*Gentianopsis thermalis*), similar to the eastern fringed gentian, which is the official flower of Yellowstone National Park. *Thermalis* refers to the plant's preference for warm spots, and while it can live in mountains more than two miles high, it also likes wet spots, particularly warm springs.

The clan is more common in European uplands. Ms. Blanchan wrote, "Fifteen species of gentians have been gathered during a half-hour walk in Switzerland where the pastures are spread with sheets of blue. Indeed, one can little realize the beauty of these heavenly flowers who has not seen them among the Alps."

Notwithstanding that lofty report, the fringed gentian has hardly gone unappreciated in its homeland. Bryant's verses for it (at left) are among the best known and the most poetic praises of a flower ever penned.

Websites

The World Wide Web offers excellent resources for researching wildflowers and related subjects. Here are some of the most useful sites.

Botanical.com

In 1931, *A Modern Herbal* by Mrs. Maude Grieve was published in England, and since then its fame has spread throughout the English-speaking world. Much of the text has been placed online, offering a wonderful reference about the uses of plants and the folklore surrounding them.
www.botanical.com

California Plant Names

Don't let the name fool you. This site will clear up the mysteries of many Latin and Greek words used in the scientific naming of plants—and not just California names. (The site also has photos and descriptions of many California wildflowers.)
www.calflora.net

Carnivorous Plants

The best place to learn about sundews, flytraps, and many other native carnivorous plants is the Website of Barry Meyers-Rice, Ph.D., a noted writer and editor on the subject.
www.sarracenia.com

Connecticut Botanical Society

There's nothing flashy about this site, but it's one of the Web's best sources of pictures and basic data on eastern North American plants. You can view more than 500 species of flowers by name (common or scientific), or by color. The photos are spectacular, great for confirming identifications.
www.ct-botanical-society.org

Digital Library Project

The University of California at Berkeley maintains a huge collection of more than 26,000 images of plants. The search form is easy to use and offers a large selection of ways to search.
elib.cs.berkeley.edu/photos/flora/

Flora of North America

This online version of a print project to describe every species of plant in North America north of Mexico contains a wealth of information, though the work is, at this writing, still far from complete. You can search for plants by name, state, or province. If a plant has been completed for inclusion, you will find both botanical and ethnobotanical information, plus a detailed map of its range.
www.fna.org

Forb Index

The U.S. Forest Service maintains a collection of profiles of wildflowers that are of interest to foresters in one way or another. The data provided for each species are extensive, but only about 150 species were covered at this writing. Still, it offers some of the more interesting and detailed information available on the Web about the covered species.
www.fs.fed.us/database/feis/plants/forb/

Glossary of Botanical Terms

GardenWeb's Glossary of Botanical Terms defines more than 4,400 words and phrases you may run across in your wildflower endeavors.
www.gardenweb.com/glossary/

Green Medicine

The U.S. National Park Service has a Website devoted, surprisingly, to the medicinal uses of native wildflowers, including many plants covered in this book. The concern is preserving and sharing information on native plants that may be of medicinal importance. "How many medicines have we already lost?" the site asks. "How many more remain to be found?"
www.nps.gov/plants/medicinal/

Lady Bird Johnson Wildflower Center

This site offers a useful national directory of recommended native plant species. For each species, there's a photo and details on its natural history, range, propagation, habitat, and more. The database is searchable by common or scientific name, state, family, or plant type (annual, perennial, vine, shrub, etc.) Look under "The Plants/Native Plants Database" on the home page.
www.wildflower.org

New England Wild Flower Society

The New England Wild Flower Society is the oldest plant conservation organization in the United States. The site describes the society and its many activities, and also is a source of links to other useful sites.
www.newfs.org

North American Native Plant Society

Originally the Canadian Wildflower Society, which created *Wildflower* magazine, the society divested itself of the magazine (see below) and concentrates on activities, including plant sales and a seed exchange. There's an online album of photos, essays on featured plants, and the usual association information.
www.nanps.org

Plant Conservation Alliance

The Plant Conservation Alliance is a group of 10 U.S. federal government agencies and more than 145 nonfederal "cooperators," such as biologists, botanists, habitat preservationists, horticulturists, resources management consultants, soil scientists, special interest clubs, and nonprofit organizations, as well as concerned citizens, nature lovers, and gardeners. While the site has a lot of boring government material, it also has a useful collection of links to native plant landscaping guides, online coloring books for kids, and an e-mail mailing list on dealing with alien plants.
www.nps.gov/plants/

USDA Plants Database

This site has information on virtually every species of plant in the United States, with the latest names, ranges, photos, and sometimes very detailed information—right down to how many of a plant's seeds equal one pound. This is an invaluable Website for anyone interested in wildflowers.
plants.usda.gov

Weed Hall of Shame

The Bureau of Land Management pictures and describes some of the worst of the invasive weeds.
www.blm.gov/education/weeds/hall_of_shame.html

Wildflower Magazine

Wildflower is North America's first and largest wildflower magazine. Alas, you won't find articles from the publication here, but you will find information on subscribing to this quarterly publication. The site also maintains a useful collection of links and a large list of native plant societies in North America, mostly by state and province.
www.wildflowermag.com

A Brief Glossary

We tried not to use many arcane terms in this book, but a few have slipped in here and there. Just in case you missed the definitions in the text, here they are in glossary form.

Calyx: The part of a flower consisting of the sepals. It is usually green.

Cleistogamous: Referring to a flower that never opens, but self-pollinates in bud form. It's from the Greek, meaning "closed."

Composite: A family of flowers, including asters, daisies, and goldenrods, whose flowers usually have central florets surrounded by florets that have given up their reproductive function and become petal-like rays. The dense mass of small flowers often looks like a single flower.

Dioecious: Referring to species that have both male and female plants.

Elaiosome: A fat-filled attachment on a seed, used to attract insects such as ants (see Myrmecochory). The word is based on Greek for "fat body."

Labellum: The main part of an orchid flower—actually, an enlarged petal and often of unusual shape.

Monotypic: Referring to a genus with only one species.

Myrmecochory: Literally, ant farming. Ants haul away seeds of certain springtime plants, eat off the elaiosomes, and toss the seed in an underground waste chamber where it sprouts, protected from foragers and the elements.

Pappus: The feathery, downy, or bristly substance attached to some seeds; it usually helps to carry them away in the air.

Pharmacopoeia: An official catalogue of drugs used as medicines, with information on preparation and use.

Pistil: The female part of a flower.

Scape: The stem of a flower growing directly from the ground.

Sepals: A green flower part, usually under the blossom. Together, the sepals form the calyx. In some flowers sepals look like petals; these are often called tepals.

Stamen: The part of a flower that produces pollen, usually made up of an anther at the end of a filament.

Stigma: The top of a pistil, where pollen is deposited, effecting pollination.

Style: The part of a pistil (usually long) that connects the stigma with the ovary, where seeds are formed.

Tepals: Sepals that look like petals on a flower; for instance, marsh marigold blossoms have tepals.

Transpiration: The process by which plants give off moisture through their leaves.

Type species: The species that is supposedly most typical of the genus.

Umbel: A flat or rounded cluster of flowers, such as a milkweed.

Bibliography

Most of the books listed here were consulted in the preparation of this book. Because books go in and out of print all the time, I have made little effort to denote which books may be currently in print. Check with your bookseller.

Most of these books, however, are probably out of print. Yet, most are probably also available from used book dealers—it's just a matter of finding the one who has what you want. Two good online sources of used books are abebooks.com and amazon.com. Both list the wares of many hundreds of used book dealers—literally hundreds of thousands of titles altogether.

Many used book dealers will also seek out editions you want, and they often advertise in the *New York Times Book Review* and other literary publications. You can also try the rec.arts.books.marketplace Usenet newsgroup on the Internet; post a message with your want list and keep an eye on the messages that dealers post.

Addison, Josephine. *The Illustrated Plant Lore.* London: Sidgwick and Jackson, 1985. A great book for legend, literature, and lore of wild plants; written by an Englishwoman, the book covers European plants, but many of them are North American immigrants. Good reading.

Ahmadjian, Vernon. *Flowering Plants of Massachusetts.* Amherst: University of Massachusetts Press, 1979. A book with 582 pages of black-and-white illustrations; relatively little text. Often seen on the used book market. Good for New Englanders.

Aiken, Senator George D. *Pioneering with Wildflowers.* Englewood Cliffs, N.J.: Prentice-Hall Inc., 1968. A highly recommended guide to growing wildflowers. Aiken, a former U.S. senator from Vermont, spent many years experimenting with ways of growing native wildflowers. Clear, informal writing style. If not in print, readily available on the used book market.

Anderson, A. W. *How We Got Our Flowers.* New York: Dover Publications Inc., 1966. Excellent background for both wildflower and gardening fans. Covers many plant explorers. Fine index.

Angier, Bradford. *Feasting Free on Wild Edibles.* Harrisburg, Pa.: Stackpole Books, 1972. A good guide for using wild plants as food.

Art, Henry W. *The Wild Flower Gardener's Guide.* Pownal, Vt.: Garden Way, 1990 and other dates. Art has produced a wonderful series of books, keyed to regions of North America and giving extensive information, including natural history, on 30 to 40 worthwhile species in each area. Texts include color and black-and-white illustrations, sources of seeds and plants, and lists of botanical gardens and native plant societies in the regions. Guides have been published in editions that cover the East, the Northwest, and the Southwest. Recommended.

Attenborough, David. *The Private Life of Plants.* London: BBC Books, 1995. Fascinating, well-illustrated account of techniques plants use to survive and procreate. 320 pages. Indexed. Recommended.

Bailey, L. H. *How Plants Get Their Names.* New York: Dover Publications Inc., 1963. A classic. Will help you understand the Latin names of plants. Great list of specific names, but not generic.

Balls, Edward K. *Early Uses of California Plants.* Berkeley and Los Angeles: University of California Press, 1965. Interesting little 103-page paperback offers lots of history on how California plants were used. Illustrated. Indexed.

Barbour, Anita, and Spider Barbour. *Wild Flora of the Northeast.* Woodstock, N.Y.: Overlook Press, 1991. Beautiful photos and interesting essay-like observations on the wildflower scene in the Northeast. Not only herbaceous plants but also trees and shrubs are covered. Indexed.

Bernhardt, Peter. *Wily Violets and Underground Orchids: Revelations of a Botanist.* New York: William Morrow, 1989. Well-written natural history of plants around the world. Color photos. Annotated bibliography. Extensively indexed. Recommended.

Birdseye, Clarence, and Eleanor Birdseye. *Growing Woodland Plants.* New York: Dover Publications Inc., 1972. A good guide for dealing with shady situations. Lots of information and tips. Clarence, by the way, is the creator of the modern frozen food system; he is the Birdseye of the brand name. Recommended.

Blanchan, Neltje. *Nature's Garden.* New York: Doubleday, Page and Company, 1900. Though her prose is somewhat Victorian and "flowery," her observations on the world of wildflowers are enlightening and entertaining. Lots of natural history from this pioneer woman naturalist. Pretty readily available at used or antiquarian bookstores at reasonable prices. Recommended.

Bliss, Anne. *North American Dye Plants.* New York: Charles Scribner's Sons, 1979. Great little guide to using wild plants as dyes.

Braungart, Dale C., and Ross H. Arnett. *An Introduction to Plant Biology.* St. Louis: C. V. Mosby, 1962. Good introductory textbook.

Britton, Lord Nathaniel, and the Honorable Addison Brown. *An Illustrated Flora of the Northern United States and Canada.* New York: Dover Publications Inc., 1970. If you are serious about identifying species east of the Rockies, you should have this on hand.

While its three paperback volumes are somewhat dated, being a reprint of the 1913 edition, it's still an invaluable source. Recommended.

Brown, Rowland W. *Composition of Scientific Words.* Washington: Smithsonian Institution Press, 1991. If you want a dictionary-like and comprehensive sourcebook on what those scientific names mean, try this. Recommended.

Burgess, Thornton W. *The Burgess Flower Book for Children.* Boston: Little, Brown and Company, 1923. Stories featuring Peter Rabbit, Jimmy Skunk, and the whole Burgess cast, introducing kids to wildflowers. Illustrated. Indexed. Recommended.

Burn, Barbara. *North American Wildflowers.* (The National Audubon Society Collection Nature Series), Avenel, N.J.: Gramercy Books, 1992. Lots of color photos, relatively little text.

Burroughs, John. *The Writings of John Burroughs.* 19 vols. Cambridge: The Riverside Press, n.d. If you are "into" nature, be it wildflowers, birds, animals, or just communing, read Burroughs. Sets of his works can be picked up reasonably in used book shops. Of course, individual volumes and collections of essays are also available.

Castleman, Michael. *The Healing Herbs.* New York: Bantam, 1995. A very detailed guide to "100 healing herbs" as well as sundry conditions they and others will treat.

Clute, Willard N. *The Common Names of Plants and Their Meanings.* Indianapolis: Willard N. Clute & Co., 1942. This book is meant to be read for its information on the many ways plants acquire their names. It is not a dictionary-style encyclopedia of names, though it is fully indexed.

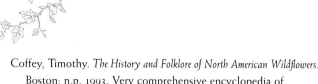

Coffey, Timothy. *The History and Folklore of North American Wildflowers.* Boston: n.p. 1993. Very comprehensive encyclopedia of American wild plants and their uses; fully indexed; extensive bibliography. Recommended.

Coon, Nelson. *The Dictionary of Useful Plants.* Emmaus, Pa.: Rodale Press, 1974. Tells the use, history, and folklore of more than 500 plant species. Lots of illustrations. Indexed. Recommended

Coon, Nelson. *Using Wild and Wayside Plants.* New York: Dover Publications Inc., 1980. More lore from Coon (above). Includes many shrubs and trees. Illustrated. Indexed.

Craighead, John J., Frank C. Craighead Jr., and Ray J. Davis. *Rocky Mountain Wildflowers.* Peterson Field Guide Series. Boston: Houghton Mifflin Company, 1963. Another excellent Peterson guide. Recommended.

Crockett, Lawrence J. *Wildly Successful Plants: A Handbook of North American Weeds.* New York: Collier Books, 1977. A guide to wildflowers that are considered pests; while it tells how to get rid of them, you almost believe that Mr. Crockett would rather keep them around to enjoy. Recommended.

Crow, Garrett E. *New England's Rare, Threatened, and Endangered Plants.* Washington: United States Department of the Interior, 1982. Technical details of about 100 very uncommon species. For those who like to stalk the rare ones.

Crowhurst, Adrienne. *The Weed Cookbook.* New York: Lancer Books, 1972. 269 ways to prepare 200 edible "weeds." Illustrated.

Culpeper, Nicholas. *Complete Herbal.* Philadelphia: David McKay Company, n.d. This is one of many editions and versions of Culpeper. They are entertaining and instructive, especially if you are interested in the historical uses of plants.

Dale, Nancy. *Flowering Plants.* Santa Barbara, Calif.: Capra Press, 1986. A fine guide to 260 species found in southern California. Includes botanical history and nomenclature origins. Indexed.

Dalton, Patricia A. *Wildflowers of the Northeast in the Audubon Fairchild Garden.* Greenwich, Conn.: National Audubon Society Inc., 1979. Nice black-and-white illustrations, so-so text. However, includes excellent time line of when northeastern plants can be expected to bloom. Indexed.

Dana, Mrs. William Starr. *How to Know the Wildflowers.* New York: Dover, 1963. Both the Dover paperback and original editions from 1893 and 1900 are widely available in used book stores. A nice friendly guide to many common wildflowers, with brief reports on natural history and folklore.

Densmore, Frances. *How Indians Use Wild Plants for Food, Medicine, and Crafts.* New York: Dover Publications Inc., 1974. A good investigation of Indian uses of plants, written by an Indian. Alas, lacks index.

Dietz, Marjorie J. *The Concise Encyclopedia of Favorite Wild Flowers.* New York: Doubleday, 1965. Lots of information on 100 well-known species. However, she annoyingly lists "assets" and "faults." An example of a "fault" is that you can't easily dig up lady's slippers from the wild and move them into your garden. Lady's slippers are best left in the wild, and that's no fault of theirs.

Durant, Mary. *Who Named the Daisy? Who Named the Rose?* New York: Dodd, Mead and Company, 1976. Entertaining look at selected wild and garden plants. No index.

Earle, Alice Morse. *Old-Time Gardens.* New York: The Macmillan Company, 1902. While primarily about gardening, includes some wildflower lore of the 19th century.

Eastman, John. *The Book of Forest and Thicket.* Harrisburg, Pa.: Stackpole Books, 1992. This is an excellent book on the wildflowers, shrubs, and trees of wooded areas of eastern North America. It contains a great deal of natural history, particularly the relationships between plants and other plants, and between plants and other creatures. This is the kind of fascinating science that is not always easy to find when dealing with wildflowers. Recommended.

Eastman, John. *The Book of Swamp and Bog.* Harrisburg, Pa.: Stackpole Books, 1992. Same as above, except plants are from the titled areas. Recommended.

Elias, Thomas S. and Peter A. Dykeman *Edible Wild Plants: A North American Field Guide.* New York: Sterling Publishing Company, 1990. Many photos, recipes, and maps in this concise guide. Indexed. Recommended.

Erichsen-Brown, Charlotte. *Use of Plants for the Past 500 Years.* Aurora, Ontario: Breezy Creeks Press, 1979. Excellent, comprehensive, and scholarly reference. Includes countless citations to recorded uses of our wild plants since the Europeans first arrived. Recommended.

Fernald, Merritt Lyndon, and Alfred Charles Kinsey. *Edible Wild Plants of Eastern North America.* Cornwall-on-Hudson, N.Y.: Idlewild Press, 1943. Extensive, 452-page illustrated guide; lots of plant lore and history.

Fitter, Alastair. *Wild Flowers of Britain and Northern Europe.* Collins New Generation Guide. London: William Collins Sons & Company Ltd., 1987. A wonderful field guide that goes way beyond just identifying plants; offers much natural history. Even though British, very handy for information on how wildflowers function in nature and includes many species that are circumpolar or that were introduced into North America. Recommended.

Forey, Pamela. *Wild Flowers of North America.* Limpsfield, Surrey: Dragon's World Ltd., 1990. Big coffee-table book, published in—of all places—England. Nice color art, but too much of the text is devoted to descriptions of the plants when it could have been about natural history and folklore. Who's going to haul a four-pound, 12-by-10-inch book into the field? Indexed.

Foster, Steven, and James A. Duke. *A Field Guide to Medicinal Plants: Eastern and Central North America.* Peterson Field Guide Series. Boston: Houghton Mifflin Company, 1990. Top-notch field guide with some of the latest medical information on plant uses, including text by physicians. Both line drawings and color photos. Plenty of warnings. Indexed. Recommended.

Fox, Helen Morgenthau. *Gardening with Herbs for Flavor and Fragrance.* New York: Dover Publications Inc., 1970. If you like to use your nose, you'll love this book. Lots of lore, planting tips, etc. Recommended.

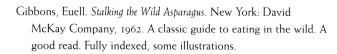

Gibbons, Euell. *Stalking the Wild Asparagus*. New York: David McKay Company, 1962. A classic guide to eating in the wild. A good read. Fully indexed, some illustrations.

Gibson, William Hamilton. *Our Native Orchids*. New York: Doubleday, Page, and Company, 1905. A classic guide to our native orchids; fine line drawings. Interesting natural history, lore. Indexed. Recommended.

Gledhill, David. *The Names of Plants*. Cambridge: Cambridge University Press, 2002. A very up-to-date guide to nomenclature.

Gray, Asa. *The Manual of the Botany of the Northern United States*. New York: American Book Company, 1889. Everyone should have one edition of Gray, even if it's antique.

Grieve, Mrs. M(aude). *A Modern Herbal*. 2 vols. New York: Dover Publications Inc., 1971. Two-volume paperback edition of a comprehensive encyclopedia, first published in 1931, of information on the uses to which plants of the world have been put. Indexed. Recommended.

Hall, The Rev. Charles A. *Wild Flowers and Their Wonderful Ways*. London: A. & C. Black Ltd., 1926. Entertaining English essays.

Harrington, H. D. *Edible Native Plants of the Rocky Mountains*. Albuquerque: University of New Mexico Press, 1967. Extensive guide, complete with recipes. Good line drawings. Huge bibliography. Indexed. Recommended.

Harris, Ben Charles. *The Compleat Herbal*. New York: Larchmont Books, 1972. An inexpensive herbal.

Harris, Ben Charles. *Eat the Weeds*. Barre, Mass.: Barre Publishers, 1971. Interesting recipes and tips on collecting and preparing common field plants for foods; information on nutritional values. Indexed.

Hatfield, Audrey Wynne. *How to Enjoy Your Weeds*. New York: Collier Books, 1973. American edition of an entertaining and extensively researched book by a British author. Covers about two dozen common "weeds" found in North America, all imported from Europe. Illustrated. Indexed. Recommended.

Hatfield, Audrey Wynne. *Pleasures of Wild Plants*. London: Museum Press Ltd., 1966. Enjoyable essays on wild British plants, many of which are found in North America. Includes recipes for eating some of them, and even for making wines and soaps. No index.

Headstrom, Richard. *Suburban Wildflowers*. Englewood Cliffs, N.J.: Prentice-Hall Inc., 1984. Readable, informative, short essays on many common wildflowers of the "suburbs." Suffers from lack of organization and an index, but grab it if you see it at a used book store.

Healy, B. J. *A Gardener's Guide to Plant Names*. New York: Charles Scribner's Sons, 1972. Short essays on the origins of many of the generic names of both garden and "wild" plants, plus a dictionary of many of the specific names. Recommended.

Hedrick, U. P., ed. *Sturtevant's Edible Plants of the World*. New York: Dover Publications Inc., 1972. Comprehensive guide to its subject; 686 pages. Indexed. Originally published in 1919. Recommended.

Hodgins, James L., ed. *Wildflower* (magazine). Various issues. Toronto, Ontario, 1985-present. The first and, for a long time, the only wildflower magazine in North America. A quarterly glossy publication, it features articles on wildflowers and other plants from throughout North America. If you like wildflowers, subscribe. (Write James Hodgins, Editor, Box 335 Postal Station F Toronto, ON, Canada M4Y 2L7, or visit http://www.wildflowermag.com .)

Hoehn, Reinhard. *Curiosities of the Plant Kingdom.* New York: Universe Books, 1980. Scads of fascinating, often offbeat facts about plants of the world. Extensively illustrated.

Houk, Rose. *Wildflowers of the American West.* San Francisco: Chronicle Books, 1987. Beautiful photographs and drawings, limited but interesting text. Very general. Indexed.

House, Homer, D. *Wild Flowers.* New York: Macmillan, 1934. Classic coffee-table book.

Hubbard, Juliet Alsop. *Wildflowers.* Burpee American Gardening Series. New York: Macmillan, 1995. An inexpensive ($9) and lushly illustrated guide to growing many varieties of wildflowers.

Hulm, F. Edward. *Familiar Wild Flowers.* London: Cassell, Petter, Galpin & Co.,1881. Wonderful old English essays on common wildflowers.

Hutchens, Alma R. *Indian Herbalogy of North America.* Boston & London: Shambhala, 1991. An extensive study of how American Indians used more than 200 plant species and—oddly enough—how that use compares with Russian uses. Extensive index by name and uses.

Hutchinson, John. *Common Wild Flowers.* Middlesex, England: Penguin Books, 1945. Comprehensive field guide to English wildflowers; black-and-white illustrations.

Hutchinson, John. *More Common Wild Flowers.* Middlesex, England: Penguin Books, 1948. See above.

Hyam, Roger, and Richard Pankhurst. *Plants and Their Names: A Concise Dictionary.* Oxford: Oxford University Press, 1995. For those who would know the meanings of the Latin and Greek names—generic or specific—applied to plants. Aimed primarily at gardeners, it nonetheless covers most wildflowers we're apt to run across in the field. The entries also tell a bit about the genera they define and where they are found. 545 pages. Recommended.

Johnson, A. T., and H. A. Smith. *Plant Names Simplified.* London: Collingride, 1964. Guide to meaning, derivation, and pronunciation of names. 120 pages.

Johnson, Lady Bird, and Carlton B. Lees. *Wildflowers Across America.* New York: Abbeville Press, 1993. The wildflower best-seller. Gorgeous photographs; text offers interesting background. Indexed.

Kalm, Peter. *Travels in North America.* 2 vols. New York: Dover Publications, 1966. Fascinating "natural history history." Kalm was very interested in the plants of this continent, "discovered" many, and found out how they were used by the natives.

Kavasch, Barrie. *Native Harvests.* New York: Vintage Books, 1979. Excellent guide to how American Indians used our plants as foods, medicines, cosmetics, tobaccos, beverages, etc.; many recipes. Illustrated. Indexed. Recommended.

Kerr, Jessica. *Shakespeare's Flowers*. New York: Thomas Y. Crowell Company, 1969. Will was a big wildflower fan.

Kingsbury, John M. *Deadly Harvest: A Guide to Common Poisonous Plants*. New York: Holt, Rinehart, and Winston, 1965. A good, readable guide to our poisonous plants.

Kluger, Marilyn. *The Wild Flavor*. Los Angeles: Jeremy P. Tarcher Inc., 1984. Loads of recipes for wild plants, arranged by season. Fully indexed.

Law, Donald. *The Concise Herbal Encyclopedia*. New York: St. Martin's Press, 1973. Loads of herbal lore and information. Unfortunately, not indexed.

Lloyd, Francis Earnest. *The Carnivorous Plants*. New York: Dover, 1976. Detailed and scholarly look at the carnivores, with many illustrations. Originally published in 1942. Indexed. Recommended.

Lubbock, Sir John. *British Wild Flowers Considered in Relation to Insects*. London: MacMillan and Company, 1890. Interesting, illustrated, and indexed. Written for the nonbotanist.

Lust, John B. *The Herb Book*. New York: Bantam Books, 1974. A classic, affordable encyclopedia of information on how our plants have been used for foods and medicines.

Martin, Alexander C. *Weeds*. New York: Golden Press, 1987. Small paperback with color illustrations of many common weeds. Okay, but not a great deal of text.

Martin, Alexander C., Herbert S. Zim, and Arnold L. Nelson. *American Wildlife and Plants: A Guide to Wildlife Food Habits*. New York: Dover, 1961. Excellent guide to how wild birds and animals, even fish, make use of our wildflowers and other plants. Great for designing a yard that will attract birds. Includes illustrations, range maps, and lists of what species eat. Cross-referenced index. Recommended.

Mathews, F. Schuyler. *Familiar Features of the Roadside*. New York: D. Appleton and Company, 1897. Turn-of-the-20th-century naturalist introduces you to the world of roadside nature. Line drawings. Indexed. Recommended.

Mathews, F. Schuyler. *Familiar Flowers of Field and Garden*. New York: D. Appleton and Company, 1915. A fine, readable guide to eastern wildflowers. Plenty of natural history and lore. Recommended.

Medsger, Oliver Perry. *Edible Wild Plants*. New York: The Macmillan Company, 1966. Extensive food guide. Has great index of edible plants by regions of the country, and then by kinds of uses (salads, beverages, nuts, etc.) Includes mushrooms.

Meyer, Joseph E. *The Herbalist*. Glenwood, Ill.: Meyerbooks, 1960. For those interested in herbs, a good basic guide. Often seen on the used book market.

Millspaugh, Charles F. *American Medicinal Plants*. New York: Dover Publications Inc., 1974. Comprehensive, detailed report on how our native plants have been used as medicines by physicians, Indians, and others. This is a reprint of an 1892 book. Recommended.

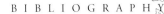

Mohlenbrock, Robert H. *Where Have All the Wildflowers Gone?* New York: The Macmillan Company, 1983. Very readable and interesting account of many of our endangered wildflowers. Illustrated. Indexed. Recommended.

Moldenke, Harold N. *American Wild Flowers.* New York: D. Van Nostrand Company Inc., 1949. Extensive guide to our wildflowers. Alas, for many species he uses scientific nomenclature that is no longer in use. Many photos. Extensively indexed.

Morris, Frank, and Edward A. Eames. *Our Wild Orchids.* New York: Charles Scribner's Sons, 1929. At 464 pages, one of our most comprehensive guides to native orchids. Written in the informal style of an explorer. Many black-and-white photos. Indexed. Recommended.

Muenscher, Walter Conrad. *Poisonous Plants of the United States.* New York: The Macmillan Company, 1939. An extensive catalogue of poisonous plants and what they can do. Indexed. Recommended.

Newcomb, Lawrence. *Newcomb's Wildflower Guide.* Boston: Little, Brown and Company, 1977. An excellent field guide. Recommended.

Nicholson, B. E., et al. *The Oxford Book of Wild Flowers.* London: Oxford University Press, 1960. Handy for seeing which of our plants are found in England. Color drawings. Indexed.

Niehaus, Theodore F., and Charles L. Ripper. *Pacific States Wildflowers.* Peterson Field Guide Series. Boston: Houghton Mifflin Company, 1976. Excellent field guide for the West Coast. Recommended.

Niehaus, Theodore F., Charles L. Ripper, and Virginia Savage. *Southwestern and Texas Wildflowers.* Peterson Field Guide Series. Boston: Houghton Mifflin Company, 1984. Another excellent Peterson guide. Recommended.

Niering, William A., and Nancy C. Olmstead. *The Audubon Society Field Guide to North American Wildflowers.* New York: Alfred A. Knopf, 1979. While many people don't like photographic field guides (they are not really comparable to drawings at pointing out field marks that are good for identifying plants), this guide has lots of information and even folklore and name origins. The photos are good and may help you confirm an ID you've selected from a Peterson or Newcomb guide. Recommended. (See under Spellenberg for West Coast edition.)

Pellett, Frank C. *Success with Wild Flowers.* New York: A. T. de la Mare Company, 1948. An old guide to gardening with wildflowers. Illustrations not very good, but growing tips may be valuable.

Peterson, Lee Allen. *A Field Guide to Edible Wild Plants: Eastern/Central North America.* Boston: Houghton Mifflin Company, 1977. Excellent field guide; not a recipe book, but does tell you in general how to use different kinds of plants as foods. Both fine line drawings and color photos. Indexed. Recommended.

Peterson, Roger Tory, and Margaret McKenny. *A Field Guide to Wildflowers.* Boston: Houghton Mifflin Company, 1968. My favorite field guide—I've worn the hardbound covers off two already. Fine line drawings. Indexed. Recommended.

Potterton, David, ed. *Culpeper's Color Herbal.* New York: Sterling Publishing Company Inc., 1983. Still in print; nicely organized and lavishly illustrated. Indexed.

Quick, Arthur Craig. *Wild Flowers of the Northern States and Canada.* Chicago: M. A. Donohue and Company, 1939. An extensive and personal look into hundreds of wildflowers, mostly natives. Arranged by time of year. Line drawings. Indexed.

Ricket, Harold William. *Wild Flowers of the United States.* New York: McGraw-Hill and the New York Botanical Garden, 1966. Massive series of coffee-table-size books offer extensive coverage of plants by region. The edition for the Northeast has 560 pages in two volumes covering more than 1,700 species. Editions exist for all regions of the country. They are out-of-print and run upwards of $100 for each region's set on the used book market, but if you are a wildflower fanatic, you'll enjoy your copies. Many color photos. Indexed. Recommended for serious wildflower enthusiasts.

Rishel, Dr. Jonas. *The Indian Physician.* New Berlin, Pa., 1828. Reprint. The Ohio State University Libraries Publications Committee, 1980. Interesting reprint, telling how folks looked on Indian medicines 175 years ago.

Roberts, June Carver. *Born in the Spring.* Athens, Ohio: Ohio University Press, 1976. A collection of concise, interesting essays on 146 spring wildflowers. Illustrated—mostly in color—by the author. Indexed.

Rose, Dixie. *Utah's Intermountain Wildflowers.* Salt Lake City: Publishers Press, 1979. Good local guide.

Saunders, Charles Francis. *Edible and Useful Wild Plants of the United States and Canada.* New York: Dover Publications Inc., 1976. Originally published in 1920, this book is arranged by uses to which the plants are put. Old lore. Some illustrations. Indexed.

Skene, MacGregor. *The Biology of Flowering Plants.* London: Sidgwick and Jackson Ltd., 1947. Comprehensive look at how many plants function. Aimed at the student; a bit technical, but a useful reference. Extensively indexed.

Skinner, Charles M. *Myths and Legends of Flowers, Trees, Fruits, and Plants.* Philadelphia: Lippincott, 1911. Lots of plant folklore. Not indexed, but organized as essays presented alphabetically by flower name.

Spellenberg, Richard. *The Audubon Society Field Guide to North American Wildflowers: Western Region.* New York: Alfred A. Knopf, 1979. See comments under Niering, William A. Recommended.

Spencer, Edwin Rollin *All About Weeds.* New York: Dover Publications, 1974. Here's a man who makes weeds so interesting, you hate to knock them off. Nonetheless, he often tells you how, but you'll love the lore anyway. Recommended.

Stack, Frederic William. *Wildflowers Every Child Should Know.* New York: Doubleday, Page & Company, 1913. Despite its name, this book by a botanist from Vassar contains much sophisticated and interesting information not readily found elsewhere. Illustrated. Indexed. Recommended.

Stark, Raymond. *Guide to Indian Herbs.* Surrey, British Columbia: Hancock House Publishers, 1984. Forty-eight-page handbook on 52 popular herbs used by American Indians.

Steffek, Edwin F. *Wild Flowers and How to Grow Them.* New York: Crown Publishers Inc., 1954. A comprehensive guide to growing wildflowers. A newer version is around, called *The New Wild Flowers and . . .* He clearly knows his stuff.

Stefferud, Alfred. *The Wonders of Seeds*. New York: Harcourt, Brace and Company, 1956. While aimed at young people, this is still an interesting book on how seeds work.

Stevens, John E. *Discovering Wild Plant Names*. Aylesbury, England: Shire Publications Ltd., 1979. Nice little British paperback guide to English names of common wildflowers.

Stevenson, Violet. *The Wild Garden*. New York: Penguin, 1985. Wonderful, extensively illustrated guide to using wild plants with a purpose—including water, rock, woods, meadow, and herb gardens. Extensively indexed. Recommended.

Stokes, Donald, and Lillian Stokes. *A Guide to Enjoying Wildflowers*. Stokes Nature Guides. Boston: Little, Brown and Company: 1985. In-depth look at some of the most popular and common wildflowers. Much natural history. Recommended.

Stokes, Donald, and Lillian Stokes. *The Wildflower Book*. Boston: Little, Brown and Company, 1992. "An easy guide to growing and identifying wildflowers." Nicely illustrated with color photos; lots of information from these veteran naturalist-writers. Paperback. (Available in editions for east of the Rockies and west of the Rockies.)

Strong, D. R., et al. *Insects on Plants*. Cambridge, Mass.: Harvard University Press, 1984. A very scientific look at the relationships between insects and plants.

Tantaquidgeon, Gladys. *Folk Medicine of the Delaware and Related Algonkian Indians*. Harrisburg: The Pennsylvania Historical and Museum Commission, 1977. A good compilation of Indian plant uses, written by an Indian from Connecticut.

Taylor, Kathryn S., and Stephen F. Hamblin. *Handbook of Wild Flower Cultivation*. New York: Collier Books, 1963. Covers many species; very simple instructions. Some line drawings. Indexed. Recommended.

U.S. Department of Agriculture. *Common Weeds of the United States*. New York: Dover, 1971. Dry, scientific identification guide to weeds. Has very good range maps. Indexed. (Originally published as *Selected Weeds of the United States*.)

U.S. Department of Agriculture. *Range Plant Handbook*. New York: Dover, 1988. Massive, 800-plus-page guide to 330 plants found on the plains, prairies, and mountains of the West; includes grasses, shrubs, trees. Lots of natural history, uses, lore. Fine illustrations. Extensively indexed. Recommended.

Uva, Richard H., et al. *Weeds of the Northeast*. Ithaca, N.Y.: Cornell University Press, 1997. A magnificent volume on weeds, with many color photos plus good natural history. Recommended.

Venning, Frank D. *Wildflowers of North America: A Guide to Field Identification*. New York: Golden Press, 1984. Useful only to casual wildflower hunters.

Vickery, Roy. *Oxford Dictionary of Plant-Lore.* Oxford: Oxford University Press, 1995. Dictionary-style, 437-page collection of lore, mostly for plants found in Great Britain. However, so many of them have made their way to North America, the book is nearly as useful on this side of the pond. Many excerpts and quotations make this work quite readable. Arranged by common names. Index is limited to scientific names. Recommended.

Vogel, Virgil J. *American Indian Medicine.* New York: Ballantine Books, 1973. Extremely comprehensive history of the uses to which Indians put countless plants. Recommended.

Wait, Minnie Curtis, and Merton C. Leonard. *Among Flowers and Trees with the Poets.* Boston: Lothrop, Lee and Shepard, 1901. An anthology of poetry about plants.

Weed, Clarence M. *Ten New England Blossoms and Their Insect Visitors.* Boston: Houghton, Mifflin and Company, 1895. What a name for a wildflower writer! Well-done essays on the natural history of a handful of common wildflowers.

Westbrooks, Randy G., and James W. Preacher. *Poisonous Plants of Eastern North America.* Columbia: University of South Carolina Press, 1986. Interesting, well-documented guide; color photos; useful "ready reference list" describing uses of the plants. Detailed bibliography. Indexed.

Woods, Sylvia. *Plant Facts and Fancies.* London: Faber and Faber, 1985. Lots of lore, but a limited number of plants. Indexed.

Woodward, Marcus. *How to Enjoy Wild Flowers.* London: Hodder and Stoughton, 1927. More enjoyable English essays.

Woodward, Marcus. *Leaves from Gerard's Herball.* New York: Dover Publications, 1969. Selections from the eminent herbalist, retaining the original Elizabethan English. Very entertaining.

Wright, Mabel Osgood. *Flowers and Ferns in Their Haunts.* New York: The Macmillan Company, 1901. Fanciful essays about searching for wildflowers in the southern Connecticut woods. Fun.

Index

A

Aaron's rod, 202
Abbott, Dr., 34
abortion, 23
absinthe, 181
Achillea: millefolium, 180–83; *ptarmica*, 181; *sibirica*, 181
Achilles, 182
acne, 163, 171, 196
Actaea: alba, 109; *pachypoda*, 107–09; *rubra*, 108; *spicata*, 108, 109
Adam's flannel, 202
adder's mouth, 125
adder's tongue, 40–43
ag-leaf, 202
Ageratina altissima, 242
AIDS, 208
Aiken, Senator George, 53, 57, 242, 252, 279
Alabama Indians, 231
Algonquin Indians, 23, 24, 154
allergies, 225
Alliaria: alliaria, 39; *petiolata*, 37–39
alum bloom, 106
amber, 209
amberbell, 40
Ambrosia: artemisiifolia, 237–39; *chenopodiifolia*, 238; *trifida*, 237–39
American Botanist, The, 212
American brooklime, 60
American Cancer Society, 70
American horsemint, 163
American mandrake, 99
American valerian, 95
Amorphophallus titanum, 5
analgesic, 118
Anaphalis margaritacea, 62
Anderson, A.W., 95
anemia, 73
Anemone: Canada, 16;

European wood, 16; wood, 14–17, 22, 49, 65
Anemone: canadensis, 16; *coronaria*, 16; *cylindrica*, 16; *hepatica*, 9; *nemorosa*, 16, 17; *occidentalis*, 16; *patens*, 16; *quinquefolia*, 15; *virginiana*, 16
Anemonella thalictroides, 15
Angier, Bradford, 29, 87, 125, 171
Antennaria: anaphaloides, 64; *neodioica*, 63; *plantaginifolia*, 62–64; *rosea*, 63
antibiotic, 84, 130, 203
antidepressants, 207–08
antiseptics, 55
antispasmotic, 104
ants, 7, 15–16, 42, 49, 52, 56, 71, 83, 139, 278
Apache Indians, 29
aphrodisiacs, 45, 52, 158, 174, 242, 254, 263
Apios: americana, 259; *apios*, 259; *priceana*, 258, 259; *tuberosa*, 259
Apocynum: androsaemifolium, 264, 266; *cannabinum*, 265, 266
apomixis, 27
appetite stimulants, 84
Aquilegia: caerulea, 33; *canadensis*, 31–33; *vulgaris*, 33
Aralia, 47
arbutus, trailing, 17
Argentina anserina, 118
Arisaema: atrorubens, 88; *dracontium*, 89; *stewardsonii*, 88–89; *triphyllum*, 86–89
aristolochic acid, 84
Artemisia, 237
arthritis, 225
artichoke, 249
Arum family, 5–6, 86

arum, titan, 5
asarabacco, 85
Asarum: canadense, 83–85; *caudatum*, 85
Asclepias: albicans, 141; *cornuti*, 138; *curassavica*, 141; *incarnata*, 141; *meadii*, 139; *purpurascens*, 141; *quadrifolia*, 141; *speciosa*, 141; *syriaca*, 138; *tuberosa*, 142–44
Asclepius, 138, 143
aspergillum, 255
ass's-foot, 20
aster, 271–75, 277; Alpine leafybract, 272; calico, 271, 274; Canby's, 272; heath, 275; large-leafed, 275; leafy, 272; Lowry's, 275; New England, 273, 274–75; New York, 275; Parry's, 272; white wood, 272, 273
Aster alpinus, 271
asthma, 5, 19, 64, 68, 87, 104, 138, 154, 165, 203, 237, 275
Astor, John Jacob, 44
astringents, 55, 106, 119, 154
Atropa belladonna, 167
avalanche lily, yellow, 43
avens, 211–12; large-leaved, 211; purple, 211; rough, 211; water, 211; white, 211; yellow, 211
Avila, Juan, 256
awn, 105
Aztec Indians, 247

B

bachelor's buttons, 159
bachelor's-breeches, 35
Bacon, Sir Francis, 119
bacteria, relation to plants, 145, 278
Baldwin, W.T., 92–93

balmony, 253
bamboo: Japanese, 197; Mexican, 197
baneberry: European, 108; red, 108; white, 107–09
Bantron, 220
Barberry family, 99
Barlett, S.R., 280
Bartram, John, 53, 162–63
bear's grape, 172
bearbind, 131, 133
bearbine, 131
beardtongue, 60
bears, 13, 43
beauty lotions, 51, 81–82
bedflower, 116
bedstraw, 115–16; boreal, 116; fragrant, 115; rough, 116; stiff marsh, 115; yellow, 115, 116
bee balm, 162–63; spotted, 163
bee guides. *See* honey guides.
Beecher, Catherine, 199
Beecher, Henry Ward, 26
beer, 183, 212, 222
bees, 4, 19, 30, 32, 35, 41, 42, 48–49, 53, 75, 76, 93–94, 114, 132–33, 145, 146–47, 148, 151, 189, 193, 227, 231, 232, 246, 249, 251, 262–63, 272
beetles, 4, 39, 42, 176, 178, 203; dogbane leaf, 266; golden tortoise, 133; Japanese, 181, 226; potato, 166
beggar grass, 194
beggar-lice, 116
beggars flannel, 202
belladonna, 164
Bellflower family, 220
Bellis perennis, 102
bells, 33

balmony, 253
belly-ache-weed, 234
bennet, 212
benzoin, 56
bergamot, wild, 161–63
Bergen, Fanny, 91
Bernhardt, Peter, 42
berries, 165
beth-flower, 56
bile, 158
bindweed, 131, 166; blue, 166; field, 133; great, 133; hedge, 131–34; hooded, 133; tuberous-rooted, 134
biological controls, 39, 176, 178
bipinnate leaves, 180
birds, 4, 30, 31, 106, 109, 113, 124, 140, 147, 151, 160, 165, 169, 171, 193, 203, 246, 250, 269. *See also* hummingbirds.
bird's eye, 52
bird's tongue, 194
birdgrass, 193
Birdseye, Clarence and Eleanor, 200
birdweed, 124, 193
Birthwort family 85
biting persicaria, 196
bitterroot, 266
bittersweet, 166, 167
bitterweed, 236
bity tongue, 195
black cohosh, 154–56
black-eyed Susans, 102, 128–30, 136
blackweed, 238
bladder ailments, 9, 91
Blakeslee, Dr. A.F., 130

Blanchan, Neltje, 3, 14, 32, 40, 53, 56, 59, 69, 70, 82, 103, 107, 125, 132, 133, 139, 150, 155, 169, 175, 186, 188, 203, 211, 213, 222, 224, 226, 230, 233, 246, 265, 272–73, 274, 280

blanket herb, 202

blasts, 256

bleeding heart, Pacific, 35

blister plant, 66

blob, 73

bloodflower, 141

bloodroot, 22–24, 37, 49, 56, 71

bloodwort, 184, 195

Blossey, Bernd, 177, 178

blowball, 25, 113

blue flag, 76–79; larger, 76. *See also* flag.

Blue Mountain tea, 232, 234

blue sailors, 159

blue-eyed grass, 79

Bluebell family, 220

bluets, 116

bog onion, 8

boils, 16, 63

bones, broken, 81, 244

boneset, 241, 243–45

books, on wildflowers, 284–94

Boone, Daniel, 45

Borage family, 122

Boston University, 38

bouncing bet, 127, 221–22

boys and girls, 35

bread, 87, 248, 258

break-bone fever, 244

breast ailments, 114, 158, 171, 225

Breathed, Berke, 30

Brewer, E. Cobham, 121

brideweed, 228

British Medical Journal, 207

bronchitis, 9, 63, 87, 143, 154, 231

brooklime, American, 60

Brooklyn Botanic Garden, 152

broomrape, 181

Brown, Theron, 205

brown betty, 130

brown dragon, 88

brown-eyed Susan, 130

bruises, 83, 104, 203

bruisewort, 222

Bryant, William Cullen, 15, 54, 276, 280

buck's beard, 114

buckwheat, 193

Buckwheat family, 193

buffalo bur, 167

buffalo weed, 239

bugbane, 65, 109, 155; Arizona, 155; Mt. Hood, 155; mountain, 155; tall, 155

bugloss, 122

bull's eyes, 73

bull's-foot, 20

bullweed, 52

bumblebee root, 56

bunk, 159

Burgess, Thornton W., 108

burns, 203. *See also* skin ailments.

Burns, Robert, 136

Burroughs, John, 3, 8, 22, 31, 34, 35, 40, 59, 91, 97, 104, 123, 140, 146, 170, 190, 192, 218, 222, 223–24, 230, 249, 272, 276

butter-and-eggs, 206, 227–29, 252, 265

butter-bur, 20–21

buttercup, 58, 65–68, 70, 74; bulbous, 66; creeping, 67; meadow, 66, 73, 74; running, 118; showy, 66; swamp, 65; tall, 66

Buttercup family, 9, 15, 32–33, 72, 74, 109, 155

butterflies, 136, 144, 240, 265, 268; American painted lady, 63; Baltimore checkerspot, 252; blue azure, 8; European cabbage, 169; fritillaries, 144; monarch, 138, 140, 266; viceroy,

138, 140; Virginia white, 37

butterfly banners, 35

butterflyweed, 142–44

Butts, Mary Frances, 32

C

cactus, 268

cadaverine, 3

caduceus, 143

calcium oxalate, 5, 86, 87

California Native Plant Society, 62

Calonyction, 133

Caltha: leptosepala, 74; *natans*, 74; *palustris*, 72–75

calve's snout, 228

Calystegia sepium, 132

calyx, 283

campions, 127, 221

Canada potato, 249

Canadian Museum of Nature, 45

cancers, 24, 51, 68, 70, 84, 98, 119, 171, 182, 219

candelaria, 202

candlewick plant, 202

candy, 51, 52, 84, 158

Canel, Dr. Camilo, 100

cankerwort, 28

capers, 73

carbuncles, 125

cardiac glycoside, 140

cardinal flower, 217–20

Carleton, Will, 245

carminative, 84, 234

carnivorous plants, 173–75

carrot, 185–87

Carrot family, 186

carrotweed, 238

carpenter's weed, 184

Carver, George Washington, 84

catchflies, 127, 221

catchfly, 266

cathartic, 98, 99

cattle. *See* cows.

celandine, 69–71; brook, 152; garden, 71; lesser, 70

centinode, 194

Cerastium vulgatum, 127

Champlain, Samuel, 97

charms, 36, 242, 245, 256, 266, 275

Cheney, Jane, 117, 119

cheese making, 115–16, 149

cheese-rennet, 116

Chelidonium majus, 69–71

Chelone glabra, 251–53

Cherokee Indians, 9, 219, 220

chew-root, 28

Cheyenne Indians, 238, 258

chick wittles, 124

Chickasaw Indians, 183

chicken pox, 182

chicken's meat, 124

chickenweed, 124

chickweed, common, 25, 58, 124–27; Indian, 125; mouse-ear, 127; star, 125

chicory, 29, 114, 157–60

childbirth, 33, 55, 73, 85, 108, 143, 154

Chippewa Indians, 9, 28, 61, 73, 84, 87, 108, 125, 130, 138, 180, 183, 231, 233, 242, 245, 249, 256, 266, 268, 275

chlorophyll, 199

Choate, Isaac Bassett, 61, 91, 126, 208

chocolate flower, 106

cholera, 106, 177, 196

Christ, Jesus, 16, 59, 148, 212

Christian, Caroline E., 52

Christie, Agatha, 133

Chrysanthemum leucanthemum, 101

churnstaff, 228

Cichorium intybus, 157–60

Cicuta maculata, 186

ciderage, 195

Cimicifuga: americana, 155; *arizonica*, 155; *elata*, 155; *laciniata*, 155; *racemosa*, 154–56

Cinquefoil, common, 118; creeping, 118–19; dwarf, 117–19; dwarf mountain, 118; old-field, 118; shrubby, 118; silverweed, 118;

sulfur, 265

Cirsium: altissimum, 269; *arvense*, 267, 268; *odoratum*, 268; *pumilum*, 268; *vulgare*, 270

Clayton, John, 13

Claytonia: caroliniana, 12; *lanceolata*, 12–13; *perfoliata*, 13; *virginica*, 12

clayweed, 20

cleats, 20

cleavers, 115, 116; yellow, 116

cleistogamous flowers, 49, 126, 151, 283

cling-rascal, 116

clock, floral, 113, 158

clock, of seeds, 20, 25, 113

cloth, 266

clover, 42, 145–49; Alsatian, 148; alsike, 148; Dutch, 148; 'four-leaf,' 148; Kate's Mountain, 146; least hop, 149; meadow, 148; purple, 148; rabbit's foot, 149; red, 146–47, 214; running buffalo, 146; suckling, 149; Swedish, 148; white, 147, 148

Clover Specialty Company, 148

Clovis, 77, 78

cluckies, 33

cluckweed, 124

Clute, Willard N., 59, 113, 144, 228

Cnicus benedictus, 269

cocum, 172

codhead, 253

coffee substitutes, 28, 79, 116, 157–58, 247

coffeeweed, 159

Coffey, Timothy, 40

cohosh, 109; black, 154–56; blue, 109; white, 109

cokan, 172

colds, 63, 143, 195, 244, 256, 279

Coleridge, Samuel Taylor, 162

colic, 46, 78, 84, 203, 212
colic root, 85
colicweed, 36
collard, 5
color, in flowers, 56, 66, 96, 118, 219, 232, 277. *See also* honey guides.
colt-herb, 20
coltsfoot, 17, 18–21, 22; false, 85
columbine, American, 22, 31–33, 65, 155; European, 32, 33; Rocky Mountain blue, 33
Commelina: communis, 188–90; *dianthifolia*, 190; *erecta*, 190; *virginica*, 189
Commelyn brothers, 188
Composite family, 26, 62, 65, 103, 114, 129, 157, 158, 180, 239, 241, 243, 268, 273–73, 283
coneflower, 129; cut-leaf, 129; tall, 129
Conium maculatum, 186
Connecticut Botanical Society, 281
conquer-john, 81
constipation, 28, 106, 125, 158, 177, 244
consumption, 154, 203, 253
contraceptive, 84, 88, 183, 187
contrastimulant, 157–58
Convention on International Trade in Endangered Species (CITES), 44
Convolvulus: arvensis, 133; *dissectus*, 134; *rhodorbiza*, 134; *scammonia*, 133; *sepium*, 132
convulsion root, 200
convulsions, 9, 200, 233, 270
Coon, Nelson, 6, 197, 203, 258
coon root, 23
corkscrew-plant, 263
corm, 41
corn root, 23
cornflower, 159

corns, 68, 70, 171, 174
Cornell University, 37, 177, 178
corpse plant, 199
cottonthistle, 269
cottonweed, 64
cough medicines, 19, 20, 24, 45, 51, 73, 87, 125, 174, 195, 203, 219, 225
coughwort, 20
cow cockle, 222
cows, 30, 36, 43, 66, 102, 104, 130, 146, 147, 171, 181, 195, 203, 222, 229, 236, 248
cow's lip, 73
cow's lungwort, 206
cowbloom, 73
cowgrass, 148, 194
Cowley, Abraham, 113
cowlily, 73
cowslip, 72, 122, 152
cramps, 233, 238
cranesbill, 105
crazy bet, 73
Cree Indians, 266
Creek Indians, 45, 219
Crockett, Lawrence J., 126
crocuses, 79
crosswort, 245
croup, 87, 154
crow's nest, 187
crowfoot, 106; cursed, 67; water, 73, 74. *See also* buttercup.
Crowfoot family, 9, 15, 32–33, 65–68, 109, 155
Crowhurst, Adrienne, 87
crowsoap, 222
crusaders, 16
crystalwort, 9
cuckoo plant, 88
cuddle me, 52
Culpeper, Nicholas, 9, 16, 28, 33, 59, 69, 104, 114, 116, 119, 125, 138, 158, 165, 182, 187, 196, 203, 212, 214, 228, 232, 270, 275, 280
Cultivator, The, 102, 116, 228, 270

Culver's root, 61
culverwort, 33
curdwort, 116
currants, 91
Cypripedin, 96
Cypripedium: acaule, 94; *calceolus*, 94; *californicum*, 96; *fairrieanum*, 95; *fasciculatum*, 96; *montanum*, 96; *pubescens*, 94; *reginae*, 95; *spicerianum*, 95

D

Dahlgren & Company, 248
daisy, blue, 159; brown, 130; bull, 104; butter, 104; button, 104; dog, 184; dun, 104; English, 102; field, 104; Gloriosa, 130; horse, 104; Irish, 28; Maudlin, 104; midsummer, 104; moon, 102; ox-eye, 101–04, 136; poorland, 104, 130; yellow, 130
dagger flower, 78
Dakota Indians, 138, 258
Dakota potato, 259
Dale, Nancy, 60
Dana, Mrs. William Starr, 7, 34, 73, 82, 83, 93, 95, 107, 142, 155, 179, 187, 194, 223, 244, 274, 279
dandelion, 18, 25–30, 58, 113, 114; blue, 159; California, 27; fleshy, 27; harp, 27; northern, 27; wool-bearing, 27
Dandridge, Danske, 23
Darwin, Charles, 151, 173–74, 179, 262, 270
Darwin, Francis, 174
Dasiphora floribunda, 118
Daucus carota, 185–87; *pussilus*, 186
dayflower, Asiatic, 188–90; birdbill, 190; common, 188–90; slender, 189–90; Virginia, 189; western, 190

de la Mare, 134
Deacon, E., 16
deadman's bones, 228
deer, 38, 42, 96, 152, 214, 225, 231, 245, 275
deer's tongue, 40
Deland, Margaret, 103, 160
Delaware Indians, 5, 45, 143, 144, 151, 183, 238, 258, 280
delphiniums, 65
dengue, 244
Denison, Elizabeth W., 166
Department of Agriculture, U.S., xvi, 27, 45, 60, 79, 100, 130, 143, 144, 148, 179, 181, 237, 258, 259, 282
depression, 207–08
Deptford pink, 135–36
de Vries, Hugo, 224
devil's apple, 99
devil's ear, 88
devil's flax, 228
devil's flower, 228
devil's head, 228
devil's nettle, 183
devil's plague, 187
devil's ribbon, 228
devil's scourge, 209
devil's vine, 133
dew grass, 174
dew plant, 174
Dianthus ameria, 135–36; *caryophyllus*, 135
diarrhea, 18, 106, 154, 177, 203, 212, 219
Dicentra: canadensis, 35; *cucullaria*, 34–36; *formosa*, 35; *spectabilis*, 34
digitalis, 61, 108, 266
dioecious species, 269, 283
Dioscorides, 122
diphtheria, 231
Dispatch, Columbus, 39
diuretics, 9, 28, 36, 59, 78, 104, 154, 196, 208, 228, 263
doctrine of signatures, 9, 122, 163, 196, 244

dog bites, 9, 266, 280
dog blow, 104
dog toes, 63
dog's cloves, 222
dogbane, 264–66; spreading, 264–66
Dogbane family, 264
doggies, 228
dogs and cats, 149
dogtooth violet, 40–43
doll's eyes, 107
doon-head, 28
douche, 200
dovedock, 20
dragon flower, 78
dragon root, 88
dragon-bushes, 228
Drayton, Brian, 38
droppers, 41
dropsy, 5, 28, 98, 167, 195, 219, 228
Drosera anglica, 175; *brevifolia*, 175; *capillaris*, 175; *filiformis*, 175; *intermedia*, 175; *linearis*, 175; *rotundifolia*, 173–75; *tracyi*, 175
Druids, 255
drunkards, 73, 74
duck, 95
Duke, James, 45
dulcamara, 166
dulcamarine, 164
dummy weed, 21
Durant, Mary, 81, 228
Dutch morgan, 104
Dutchman's breeches, 34–36, 37
Dutchman's pipe, 200
dyes, 23, 52, 68, 78, 115, 138, 151, 172, 195, 203, 229, 232, 247
dyspepsia, 28, 98, 143, 253
dysentery, 63, 143, 177, 183, 195, 212, 219

E

ear jewel, 152
earaches, 183, 203
eardrops, 34

Earle, Alice Morse, 95, 137, 155, 199, 244
earth apple, 249
Eastman, Elaine Goodale, 94, 147;
Eastman, John, 96, 167, 178, 277
eczema, 70, 143, 171, 225
Edison, Thomas, 231
eggplant, 167
eggs-and-collops, 228
elaiosomes, 15–16, 42, 49, 71, 83, 283
Emerson, Ralph Waldo, 33, 158
emetics, 24, 78, 171, 219
enchanter's plant, 255
endive, 157, 159
English bull's eye, 130
enteritis, 78
epilepsy, 51, 115, 195
epiparasite, 198–99
Erigeron philadelphicus, 53
Erynnis lucilius, 32
Erysimum alliaria, 39
Erythronium albidum, 41; *americanum*, 40–43; *californicum*, 43; *dens-canis*, 40, 41; *elegans*, 43; *grandiflorum*, 43; *propullans*, 41; *tuolumnense*, 43
esclepain, 138
ethnobotany, xv
etoposide, 98
Eupatorium: compositifolium, 245; *fistulosum*, 240; *maculatum*, 240; *perfoliatum*, 243–45; *purpureum*, 240; *rugosum*, 242; *urticaefolium*, 242
Eurybia: divaricata, 272; *macrophylla*, 275
Euthamia graminifolia, 233
evening-primrose, 102, 223–25; common, 223-25
Evening-Primrose family 224–25
evening-star, 225
everlasting, 62–64, 90; early, 63; pearly, 63–64; pearly mouse-eared, 63;

plantain-leaf, 63
evil spirits, 202, 219, 256
expectorants, 55, 59, 143, 154
eye ailments, 16, 28, 51, 69, 71, 87, 125, 158, 177, 200, 219, 228, 247, 263
eyebright, 200

F

fabrics, 79, 247
Fagopyrum esculentum, 193
fainting spells, 200
fairy candles, 154–56
fairy-smoke, 200
fairy-spuds, 13
false bindweed, hedge, 131–34
false Solomon's seal, 82
fawn lily, 40–43; California, 43; coast range, 43; Minnesota, 41; mother lode, 43; Tuolumne, 43; yellow, 43
felonwood, 166
felonwort, 71, 166
feltwort, 202
fertilizer, 248
fertility treatments, 45
fetid hellebore, 5
Fetrow, Charles, 256
fever-plant, 225
fevers, 33, 68, 119, 163, 177, 208, 212, 238, 244, 249, 256, 275
feverwort, 244
fibers, 79, 143, 247, 266
Fields, Annie Adams, 182
Figwort family, 60, 206, 229, 252
filius-ante-patrem, 21
finger leaf, 118
fish, 84, 85, 134, 203, 213
fish mint, 213
fishmouth, 253
Fissipes acaulis, 96
fitroot, 200
fits, 73
five-finger, 118
five-leaf grass, 117

flag, blue, 76; harlequin blue, 79; larger blue, 76; poison, 78; western blue, 79
Flathead Indians, 186
flatulence, 187
flavorings. *See* seasonings.
flaxweed, 228
fleawort, 116
fleur-de-lis, 77–78
flies, 3, 55, 56, 83, 87, 155, 169, 172, 199, 265
Flora of North America Association, 53
floral clock, 113, 158
flour, 193, 256
flowering sally, 177
flu, 24, 143, 244
fluellein, fluellin, 60, 228
fluffweed, 202
flyflower, 35
flytrap, 266
foalsfoot, 20
foalswort, 20
fodder, 247, 248
Food and Drug Administration, U.S., 70, 84, 208, 220
Forest Service, U.S., 139, 281
forget-me-not, 120–23; Asian, 122; bay, 122; spring, 122; water, 121
Forman, Emily Shaw, 263
Foster, Steven, 45
four toes, 63
four-leaf clover, 148
four-o'clock, 225
foxglove, 61, 229
foxtail, 177
Franklin, Benjamin, 171
fresheners, 64
Friendly Botanical Societies, 219
frog's feet, 255
fuller's herb, 222
Fumitory family, 35
fungi, plants and, 93

G

gagweed, 220
Galium: aparine, 115, 116;

asprellum, 116; *kamtschaticum*, 116; *tinctorium*, 115; *triflorum*, 115; *verum*, 115
gall bladder ailments, 78
gallstones, 28, 115, 158
gallwort, 228
gamma linolenic acid (GLA), 225
gangrene, 56
garget, 171
garlic mustard, 37–39
garlic root, 38
garlicwort, 38
gastritis, 78, 167
Gay, John, 129, 130
gentian: barrel, 278; blind, 278; bottle, 276–80; closed, 278; fringed, 276–80; soapwort, 222; striped, 280; western fringed, 280; white closed, 253
gentian bitters, 280
Gentian family, 280
Gentiana: andrewsii, 278; *clausa*, 278; *crinita*, 278; *villosa*, 280
Gentianopsis: crinita, 278; *thermalis*, 280
geranium: Carolina, 106; dove's foot, 106; wild, 55, 105–06
Geranium: carolinianum, 106; *maculatum*, 105; *molle*, 106; *robertianum*, 106
Geranium family 106
Gerard, John, 38, 49, 51, 68, 69, 71, 82, 108, 113, 114, 115, 122, 124, 136, 165, 209, 214, 232, 236, 255
German scammony, 133
Geum: aleppicum, 211; *canadense*, 211; *macrophyllum*, 211; *triflorum*, 211; *urbanum*, 211, 212; *virginianum*, 211
ghost flower, 199
Gibbons, Euell, 28, 97, 170, 194, 197, 203, 214, 216, 234, 247

Gibson, William Hamilton, 7, 93, 98, 105, 125, 133, 150, 239, 262, 277
Gill, Dr. Douglas E., 94
gill-over-ground, 58
ginger, 20, 83, 84, 85
ginger, long-tailed wild, 85; wild, 49, 83–85
Ginsana, 46
ginseng, American, 44–47, 55; dwarf, 44–47
Ginseng family, 47
Gledhill, David, 60
Gloriosa daisy, 130
Glycine apios, 259
goatsbeard, 113–14
goatweed, 209
godfathers and godmothers, 52
golden Jerusalem, 130
golden marguerites, 104
golden trefoil, 9
goldenrod, 230–35; anise-scented, 232; Atlantic, 233; blue-stemmed, 233; Canada, 233; early, 233; fragrant, 232; gray, 233; lance-leaved, 233; meadow, 233; narrow, 234; rough-stemmed, 233; sharp-leaved, 233; stiff, 232; sweet, 234; tall, 233; white, 234
goldenseal, 55, 82
gonorrhea, 106, 222
Goodale, Dora Read, 8
goolriders, 101
gools, 73, 101
gooseberries, 91, 162
goosegrass, 116, 193
goosethaw, 3
Gosnold, Bartholomew, 258
gout, 16, 46, 187, 195, 196, 203
gowan, horse, 104; meadow, 73; milk, 28; water, 73; yellow, 28
grace of God, 209
grapewort, 109
grass polly, 177

grass-of-Parnassus, 91
grass-pink, 136
gravel root, 242
Gray, Asa, 34, 93, 98, 172, 179, 215, 258, 262
great bitterflower, 73
great ox-eye, 104
green dragon, 89
Grieve, Maude, 20, 29, 38, 51, 66, 70, 87, 98, 104, 108, 113, 124, 134, 174, 185, 214, 243, 249, 268, 281
grip-grass, 116
Gronovius, Johann Friedrich, 13
ground lemon, 99
ground pea, 259
groundhele, 60
groundnut, 257–60; Price's, 258
gum disease, 24, 106
gypsy weed, 60
Gyrostachys, 262

H

hag's taper, 202
halictids, 109
Hall, Pamela, 93
hangovers, 50, 225
hard-hay, 209
Harding, A.R., 44
Harlan, Kentucky, 170
hare's beard, 202
hare's foot, 149
Harris, Ben Charles, 171, 253
Hatfield, Audrey W., 67, 118, 125, 204
hawkweeds, 102, 114
Hawthorne, Nathaniel, 17
hay, 101, 102, 159, 236
hay fever, 232, 236–38
hay fever weed, 238
headaches, 16, 33, 46, 50, 64, 68, 78, 87, 96, 163, 182, 203, 256
heal-all, 58
heart diseases, 52, 55, 63, 143
heart-leaf, 85

heart-snakeroot, 85
heartburn, 78, 114
heartsease, 53
hedge garlic, 38
hedge taper, 202
Helianthus: annuus, 246, 250; *giganteus*, 246, 250; *tuberosus*, 248, 249
heliotropes, 122
hemlock, poison, 186; water, 186
hemorrhages, 55, 59, 106
hemorrhoids, 183, 228
Henry IV, King, 121
hepatica, 7–10, 17, 22, 49, 56, 65; round-lobed, 8; sharp-lobed, 8
Hepatica: acutiloba, 8; *americana*, 8, 9; *hepatica*, 9; *nobilis*, 8; *triloba*, 9
Hera, 50
herb bennet, 211, 212
herb bonnet, 212
herb Christopher, 109
herb grace, 255
herb Margaret, 104
herb of the cross, 255
herb Robert, 106
herb trinity, 52, 56,
Herba benedicta, 212
Herba fullonum, 222
Herba sacra, 255
Herba veneris, 254
herbalists, xv
heucheras, 91
Higginson, Mary Potter Thacher, 201
high taper, 202
hives (ailment), 46
hog apple, 99
hog's physic, 217
hogweed, 194, 236
Holmes, Oliver Wendell, 218
holy herb, 255
hoofs, 20
Hooker, Joseph, 126
honey guides, 11, 48, 53, 76, 106, 118, 122, 277
honeybloom, 266

Hopi Indians, 138
horse-cane, 239
horse blobs, 73
horsefoot, 20
horsehoof, 20
horsemint, 163
horsenettle, 167
horses, 102, 104
horseweed, 239
Houma Indians, 167, 233
House, Homer D., 99
Hulme, F. Edward, 121, 212
hummingbird tree, 253
hummingbirds, 31, 32, 151, 162, 163, 203, 217–18, 253
Huron Indians, 98, 247
Hutchinson, Dr. John, 126
hyacinth bean, 259
Hyam, Roger, 60
hydrangeas, 91
hydrophodia, 125
Hypericin, 208
Hypericum: perforatum, 207–10; *punctatum*, 210; *spathulatum*, 209, 210
hysteria, 5, 96, 115

I

Ibidium, 262
Ictodes foetidus, 5
Illinois Indians, 183
Impatiens: biflora, 151; *capensis*, 151–52; *fulva*, 151; *pallida*, 151
impetigo, 51
impudent lawyer, 228
Indian apple, 99
Indian balm, 56
Indian chickweed, 125
Indian chocolate, 212
Indian ginger, 85
Indian hemp, 265, 266
Indian lettuce, 13
Indian paint, 23
Indian pipe, 198–201
Indian Pipe family, 198
Indian potato, 259
Indian sage, 243
Indian shamrock, 55

Indian shoe, 95
Indian tobacco, 63, 219–20
Indian turnip, 87
indigestion, 46, 130, 143
inflammations, 19
inkberry, 172
insect bites, 19, 125, 138, 163, 232, 256
insect enemies, 39, 193–94
insect repellants, 23, 98, 103, 155
insectivorous plants, 88
insomnia, 28, 51, 167, 256
Internet, xvi, 281–282
Io, 49
Ion, 50
Ipomoea: batatas, 134; *pandurata*, 132; *purga*, 134; *purpurea*, 131; *tricolor*, 131
Iridin, 78
Iris, 77
Iris: florentina, 78; *hexagona*, 79; *missouriensis*, 79; *pseudocorus*, 79; *versicolor*, 76
Iris family, 79
irises, 76–79
Irish daisy, 28
Irisin, 78
ironweed, 255
Iroquois Indians, 183, 219
Ives, Ella Gilbert, 235
ivy flower, 9

J

Jack-by-the-hedge, 38
Jack-go-to-bed-at-noon, 113
Jack-in-the-bush, 38
Jack-in-the-pulpit, 5, 86–89; northern, 89; swamp, 88; woodland, 88
Jack-in-trousers, 33
Jack-jump-up-and-kiss-me, 52
Jacob's ladder, 228
Jacob's staff, 202
jalap, 134, 172
jam, jelly, 138, 162, 163, 197
James, Edwin, 206

jaundice, 9, 28, 51, 70, 104, 158, 165, 195, 228, 233, 253
Jefferson, Thomas, 159
Jerusalem artichoke, 249
jewelweed, 150–53; spotted, 151
Job's tears, 82
Joe-Pye weed, 240–42; hollow, 240; spotted, 240; sweet, 240, 242
Johnny jump-up, 52
Johnson, A.T., 60
Johnson, C.P., 125
Joseph's flower, 114
Journal of the American Medical Association, 207
Juno's tears, 255

K

Kalm, Peter, 64, 87, 137, 152, 247
kapoc, 137–38
Kavasch, Barrie, 125
kenningwort, 71
kicking colt, 152
kidney ailments, 9, 28, 165, 183, 187, 242, 263, 279
kidney root, 242
killweed, 177
killwort, 71
king cups, 73, 75
king's cure-all, 225
Kingsbury, John M., 108, 172
kiss-her-in-the-buttery, 52
kit-run-in-the-fields, 52
kitten-breeches, 35
Klamath weed, 209
Kluger, Marilyn, 170
knap, 148
Knoll, Fritz, 277
knotgrass, 192
knotweed, 192–97; Japanese, 193, 196–97; prostrate, 194
Kunze, R.E., 200

L

labellum, 93, 283
lace-flower, 187
ladies' ear-drop, 152
ladies' tobacco, 63, 64
ladies'-slipper, 152
ladies'-tresses, 261–63; fragrant, 261; green-lipped, 263; hooded, 262; Irish, 262; nodding, 261; northern slender, 261; Ute, 263; Western, 262
lady neverfade, 64
lady's nightcap, 133
lady's slipper: California, 96; clustered, 96; mountain, 96; pink, 92–96; showy, 95, 217; yellow, 92–96
lady's thumb, 195
lamb mint, 213
lamb's tongue, 40
lambs quarters, 56
Landon, Alf, 249
larkspur, 65, 155, 228
latex, 28, 138, 231
latherwort, 222
Laurance, Ray, 56, 140, 151, 187
Law, Donald, 70, 232
lawns, wildflowers for, 58, 62
laxative, 51, 78, 97, 238, 253
leafminers, 32
leather-breeches, 35
Lee, Penny, 57
lemonmint, 163
Leontodon taraxacum, 27
leopard's foot, 73
leprosy, 16
Leucanthemum vulgare, 100
Lewis, Meriwether, 84, 85, 247
Lewis, William, 208
Library of Congress, 45, 46
Lilium philadephicum, 53
lily: fawn, 40–43; ground, 56; harvest, 133; hedge, 133; liver, 78; snake, 78; trinity, 56; trout, 40–43; yellow, 40

Lily family, 56, 80
Linaria vulgaris, 227–29, 265
liniment, 87
Linnaeus, Carolus, 16–17, 53, 55, 104, 109, 128–29, 138, 183, 188, 259
linoleic acid, 249
lion's mouth, 228
lion's tooth, 28
little boy's breeches, 35
live-forever, 64
liveman, 116
liver ailments, 9, 70, 78, 98, 114, 125, 177, 183, 228, 270
liver-moss, 9
liverleaf, 9
liverwort, 9
Llewelyn's herb, 60
Lloyd, John Uri, 220
lluellin, 60
L'Obel, Matthias, 220
lobelia: great blue, 219; pale-spike, 220; red, 217
Lobelia: cardinalis, 217–20; *inflata*, 219–20; *spicata*, 220; *siphilitica*, 219
lobeline, 220
Lombard, Lucinda Haynes, 212
London pride, 222
Longfellow, Henry W., 77, 121
loosestrife: California, 176; Florida, 176; purple, 176–79; yellow, 177; whorled, 177
Louis VII, King, 77
lousewort, Furbish's, 206
love potions, 45, 52, 67, 183, 187, 219
love idol, 52
love's nest, 63
love-lies-bleeding, 52
love-me, 121
Lowell, James Russell, 26, 30, 67
Lubbock, Sir John, 53, 114, 123

lunacy, 68
lung ailments, 16, 19, 24, 81, 138, 143, 149, 183, 202, 249
lungwort, 202, 206
Lust, John, 125, 143, 228
Lycopersicum esculentum, 167
Lysichiton americanus, 5
Lythrum, winged, 176
Lythrum: alatum, 176; *californicum*, 176; *flagellare*, 176; *salicaria*, 176–79

M

macaroni, 77
mackerel mint, 213
madder, 115
Madder family 116
Maianthemum racemosa, 82
maidshair, 116
malaria, 87
Malecite Indians, 253
man-under-ground, 132
mandrake, 99
Mangosteen family, 209–10
marigold, marsh, 21, 72–75
marlgrass, 148
marsh marigold, 72–75; floating, 74; white, 74
marsh turnip, 88
Marybuds, 73
Mather, Rev. Cotton, 70
Mathews, F. Schuyler, 7, 23, 33, 34, 62, 82, 93, 107, 115, 116, 123, 131, 137, 200, 217, 221, 230, 233, 234, 239, 241, 245, 264–65, 277
maudlinwort, 104
May apple, 97–100
May blobs, 73
May-flower, 90
meadow cabbage, 5
meadowbouts, 73
measles, 182
meat tenderizer, 138
Medsger, Oliver Perry, 170
meeting houses, 33
Melilotus, 149

Menominee Indians, 5, 36, 98, 143, 183
menopause, 154
Mentha: aquatica, 216; *arvensis*, 213, 215; *piperita*, 215, 216; *spicata*, 213–16; *viridis*, 215
Merremia dissecta, 134
Meskwaki Indians, 16, 33, 45, 84, 85, 108, 183, 219, 232, 233, 275
Meyer, Joseph and Clarence, 125
Meyers-Rice, Barry, 281
Miami Indians, 183
Micmac Indians, 5, 183
microspecies, 27
Midas ears, 5
milfoil, 180
milfoil tea, 182–83
milk, breast, 138
milk gowan, 28
milkthistle, blessed, 270
milkweed, 137–41; common, 137; four-leaved, 141; marsh, 242; Mead's, 139; purple, 141; showy, 141; swamp, 138, 141; wandering, 266; white-stemmed, 141
Milkweed family, 139
Millspaugh, Charles F., 26, 28, 47, 66–67, 73, 138, 143, 154, 171, 199, 223, 244
miners' lettuce, 13
mint: brown, 215; common, 215; green, 215; Our Lady's, 215; spire, 215; water, 216; wild, 213
Mint family, 161, 213–16
mint sauce, 214
Mithridates Eupator, 241, 242, 243
mitreworts, 91
Miwok Indians, 144
moccasin flower, 93
mock orange, 91
mock-gilliflower, 222
Mohammed, 51

Mohawk Indians, 66, 183
Mohegan Indians, 23, 45, 63, 87, 268
Mohlenbrock, Robert H., 258
Moldenke, Dr. Harold, 5, 48, 88, 217
mollyblobs, 73
Monarda: didyma, 162–63; *fistulosa*, 161–63; *punctata*, 163;
Monardella macrantha, 163
Monardes, Nicolas, 161, 163
moneywort, 177
monk's head, 27, 35
monkeyflower, 60
monophagous insects, 39
Monotropa: hypopithys, 198; *uniflora*, 198–201
monotypic species, 71, 283
Montagnais Indians, 84
moon flower, 104, 133
moon penny, 104
moonshine, 64
moonwort, 174
Moore, John, 75, 248
More, Thomas, 4
morning glory, 131
Morning Glory family, 131–32
motherwort, 242
moths, 32, 205, 221, 223, 265, 277; crepuscular, 132; gypsy, 178; iris borer, 78; sphinx, 132, 221; yellow-banded wasp, 133
mourning doves, 169
mouse-ears, 9
Moxie, 278
Muehlenberg, Heinrich, 194
Mueller, Fritz, 144
Muellerian mimicry, 138
Muenscher, Walter Conrad, 108
Muir, John, 123

mullein, 60, 202–06, 229; common, 204–06; great, 202–06; moth, 205; purple, 205
mullein tea, 203
multiple sclerosis, 225, 249
mumps, 203
mutants, mutations, 224
mustard, garlic, 37–39
Mustard family, 37–39
mustard root, 38
Myosotis: alpestris, 122; *laxa*, 122; *scorpioides*, 121; *verna*, 122
myrmecochory, 7, 15–16, 42, 49, 52, 56, 71, 83, 283

N

Nanticoke Indians, 5, 151, 238
Napoleon, 50–51
narcotics, 167, 171, 203, 219
National Institutes of Health, 207
National Park Service, 37, 282
native plant nurseries, 12
natural enemies, 37–38
Nature Conservancy, The, 178
National Sunflower Association, 247, 248
nausea, 231
necklace weed, 109
nectar, 75, 122, 147, 193, 277
nerve root, 95
nervines, 220, 275
Nesom, Guy, 271
neuralgia, 106
New England Wild Flower Society, 282
New York Botanical Garden, 5, 88, 217
New York Times, 242, 277
nightshade, American, 170; bittersweet, 164–67; black, 166; climbing, 164–67; deadly, 164, 166, 167; garden, 166;

silver-leaf, 167; woody, 166
Nightshade family, 167
nine-joints, 194
nitrogen, 145
Noah's ark, 95
none-so-pretty, 64
noonflower, 113
North American Native Plant Society, 282
nosebleed (ailment), 56, 61, 182, 219, 256
nosebleed (plant), 56
Nova Scotia Agricultural College, 199
noyau, 134
nurseries, native plant, 12
Nutting, Wallace, 25

O

obesity, 78, 125
obligate plants, 4
Oenothera: biennis, 225; *rosea*, 225
Ojibwa Indians, 16, 108, 183, 225, 242, 247, 275
old maid's nightcap, 106
old man's nightcap, 133
old man's pepper, 183
Oligoneuron rigidum, 232
Olson, A. Randall, 199
Omaha Indians, 258
Onopordum acanthium, 269
opium, 24
Orchid family, 79, 92–96, 261, 262
orris root, 78
Osage Indians, 87, 258
Oswego tea, 162
Our Lady's flannel, 202
Ovid, 214
Oxford English Dictionary, 73, 85

P

pain relievers, 51, 118
palsywort, 73
Panax: quinquefolius, 44–47; *schin-seng*, 44; *trifolius*, 46

Pankhurst, Richard, 60
pansies, 51
pappus, 63, 137, 140, 283
paralysis, 63, 98
parasites, 198
Parkinson, John, 182, 214
Parsnip family, 186
parson in a pillory, 5
Parsons, Frances Theodora, 155
pasque flowers, 16
passenger pigeon, 169
patten and clogs, 228
Paul's betony, 60
Pawnee Indians, 87, 258
Pea family 146
pear vine, 133
Peattie, Donald Culross, 271
pelargonium geraniums, 105
Pellett, Frank C., 12, 250
penny-hedge, 38
Penobscot Indians, 143
peony flowers, 23
pepper turnip, 88
peppermint, 215
pepperplant, 195
peppers, 167
Percival, James Gates, 15
percum-leaves, 209
perfumes, 52, 78, 79, 84, 163, 213–14
Peter's rod, 202
Peterson, Lee Allen, 87
Peterson, Roger Tory, 217, 274
Pharmacopoeia, U.S., 78, 96, 138, 143, 154, 171, 183, 234, 243, 266, 283
Pharmaton Natural Health Products, 46
phlebitis, 19
Phytolacca: americana, 168–72; *decantra*, 172
pig potato, 259
pigeon grass, 255
pigeon-berry, 169
pigrush, 194
pigtail, 116
pigweed, 194

piles, 70, 81
Pilgrims, 258
pinesap, 198, 199
pink: chimney, 222; Deptford, 135–36; hedge, 222; old maid's, 222
Pink family, 127, 135, 221
pink-eyed john, 52
Pinkham, Lydia E., 156
pinkweed, 194
pissenlit, 28
pistil, 283
pitcher plants, 175
Piute Indians, 183
plague, 68
plantain, white, 63
Plant Conservation Alliance, 282
Plants Database, USDA, xvi, 282
pleurisy, 51, 143
pleurisy root, 142
Pliny, 71, 85
pneumonia, 68, 154
pocan, 168, 172
pocanbush, 24
pocketdrop, 152
podophyllin, 98
podophyllotoxin, 98, 100
Podophyllum: hexandrum, 99; *peltatum*, 97–100
poison ivy treatments, 82, 150–51, 222, 238
poisonflower, 166
poisons, 98, 108, 138 164, 167, 172, 186, 212, 228–29, 242, 266
pokan, 24
poke, 167–72
poke-root, 24
pokeweed, 24, 168–72
polecatweed, 5
Polhamus, L.G., 231
polk, 171
polkweed, 5
pollen, 123, 236–39, 263. See also pollination.

pollination, 3–4, 14, 32, 49, 56, 59, 63, 65–66, 75, 76, 80, 83, 87–88, 93–94, 97, 103, 106, 122–23, 129, 132, 139–40, 147, 151, 161–62, 179, 199, 215–16, 217, 236–37, 251–52, 262–63. See also self-pollination, bees, flies *and* hummingbirds.
pollinia, 139
pollinosis, 238
Polygonatum: biflorum, 80–82; *cobrense*, 81; *commutatum*, 80; *hirsutum*, 81; *multiflorum*, 81–82; *pubescens*, 81
Polygonum: amphibium, 195; *aviculare*, 192, 193; *cespitosum*, 193; *cuspidatum*, 196–97; *hydropiper*, 195; *hydropiperoides*, 195; *muhlenbergii*, 194; *pensylvanicum*, 53, 192; *persicaria*, 195; *sagittatum*, 194
poor man's mustard, 38
poorweed, 116
Poppy family, 23, 36, 71
Portulaca family, 13
postage stamps, wildflower, 19, 247
potato, 164, 167, 258
potato bean, 259
Potato family 167
Potawatomi Indians, 84, 108, 242
Potentilla: anserina, 118; *canadensis*, 117–19; *fruticosa*, 118; *recta*, 265; *reptans*, 118–19; *robbinsiana*, 118; *simplex*, 118
poultices, 5, 43, 51, 63, 78, 82, 125, 151, 158, 231, 238, 242, 247
poverty weed, 63, 104
prairie smoke, 211
Pratt, Anne, 66
praying mantis, 231
Preacher, James, 108

preservatives, 84
pretty maids, 89
Price, Sadie, 258
Price's groundnut, 259
priest's crown, 27
priest's pintle, 88
Primack, Richard B., 38, 93
protandric, 252
protopine, 24
psoriasis, 171
Puck's foot, 99
puccoon, 23, 122
puffball, 28
pukeweed, 220
purgative, 98, 99, 133, 134, 172
purple grass, 177
purple willowherb, 177
Purslane family, 13
purvain, 255
pussies, 149
pussy clover, 149
pussytoes, 62–64; pearly, 64; plantain-leaved, 63; rosy, 63; smaller, 63
Pye, Joe, 240
pyrethrum, 103

Q

Queen Anne's lace, 18587
queen of the meadow, 242
Quick, Arthur Craig, 33, 200–01, 225
quillwort, 242

R

rabbit's weed, 228
rabbits (plant), 228
raceme, 82
raccoon berry, 99
ragged sailors, 159
ragged-robin, 127, 221
ragweed, common, 236–39; great, 236–39; San Diego bur, 238
Raleigh, Sir Walter, 258
rampion, German, 224
ranges, for wildflowers, xv–xvi

ranstead, 228
rantipole, 187
Ranunculus: acris, 66; *bulbosus*, 66; *ficaria*, 70, 71; *hispidus*, 65; *repens*, 67; *sceleratus*, 67
Rappahannock Indians, 167
rattlesnakeweed, 186
rattletop, 154
Raudot, A.T., 98
red benjamin, 56
red betty, 217
red dot, 174
red knees, 195
red monardella, 163
red robin, 194
red root, 23
red sally, 177
red-ink plant, 172
redroot, 211
redshanks, 195
redweed, 172
Reese, Lizette Woodworth, 269
refrigerant, 280
rheumatism, 5, 51, 143, 154, 165, 171, 196, 244, 266
rheumatismwood, 266
rhizoctonia fungi, 93
rhizome, 78
rhodium, oil of, 134
ringworm, 23, 70, 171, 203, 244
Roberts, June Carver, 11
rock bells, 33
rock lily, 33
rockfoil, 90
rockweed, 5, 106
Roelofson, Emily Bruce, 122
rope, string, 79, 266
Rose family, 117, 211
rose sundrops, 225
rosin weed, 209
Rudbeck, Olaus, Sr. and Jr., 128
Rudbeckia: fulgida, 130; *hirta*, 128–30; *laciniata*, 129; *tetra*, 130
rue-anemone, 14–17

S

Saftmal, 122
sailor's knot, 106
St. Anthony's turnip, 66
St. Benedict, 212
St. John's grass, 209
St. Johnswort, 102, 207–10; common, 207–10; shrubby, 209, 210; spotted, 210
St. Mary's herb, 215
salad greens, 12, 29, 39, 51, 60, 84, 91, 116, 125, 157, 159, 163, 170, 189, 268, 275
salicare, 177
salsify, 114; yellow, 114
salt-rheum weed, 253
sang diggers, 44–45
Sanguinaria canadensis, 22–24
sanguinary, 184
Saponaria: officinalis, 221; *vaccaria*, 222
saponin, 222
saprophite, 198
Sarrazin, Michel, 98, 108
sarsaparilla, 47
Satin, 212
satinflower, 125
sauce alone, 38
sauces, 38
Saunders, Charles F., 97, 222, 234
Saxifraga: granulata, 91; *micranthidifolia*, 91; *oppositifolia*, 90; *pensylvanica*, 91; *virginiensis*, 90
saxifrage, 90–91; early, 90; European meadow, 91; lettuce, 91; purple mountain, 90; spring, 90; swamp, 91
Saxifrage family, 91
scabish, 225
scammony, 133–34
scape, 283
scarlet fever, 24
scarletberry, 166

scent, 3–4, 8, 52, 56, 78, 93, 97, 116, 155, 199, 212, 221, 258
sciatica, 196, 275
Schemske, Douglas, 42
scoke, 172
scorpion bites, 122
scorpion-grass, marsh, 121; mouse-ear, 121
Scott, Sir Walter, 50
scratch-grass, 116
screw-auger, 263
scrofula, 40, 43, 59, 61, 70, 78, 138, 266
scrofula root, 40
scurvish, 225
sealwort, 81
seasonings, food, 19, 54–55, 84, 149, 183, 186, 187, 212, 213, 214–15
seasons, for wildflowers, xvi
sedative, 154, 220
seed bank, 39
seeds, 7, 15–16, 42, 49, 71, 93, 94–95, 103, 105–06, 113, 116, 124, 126, 140–41, 150, 152, 186, 269
self-pollination, 19, 24, 59, 63, 169, 241
Semple, John C., 274
Seneca Indians, 247
sepals, 42, 283
serpent's tongue, 40
Shakers, 275
Shakespeare, 50, 51, 52, 66, 73–74, 78, 99, 102, 147, 177, 279
shameface, 106
shampoo, 222
shamrock, 149
Shawnee Indians, 87
sheepweed, 222
shellflower, 253
shepherd's club, 202
shining-grass, 152
Shiraz, 121
shoe of Mary, 93
sickleweed, 195

sightwort, 71
Silene pensylvanica, 53
silver cap, 152
silverbutton, 64
silverleaf, 64, 152
silverrod, 234
silverweed, 118, 152
Silybum marianum, 270
simpler's joy, 255, 256
simplers, 256
sinkfield, 118
sinus ailments, 78
Sioux Indians, 138, 143, 258
Sipes, Sedonia, 263
Sisymbrium alliaria, 39
skatole, 3
skin ailments, 23, 36, 55, 59, 70, 78, 151, 163, 165, 167, 222, 225, 253, 263, 275, 279
Skinner, Charles M., 45, 74, 208, 262, 270
skirt and buttons, 125
skoke, 172
skunk cabbage, 3–6, 9, 17; American, 5; yellow, 5; skunkweed, 5
sleep inducers, 23, 28, 50
slinkweed, 217
slipper root, 95
slipperweed, 152
smallpox, 143
smartweed, amphibious swamp, 195; long-bristled, 193–95; longroot, 195; Pennsylvania, 192, 194; shoestring, 194; smarting, 195; swamp, 194
Smilacina racemosa, 82
Smith, H.A., 60
Smith, Huron H., 36
Smith, Capt. John, 52, 97
snake grass, 121
snakeberry, 166
snakebite (plant), 23, 108
snakebites, 55, 122, 154, 244, 256, 275
snakehead, 253

snakeroot, 40, 65, 241; black, 154; Canada, 85; Vermont, 85; white, 242; whiteberry, 109
snakeweed, 195
snapdragon, 152, 206, 227, 228
snapweed, 152
sneezewort, 181
soap, 79, 222
soaproot, 222
soapwort, 222
soil conditioners, 145, 238, 239, 248
solanine, 164
Solanum: americanum, 166; *dulcamara*, 164–67; *elaeagnifolium*, 167; *melongena*, 167; *nigrum*, 167; *rostratum*, 167; *tuberosum*, 167
soldier buttons, 73
soldier's cap, 34
Solidago: altissima, 233; *arguta*, 233; *bicolor*, 234; *caesia*, 233; *californica*, 231; *canadensis*, 233; *graminifolia*, 233; *juncea*, 233; *nemoralis*, 233; *odora*, 232, 234; *rigida*, 232; *rugosa*, 233; *simlex*, 234; *spathulata*, 234; *virgaurea*, 232
Solomon's plume, 82
Solomon's seal, 80–82; broadleaf, 81; dwarf, 81; false, 82; giant, 81; great, 80; hairy, 81; McKittrick's, 81; smooth, 81
solsequia, 73
sore throat, 24, 33, 63, 87, 106, 163, 177, 212, 231
soup, 247
sowfoot, 20
spadix, 86, 87
sparrow tongue, 194
spathe, 4, 86, 87, 88
Spathyema foetida, 5
spearmint, 213–16
speckled jewels, 152
speedwell, 58–61, 206, 229;

American, 60; bird's eye, 60; common, 58–61; corn, 60; Cusick's, 60; slender, 60; spiked, 59; thyme-leaved, 60; water, 60
Spellenberg, Richard, 165
Spencer, Edwin Rollin, 132, 256, 267
spiders, 4
Spiderwort family, 189
spiderworts, 161, 189
spiked soldiers, 177
spikenards, 47, 85
spines, 268
Spiranthes: cernua, 261, 263; *diluvialis*, 263; *lacera*, 261, 263; *odorata*, 261; *porrifolia*, 262; *romanzoffiana*, 262
spleen ailments, 158
sprains, 63
Sprengel, Christian, 106, 122
spring beauty, 9
spring-beauty, 11–13, 17, 37; Carolina, 12
squawroot, 154
squirrel corn, 35
squirrel cup, 9
Stack, Frederic William, 7, 9, 34, 74
stamen, 283
stammerwort, 238
staphylococcus infections, 130
star of Jerusalem, 114
starch, 87
starchwort, 88
starflower, 118
starstriker, 40
starweed, 125
starwort, 125
staunchweed, 184
Steffek, Edwin, 245, 278
Stellaria media, 124–27
Steyermark, Julian and Cora, 8
stick-a-back, 116
stickweed, 238
stickywilly, 116

stigma, 283
stinking benjamin, 56
stitchwort, 124
stolon, 67
stomach ailments, 28, 43, 46, 78, 81, 84, 114, 195, 212, 214, 231, 280
stomata, 20, 146
stonecrops, 91
storksbill, 106
strawberry, barren, 118
stress, 45
stuffing, pillow, 137
sturgeon plant, 84
sturgeon potato, 84
Sturtevant, Edward Lewis, 38, 125, 186, 214
styptic, 106
succory, 158
sugar plums, 148
sundew: dwarf, 175; pink, 175; round-leaf, 173–75; slender-leaf, 175; spoon-leaf, 175; thread-leaf, 175; Tracy's, 175
sunflower, 246–50; common, 246, 250; giant, 246, 250; mammoth, 247; Russian, 247; tall, 246, 250
sunflower cookies, 247
style, 283
Swain, Ralph B., 133
swallowwort, 71
swamp cabbage, 5
sweating plant, 244
sweet betty, 222
sweet clover, white, 149; yellow, 149
sweet potato, 134
sweet William, wild, 222
sweet Wilson, 91
sweethearts, 116
swine's grass, 194
swine's snout, 26
Symonds, George W.D., 196
Symphyotrichum: foliaceum, 272; *lateriflorum*, 273, 274; *novae-angliae*, 274–75; *novi-belgii*, 275
Symplocarpus foetidus, 3–6

syphilis, 78, 219, 220, 222, 266

T

Tallant, Robert, 82
tannin, 106, 118, 119
tansy, white, 181
Tantaquidgeon, Gladys, 23
Taraxacum: californicum, 27; *carneocoloratum*, 27; *eriophorum*, 27; *kok-saghyz*, 28; *lyratum*, 27; *officinale*, 25–30; *phymatocarpum*, 27
tattoos, 5
tea, herbal, 19, 20, 59, 96, 118, 149, 162–63, 182–83, 190, 203, 214, 232, 233, 238, 244, 256, 280
teak, 255
tearthumb, arrow-leaved, 194
teasel, 230
teniposide, 98
Tennyson, Alfred Lord, 58–59, 120
tepals, 42, 74, 283
Tepedino, Dr. Vincent, 263
tetterwort, 23, 71
textiles, 79, 143
Thalictrum thalictroides, 15
thermogenesis, 4
thimbleweed, 16
thistle, 267–70, 279; blessed, 269; bull, 267, 270; Canada, 267, 268, 270; cotton, 269; fragrant, 268; pasture, 268; roadside, 269; Scotch, 268, 269; tall, 269
Thomson, Samuel, 219
Thoreau, Henry David, 3, 76, 77, 165, 169, 258, 274, 276
thoroughwax, 245
thoroughwort, 244
thousand weed, 184
thousand seal, 184
throatwort, 212
throughstem, 245
thrush, 106
thujone, 181

tipton weed, 209
toadflax, 60, 227–29, 252
toadroot, 109
tobaccos, smoking, 19, 33, 63, 64, 149, 164, 167, 249, 275
tomato, 164, 167
tonics, 45, 46, 104, 183, 253, 270, 280
tongue grass, 125
toothaches, 5, 70, 96, 104, 106, 119, 196, 203, 232
toothpaste, 24, 222
toothworts, 37
torches, 202
tormentil, 118
touch-me-not, pale, 151
Touch-me-not family, 151
Tradescant, John, 31, 161, 218
Tragopogon: dubius, 114; *porrifolius*, 114; *pratensis*, 113–14
trailing pea, 259
tranquilizers, 50, 96, 220, 256
transpiration, 146, 249, 283
traveler's delight, 259
trees, relationship of wildflowers to, 92–93, 199
Trifolium: arvense, 149; *dubium*, 149; *hybridum*, 148; *pratense*, 146–47, 214; *repens*, 147; *stoloniferum*, 146; *virginicum*, 146
trillium: dwarf, 57; large-flowered, 57; painted, 57; purple, 56; red, 4, 49, 55–57; western, 57; wetdog, 56
Trillium Complex, 55
Trillium erectum, 55–57; *grandiflorum*, 57; *nivale*, 57; *ovatum*, 57; *undulatum*, 57
trimorphism, 179
trout lily, 40–43; white, 41
true-love, 56
trumpet flower, 242
tuberculosis, 231
tumors, 43, 55, 253, 266

turkey corn, 35
turmeric, 23
Turner, Cordelia Harris, 142
turtle, box, 98
turtlebloom, 253
turtlehead, 60, 206, 229, 251–53
Tussilago farfara, 18–21
tutsan, 209
twisted-stalk, 263
typhoid fever, 138, 240

U

Ukrain, 70
ulcers, 19, 23, 43, 51, 55, 59, 104, 119, 125, 182, 253, 279
umbel, 283
University of California, 281
University of Colorado, 24
University of Maryland, 94
University of Mississippi, 99–100
University of Pennsylvania, 265
University of Waterloo, 274
urinary ailments, 115, 242
Ute Indians, 182, 183

V

van Gogh, Vincent, 250
vegetable calomel, 99
vetetable mercury, 99
vegetables, wildflowers as, 72, 91, 114, 125, 134, 138, 143–44, 151, 158, 167, 170, 197, 225–26, 248, 249, 257–58, 268
vegetative reproduction, 71
velvet dock, 202
velvet plan, 202
Venus flytrap, 175
Verbascum: blattaria, 205, 206; *phoeniceum*, 205; *thapsus*, 202–04, 206
Verbena: bracteata, 256; *hastata*, 254; *officinalis*, 254; *stricta*, 256; *urticifolia*, 256

Vermont Ladyslipper Company, 95
Veronica: americana, 60; *anagallis-aquatica*, 60; *arvensis*, 60; *chamaedrys*, 60; *cusickii*, 60; *filiformis*, 60; *officinalis*, 58; *serpyllifolia*, 60; *spicata*, 59; *virginica*, 61
Veronicastrum virginicum, 61
verrucaria, 73
vertigo, 165
vervain, 254–56; American, 255; big-bract, 256; blue, 254–56; hoary, 256; swamp, 256; white, 256
Vervain family, 254
Viadent, 24
Vickery, Roy, 79
vinegar, 183
Vineland, N.J., 28
Viola: blanda, 53; *canadensis*, 53; *conspera*, 53; *cucullata*, 53; *guadalupensis*, 53; *lanceolata*, 53; *nuttallii*, 54; *odorata*, 52; *palmata*, 53; *papilionacea*, 49; *pedata*, 53; *primulifolia*, 53; *pubescens*, 54; *rotundifolia*, 54; *tricolor*, 49
violet, 48–54; American dog, 53; birdfoot, 53; bog white, 53; Canada, 53; dogtooth, 40–43; downy yellow, 54; early blue, 53; lance-leaved, 53; marsh blue, 53; palm, 53; prairie yellow, 54; primose-leaved, 53; rattlesnake, 40; round-leaved yellow, 54; sweet white, 53; sweet-scented, 52
violet bloom, 166
violet plates, 52, 158
Vipont Pharmaceuticals, 24
Virgil, 214, 273
Virgin's shoe, 93

Virginia Native Plant Society, 12
vitamins, in wildflowers, 13, 29, 38, 49, 125, 182–83, 225, 248
Vogel, Virgil J., 16
voodoo, 82
vomiting, 23, 68, 78, 143, 266
vomit-weed, 219–20

W

Wahl, Stacey, 188
Wait, Minnie Curtis, 99, 130
Wall Street Journal, 45
wake-robin, 55, 88
warts, 69, 73, 98, 174, 203
wartwort, 71
water blobs, 7
water crowfoot, 73
water dragon, 73
water gowan, 73
water-pepper, 195, 196 mild, 195
wax plant, 199
weather-cock, 152
Websites, 281–82
weed, definition of, xiv
Weed, Clarence M., 66, 76
weevils, 39, 178
Westbrooks, Randy, 108
western wallflower, 266
whippoorwill's shoe, 95
white apple, 259
white bird's eye, 125
white hearts, 34
white man's weed, 104
white tansy, 181
whiteheads, 109
whiteweed, 101
Whittier, John Greenleaf, 88, 234, 257
whooping cough, 24, 87, 104, 149, 154, 165
wild balsam, 152
wild bean, 259
wild beet, 225
wild bergamot, 161–63

wild buckwheat, 194
wild carrot, 185–86
wild celandine, 152
wild flax, 228
wild ginger, 83–85
wild hyssop, 255
wild ipecac, 266
wild jalop, 99
wild lemon, 99
wild licorice, 116
wild madder, 115
wild morning glory, 131
wild potato, 13
wild sage, 245
wild succory, 159
wild tobacco, 220, 228
wild tube-rose, 263
wild turnip, 88
wildflower, definition of, xii
Wildflower magazine, 24, 57, 282
Williams, Alfred, 19
willowherb, night, 225
windflower, 14
wine, 50, 116. 171, 187, 225, 232
Winnebago Indians, 43, 183
winterweed, 125
wire weed, 194
witchcraft, 165
witches, 119, 183, 202, 232, 255
witches' herb, 209
witloof, 29, 159
wolfbane, 65
woman's tobacco, 63
woodbind, 133
woodruff, 116
Woodward, Marcus, 102, 131
woolen, 202
Wordsworth, William, 70
World Wide Web, xvi, 281–82
worms, 220, 253, 279
wormwood, 181; Roman, 238
wound treatments, 5, 59, 81, 84, 104, 119, 125, 143, 151, 182, 208, 214, 225, 231, 280

woundwort, 182
Wright, Mabel Osgood, 36, 77, 230, 232, 258, 274
Wrigley, 213, 215

Y

Yankee weed, 245
yarrow, 180–83; California, 181; Siberian, 181; western, 181
yellow bastard-lily, 40
yellow bells, 40
yellow bird's nest, 199
yellow snakeleaf, 40
yellow snowdrop, 40
yellows, 95
yellowthroat, 4

Z

Zeus, 49–50
Ziska, Lewis, 237
Zuni Indians, 183, 231